First published in 2012 by Motorbooks, an imprint of MBI Publishing Company, 400 First Avenue North, Suite 300, Minneapolis, MN 55401 USA

Motorbooks titles are also available at discounts in bulk quantity for industrial or sales-promotional use. For details write to Special Sales Manager at MBI Publishing Company, 400 First Avenue North, Suite 300, Minneapolis, MN 55401 USA.

To find out more about our books, visit us online at www.motorbooks.com.

ISBN-13: 978-0-7603-4343-2

Photo credits:
cover: Sixties-era big-bore Corvettes scream around a turn at Pomona (top), while the modern C6R accelerates in the 24 Hours of Le Mans race (bottom).

back cover: On the back cover: In 1972, John Greenwood built two ZL1-powered Corvettes from recycled 1969 convertibles (top). In the yellow No. 3 car, Corvette racers Ron Fellows, John O'Connell, and Franck Freon outlast Prodrive's red Ferrari 550 Maranello at Sebring in 2003 (bottom).

right flap: The Corvette SS started life as Project XP-64.

spine: Though their appearances have changed over the years, ZR1-equipped Corvettes still get it done on the racetrack.

Editor: Jordan Wiklund
Design Manager: James Kegley
Designer: John Sticha
Cover design: Rob Johnson

Printed in China

# CORVETTE RACING

## The Complete Competition History
## from Sebring to Le Mans

**David Kimble**

**motorbooks**

# CONTENTS

# 1
## 1953-1957
## FIBERGLASS DREAM TO RACING SUCCESS

**After World War II,** a growing number of car magazines and returning GIs slowly raised America's awareness of British and European sports cars. A few clever entrepreneurs began importing these exciting cars, and amateur sports car racing started growing in popularity with the Sports Car Club of America (SCCA) leading the way. In an unprecedented move, General Motors (GM), the world's largest automaker, decided to enter this market segment, which in 1953 amounted to a mere 0.027 percent of new car sales. Harley Earl, GM's first vice president of styling, was the driving force in GM's decision, deciding to design a sports car that would appeal to American buyers.

Earl intended the car to be part of GM's 1953 Motorama Traveling Dream Car Road Show and gave a few concept sketches to Bob McLean. A recent Cal Tech engineering graduate, McLean was also a stylist, and his assignment was to layout the new GM sports car. McLean based the proportions—but not the styling—on the popular XK120 Jaguar, a car that also offered a front-engined six-cylinder-powered layout. Like the Jaguar, he rear-biased the engine location low in the frame and pushed the low seats almost against the rear wheelhouses. The XK120 had a 92-inch wheelbase, but McLean was designing a sports car for American drivers and roads, so not surprisingly, his version ended up larger with a wheelbase measuring 102 inches.

Chevrolet's chief engineer, Ed Cole, was one of the first to see a completed mockup of the car, and it matched his vision to revitalize the division's products. Cole had overseen the design of Cadillac's modern overhead valve V-8 before moving over to Chevrolet, where he had a similar engine in the works. He saw the new sports car as something exciting that could be in Chevrolet showrooms at least a year before the passenger cars with the new V-8 engines, and he gave it his enthusiastic support. After a formal review of the mockup, GM President Harlow "Red" Curtis gave Earl the go ahead for Motorama, but Cole came away with only tentative production approval. Chevrolet General Manager Tom Keating supported the sports car, and Cole had an almost free hand with his vast engineering budget, so he didn't wait around for a final approval.

Cole recruited Maurice Olley from GM's Vauxhall Motors in England and put him in charge of Chevrolet Research and Development (R&D). Olley first saw the sports car mockup on June 2, 1952, and Cole asked him to design a chassis for the car on a compressed time frame. Olley had served as Rolls-Royce's chief engineer in the United States before joining GM in 1930 where his work on vehicle handling led to the General's adaption of independent front suspension. Olley went to work on the sports car project and in 10 days did a sketch of the chassis very close to its final configuration under the code name "Project Opel." He had mockups underway while Cole worked to remake Chevrolet's Blue Flame Six into a sports car engine.

Jaguar's XK 120 provided the performance baseline. Its 160-hp straight six displaced 3.4 liters, had double overhead cams with hemispherical combustion chambers, and breathed through a pair of side-draft carburetors. By comparison Chevrolet's Powerglide Six displaced 235ci (3.8 liters), had a hydraulic lifter pushrod valve train with wedge combustion chambers and a single-barrel downdraft Carter, and produced a rather paltry 115 hp. For the sports car version, compression was raised from 7.5 to 8:1 and the solid-lifter truck cam was fitted. Three sidedraft Carter carburetors fed more fuel to the engine, helping to increase output to a respectable 150 hp.

The inline six had been backed by the two-speed Powerglide automatic since 1950, and it would remain the only transmission available until late in the 1955 model year. This availability acted as an expedient for Motorama and simplified production startup. Chevrolet rationalized that most American car buyers would consider a manual transmission old-fashioned. The suspension and other

The Corvette was conceived by Harley Earl, GM's first vice president of styling, as a low-cost alternative to the foreign sports cars with greater appeal to American buyers. This would lead to the world's largest automaker making the unprecedented move to enter a new market segment that represented only .027 percent of U.S. new car sales in 1952. *GM Media Archive*

The show car's hot-rodded Blue Flame Six sparkled with chrome and breathed through an impressive looking trio of sidedraft, single-barrel Carter carburetors. The compression ratio was raised from 7.5 to 8:1, and a solid-lifter cam from the 261ci truck engine, along with a split pair of exhaust manifolds, raised the engine's power output from 115 to 150 hp. *GM Media Archive*

## What's in a Name?

The show car needed a name, but Chevrolet and its advertising agency Campbell-Ewald were drawing a blank. The name of a small, fast naval vessel was suggested to Ed Cole, and Chevrolet's sports car thus became the Corvette. The new Corvette was a sensation at its January 1953 Motorama debut at the Waldorf Astoria in New York City. Among the thousands captivated by the Corvette was Zora Arkus-Duntov, a performance-loving Belgian-born Russian with a German engineering degree. Duntov was looking for a job in the U.S. auto industry, and seeing the Corvette inspired him to write Olley to inquire about work with GM. Duntov joined Chevrolet R&D on May 1, 1953, fated to become a central figure in Corvette development.

driveline components were also sourced from the passenger car parts bin with minor modifications to sharpen handling.

The styling staff used glass reinforced plastic (GRP) for EX 52, the Motorama show car's body, because it could be quickly and inexpensively produced. Olley had been experimenting with this material for production bodies and recommended it as the only way to meet the production schedule for 1953.

Chevrolet received letters from about 7,000 other visitors to Motorama, each assuring that if the Corvette became available they would buy one. This convinced GM's president to approve the car for production, but the company would body it in

This see-through profile is of Ex-122, the Motorama show car, which certainly looked like a sports car with its set-back engine and low profile body, but looks could be deceiving. The substantial ladder frame was a solid foundation, but it would be three model years before the Corvette could be taken seriously as a sports car. *GM Media Archive*

steel instead of the fiberglass used in the first 300 Corvettes that came off a temporary pilot assembly line in Flint, Michigan.

Ed Cole's objectives for the Corvette were met, if only in a limited way, with a few cars in the hands of high visibility owners or on display at Chevrolet dealers by the fall of 1953. Full-scale production of the 1954 Corvette started in St. Louis on a permanent assembly line during December 1953. This line was designed to turn out an optimistic 10,000 cars a year, but by the time it was up to speed, demand had fizzled and America's fiberglass dream had turned into an orphan stepchild seemingly overnight.

Riding the crest of the wave whipped up by Motorama, Chevrolet dealers were inundated with requests for the Corvette. The dealers in turn bombarded Chevrolet General Sales Manager William Fish who decided to allocate the trickle of cars available only to select high-volume dealers. Fish told them to invite only celebrities and the most socially prominent people in their communities to buy new Corvettes. He presumed they would tell their friends what a great car it was, but this strategy didn't really pan out. It's doubtful any of these early customers thought about racing, and even Olley never envisioned the Corvette being raced. Still, it had two seats, a convertible top, and Chevrolet called it a sports car.

### Sports Car or Racer?

Classified by its displacement, the Corvette's 3.8-liter engine put it in Class C, up against its performance baseline the Jaguar XK 120 and, worse yet, the faster XK 120M. The Corvette wasn't far off in acceleration or cornering speed compared to the base Jag, but its brakes were hopelessly inadequate. This deficiency was exacerbated by minimal engine braking through the Powerglide, which converted the energy it sucked up into heat and often blew seals. In 1954, amateur sports car racing involved a low level of commitment with show room stock cars usually driven to the track, but few Corvette owners gave it a try.

In 1953, there were only a few permanent road courses in the United States, but racing enthusiast General Curtis Lemay, head of the Strategic Air Command (SAC), opened up a handful of air force

## It had two seats, a convertible top, and Chevrolet called it a race car.

This was the first time that volume production of fiberglass bodies had been attempted and a lot of problems had to be overcome. This photo shows only the largest of 62 individual pieces. These moldings were rough and uneven on their reverse side, requiring a lot of grinding and fitting to bond them together, and worse yet they were peppered with porosity, which made painting a nightmare.
*GM Media Archive*

Corvette production started less than six months after its introduction close to home on a temporary pilot assembly line in Flint, Michigan, where the first 300 examples were built. All of these cars were white with red interiors and black canvas convertible tops; the first two rolled off the line on June 30, 1953, with production moving to the permanent plant in St. Louis, Missouri, in December. *GM Media Archive*

bases to SCCA racing. Two 1954 Corvettes were entered in a race at March AFB near Riverside, California, and at Andrew's AFB in the Washington D.C. area. Dr. Dick Thompson, a dentist off the racetrack, had been racing a Porsche 356 and was well on his way to winning a SCCA National Championship when a young Chevrolet dealer, Bob Rosenthal, asked him to try a Corvette during a practice session. Thompson was favorably impressed and got in some competitive laps before, predictably, the brakes and transmission failed. Still, he decided to race a much-improved Corvette for Chevrolet two years later.

The most ambitious early attempt at racing a '54 Corvette has to be Bill Von Esser's entry in the November 1954 Mexican road race, the Carrerra Panamerica. He left the starting line with co-driver Earnest Pulz but blew the engine before completing the first leg. It seemed the Corvette's fate to be an also-ran.

## Saved by a Rival

To the bottom line–oriented GM upper management, the Corvette was all but gone when Ford inadvertently saved it with the introduction of the two-seat Thunderbird in September 1954. Chevrolet's crosstown rival sold about the same number of cars through an equal number of dealers, and to cancel the Corvette when Ford came out with a rival would have been an embarrassment. Both cars had a 102-inch wheelbase, but Ford took a more conventional approach with a steel body and less aggressive styling. Ford came out with its first overhead valve V-8 in 1954 and offered it in the new 1955 Thunderbird, but Chevrolet could maintain the balance of power by offering its new V-8 in the Corvette. The Corvette, however, needed much more than a V-8 engine to overcome a reputation for the dismal build quality established in its first two years of production.

Chevrolet's sales department insisted that 1955 production could not start up again until most of the unsold '54s were out of the way. The decision to continue building Corvettes came too late for a restyle and the new V-8 didn't help sales. When the St. Louis plant finally began manufacturing 1955 Corvettes, it was on a very limited basis with only 700 produced to fill orders and keep the nameplate alive. The 265ci (4.3 liter) V-8 improved both acceleration and drivability, but hardly anyone seemed to notice or care. The optional V-8 was equipped with the passenger cars' power pack four-barrel Carter WCFB carburetor and a hotter camshaft making 195 hp. Equipped with the standard Saginaw 3-speed manual transmission, the Corvette saw real performance improvement thanks to the 41-pounds-lighter V-8 and the 95-pounds-lighter transmission. Additionally, the V-8 provided a lower center of gravity than the Blue Flame 6.

## Wowing the Competition

Even with the V-8, the Corvette was still in Class C, but it was a better race car despite the fact that most cars were still equipped with the Powerglide and weak brakes. The new T-bird raced in Class C as well, and its 4.8-liter 292ci Power Pack–equipped Y-block V-8 gave it a slight horsepower advantage. But the T-bird carried about 300 pounds more weight than the Vette, leaving its acceleration only slightly better than the six-cylinder Corvette, and its resultant lap

Ford inadvertently saved the struggling Corvette from cancellation with the introduction of their rival two-seater 1955 Thunderbird, and Chevrolet could match its optional V-8 with their 265. A powerpack version of Chevy's new V-8 with a four-barrel carburetor and solid-lifter cam was available for passenger cars, with Corvettes getting a hotter cam bringing their 265s up to 195 hp. *General Motors*

David Kimble

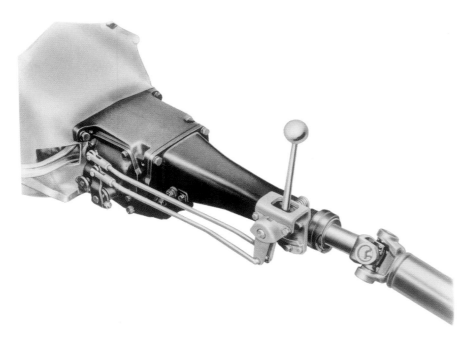

The passenger car Saginaw three-speed manual transmission was listed as standard equipment, but only about 75 of them equipped with floor shifters were installed in Corvettes late in the 1955 model year. This combination not only added 40 hp, but the V-8 was also 41 pounds lighter than the Blue Flame Six, with the manual transmission taking off an additional 95 pounds. *GM Media Archive*

times around a road course weren't even close. On a race course, the Thunderbird was a nonissue for the Corvette. The real C-Class competition came from Jaguar's XK 120M and XK 140, and the car to beat for overall wins was the Mercedes-Benz 300SL.

By this point in time, several Corvettes were racing around the country. Usually the best they could hope for was to simply finish, but Chevrolet dealer Addison Austin was actually doing quite a bit better than just straggling across the finish line. He entered an SCCA national event at Watkins Glen in September, finishing 7th in class, 10th overall, against Jaguars and 300SLs. With careful preparation and the addition of Raybestos brake linings, Austin managed a 3rd-in-class podium finish at Thompson and a class win at Hagerstown.

## Bold Predictions

With production only a trickle, Chevrolet used 1955 to give the Corvette a much-needed mechanical and styling makeover. The 1956 body was a very effective reskin over the existing support structure and featured a 300SL-influenced front end and

The decision to continue producing Corvettes on a limited basis in 1955 came too late for a much-needed restyling to help make a break with the past and start overcoming a bad reputation. The only exterior clue to V-8-equipped Corvette's newfound power was a large gold "V" covering the small "V" in the Chevrolet finder script, which is missing on this engineering car. *GM Media Archive*

customer-demanded niceties like roll-up windows, exterior door handles, and an available removable hardtop. The powertrain was upgraded with a pair of more powerful 265ci V-8s to choose from. Both engines benefited from dual point distributors with centrifugal advance, new high-performance cylinder heads with a 9.25:1 compression, and freer-flowing exhaust manifolds. The early production 1956 Corvette engines all

had aluminum intake manifolds with a pair of Carter WCFB four-barrel carburetors and were rated at 225 hp. Later in the year, the 210-hp base engine with a single four-barrel Carter returned. The company ordered 111 base engines with Racing Production Order (RPO) 449—a camshaft recommended for racing purposes only—bringing engine output up to an unpublished 240 hp.

If racing improves the breed, then no part saw greater benefit than the cast-iron Saginaw manual transmission, which now had a close-ratio gearset far more effective for racing coupled to a coil spring–design clutch that offered far more clamping pressure. Unfortunately the same could not be said for the brakes, which remained unchanged except for more fade-resistant linings. They would remain a problem into the next decade.

The frame and suspension were the best parts of the original Corvette, though minor but important modifications to the chassis were made based on Duntov's handling evaluation of the Corvette not long after he joined Chevy R&D. Duntov remarked that it was a car in which the two ends were fighting each other, but he found a relatively simple fix: by adding tapered shims between the bolts on the front crossmember and the frame, he increased stability and diminished some of the roll oversteer. He also raised the rear spring mounts, and a shallower angle decreased the roll understeer. The handling was much improved.

It wasn't long until Duntov was removed from working on the prototype and forced into a lesser position, even though he had worked for Sydney Allard in England and co-drove one of his cars at the 24 Hours of Le Mans in 1952; his boss, Olley, would not give him permission to drive for Allard in the 1953 race. Duntov was furious. In a breach of GM etiquette, he went over Olley's head directly to Cole. When Duntov returned from France, he was still attached to R&D, but was relegated to engineering purgatory at GM's remote proving grounds in Milford, Michigan, where he worked on minor projects like school bus driveshaft vibration problems. But Cole had larger plans for him.

Duntov's steady driving and position as a GM engineer interested Porsche, and they invited him to be a 550 Spyder team driver at Lemans in 1954. He co-drove one of their 1100cc Spyders to a class win in the 24-hour race and drove for them again in 1955, even though he was working on a secret project for GM. Cole's main interest in Duntov was his experience with high-performance engines and fuel injection, and he asked the engineer to shift his primary focus and work with John Dolza as a part of the GM engineering staff. Dolza was developing a production fuel injection system, and even though Duntov was working with Dolza around the clock on his engineering staff, he still managed to win another 1100cc class race for Porsche at Le Mans in 1955 and followed that up with a record run up Pike's Peak later that year.

An increasing number of adventurous owners were participating in amateur club road racing at tracks around the country in 1955, with the new 4.3-liter V-8 powered Corvettes remaining in Class C. The 55 Corvette was a better race car, even though most of them were still equipped with Powerglides, and nothing had been done about the brakes, which remained their Achilles' heel. *Dr. Peter Gimenez*

## For Corvettes to be taken seriously as sports cars, they needed road-racing credentials.

After the Pike's Peak celebration dinner, Duntov wanted to publish the impressive performance of the rejuvenated 1956 Corvette. He suggested to Ed Cole that the world be shown just how fast the new Corvette could go, and when Cole asked how fast that was, Duntov made a bold prediction: 150 mph. With a reminder that fuel injection was still his primary assignment, Duntov began figuring out how to reach 150 mph on the sand at Daytona Beach, the place where Corvettes first achieved widespread publicity in 1955. He equipped a 1954 engineering car with a 225-hp engine and aerodynamic fairings and a stabilizer fin, but it wasn't enough; he needed more power.

A Chevy engineer named Fred Frincke was working in the drafting room when Duntov gave him a set of camshaft specifications originally intended for his Ardun Ford. Frincke's instructions were to convert the dimensions of the camshaft from metric to SI and have some cams ground while Duntov traveled to GM's Mesa, Arizona, proving grounds. Duntov installed one, known as Duntov cams, in the Corvette test mule's engine and hit the accelerator. The cams helped produce about 240 hp in a dynamometer test—enough power for Duntov to lap Mesa's banked 5-mile circle at 163 mph in December of 1955, 13 mph more than he had boasted to Ed Cole. Duntov was sure he could reach 150 mph atop the higher rolling resistance of packed beach sand. Across the country in Warren, Michigan, Duntov cams were installed, the engine was freshened up, and that assembly, along with several other special components, was swapped into a red 1956 Corvette body that had white side coves.

The 1956 Corvette was introduced late, not breaking cover until January 1956 at New York City's Motorama at the Waldorf-Astoria. Though the car lacked credibility, Chevrolet was prepared to run it at Daytona once the beach conditions were right. It took some time, but Duntov was patient. He finally made a two-way run timed by the National Association for Stock Car Auto Racing (NASCAR) and held his breath until the final speed was declared—150.583 mph. It was little more than

The restyled 1956 Corvette was an effective reskin over the existing body support structure featuring roll-up windows, exterior door handles, and an optional auxiliary hardtop. This makeover didn't break cover until Motorama opened at the Waldorf in January, and at a press conference late in the month Ed Cole announced that factory-backed Corvettes would be raced by Chevrolet dealers.
*GM Media Archive*

a breath over his prediction, but a breath was all he needed. Corvette was quick to pounce on Duntov's promise and entered three factory Corvettes at NASCAR's speed weeks on Daytona Beach in February 1956. It was Ford versus Chevy, and the Thunderbirds matched the Corvettes' 225 hp with a 312ci version of their Y-block. The Corvette team cars were erected atop 1955 chassis with '56 bodies painted in an interpretation of American International racing colors—white with a pair of blue stripes down the center and blue side coves.

The drivers were famous road racers John Fitch and self-proclaimed "aerobatic aviatrix" stunt pilot Betty Skelton (of Campbell-Ewald), and they drove production-class Corvettes with Duntov in a modified class car. The event was a standing mile acceleration run, and the heavier T-birds had the advantage. Fitch even tried a six-cylinder engine block in the trunk of his Corvette, but because of poor reception from the press, he competed without it. He finished third behind a pair of Thunderbirds.

Duntov's Corvette was the only one to do well in the standing mile. Featuring bullet-shaped farings over the headlights, a tall fin, and experimental 10.3:1 high compression heads, Duntov's Corvette achieved 89.753 mph, winning the modified class.

The other competitive event was the flying mile, and Duntov won again with a speed of 147.30 mph against unfavorable winds.

Fitch had the fastest production sports car at 145.543 mph, and Skelton was next with 137.773 mph, giving the future owners of '56 Corvettes bragging rights of splintering top speeds.

## Off to the Races

For Corvettes to be taken seriously as sports cars, they needed road-racing credentials. Cole called a meeting to determine what it would take to make the Corvette competitive. On November 30, 1955, at the Milford proving grounds, the minutes were taken by Mauri Rose, a three-time Indy 500 winner and Chevy R&D engineer. Briggs Cunningham and Fitch, two of America's best known road racers, were there to evaluate a 1955 V-8-powered Corvette with a manual transmission. For comparison, there was also a Mercedes-Benz 300SL. Duntov began the trials with a demonstration run with the Corvette. Cole stated that he would like to have two or three Corvettes run Florida's Sebring Road Race in the stock sports car class. Cole and Duntov knew that the production 1956 Corvette would correct some of the deficiencies that Cunningham and Fitch pointed

For 1956 Chevrolet got serious about making the Corvette into a real sports car, finally making the minor but important modifications to the chassis suggested by Zora Arkus-Duntov not long after he joined Chevy R&D. The manual transmission was now readily available, equipped with a close ratio gearset and coupled to a dual-quad equipped Z65 by a 10 1/2-inch diaphragm clutch on this early '56 chassis. *GM Media Archive*

For its second year, the Corvette V-8's compression ratio was raised from 8.0 to 9.25:1, which, combined with freer flowing "Rams Horn" exhaust manifolds, brought the base version's power output up to 210 hp. Adding RPO 469 increased this to 225 hp by adding a pair of four-barrel carburetors on an aluminum intake manifold, which was Chevrolet's first optional speed equipment. *General Motors*

out after driving the '55, but winning Sebring was still an entirely different matter.

### Daytona and Sebring

Fitch was the only American on the Mercedes-Benz all-conquering 300SLR team until it abruptly pulled out of racing. Mercedes' knee-jerk reaction to a disastrous crash at Le Mans in June 1955 prompted Fitch to action. Encouraged by his meeting with Cole, he wrote Cole a letter late in December expressing genuine interest in helping to develop the Corvette. Cole responded with an offer to drive a

Corvette at Daytona Beach. Duntov was at Daytona in January, and while waiting for favorable weather, traveled south with the car to Sebring. With several talented drivers, the Corvette posted respectable lap times, and this was enough for Cole to enter a four-Corvette team in the 12-hour race. He hired Fitch as both a driver and team manager.

At a press conference in late January 1956, Cole announced there would be two models of the 1956 Corvette: a standard production model and a special racing version with magnesium knock-off wheels and oversized brakes. He also said that the cars would be

David Kimble

raced through local dealers. By the time Fitch was set up at Sebring, he would have five weeks before the race to develop the special racing version. To make matters worse, this seemingly impossible task had to be developed from both ends of the country, in both Florida and Michigan. Fitch, PR guy Walter Mackenzie, and Rose were the key players in Florida. In Michigan, Duntov was up to his ears with the fuel injection project, but joined by Maurice "Rosie" Rosenbeger and Russ Sanders, he still managed to help. The two groups were linked by daily flights, and the project was made even more difficult by production-class racing rules requirements: to be legal, parts developed in Florida had to be conceived, catalogued, manufactured, and assigned parts numbers in Michigan.

The three Daytona Corvettes were shipped back to Michigan to be rebuilt for Sebring and were accompanied by a new '56 that was to be equipped with the special racing parts as they became available. Engineering cobbled together a test model for Fitch from a worn development 1956 chassis and a spare '55 body. It was tough going; it was Fitch's first experience as a team manager, but he was also the development driver and spent many hours pounding around the bumpy 5.2-mile Sebring airport circuit. As parts fell off his vehicle and broke, his team of Chevrolet mechanics literally worked around the

clock to fix them. By the time the race cars arrived in Florida, some of the problems had been sorted out, but the cars were still very much a work in progress.

Sebring was the only international endurance race in the United States during the 1950s, and Duntov was probably the only one at Chevrolet who understood the Federation Internationale de l'Automobile (FIA) paperwork. He exercised a little entrepreneurial creativity while filling out the homologation forms to allow the modified Corvettes to compete as production cars. Many of Cole's proclamations were seen: the magnesium knock-off wheels from Halibrand, the oversize brakes and finned cast-iron drums, the Bendix Cerametallix linings. . . . By race day they looked ready, even though the cars were still being assembled during the night. With months of development crammed into five weeks, the drop of the green flag would be a step into the unknown.

Fitch chose Firestone Super Sport 170 tires for his racer in order to match the 37.5-gallon fuel tanks fitted to cover more miles between pit stops. Corvette steering was too slow for competitive driving, so a quick-steering adaptor extension was added to the central combined steering and idler arm. The steering columns were shortened, and tachometers reading to 7,000 rpms replaced speedometers. Rear axles had hi-torque limited-slip

Betty Skelton was a well-known stunt pilot famous for cutting ribbons while inverted 10 feet off the ground, and at the same time she was working for Campbell-Ewald as the Corvette's spokesperson. She had set a stock car flying mile record for Dodge at Daytona in 1954 and did a credible job for Chevrolet running the flying mile with a 137.773 average speed. *GM Media Archive*

differentials and longer axle shafts with threaded ends for the center-lock wheels knock-off wing nuts. Tubular shocks, springs, and the anti-roll bar were stiffened by an additional pair of Hodaille van-type rear shocks. These were curiously mounted to the leaf springs' U-bolt plates, adding them to unspring weight, but they eliminated persistent wheel hop problems. The designers, engineers, and pilots were about to experience an entirely new Corvette.

Flint V-8 built the race engines, and it's believed they arrived at Sebring by way of Smokey Yunick's "Best Damn Garage In Town" after some additional tuning. Chevrolet's team of four white Corvettes with blue graphics was entered in the 12 Hours of Sebring race by Dick Doane's Raceway Enterprises, keeping with Cole's press conference statement that Chevrolet wanted to remain in the background.

Chevrolet's first try at the 12 Hours of Sebring was a limited success, but ad man Barney Clark, who paid the drivers through Campbell-Ewald, knew how to make the most of it. This photo taken of a pit stop during the race proclaimed the B modified Team Corvette to be "The Real McCoy" in an ad that ran after the car's class win in the 12-hour event. *GM Media Archive*

It was decided that the best way to capitalize on the win at Sebring was to campaign a Chevrolet-backed Corvette in amateur sports car races, and Barney Clark recruited Dr. Dick Thompson. He was a Washington D.C. dentist with an SCCA National Championship, and Barney used this photo of him winning his first race in the car at Pebble Beach in 1956 for another hard hitting ad. *GM Media Archive*

The Dundee, Illinois, Chevrolet dealer had a fifth Corvette in the race, and like three of its factory cars, it was a '56-bodied 1955 engineering car. It was painted Doanes' racing color: Arctic Blue. The engine was prepared by Chevrolet but didn't have any special racing components. All of the engines breathed through dual Carter four-barrels, and one of the Class-C production 265s had a mild cam chosen for low-end torque and durability. Another engine was bored to 3.81 inches and stroked to 3.30 for 307ci, with ported high-compression heads and a ZF four-speed transmission to run in Class B modified. The only cars entered in Class B were Ray Crawford's Kurtis, and some 312ci Thunderbirds and a Corvette equipped with an engine to keep Ford from winning anything while increasing Chevrolet's chances. The blue Corvette was officially entered by one of the drivers, Don Davis from Chicago. In this grueling race where typically less than half the

This magazine ad announced the introduction of an engineering advance of great significance available on the 1957 Corvette: fuel injection that permitted a level of efficiency hitherto unrealized. Potential customers were invited to examine this wonder of since for themselves by driving the 283 hp Corvette with 1 hp/ci. *GM Media Archive*

1957 Corvette bodies were a carryover from '56 with the recessed side covers offering an opportunity for two-tone paint schemes, which were very popular in the 1950s. This Venetian Red car had beige coves, along with the auxiliary hardtop, and if RPO 579 had also been ordered, it would have had fuel injection script in its coves and on the rear deck. *GM Media Archive*

cars ever completed the 12 hours, it was 5 fledgling Corvettes in a 60-car field.

As team manager, Fitch had hired the drivers and worked out the race strategy. But he also co-drove the No. 1 modified Corvette with Walt Hansgen in Class B. Dick Doane's blue Class C Corvette was No. 3, with the other factory cars numbered 5, 6, and 7, which were also their starting positions. After a promising start to the race, Fitch found trouble in the form of a slipping clutch on the second lap, but he saved the situation by deliberately slipping it in high gear until the cockpit filled with smoke. After cooling down under a light load, the clutch gripped well enough to continue, and since the Thunderbirds withdrew before the race, if the No. 1 Corvette could stagger to the finish, it would win Class B. Dale Duncan started the race in the No. 5 car, the fastest of the Class C Corvettes. He ran flat-out at 6,000 rpm and all three gears, but the hammering on the bumpy circuit broke an axle shaft in eight laps. His race was over.

After the race clock elapsed two hours, all four factory Corvettes were casualties, while the blue No. 3 with Davis and codriver Bob Gatz was functional but not competing. No. 7 was the new 1956 Corvette driven by Ernie Ericson with William Earger, and even with a Duntov cam, it was limited to 5,500 rpms using only second and third gears. Even though the engine wasn't being pushed to the limit, it burned or broke a piston, laid down a smoke screen, and retired from the race. In the No. 6 car, Ray Crawford and Max Goldman were having transmission problems even though they also weren't using first gear on the track because it wasn't synchronized. They had to run most of the race in third gear, but fortunately this car had a conservative camshaft and could rev to 5,000 rpms. It didn't lag, coming around even the slowest corners.

Chevy's little 265ci V-8 got its first displacement increase in 1957 with its cylinders bored out from 3.75 to 3.87 inch for 283ci and, topped by the Ramjet fuel injection unit, it produced 283 hp with a solid-lifter cam. The fuel injection system was still undergoing intensive development when production started in November 1956, and the illustration is one of the early 283 hp engines with the cool-looking but restrictive louvered air filter housings. *General Motors*

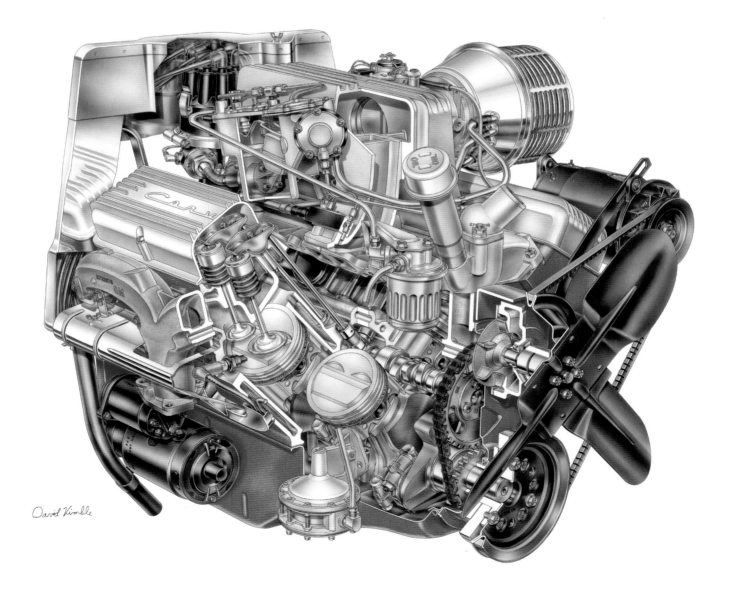

## Thompson "charged through the field like a rhino in heat."

*—Barney Clark, GM Advertising*

Only 24 cars finished at Sebring in 1956, and 3 of them were Corvettes. The Fitch/Hansgen No. 1 car won Class B, finishing 9th overall. Class C was won by a Ferrari driven by the Fangio/Castellotti team. The No. 6 Corvette of team Crawford/Goldman placed 15th overall, and the Davis/Gatz team finished 23rd in the No. 3 Corvette. John Fitch felt that his car's slipping clutch and the No. 6 running with only third gear had prevented their engines and drive lines from being overstressed. In other words, the problems that held them back during the race may have also allowed them to finish, turning what could have been an embarrassing disaster into a limited success. Barney Clark at Campbell-Ewald knew just what to do with the Corvettes' first glimmer of racing success and wrote the copy for a memorable print ad with the headline "The Real McCoy."

The production version of the factory Sebring Corvettes was model 2934 SR. Only six were assembled at the St. Louis plant in June 1956. Chevrolet engineering had SR parts—and a few may also have been assembled there—but the FIA required 25 models for a car to be classified as production. Duntov's fanciful homologation paperwork was upheld at Sebring, but the few times the Sebring Corvettes raced in SCCA, they had to compete as modifieds ("mods"). There were plenty of Corvettes racing in Class C by the summer of 1956, but they were legitimate production cars, and some of them did very well.

Two additional SR chassis were built in GM's mechanical assembly shop for the SR-2s. One was intended as a race car for Harley Earl's son Jerry. The restyled Corvette's most prominent feature was an extended nose, as well as large rear-brake cooling scoops in the side coves. Built like a show car, a finned headrest was added later to the body without giving a thought as to how much it weighed. For its racing debut, Jerry Earl entered the SR-2 in the June sprints at Elkhart Lake, Wisconsin, as a modified driven by Thompson. He campaigned for a production Corvette and found the SR-2 too heavy to be competitive, finishing 16th in B/C modified. GM styling applied the vehicular equivalent of a liposuction treatment, and it lost about 300 pounds. A second SR-2, this one with a street chassis, was built for GM President Red Curtis, and a third one for Bill Mitchell, which was also raced.

### The Flying Dentist

How to leverage Corvette's performance at Sebring was the question on Mackenzie's mind. Mackenzie had become Chevrolet's de facto racing director, while Clark worked with the drivers. It was decided that the best way to build on the success of Sebring was to campaign a Chevrolet-backed Corvette in amateur sports car races across the country. These events drew huge crowds, and those crowds represented scores of potential buyers, however, the SCCA did not allow factory entries or even sponsorship. Barney next approached Thompson with an offer he couldn't refuse. Thompson had won an SCCA National Championship and garnered many other victories behind the wheel of other high-performance cars like Porsches and Jaguars. The terms of the offer were unprecedented: Thompson would still have to pay his own travel expenses and would have to buy the Corvette, but it would be prepared and maintained by Chevrolet. Also, anywhere in the country he wanted to race, Chevrolet would provide the vehicle and

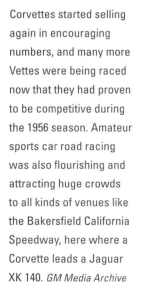

Corvettes started selling again in encouraging numbers, and many more Vettes were being raced now that they had proven to be competitive during the 1956 season. Amateur sports car road racing was also flourishing and attracting huge crowds to all kinds of venues like the Bakersfield California Speedway, here where a Corvette leads a Jaguar XK 140. *GM Media Archive*

engineer Frank Burrell. After each race, Thompson would relinquish the car once more to Chevrolet.

Thompson's first venue was the Pebble Beach National Road Races near San Francisco on April 22, 1956, where he competed in the over 1500cc production race. His main opposition was the formidable Mercedes-Benz 300SL, which was equipped with independent rear suspension and a 2995cc inline-six with direct cylinder fuel injection rated at 215 hp. Even though these cars were in Class D, they were very fast and very popular, usually competing among themselves for an overall win. Thompson's Corvette had the springs, tubular shocks, front anti-roll bar, and some of the transmission parts from one of the Sebring cars, but otherwise was considered almost stock, with an open differential and production brakes. He liked everything about the car but the brakes; however, the Sebring brake package could not be used and the stock ones almost ruined his race.

The 300SLs, like most European cars, had four-speed transmissions, while the Corvette's three-speed had well-spaced ratios; it was its 25 extra hp with an additional 70 lbs/ft of torque that made up for the missing gear. After starting poorly, Thompson led the race on the second lap and stayed in front even as his brakes started fading. When they failed completely, a factory 300SL driven by Rudy Cleye finally passed him. Thompson's brake drums were pulled after the race, and the charred brake shoes fell apart.

For Corvette, the results were still impressive: second overall and first in Class C. Clark wrote another ad trumpeting this achievement and sent Thompson to selected SCCA Nationals and hill climbs, primarily in the East and Midwest, which he usually was able to win. Clark was worried when he first met the mild-mannered dentist, but he later declared that Thompson "charged through the field like a rhino in heat."

Corvette sales grew, and more of them were being raced, including entries from Chevrolet dealers like Rosenthal. He had given Thompson his first chance to try a Corvette in 1954 and also had a winning two-car team with drivers Bark Henry and Fred Windridge. W. G. "Racer" Brown from *Hot Rod Magazine* and Bob D'Olivo, a Peterson Publishing staff photographer, watched Thompson's Corvette whip the 300SLs at Pebble Beach, and after telling Duntov that they could make one that was better, the engineer must have been intrigued because

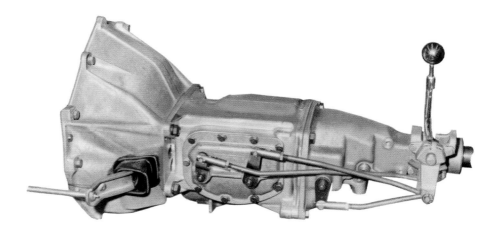

Brown and D'Olivo received a car. Cal Club had liberal modification rules, and it was a good fit for a couple of hot rodders. Brown wrote an article about preparing the Corvette for racing, and how one driver, Peterson ad man Bill Pollack, inadvertently bashed in competitors' bodywork while leaving only minor cracks in the Corvette's durable fiberglass fenders.

Thompson traveled west to drive Brown's mod car to victory at Seattle Seafair Raceway in June, where he finally beat the hot 300SL driver Paul O'Shea. He also won at the Cal-Club Palm Springs Race in November. He finally won the SCCA's 1956 Class C production championship, proving the Corvette sports car as "the real McCoy."

Little did he know, though, that in 1957, developments were underway that would enable the Vette to dominate. Corvette sales totaled 3,407 for the model year, a huge improvement over 1954, the only other year of full production when 2,540 were actually sold. Sales were rising. Ford sold 15,631 Thunderbirds in 1956, down from 1955 but still amazing for a two-seater. The Corvette, however, was no longer threatened. Its place in Chevrolet's product line was secure, and it was becoming the halo car that Cole and Harley Earl had in mind.

On Sunday, July 1, 1956, Cole became a GM vice president and general manager of Chevrolet, and his assistant, Harry Barr, became chief engineer. The following year was Cole's first on the corporate scoreboard as general manager. He wanted something more to showcase technical innovation than a displacement increase for the V-8 and a four-speed transmission; he wanted the fuel injection that had been under development for several

Corvettes needed a four-speed but it had to be sourced from existing high-volume components and GM's Saginaw three-speed was not a suitable starting point because first gear wasn't synchronized. Borg-Warner's T-85 three-speed was, and Chevrolet Engineering worked out a conversion by moving the reverse gear into the tail shaft creating the T10 fully synchronized four-speed manual transmission.
*GM Media Archive*

years. Cole told Barr to make sure the fuel-injected V-8 was ready for 1957, and he ordered Duntov, who was recovering from a broken back, to complete fuel injection research immediately.

Chevrolet and Pontiac were the only GM divisions to put fuel injection into production. By this time, Duntov had a small group at Chevrolet working with the Rochester products division where the system would be manufactured. Even though problems still existed, production of the fuel injection unit was frozen at the end of August, which was late for 1957, but could still be squeezed in.

GM's fuel injection was constant flow with fuel spraying continuously from eight injection nozzles directly into the ports, and Chevrolet's version was called Ramjet fuel injection. Its advantages over carburetors were more power with better fuel mileage and improved throttle response. Despite not being quite ready, Cole made it available on passenger cars in addition to the Corvette. In 1957, Chevrolet's V-8 cylinders were bored from 3.75 inches to 3.87 inches for 283ci or 4.6 liters; the solid-lifter Duntov cam dual four-barrel carburetor version was rated at 270 hp, and with different heads, pistons, and fuel injection 283 hp, 1 hp/ci. To get

the most out of this additional muscle, a four-speed transmission was released for sale in April with a limited slip differential.

Chevrolet engineering worked out a four-speed conversion of Borg-Warner's cast-iron T-85 three-speed transmission. Except for the engine and drive line, the 1957 Corvette was essentially the same car as the '56; however, its sizzling performance and growing reputation as a sports car almost doubled sales that year.

Production of RPO 579 and the fuel-injected 283 began at Flint V-8 on November 1, 1956, and fuel-injected Corvettes were being assembled in small numbers at St. Louis a few days later. Cole, now general manager of Chevrolet, wanted to start an aggressive racing program to show off his Corvettes' performance, and he wanted to start with Nassau. The Nassau races were a unique nonchampionship series held during a two-week-long party in the Bahamas. Racing around a rough 4.5-mile airport circuit attracted the big league European teams and drivers. It was the perfect opportunity for the Corvettes' return to Sebring, and three fuelies were allocated from early production and prepared for racing.

## Sebring and Nassau, 1957

Two of these cars were factory entries; the third was privately entered but still considered part of the team. All were prepared at the Chevrolet engineering center. The most obvious changes to the Corvette's racing package from early in the year were the lack of rear brake cooling scoops and bolt-on steel wheels. Air to cool the rear brakes entered ducts on both sides of a radiator that carried it through the engine compartment to rocker panel ducts, which sent the air to the rear wheel wells. After a disagreement between Cole and Ted Halibrand (the knock-off magnesium wheels manufacturer), they weren't used on the 1957 production-class Corvettes and started appearing on the racing Thunderbirds.

Fitch was the production-class Corvette's team manager at Sebring in 1957, but it was Thompson who pounded the Nassau Corvettes around Sebring's bumpy 5.2-mile track. Thompson drove the car through this marathon test session until something went wrong and he was forced to grab a new vehicle while his was being worked on. The Corvettes were equipped with 37.5-gallon metal fuel tanks, quick-fill gas caps, roll bars, and hardtops. The steel wheels were .50 inch wider than standard, and Firestone super sport racing tires were mounted on them for both Nassau and Sebring.

Altogether, five Corvettes presented at Nassau for Speed Week, with the three Chevrolet-engineered cars painted white with the same blue graphics as the 1956 factory-racing Corvettes. Red steering wheels completed the patriotic look, as the Yanks hoped to showcase a little American muscle and capture the imagination of the racing world. Thompson drove the No. 15 car, Jim Jeffords in No. 36, and No. 72 was handled by Windridge. Mitchell's red SR-2 joined them as a modified No. 117 shared by Pete Lovely and O'Shea, and the No. 43 blue Corvette was driven by Warren Flichinger. Mitchell's SR-2 was powered by a fuel-injected 283 with an early version of the cold air induction setup that would soon become an RPO. Nassau Speed Week started on December 3, 1956, and unfortunately the fuel-injected Corvettes' racing debut was less than spectacular.

Nassau served its purpose, and Chevrolet resolved that the cars would be ready for Daytona and Sebring. All three factory-prepped Corvettes returned to Chevrolet engineering, and the SR-2 returned to styling. Mitchell's SR-2 was aero-dynamized for Daytona, losing its large rear brake

Before the Speedweek time trials, NASCAR also held a road race at nearby New Smyrna Beach Airport, and another NASCAR regular from the Corvette team, Paul Goldsmith, was entered to deal with some factory T-Birds. The windshield, roll bar, and hardtop were back on his Corvette for this event, and surprisingly Goldsmith spent most of the main event trying to get by Ford ace Marvin Panch in a very fast 312ci T-Bird, finishing fourth overall.
*GM Media Archive*

## Project XP-64 became the Corvette SS.

With less than six months to design and develop the Corvette SS sports racing car, Zora Arkus-Duntov had to use the assembly mockup with incomplete fiberglass body as a test mule. Here the mockup is being rolled out for a run at GM's Milford, Michigan, proving grounds with Duntov, who logged most of over 2,000 miles of testing behind the wheel. *GM Media Archive*

cooling scoops and getting, among other wind-cheating devices, a full Plexiglas canopy for the driver. Since it would have to run as a modified anyway, an experimental fuel-injected 283 with two air meters (throttle bodies) and eight individual exhaust pipes was installed, raising the horsepower to 310. The Nassau production-class Corvettes were shipped to Smokey Yunick's garage in Daytona Beach to get them ready for NASCAR's version of Speed Week on the Florida sands.

The year 1957 saw a general reduction in Daytona speeds in the flying mile, but that didn't keep the factory Corvettes from sweeping their classes in both events, running without their windshields and hardtops. NASCAR driver Paul Goldsmith was in Thompson's Nassau car and set a new class record, winning the standing mile acceleration runs with an average speed of 91.301 mph. His teammates finished behind him: Johnny Beauchamp took second and Betty Skelton finished third in dominating performances. In the flying mile event, Goldsmith won again with a speed of 131.941 mph, and Skelton finished second ahead of Beauchamp. Skelton tried the SR-2, but it was NASCAR legend Buck Baker that drove it to both modified class wins, with 93.047 mph in the standing and 152.866 over the flying mile. The fuel-injected Corvettes made a clean sweep of Daytona Beach.

Before Speed Week, NASCAR also held a road race at nearby New Smyrna Beach airport, and Goldsmith entered to help the other Corvettes compete with some very fast factory Thunderbirds. Goldsmith's Corvette, with its hardtop back in place, was assigned No. 9, and after qualifying third for the main event, he spent most of the race trying to wrench second place overall away from Marvin Panch, another NASCAR driver in a 312 Thunderbird. After squealing into the pits for a tire, Goldsmith finished first in class and fourth overall, four laps ahead of second place, an XK 140 Jaguar.

This time, Duntov was not directly involved. The fuel injection system had been released for production before it was ready, and development was still underway; however, the engineer's role was winding down, and he was consumed with another project.

### Duntov and the SS

Harley Earl had plans for Duntov. He would soon be maneuvered into an assignment that he had hoped for since starting to work at Chevrolet—the chance to design a sports racing car with GM's resources behind him. Like Cole and Duntov, Earl wanted to see Corvettes contending for overall wins in international endurance racing, so he had a D-type Jaguar sports racing car brought into styling for evaluation . . . and for bait. He made sure the word spread that he intended to rebody the Jag as a Corvette and race it at Sebring with a Chevy engine. Earl knew that his idea would be unacceptable to Cole and Duntov, and he soon found both of them telling him why his plan wouldn't work. But Duntov's plan worked: from these discussions came the authorization to style a bold new Chevrolet sports racing car. Duntov would design the chassis.

Project XP-64 became the Corvette SS, and like the original Corvette, its starting point was a Jaguar D-type blended with futuristic Corvette styling details. Jaguars had also served as Duntov's inspiration for the tail fins on his Daytona Beach Corvettes, and as Earl's with the SR-2 when he won Le Mans in 1955 and 1956. Jaguar was the ideal car to follow starting from scratch. The wheelbase was shortened from the production Corvette to 92 inches, bringing it in line with cars it would be racing against. A wind tunnel comparison was conducted between the SS styling clay and the D-type.

Zora Arkus-Duntov had an area walled off in Chevrolet engineering where he worked around the clock overseeing a small group of draftsmen and fabricators, living the realization of a dream—designing and building an all-out sports racing car with the resources of GM behind him—and in this publicity photo, the Corvette SS chassis is nearing completion.
*GM Media Archive*

Cole wanted the car to be ready for Sebring on March 23, 1957. The body design was almost finalized by the time Duntov started developing the chassis less than six months before the race. He walled off a private area at Chevrolet engineering and oversaw a small group of engineers working around the clock behind closed doors. There would be no distractions.

The D-type had a center monocoque tub with its in-line six-cylinder engine and independent front suspension carried by a tubular steel subframe bolted to the firewall. With so little time, Duntov took a more expedient approach and had the body removed from a Mercedes-Benz 300SL, revealing its advanced tubular steel space frame for ideas in designing the primary structure of the SS. Hand-fabricated, unequal A-arms were used for the front suspension like the Jaguar, but for the rear suspension he went one better with a De Dion tube instead of a live

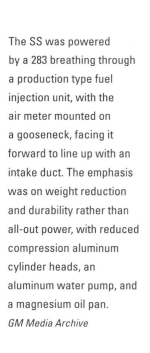

rear axle. This arrangement was still a solid axle but reduced unsprung weight by allowing the rear end to be mounted to the frame with drive to the rear wheels through half shafts.

Like Ferrari, and most of the other European race car builders, Duntov stuck with what he knew and used drum brakes instead of the early Dunlop four-wheel disc brakes on the D-type. Cerametallix linings were put on Chrysler center plane front brakes at all four corners with drums fabricated from cast-iron 12-inch-diameter rings with steel face plates and aluminum cooling fins bonded by the All-Fin process. Like the 300SL's lower unsprung weight, the rear breaks were located inboard taking advantage of the De Dion suspension. To save time, a modified Halibrand quick-change rear end housing was used with special side cover castings to mount the brakes and gears produced at the engineering

center. The magnesium knock-off wheels were also from Halibrand, and the SS along with the SR-2s were the only Chevrolet racing Corvettes to run them in 1957.

The SS was, of course, powered by a fuel-injected 283 with modifications made primarily to save weight and adapt it to this unique application rather than to produce more power. The fuel injection unit was the production type with a single air meter, but it was mounted to the side of the intake manifold plenum chamber by a gooseneck facing it forward. This lined up with an intake air duct from the grillee that was said to be good for an additional 10 hp at 150 mph from the ram effect. Cylinder heads were cast in aluminum with a reduced compression ratio of 9:1 down from 10.5:1 for durability, and the water pump was also aluminum with a special baffled magnesium oil pan. The water pump and frame-

The SS was powered by a 283 breathing through a production type fuel injection unit, with the air meter mounted on a gooseneck, facing it forward to line up with an intake duct. The emphasis was on weight reduction and durability rather than all-out power, with reduced compression aluminum cylinder heads, an aluminum water pump, and a magnesium oil pan.
*GM Media Archive*

The Corvette SS was so late reaching Florida that all of the potential co-drivers John Fitch had talked to took other rides, so John contacted his former Mercedes-Benz teammate, Piero Taruffi. As it turned out, the "Silver Fox" made a long flight from Italy for a short drive at Sebring, which included a few laps in practice when this photo was taken, and the car's last two laps in the race. *GM Media Archive*

Having the largest displacement engine in the field, the Corvette SS was lined up first for the run and jump start at Sebring in 1957, with John Fitch winning the foot race across the track. Unfortunately the 283 was slow to start, and Fitch came around in 6th place after the Lap 1 with things just starting to go wrong. Taruffi retired the SS after 23 laps with the rear axle steering the car. *GM Media Archive*

After using the Nassau Corvette for practice, a brand new pair of thoroughly prepared cars arrived from Chevrolet the day before the race for the 3.0- to 5.0-liter GT class, joining the team's modified class SR-2. The new Corvettes stayed with the red, white, and blue color scheme, and they both performed flawlessly in the race, with Dave Duncan, John Kilborn, and Jim Jeffords finishing 15th overall driving the No. 3. *Dr. Peter Gimenez*

mounted generator were driven by two V-belts and the mechanical fuel pump pad on the side of the block had a cover over it.

Four-speed transmissions wouldn't go into production at Borg-Warner until April, but the SS had one of the gear sets with special ratios in an aluminum housing, and there was also a matching aluminum bell housing. Every part of the SS was designed with weight in mind, and the completed race car, wrapped in its magnesium body, weighed in at 1,850 pounds, about 100 pounds lighter than the D-type Jaguar. This lower weight was essential because the conservative 283's output of 307 hp was about the same as the latest 3.4 liter Lucas fuel-injected Jaguar straight six and less power than the heavier V-8 and V-12 Italian opposition. In contrast to the European perception of American racing cars, the Corvette SS would have to rely on superior road holding and a weight advantage to win races.

The project was, by necessity, designed on the fly—parts were fabricated as they were drawn up and assembled on a mock-up with a preliminary version of the engine. With time running out, the mockup became the test model. Though it weighed over 150 pounds more than the final SS car and commanded

less horsepower, it still proved to be very fast and racked up over 2,000 miles of testing, most with Duntov behind the wheel. No one involved except Duntov had ever worked on a racing car before, and even behind schedule, the model amazed everyone at the track with its performance.

John Fitch was not only team manager of the three GT-Class Corvettes, but he was also signed to drive the SS. He had a problem, though: his co-driver was nowhere to be seen. The race car arrived in Florida so late that Fitch was forced to ask other drivers about driving with him. He finally contacted former Mercedes-Benz teammate Piero Taruffi, who flew over from Italy. With the SS problem solved, a pair of new fuel-injected Corvettes arrived at Sebring a day before the race to compete in the 3.0- to 5.0-liter GT class. All three Nassau Corvettes were used as practice cars, with Mitchell behind the wheel of the SR-2 modified class Corvette in the GT heats.

As car No. 1, the SS was in first position for the run-and-jump Le Mans start, but the engine was slow to fire up and Fitch was in sixth place after the first lap of the race. Persistent problems with the brake-balancing system led to a flat-spotted front tire, but after a pit stop on Lap 4, things came apart even more.

Soon, the engine stopped running—twice—and the car's magnesium body acted as a heat trap, turning the cockpit into a toaster oven. The rear axle started steering the car. With the engine overheating and the SS all but undriveable, Fitch pulled into the pit stop and relinquished the SS to Taruffi. After just a few laps, Taruffi agreed—there wasn't any point in continuing.

On the surface, the Corvette SS's racing debut could be seen as a disaster, but for a few laps during the race, Fitch matched 1956 winner Mike Hawthorne's lap record, despite the SS's erratic brakes. Cole watched the race and saw the car's potential, realizing that the actual racing car had very little track time before the race to sort out its problems. He

authorized a three-Corvette SS team for Le Mans. The GT Corvettes performed flawlessly throughout the 12-hour race and had some luck with their only real threat—a Ferrari Europa that retired from the lead after 9 hours. Thompson shared the winning Corvette No. 4 with Gaston Audrey, finishing 12th overall. Finishing 2nd in class was the No. 3 Corvette driven by Jeffords with John Kilborn and Duncan followed by O'Shea with Lovely in the SR-2 No. 2 finishing 16th.

## The AAMA Ban

Cole's racing program was gaining momentum, but at Sebring, it was already doomed by an agreement signed at the annual board meeting of the American

Zora Arkus-Duntov was finally able to give John Fitch a look at the late arriving SS race car, with enough time left before the race for him to get a little time in the car, which had never turned a wheel. The magnesium bodywork pivoted out of the way at both ends, which was handy, but it created an unforeseen problem by trapping heat in the cockpit that dissipated through the fiberglass body.
*GM Media Archive*

Automobile Manufacturers Association (AAMA) in February 1957. The AAMA voted unanimously that its member companies take no part in automobile racing and that they refrain from suggesting speed in their advertising or publicity. This motion took effect immediately, but GM, Ford, and Chrysler all had big racing programs, as their drivers and teams were under contract. They were given until June of the same year to wind down these activities. Incredibly, GM President Curtis, who supported increasing performance and the Corvette, proposed this repressive action.

GM was the world's largest corporation and accounted for over 50 percent of the U.S. car market. It had been under threat of a Federal antitrust suit for years, and the escalating Detroit horsepower war created more bad press. GM's upper management believed that if any doubt was cast on their activities, the antitrust suit might follow; the new ban could serve to quiet complaints from the National Safety Council and insurance companies. Ford's new president, Robert McNamara, saw racing as an expensive nuisance. He enforced the ban to the letter while Curtis allowed racing to continue under the table and out of public view.

The unloved AAMA ban was really only a voluntary guideline, and seeing what GM was doing, the other auto manufacturers returned to racing in 1958, but at GM, it was corporate policy for the next 14 years. The highly visible Corvette Super Sport program was specifically targeted for extension in May when the program was dealt a devastating blow: the three chassis under construction, along with the model, were ordered to be scrapped, saving only the SS race car. The model was quietly hidden away, and with factory racing at an end, Chevrolet moved to start helping their customers compete with the Corvette's first racing RPOs, coincidentally becoming available that month.

Most car magazines found the fuel-injected 283-hp Corvettes the fastest accelerating cars they had ever tested, usually covering the standing quarter mile in under 15 seconds. In 1957, the SCCA started factoring in cars' racing performances and not just classifying them by displacement, and even though the fuel-injected Corvettes' 4.6-liter engines were still below 5.0 liters, they put them in the new B-production class. Racers could order a near duplicate of the factory Sebring Corvette's chassis framework. This RPO 684 heavy-duty racing

suspension included stiffer springs and front anti-roll bar, stiffer larger diameter shocks, and a quick steering adaptor. The racing brakes were also part of this package; the finned cast-iron drums had scoops on their backing plates, Cerametallix linings; and the internal ducting system carrying cooling air from the front of the car to the rear brake scoops.

This option was only available with a manual transmission and required that the Positraction rear axle along with the fuel-injected or dual four-barrel solid-lifter engines be ordered as well. The 15x5.5 wheels on the RPO 276 also had to be included because the standard wheels wouldn't fit over the finned drums. RPO 579D was the same fuel-injected 283-hp engine as the 579C but with a cold air induction system and an 8,000 rpm steering column mounted AC mechanical tachometer. A flat three-sided fiberglass duct was mounted to the inner fender panel forming an air box that picked up cool intake air next to the radiator. The filter element was at the back of this duct connected to the air meter (throttle body) by a short round duct, and this setup could be combined with RPO 684 creating the ultimate 1957 customer racing Corvette. The four-speed transmission was still scarce, but in May, it was normally added to this already bewildering array of regular production options.

## Racing Under the Ban

In the full grip of the AAMA ban, Chevrolet was paralyzed, but to the huge crowd watching a regional SCCA race at Cumberland, Maryland, on Sunday, May 19, it seemed that nothing had changed. In the seventh race of the day, there were plenty of Jaguars and 300SLs, but they were completely outclassed by the latest fuel-injected Corvettes.

A notable pair of Corvettes built less than a week before the race went head-to-head with the first RPO 579 C/684 No. 164, driven by Henry, with Bill Howe Jr. in the pilot RPO-579 D air box Corvette No. 253. Both Sebring Corvettes were also in the race—with hardtops in place and pink side coves. The No. 64 car was driven by Carroll Shelby and Ebb Rose Jr., who had bought the cars from Cole, himself in the No. 65 car. There were also several significant drivers in less significant Corvettes, including Thompson in No. 11 and Don Yenko driving No. 193.

When the checkered flag fell, it was the Corvettes holding the first three places in Class B production with Thompson overall in first. Carroll Shelby finished second—his first time in a Corvette—and Howe finished third. Henry, driving Rosenthal's new RPO-684 Corvette, had been in third before a rain delay but ran into trouble and didn't finish. Mercedes-Benz 300SLs took the next three positions, and the best Jaguar only finished *ninth*. The Corvette's time had come, and the American racer became even more dominant in the summer and fall of 1957.

At the SCCA National in Elkhart Lake, Wisconsin, on June 23, Corvettes took the first four positions in B-production, with Jeffords finishing ninth overall (first in class), while

Thompson uncharacteristically finished toward the back of the field. On July 14, in another national at Marlboro, Maryland, Thompson won overall with Rosenthal's pair of Corvettes following him. In August, the Montgomery New York Air Force Base was the scene of a six-Corvette sweep. In California, Dan Gurney drove a Corvette for the first and only time to a class win in September at Riverside Raceway's inaugural event, and Jerry Austin was first overall with his Corvette at Palm Springs, the November finale to the SCCA racing season. Cole was a happy man.

It didn't stop there. In 1957, and for the second year in a row, Thompson won an SCCA National Championship with a Corvette. Duntov was recognized within Chevrolet as the resident sports car expert and was closely identified with the Corvette by the press and public. He rose to his first executive position as Director of High Performance for Chevrolet, responsible primarily for developing performance engine parts and covertly helping to maintain Chevrolet's dominating presence in motorsport from behind the scenes. Duntov's small group also became responsible for Corvette engineering, but it would be years before he had any authority over it.

Corvette sales almost doubled in 1957 to 6,339 but were still well under the original 1954 projection of 10,000 a year. Ford Thunderbird sales also increased to 21,380, but even though a few T-birds were still racing, Ford had given up trying to position it as a sports car and decided to stop fooling around producing a low volume two-seater. The T-bird carried something of a performance image, and Ford capitalized on it, turning the T-bird into a sporty four-seater, selling a whopping 80,938 the first year. The Corvette also went through a metamorphosis for 1958, equipped with an entirely new body; sales approached the 10,000-per-year goal, but it remained very much a sports car at heart.

The No. 4 put in the best performance of the 4-car Corvette team at Sebring, with Dick Thompson, the racing dentist, and Gaston Audrey coming in 12th overall, 1st in GT. Their Corvette had an international flavor, with Swiss shields for Andrey and American shields for Thompson on the front fenders. *GM Media Archive*

**Quad headlights first appeared** on American cars in 1957 with the Chrysler Corporation products leading the way. By 1958, they had become a fad, along with flashy chrome detailing. The four-eyed chrome-barge look swept through the industry, and the Corvette wasn't left out: the new body and interior featured four headlights and more panache. Sitting atop the same chassis, the all-new 1958 Corvette was 9.19 inches longer, 3.34 inches wider, and a little heavier than its predecessor, with the bumpers mounted to the frame instead of the fiberglass body. Aluminum bracing had been gradually added to the Corvette's body starting in 1956, and perpetual revisions evolved the body into a complete cowl support structure with additional bracing in the nose, front fenders, and other high-stress areas by 1958.

Inside the car, the steering wheel and shifter looked familiar, but their surroundings were entirely new, including a grab bar in front of the passenger seat and seat belts as standard equipment. Seat belt anchors had been installed since 1956 when they became a dealer accessory, but in 1958, seat belts were installed at the factory, and along with the grab bar, made welcome additions—the new seats didn't offer any more lateral support than those they replaced. Another important improvement, which made the cockpit more suitable for high-performance driving, was relocating the gauges, which were strung out across the instrument panel within the driver's field of vision below the speedometer. Like the factory-racing Corvettes, the tachometer was above the steering column so the driver could keep an eye on it as he cycled through the gears.

Many other improvements less visible to the naked eye were implemented: the 283-hp fuel-injected 283's power output increased to 290 hp through improvements in fuel metering; redesigned

Opposite page: Even though it was sitting on the same chassis, the 1958 body was 9.19 inches longer, 3.34 inches wider, and a little heavier, with the bumpers mounted to the frame instead of to the fiberglass body. This early '58 cruising around the GM Tech Center campus is probably an engineer car, and the pair of chrome strips on its deck lid were unique to that year. *GM Media Archive*

The front fenders had to get wider to accommodate the quad headlights, which were surrounded by a chrome bezel with chrome strips trailing back on top of the fenders. Simulated air outlet louvers on the hood disappeared in 1959, but the nonfunctional outlets, at the front of the side coves, stayed in place to maintain the busy look that Chevrolet felt sold cars. *GM Media Archive*

injection nozzles and cold air induction ducts made the vehicle run smoother and cleaner; the generator switched to the right side of the engines, wrapping the fan belt more fully around the water pump pulley; and much, much more. The total vehicular overhaul produced an altogether superior Corvette.

Chevrolet's V-8 was joined in production by a larger engine in 1958: the W-motor with an initial displacement of 348ci. It became the famous 409 in 1961, and the terms *big block* and *small block* were coined to differentiate between them. The solid-lifter 348 with three two-carburetors was rated at 315 hp, making it Chevrolet's most powerful engine in 1958, but Zora Arkus-Duntov successfully argued against making it available in the Corvette. His point was that the W-motor was over 100 pounds heavier than the small block, and the extra weight on the front end would compromise the Corvette's handling. Still, Duntov's misgivings didn't stop him from having one installed for evaluation. Denny Davis, one of Duntov's engineers at the time, drove the W-equipped Vette home one night and encountered a ready-to-street-race fuel-injected Corvette. Davis remembers the guy was good, but he was able to stay with him, even though the 348 was hooked up to a Powerglide. His opponent almost lost it when Denny opened the hood.

## Racing under the Radar

Chevrolet could no longer be involved directly in racing, but proponents of the Corvette continued to build its reputation by providing covert support to the teams and drivers (among others) that they had worked with in the past. Corvettes finished first and second in GT at Sebring for the second year in a row; Dick Doane and Jim Rathmann placed 1st in 5000 GT, 12th overall, and were followed by Dick Thompson and Fred Windridge with John Kilborn taking 2nd in class, 33rd overall. Dick Doane's Raceway Enterprises entered the factory team cars in 1956, while in the new '58, his co-driver Rathmann managed the Advanced Marine Corporation covert supplier of Chevrolet cars and parts to the National Association for Stock Car Auto Racing (NASCAR) teams. Thompson won Sebring in 1957 driving a factory entry and found himself in the '57 Corvette Windridge had raced for Bob Rosenthal in the Sports Car Club of America (SCCA) competition the previous year.

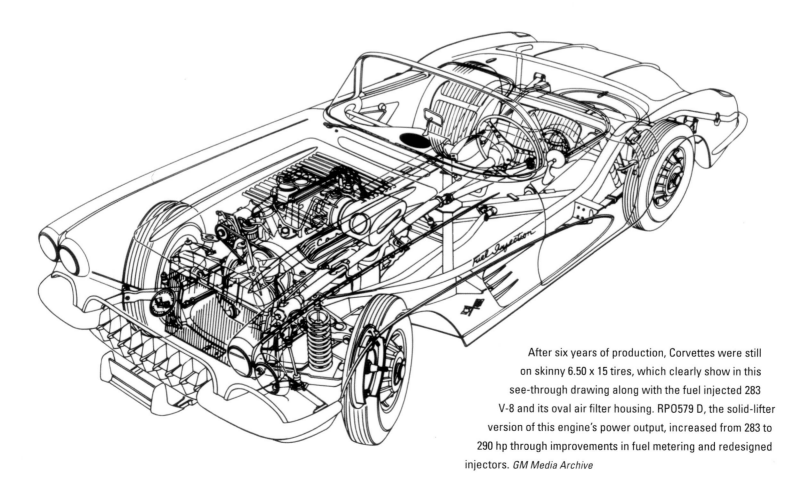

After six years of production, Corvettes were still on skinny 6.50 x 15 tires, which clearly show in this see-through drawing along with the fuel injected 283 V-8 and its oval air filter housing. RPO579 D, the solid-lifter version of this engine's power output, increased from 283 to 290 hp through improvements in fuel metering and redesigned injectors. *GM Media Archive*

Amateur sports car racing was practically a year-round activity in southern California with events organized by two rival clubs—the LA region of the SCCA and Cal Club—which created a lot of friction. On March 8, 1959, in a Cal Club Regional at the Pomona L.A. Fairgrounds circuit, Bob Hoffman, Scott Bailey, and Bill Gaskins lead a menacing Ferrari 250 GT Berlinetta through Turn 3 under the foot bridge. *Bob Tronolone*

Chevrolet was also still quietly assisting SCCA amateur racers with Corvettes, which had suddenly become as numerous as MGs and Triumphs; they helped to ensure Vettes remained the car to beat in big-bore competition.

## Monsters and Marine Life
### The Purple People Eater

Nickey Chevrolet in Chicago decided to get in on the fun and contacted the factory about preparing a Corvette for SCCA racing. Duntov recommended signing Milwaukee ad executive Jim Jeffords as the driver. In 1956, Jeffords had contacted Ed Cole and experienced a few rides in a Sebring Corvette later in the season and drove a factory team car at Nassau in December. In 1957, when Jeffords got the call from Nickey's sales manager, Lionel Lindhimer, he wasn't shy telling Lindhimer that if he got the deal, the Nickey-backed Corvette would win the national championship. The car was painted a livid purple and soon became known as the *Purple People Eater* after the popular song. Jim wasn't lying: his car won two back-to-back national championships for Nickey in 1958 and 1959.

Corvettes were big, powerful cars and, with their tough fiberglass bodies, tended to be driven more

Cal Club and the SCCA managed to cooperate in jointly sectioning the Kiwanis Grand Prix held at Riverside in July 1959, with Cal Club hosting the event that counted for SCCA national points. The production sports car support race was a wild one that was finally red flagged after multiple wrecks, with Tom Frank's shattered 1958 Corvette having to be dragged back to the pits. Bob Bondurant was declared the wiunner. *Bob Tronolone*

Bob Bondurant was one of the hottest Corvette drivers on the West Coast, winning 18 of the 20 races he entered in 1959, including this Cal Club Regional at Del Mar on September 19, 1959. This popular temporary circuit ran through the large Del Mar Fairgrounds parking lot north of San Diego, and Bob has obviously had to tape over his sponsor's name to satisfy the track stewards. *Bob Tronolone*

aggressively than the SCCA would have liked—but the fans loved it. This was especially true in Southern California Cal-Club events: the racing was wild and the rules liberal, with plenty of slam-bam fiberglass-crunching action. Bob Bondurant joined the West Coast Corvette wars early in his impressive driving career, buying a '57 from Jerry Austin that had been sponsored by Mead Chevrolet. Bob's first race in the car on his way to fame was at the Santa Barbara Road Races in August where he finished second behind Skip Hudson, whose '58 was now sponsored by Mead Chevrolet.

As Ford's Thunderbird became a four-seater, Chevrolet hoped that many former T-bird buyers would now favor the Corvette; no doubt some of them did, but sales numbers still didn't approach the two-seater T-Bird. With the new body, Corvette sales dramatically increased from 6,339 in 1957 to 9,168 in 1958—close to Cole's goal of 10,000 per year—but the '57 T-Bird's 21,380 sales mark wouldn't be reached until 1963 with 21,513. Harley Earl retired on December 1, 1958, and was replaced by

Bill Mitchell as vice president of styling, but Mitchell never liked that term and quickly changed his group's name to Design Staff.

Mitchell had been Earl's second in command for years; he had every bit as big an ego and bad as temper as his former boss, along with the same freedom to oversee the future design of Corvettes. Corvette styling had been his responsibility since 1955, and only minor changes were made to the 1959 model, with removal of the chrome strips on the rear deck lid and phony louvers on the hood. The gauges were redesigned to make them easier to read, and the door panels were rearranged for more elbow room with a T-handle reverse lock-out added to the four-speed's shifter. Another functional change was the addition of cooling slots to the simulated knock-off wheel covers, allowing air to reach the brake drums through openings in the wheels.

Duntov's group added gas-pressurized shocks and rear axle traction bars (trailing radius rods) that kept the leaf springs from winding up during hard acceleration, controlling wheel-hop and chatter.

Unfortunately for cars equipped with RPO 684, the traction bars conflicted with the rear brakes' cooling air deflectors, so the through-the-car ducting was cancelled. Sintered metallic brake linings were developed by GM's Delco Moraine Division and became available for street Corvettes as RPO 686 with heavier unfinned drums. The racing brakes' Bendix Cerametallix linings were terrible on the street, pulling from side to side, until they came up to a temperature that was never reached in every day driving. The metallic linings were also best when hot but offered good overall performance, which meant that the Corvettes' brakes were the first that could be used enthusiastically away from the race track.

Mitchell's SR-2 enjoyed an active competition career, but with its streamlined body, it had to race as a modified with a production Corvette chassis against some of the hottest sports racing cars. It was rarely competitive. In 1957, the Corvette SS Mule was a sports racing car that had been competitive during practice at Sebring against similar cars, but it was hidden away in storage without notice, which frustrated both Mitchell and Cole. Mitchell made a curious deal with Cole: for $1, he bought the car from Chevrolet and entered it in competition with a new body, but GM President John Gordon only agreed to the purchase with the understanding that it would in no way be associated with Chevrolet or the Corvette.

## The Sting Ray

Mitchell enjoyed deep sea fishing, so the only name that appeared on the new body was "Sting Ray"; he intended it to be an unannounced preview of the next generation Corvette. The SS wheelbase was 10 inches shorter than an existing Corvette; however,

Cal Club was back at Pomona in March of 1960 for a regional event that, as usual, attracted a large field of Corvettes, which are charging through Turn 2. The leader of the pack in the No. 13 is Dean Geddes, followed by Buford Lane No. 614, Don Steves No. 161, and Dave MacDonald No. 288, who's just starting out, with David Saylor No. 125 bringing up the rear.
*Bob Tronolone*

The foot bridge between Turns 2 and 3 at Pomona was very popular with photographers during the races until one of them dropped a camera on the track, and the police started kicking everyone off. On June 26, 1960, it's all four-headlight Corvettes at the head of the big-bore race with Vince Mayell No. 222, leading Buford Lane No. 50, followed by Mercedes-Benz dealer Tony Settember driving No. 58. *Bob Tronolone*

Dave MacDonald, a former drag racer, jumped into Corvette racing seemingly from nowhere in 1960 and was fast right away with his signature No. 00 sponsored by Don Steves Chevrolet. Davey's spectacular sideways driving style attracted attention wherever he ran, and here he's drifting through a high-speed turn at Marchbanks Speedway in Hanford, California, on September 17, 1960. *Bob Tronolone*

he intended the second generation to also be shorter, and this allowed Mitchell to legitimately put his design staff's resources to work. Over the winter of 1958–1959, the styling was pinned by Larry Shinoda and based on the stillborn Q-Corvette. The design broke completely from the 1950s futurism of the SS—flat as a single, with an upturned nose in profile that was supposed to create downforce. The new body was hand-layed up in 1/8-inch-thick fiberglass, about the same as a production Corvette, with aluminum supports and body mounts. It was heavy but plenty strong to stand up to competition.

As agreed, Mitchell paid for the Sting Ray out of his own pocket (as a GM vice president, his pockets were deep but limited). With the addition of a Harrison aluminum radiator and oil cooler, the SS mule chassis had to be run as it came out of storage. The first event for Mitchell's personal racing program was the President's Cup at Marlboro, Maryland, on April 18, 1959, and his volunteer driver for the bright red Sting Ray was Thompson. Like the Corvette SS at Sebring, its first shakedown was a practice run for the race, with no time to correct any problems that emerged on the track. Thompson quickly discovered that the brakes were erratic and prone to locking the front wheels, while the inverted airfoil nose generated lift—not downforce—and the front end started to fly at speeds above 100 mph.

The Sting Ray had a pair of grillees on its hood to allow heated air to escape, and cutting them out helped a little with the front-end lift, but nothing could be done about the brakes. Another challenge facing the racing dentist was wet roads: the main event was run in intermittent rain and the car didn't

# Mitchell paid for the Sting Ray out of his own pocket.

Rebodied as Bill Mitchell's Sting Ray racer, the Corvette SS mule's chassis had covered a lot of racing miles by the last time Dick Thompson drove it in competition at Riverside in 1960. With the SCCA C-modified championship won, the car traveled west to the *LA Times* Grand Prix in October, where Thompson ran as high as 7th and finished 9th after losing his brakes. *Bob Tronolone*

The Sting Ray made an encore appearance at the 1961 LA Times Grand Prix as a show car on display in the pits, badged as a Corvette for the first time. This pointed the way to the future, suggesting that it previewed the styling team for the next generation, which was how Bill Mitchell could justify Design Staff building the body. *Bob Tronolone*

Spiffed up for the car show circuit, the retired race car had lengthened chrome-plated grilles on the hood, chrome side exhaust pipes, a pair of bullet-shaped outside mirrors, and a passenger's wind screen. The Spartan interior included full gauges, with a wood rim steering wheel and complete upholstery in gray to match the silver gray exterior paint.
*Bob Tronolone*

have a limited-slip differential, so he also had to deal with wheel spin. Thompson was a fearless competitor in an era when safety equipment was limited to a seat belt, roll bar, and helmet, and he zoomed to the lead at the start of the race. Soon, though, a Lister-Corvette overtook him. He regained first position when the Lister retired, but then he spun, lost half a lap, and finally finished fourth behind two Porsche RSKs and the winning Lister-Jaguar. Despite the setbacks, it wasn't a bad performance for a new race car the first time out.

With the brakes jerking the car from side to side between lockups and the front tires barely skimming the track at high speed, Thompson put on quite a show; the Sting Ray bounced off several competitors, barely under control. Mitchell was thrilled because its performance proved that the Sting Ray wasn't just a racing show car like the SR-2s; track stewards, however, were less than pleased. At a formal hearing, Thompson's SCCA license was suspended for 90 days for erratic driving and contact with other cars, but Mitchell was undaunted and called John Fitch for the next race. Bill also picked up Dean Bedford Jr., a team manager and engine development engineer,

and the Sting Ray was put back in shape, but nothing more was done about the front-end lift or the brakes.

Fitch must have had some fond memories of the SS Mule when he got behind the wheel of the Sting Ray for the June sprints at Elkhart Lake, Wisconsin, but the brakes functioned as poorly as the SS race car. The culprit was an automatic front-to-back balancing system with a vacuum booster for each end. It had worked well enough on the mule until it was rebuilt and put into storage. Now the brakes were failing, like the SS race car at Sebring, but Fitch still managed a respectable start. He ran between fourth and fifth places until he spun under braking, swerving the Sting Ray off the track and out of the race. Something had to be done, but the fundamental problem couldn't be tackled until the car was taken completely apart, so the drums and shoes were simply replaced.

The Sting Ray was back at Elkhart Lake in August. Thompson was behind the wheel with Design Staff Stylist Anatole Lapine as his co-driver. They had a reasonably good race until, with Thompson in fifth overall, he was forced to retire—more brake trouble.

The Sting Ray needed a complete rebuild, and the quirky dual-vacuum Survo brake system was

With its hood raised to wow passers-by, the Sting Ray's production-based 283 V-8 is surrounded by heat shielding, with long tubular exhaust headers exiting through the rocker panels. The car's Corvette SS origins were still evident, with its frame-mounted generator and forward-facing fuel injection system air meter. *Bob Tronolone*

Chevrolet's small-block V-8 received its second displacement increase in 1962 with the 283, both bored and stroked to reach 327ci, which required reworking the block's casting patterns to accommodate 4-inch bores. The only remaining fuelie, RPO 582, still breathed through the same intake manifold with an extended flattop plenum, but with a higher flow air meter, along with an 11.25:1 compression ratio, it was rated at an impressive 360 hp.
*GM Media Archive*

finally replaced. One of the Hydrovac power brake boosters was modified for a new single Survo setup. After further modifications, the Sting Ray was almost 1,000 pounds lighter, with much lower drag and higher top speed than a production Corvette. The brake system, however, continued to overwhelm them. After a few more SCCA races, Mitchell's red Sting Ray traveled to Nassau for Speed Week in December, where the former Harley Earl SR-2 was also entered; it was now owned and operated by Chevrolet dealer Bud Gates.

Rules for nonchampionship races were patterned after the Federation Internationale de l'Automobile (FIA) to accommodate the international field they attracted—some of the hottest cars and drivers from Europe were frequent competitors in America. The Sting Ray and SR-2 were in different classes; Thompson's 283 pitted him against the fastest

sports racing cars, while Gates' punched-out 331ci small-block Chevy faced lesser opposition. In the Governor's Trophy Race, Gates took 3rd in class, and Thompson finished 11th. There was much to celebrate, but the main event—the Nassau Trophy Race—loomed large. History repeated itself, as Gates came in 3rd and Thompson 11th once more. These results were hardly headline material, but considering the competition, the much-improved Sting Ray looked ready for SCCA C-modified competition in 1960.

After three class wins in a row, no Corvettes entered the 1959 12 Hours of Sebring race. Direct factory involvement ended in 1957, and the '58 win was considered a carry-over with factory connections. The SCCA returned to big-bore racing, and 283 fuel-injected Corvettes won in every region. Duntov, along with other Chevrolet engineers, occasionally showed up at the bigger events while on vacation. In southern California, racing started immediately in January, and stars like Andy Porterfield, behind the wheel of his symbolically numbered 283, were already banging fenders with rivals like Bondurant. The SCCA was based on the East Coast, and most of the Cal Club Races only drew competitors and crowds from the region, but the competitors were serious and the crowds were large. The Cal Club races received extensive newspaper coverage; some were even televised.

Jeffords successfully debuted the 1959 edition of the *Purple People Eater* in the East and Midwest, defending his B-production title. He decided to make a surprise appearance at Riverside, California, in July. Contact between drivers from different parts of the country was minimal, but competitive rivalry among drivers was plentiful, and with most national championship events held in the East, Jeffords' appearance gave the California Corvette cowboys a rare shot at a national championship.

The production support race for the one and only running of the Kiwanis Grand Prix was a SCCA national hosted by Cal Club, and Jeffords was less than pleased that it was going to be run under their liberal rules. Many cars were lightened, and any oversized Gumball-recapped tires had their bumpers stripped off, even though California Corvette racing was a contact sport.

The field of racers was so large it stretched the length of Riverside's infamous Esses. A thin-skinned 300SL and Jaguar stood out among a larger crop of big bad Corvettes, and Jeffords, behind the wheel of the *Purple People Eater,* quickly took the lead. As the reigning champ, Jeffords car was No. 1. Bob Bondurant still drove his '57 Vette No. 51, in which he had won 18 of the 20 races he entered that year. Bondurant made his move after drafting Jeffords down Riverside's long back stretch; he out-braked Jeffords entering the high-speed 180-degree Turn 9, and took the lead. Jeffords stayed in contact, but he never got a chance to rally because the race

On February 11, 1962, the FIA added a new season opener to their international endurance racing series, the Daytona Continental 3 Hour Run on the 3.81 mile combined infield and tri-oval road course at Daytona. A. J. Foyt, driving a Pontiac Tempest No. 59, and Bob Johnson in the No. 17 327 Corvette, started on the front row, followed by Ford star Marvin Panch No. 20, driving a Corvette for the first and only time.
*GM Media Archive*

Overall winner Dan Gurney, driving Frank Arciero's Coventry Climax–powered Lotus 19, blows past Jack Knab's No. 75 Corvette, which came in 5th in class, 23rd overall in the 3-hour race. The sparse crowd was typical of this event and never improved very much over the years, but it remains an important part of Daytona Speed Week. *GM Media Archive*

Dave Morgan, in a new 1962 327 Corvette No. 25, overtakes a Jaguar XKE on the tri-oval banking; he would finish 21st overall, 5th in class at the inaugural Daytona Continental. This event was lengthened to 2,000 kilometers in 1964, which took about 11 hours, and finally became the 24 Hours of Daytona in 1966, joining Sebring and Le Mans as part of the Triple Crown. *GM Media Archive*

was red-flagged for a bad wreck, bringing it to an early end.

Through her steady race performances and cadre of dedicated Chevy drivers, engineers, and visionaries, the Corvette continued gathering momentum in 1959, both on the track and in the showroom. The sales numbers totaled 9,670, compared to 9,168 the year before. Slowly but surely, the Corvette was inching closer to Cole's bold sales projection.

## Looking for Le Mans

Preparing a Corvette for amateur production sports car racing in 1960 hadn't changed very much since it entered competition in 1954 with the addition of a wide, quick-release, World War II–style aircraft seat belt. Roll bars started appearing in 1957 (they became mandatory by 1960) and were installed in a complete interiorm, including the passenger's seat and carpet. The windshield could be cut down or removed, usually replaced by a Plexiglas racing windscreen. All other parts except replaceable components, like tires, were required to have factory part numbers and be correct for the car. Rules varied between SCCA regions, but mufflers and engine cooling fans could usually be removed for racing and replaced on cars driven to the track after the event.

Even if the Corvette SS team had made it to Le Mans in France in 1957, it would have been for the first and last time. In 1958, all entries were limited to a displacement of 3.0 liters. The possibility of winning the world's most famous endurance race with a big-bore American car returned in 1960; limitations on engine size were removed, and Corvettes were entered for the first time. Both Cole and Duntov had wanted to enter Corvettes at Le Mans since Chevrolet started racing them, and they came within a few months of their dream in 1957 before the American Automobile Manufacturers Association (AAMA) ban made that dream impossible. To cover Chevrolet's involvement at Le Mans, engineering development contracts were

With the No. 1 prototype Ferrari passing on the low side, Dick Thompson, driving Grady Davis' No. 11, is on his way to winning the 327 Corvette's GT class, finishing 13th overall. Thompson's teammate, Don Yenko, driving the Gulf Oil executive vice president's other immaculately prepared 62 Corvette, No. 10, came in second in class. *GM Media Archive*

For the annual 12-hour grind at Sebring in March 1962, the Corvette entries were numbered 1 through 7 and lined up at the front of the field in that order. The No. 7 Corvette was one of the first cars to be rolled into position before the start. Driven by Harry Washburn and Bill Fuller, it finished fourth in class, 31st overall.
*GM Media Archive*

signed for two teams, and the plan was for each team to run a pair of cars first at Sebring and then at the big one in France.

The two groups couldn't have been more different. Lloyd "Lucky" Casner's Camoradi Team had never been to Le Mans, while Briggs Cunningham had entered every race since 1950 and built his own cars from 1951 to 1955. Casner was a promoter and freewheeling business man with many diverse enterprises: *Camoradi* was an amalgam crafted from Casner Motor Racing Division. (In 1959, Duntov had the opportunity to drive Casner's 250F Maserati Formula One car in a race at Lime Rock, which may have indirectly led to Camoradi's involvement in Chevrolet's Le Mans effort.) Cunningham, on the other hand, had 10 years' racing experience at Le Mans and even more as a racing consultant to Chevrolet.

All four cars were white and equipped with the LPO 1625 A 24-gallon fiberglass fuel tank, only available with the hardtop required for GT endurance racing. Casner's cars were completed first, then delivered through Don Allen Chevrolet in Miami, Florida; Camoradi mechanic Lee Lilley oversaw race preparation. Cunningham's Corvettes were sent from St. Louis, Missouri, to the Chevrolet Engineering Center, where a stack of engineering work orders were filled before shipping them to Brigg's mechanic Alfred Momo and his shop in Long Island, New York. The cars came equipped with cast-iron big valve .194-inch heads, 1956 SR-type front hubs, and axle shafts mounted to Halibrand knock-off magnesium wheels rolling on Firestone T170 Super Sport racing tires.

Six 37-gallon center-fill fiberglass fuel tanks were constructed from a later engineering work order and shipped to both teams, leaving them to complete the installation and modify the hardtops' rear windows. The fuel filler caps for these big tanks were on the convertible top storage compartment covers and could only be reached through an opening in the rear window. A Plexiglas enclosure isolated them from the interior (and the driver). The teams also installed the roll bars and other safety equipment and stripped their new Corvettes' front bumpers, grillee bars, and most of the chrome trim, adding their individual interpretations of American racing colors.

The Camoradi cars remained relatively stock, while Momo made additional modifications to Cunningham's vehicles. He added several doodads, like backup batteries, ignition coils, and electric fuel pumps. Duntov was directly involved with Briggs' team and oversaw the cars' preparation. Under his eye, the cars tried the silicon alloy aluminum heads, but unfortunately, in a 24-hour track test, they didn't even last 12 hours. On Casner's little team, Lilley was not only the mechanic, but also one of the drivers, with PR specialist Fred Gamble driving as well. Aside from Chevrolet support, Casner had wrangled sponsorship from Goodyear, raising the stakes of the race; Chevrolet and Corvette wanted to challenge rival Firestone in racing and also wanted to compete against the European tire manufacturers. There was no better stage than Le Mans for an international showdown.

Even though Chevrolet was compelled to stay under the radar, this was the first factory Corvette racing effort since 1957, and they stood out. Corvettes entered at Sebring that weren't part of the program. Chevrolet dealer Delmo Johnson raced his black 1959 No. 5 with codriver Dave Morgan, and a new white Corvette No. 6 was picked up at the factory on the way to Sebring by Chuck Hall and Bill Fritts. They drove from Chicago to St. Louis and trailered the race-optioned car to Florida with minimal preparation after they arrived at the track. Sixty-five cars entered the 12 Hours of Sebring that year. Six Corvettes boasted the largest engines, and they were ready to roll for the run-and-jump start.

The race was a disaster for Cunningham's cars. Behind the wheel of the No. 1 car, Briggs jumped to the head of the line but soon fell off course and rolled without major damage, but he was unable to continue and his race was over. The No. 2 Corvette, shared by Thompson and Windridge, had ignition problems before crashing out on Lap 41. Both of the more conservative Camoradi cars were able to

finish. After 12 hours, Chuck Hall and Bill Fritts demonstrated just how good a competition-optioned stock the 1960 Corvette could be on the bumpy airport circuit; they won the 5000 GT and placed 16th overall. The Camoradi Corvettes finished 2nd and 3rd in class. The No. 3 team of Jeffords/Bill Wuesthoff finished 26th overall, followed by the No. 4, driven by Fred Gamble for most of the race, finishing 32nd overall.

The drama wasn't over, however. The Camoradi No. 4 Corvette was forced to borrow a fuel line to replace a broken one on the engine, and it was returned to a spectator's car afterward. This left the camshaft-driven pump connected to the fuel tank with nothing but air between it and the injection unit's fuel filter. Word of this dangerous situation didn't get back to their shop until it was too late. After the car was run, fuel began gushing from the pump, and the resulting fire destroyed the car. With this experience, both teams regarded the long unsupported fuel lines on 1960 injected Corvettes as fires waiting to happen and retrofitted the '59 versions with two shorter lines and the filter in between.

The Le Mans entry for Camoradi's incinerated Corvette was filled by a third new car added to the Cunningham team. They sent a single car to France for the Le Mans prerace test on April 9, accompanied by a vacationing Duntov. With his Goodyear sponsorship, Casner's Corvette and birdcage Maserati went to Europe in May to run the Nurburgring 1,000 kilometer race. In Germany, it was one up, one down for the Camoradi team: Sterling Moss and Dan Gurney won overall in the Camoradi Maserati, but a wheel-bearing failure ended Gamble and Lilley's race early in the Corvette.

Early in the race, with nothing but a row of hay bales separating the pit lane from action on the track, the No. 5 Corvette roars past, closely tucked up behind the No. 4. Delmo Johnson and David Morgan finished 21st overall in the No. 4 Corvette, which put them 3rd in class, while Jerry Grant, co-driving the No. 5 with Pat Piggott, had bad luck and failed to finish. *GM Media Archive*

During a pit stop, Dallas Texas Chevrolet dealer, Delmo Johnson, and his regular co-driver, Dave Morgan, are getting ready to trade off when refueling is completed. Delmo's No. 4 1962 327 Corvette has the "Le Mans" hood developed by Chevrolet from his 61, with an air deflector ahead of an opening in the hood to reduce front-end lift.
*GM Media Archive*

Duntov was painfully aware that Corvettes were about as aerodynamic as bricks. There wasn't much that could be done about drag, but wind tunnel testing revealed some areas that could be improved. An air deflector was added to the hoods of the Cunningham cars, with two rows of six louvers behind it to reduce high speed front end lift and raise airflow over the windshield for improved visibility in the rain. Lilley didn't install the louvers and positioned the deflector farther back on the Camoradi Corvette's hood. He and Gamble found out the hard way that this arrangement didn't work during a run in the rain soon after.

Cunningham listed Duntov as a reserve driver, and he was highly visible in the pits at Le Mans hoping for some time behind the wheel. Cole valued him too much, however, and had asked Cunningham to not let him drive. Thrust into an awkward position, Cunningham was finally able to explain to Duntov why he didn't let him drive during his retirement

dinner 15 years later in 1975. In the Corvettes' first appearance at Le Mans, the four big, white-and-blue striped American cars looked awfully impressive as they lined up at the front of the starting grid. Unable to call on Duntov, Fitch was the only other driver with Le Mans experience, so Cunningham was assigned to another car.

The No. 1 car at Le Mans raced as No. 2 at Sebring, and the European race found Bill Kimberly sharing the car with Cunningham. Thompson and Windridge were in the new No. 2 car; this left the No. 1 from Sebring with a new left front fender and top. This Corvette was No. 3 at Le Mans, shared by Fitch and his co-driver Bob Grossman with Gamble and Lilley continuing to drive for Casner, who also had three birdcage Maseratis entered in the race. The Camoradi car was the lightest but also paradoxically the slowest of the quartet. Lilley set a 5,000 rpm red line to improve their chances of lasting 24 hours, and Lilley's car was one of two Corvettes running at the finish.

Just moments after the race started, Fitch and Gamble were side by side through the Dunlop curve, leading the field. Cunningham was not far behind, gunning his engine around a dry track. A rain squall hit in the second hour, and when Cunningham brought the No.1 Corvette in for a routine pit stop, Kimberly took the car next and promptly rolled it at Maison Blanche. Thompson and Windridge's race turned into a prolonged ordeal—they also spun out in the rain at Maison Blanche, and later the brakes failed at Tertre Rouge. The No. 2 car lost precious time during the night while being dug out of the sand before continuing with pieces missing from its battered bodywork and seeping head gaskets. The rules stipulated that liquids could only be added at 25-lap intervals during the race, and the No. 2 car's

oil consumption became too much to handle. At 11:15 in the morning, Windridge came past the pits in the No. 2 car, trailing smoke and out of oil as he bowed out of the race.

In 1953, Fitch finished 2nd overall at Le Mans, co-driving a Cunningham C4. The L.A. Sarth circuit veteran co-drove the No. 3 Corvette with Bob Grossman, steadily working through the rain-slicked track, placing an incredible 3rd overall before midnight. The car was still in 6th overall in the afternoon when it came into the pits, sputtering and overheated. Too late in the race to add water, Chevrolet engineer Frank Burrell—Thompson's first Corvette mechanic—saved the day after the radiator cap was left off. He packed the engine with ice bought from the concessions. With the car iced down

Both Delmo Johnson's and Grady Davis' Corvettes continued to use the 37-gallon, center-fill fiberglass fuel tanks from 1960, with their filler caps on the convertible top storage compartment cover. These cars had to be refueled through an opening in the hardtop's rear window, isolated from the interior by a Plexiglas enclosure, by a crewman perched on the rear deck. *GM Media Archive*

but functional, Grossman's instructions were to stop every four or five laps, giving Corvette a chance to maintain the class lead.

It wasn't pretty, but it was dramatic—the crowd cheered with every bucket of ice thrown on top of the overheated engine. They stayed ahead of the second-place Aston Martin who had won GT in 1959. After 24 hours, Fitch and Grossman had covered 2,363.5 miles. Their average speed was almost 98 mph. It was good enough to take 8th overall and win the GT class at Le Mans . . . in a Corvette. The Camoradi Corvette finished 10th overall, but Gamble and Lilley didn't manage to complete enough laps to be scored as finishers and had fallen off the index of performance. All wasn't lost, however—they were still paid for their place. Casner's trio of Maseratis was also in the race but failed to finish, along with a prototype E2A XKE Jaguar entered by Cunningham.

With their Chevrolet contracts at an end, both teams sold their Corvettes.

## The Sting Ray Attacks

Back in the United States, Thompson continued racing the Sting Ray, now with a lightweight body painted silver for the 1960 season. Bedford was still the team manager, and Design Staff employee Ken Eschebach joined Mitchell's team of unpaid volunteers as a mechanic. Together, they planned a campaign to win the C-modified national championship. This class was for sports racing cars with between 3.0- and 5.0-liter engines, and the main opposition would come from the Lister Corvettes and Jaguars, along with numerous American-built Chevy-powered specials. All of the modified classes usually ran together in the same race, and with the big-bore cars handicapped by

With the 5.3-liter 327s classified in A-production, and the 4.3-liter 283s staying in B-production, Grady Davis campaigned an identically prepared Corvette in both classes, with a pair of distinctive air horns on their hoods. Grady's cars swept the A- and B-production race at the June Sprints in Elkhart Lake, with Don Yenko's No. 1 winning B-production and Dick Thompson's No. 11 winning A-production, taking both classes' national championships. *GM Media Archive*

their skinny tires, the smaller, lighter ones were often the overall winners.

The Sting Ray was rarely the fastest car on the track. It placed third overall at Marlboro in April behind a pair of Porsche RSKs. Its next two races in May were also won overall by RSKs. On May 30, at Bridgehampton, New York, Thompson finished second to a birdcage Maserati ironically owned by Cunningham, and in June, he came up against the hottest modified in the country—the Meister Brauser Scarab. With Augie Pabst behind the wheel and weighing in at 1,750 pounds, it was powered by a 5.56-liter Hilborn fuel-injected small-block Chevy said to be capable of 390 hp. The Sting Ray weighed about 2,000 pounds, and its Rochester fuel-injected 4.6-liter small-block only reached about 300 hp, but Thompson was able to compete with the Scarab.

Pabst and Thompson treated the crowds to epic battles at Elkhart Lake on June 18 and again at Meadowdale on July 24, trading the overall lead many times. While the Sting Ray finished second, Thompson's spectacular driving overshadowed Pabst's victories, and the season was going according to plan for Mitchell's team. All of these races were C-modified class wins, and with more experience than many of the other contenders, Thompson clinched the national championship after Meadow Dale. Even with a volunteer crew and driver, Mitchell must have been feeling the high cost of racing as he competed in so many events. Even with the championship won, he still sent the Sting Ray west to California in the fall to make an appearance in a couple of well-publicized races at the end of its competition career.

The Times Grand Prix was a huge international event at Riverside in October, co-sanctioned by the United States Auto Club (USAC) and the FIA, that attracted well-known European drivers. The Sting Ray qualified ninth and held seventh place for much of the race. Fading brakes forced the car back to ninth once more until it finished without any brakes at all. A week later, the Pacific Grand Prix at Laguna Seca looked more promising, and Thompson held fourth during the first of two heats. Walt Hansgen, in the Cunningham birdcage, squeezed by him, slamming his disc brakes through a turn only to end in ruin; Thompson's terrible drum brakes couldn't handle the slowdown, and the Sting Ray slammed into the back of the Maserati, ending the race for them both.

From Laguna, the Sting Ray returned to Design Staff at the GM Tech Center to be rebuilt as a show car and became a sensational hit across the country. It returned to Riverside for the Times Grand Prix in 1961, albeit as a display car finally badged as a Corvette. Vettes were competing in all popular forms of motorsports, from drag strips to hill climbs, even broad-sliding up Pikes Peak in the dirt and making top speed runs on the Bonneville salt flats. Corvette owned SCCA B-production racing as Bob Johnson won the 1960 national championship, and Corvettes were also winners in the showroom. Sales continued to climb, and in 1961, the original sales projection was met: 10,261 Corvettes had been sold. After seven years, they had done it.

After an almost-stock, racing-optioned Corvette won its GT class at Sebring in 1960, five Corvettes started the 12-hour race in March of 1961. They were all duck tailed 1961 models. Grady Davis, executive vice president of Gulf Oil, entered two cars, which utilized the Le Mans louvered hoods, air deflectors, and center-fill 37-gallon fuel tanks. Indianapolis Chevy dealer Bud Gates had extensive racing experience, but his fawn beige '61 Corvette arrived without the hardtop required for FIA GT class racing.

Delmo Johnson, another Chevrolet dealer out of Dallas, also had the 37-gallon fuel tank along with a Le Mans hood on his No. 4 Corvette. He ran a conservative race with co-driver Morgan. They finished 1st in class, 11th overall, keeping to a 6,100 rpm red line. They gambled on their injection unit's fuel meter ratio, running a little rich, trading reliability for power. Gates and Harry Heuer, in Bud's fawn-and-red No. 83, finished 2nd in class, 23rd overall, followed by Gardy Davis in the No. 1 car, with Ben Moore and Don Yenko finishing 3rd in class, and a distant 32nd overall. The No. 3 Corvette driven by George Robertson and Bill Warren was still running after 12 hours, but they didn't complete enough laps to be classified. Davis' No. 2 car, with Kilborn and Ray Rairdon, didn't finish.

Don Yenko was also driving one of Davis' Corvettes in SCCA B-production, and three races

> # The Sting Ray was rarely the fastest car on the track, but Vettes were competing in all popular forms of motorsports.

## 1962 was the high-water mark of Corvette's first period of SCCA dominance.

into the season he was busted when his car was discovered still equipped with a lightweight flywheel from Sebring. After this major rules infraction, Yenko's SCCA license was suspended, and Grady asked Thompson to take over for the rest of the season. Back in a production Corvette, it was like 1956 and 1957 all over again for the racing dentist, and he won the B-production title.

It was his eighth SCCA national championship, and he had won half of them in Corvettes (including the Sting Ray).

Corvette racing in the Wild West got even wilder in the fall of 1961 with the debut of the Simpson Corvette special sports racing car driven by Dave McDonald. Jim Simpson sold a lot of Corvettes at Bob Sorenson Chevrolet in Whittier, California, and was a good friend of McDonald, who had won the 1961 Pacific Coast B-production championship with his spectacular tail-out driving. McDonald and Sorenson Chevrolet wanted a Corvette that could win overall in the main events at these races, which were for sports racing cars called modifieds by the SCCA and went to Max Balchowsky. His series of "Old Yeller" Buick nailhead-powered specials had been humiliating the local Ferraris and Maseratis in modified class racing for years, so Simpson bought one of his Old Yeller Mark IV chassis as a starting point.

They built the car with Balchowsky's assistance in his shop on Hollywood Boulevard. They started with the lightweight body made by Jim Burell of Fiberglass Auto Body and used molds pulled from a new 1961 Corvette borrowed from Sorenson Chevrolet. The body was shortened by 17 inches and narrowed by 5 inches to fit the Old Yeller chassis, which had plenty of room to accommodate one of the new 327ci fuel-injected Corvette engines. The simple ladder-truss tubular steel frame had independent, unequal-length A-arm front suspension and a Studebaker rear axle with Pontiac front and Buick rear finned brake drums. They used a Borg-Warner T-10 4-speed transmission.

The 1,750-pound Corvette was killer fast. Exhaust bellowed from a pair of motorcycle megaphones on both sides, and it hit 180 mph on Riverside's long back stretch. As No. 00, its first outing was

at Laguna Seca in October. The car's debut in the Pacific Grand Prix was cut short when, after spinning twice, Davey bowed out with mechanical problems. But the first of many wins came at Cotati, California, in November. Jim Simpson had paid for building the B-modified Corvette with money he had saved to buy a house and managed to get his employer, Sorensen Chevrolet, to sponsor it. He later found other sponsors during 1962 for numerous additional victories.

### New Management

The tenure for a GM divisional general manager was typically five years; Cole had been in charge of Chevrolet since July of 1956, and hewas promoted to automotive group vice president in December 1961. Semone "Bunkie" Kundsen, after saving Pontiac from extinction and getting the division up to number three in sales, was also promoted to general manager of Chevrolet, GM's largest division. Kundsen had pushed the corporate "no racing" policy even further at Pontiac than Cole had at Chevrolet, and he planned to continue in the same manner with his new position. Corvette sales continued to increase in 1961, reaching 10,939. Under new management, 1962 would be a year of building toward the biggest Chevrolet racing program since the preban months of 1957.

In its last year of production, the solid-axle Corvette body received some final appearance enhancements with a blacked-out grillee, and the chrome strakes in the side coves were replaced by finned inserts in the vents. The coves also lost their stainless-steel outline trim—and with it the option to have them painted a contrasting color—however, ribbed chrome rocker panel moldings added a little glitter to the sides. Of interest to the racers were the heavy-duty brake and steering package, which now included stiffer redesigned shocks, and a heater was standard equipment for the first time.

Hot rodders had been boring out the 283's 3.87-inch diameter cylinders to 4.00 inches for years, but it required redesigned cores for production, and this finally happened for the 1962 model year. For its second displacement increase, the small-block V-8 was given a 4.00-inch bore with the crankshaft stroked 0.25 inch to 3.25 inches for 327ci, or 5.3 liters, for an additional 44ci. The solid-lifter carbureted 283's pair of Carter WCFBs was replaced with a single larger Carter AFB for the 327 with a

.25 higher 11.25:1 compression ratio; it was rated at 340 hp. The only remaining fuelie, RPO 582, still breathed through the same intake manifold with its expanded flat top plenum, but it had a higher flow air meter with a choke plate added to its annuler venture cone. With the same pistons, heads, and cam as the 340-hp carbureted engine, the fuel-injected 327 produced an impressive 360 hp.

The 4.6-liter 283 Corvettes continued competing in SCCA B-production and 5000 GT in FIA races like Sebring. The 5.3-liter 327 Corvettes moved up a class in both racing series. The SCCA soon saw hordes of Corvettes competing in two classes during the same races, and the "BP" that had started appearing on the sides of some Corvettes in 1957 was joined by "AP" on the sides of most of them. The SCCA frowned on sponsorship in amateur racing and had formerly required sponsors' names on cars to be taped over, but by 1962, with the increasing cost of racing, they usually allowed them to be left unobscured.

### Class Acts

On February 11, 1962, the FIA added a new season opener to their international endurance racing series: the Daytona Continental three-hour run on the 3.81-mile combined infield and tri-oval road course. Superstars from Formula 1, the Indy cars, and NASCAR were there; Moss and "Fireball" Roberts, in a pair of Ferrari 250GT SWB Berlinetas, finished first and second in GT overall. The Corvettes were split between the two largest displacement GT classes, and the Ferraris' 2953cc V-12s put them in third. Even though they only had about 275 hp, the 250GTs were lightweight and very fast. Davis had a new pair of 62 327 Corvettes at Daytona with the Le Mans hoods and 37-gallon fuel tanks, and they were driven by Yenko in No. 10 and Thompson in No. 11.

Grady's cars were the highest finishing Corvettes. Thompson finished 3rd in GT behind the Ferraris' 1st in class and 13th overall, followed by Yenko 2nd in class and 19th overall. NASCAR star Marvin Panch was a Ford guy, but he drove the No. 20 Corvette to 3rd in class, 20th overall, with Corvette regular Morgan 21st overall in the No. 25 car finishing 4th in class. The last Corvette to finish the 3-hour race was No. 75, handled by Jack Knab, who finished 5th in class, 23rd overall. No. 17 Bob Johnson and No. 35 Skip Hudson didn't make it to the end of the race that would become the 24 Hours of Daytona in 1966.

For the annual 12-hour grind at Sebring in March 1962, the Corvette entries were numbered an orderly 1 through 7, with Davis' cars finishing 1st and 2nd in class. Detroit was also represented by a Falcon Sprint No. 9 with a 260ci Ford small-block driven by Panch and Joko Maggiacomo, but the first American car to finish was a Corvette. It was the No. 2 car, driven by Duncan Black and M. R. J. Wyllie, followed by Davis' other car, the No. 1, driven by Yenko and Ed Lowther, who took 2nd in class. Three other Corvettes finished, and two others did not. These two FIA races were followed by a single Corvette entry at Le Mans driven by Tony September and Jack Turner. They competed about 19th overall until the 14th hour, when Turner accidentally lifted the reverse lockout, downshifting and blowing the engine, ending the last attempt for a Corvette until 1967.

### The Legend Begins

The year 1962 was the high-water mark for Corvette's first period of domination in SCCA amateur sports car racing, but there were a few pesky foreign cars that occasionally beat them. On the tighter courses, Porsche Carrera 356 coupes sometimes drove the B-production Corvette drivers crazy, and Jaguar produced a new contender in the XKE. The new Jags were rarely competitive; however, the Ferrari 250GT SWB Berlinetas were. There were only a handful of these cars racing in the United States (some with aluminum bodies), but with their lightweight and high-winding 3.0-liter V-12 275-hp engines, they were capable of winning A- and B-production races overall.

The SCCA National B-Production champions had won their titles driving 283 Corvettes since 1957, and in 1962, the title went to Yenko. Thompson won the A-production class driving a 327 Corvette. Corvettes also continued to impress in showrooms across America. Knudsen, Chevrolet's general manager, added a second shift at the St. Louis plant, and Corvette Sales Manager Joseph Pike stepped up promotion. With more cars available for dealer stock and customer orders filling quickly, sales made its biggest jump in Corvette's 10-model year history to 14,531, a 3,592 increase from 1961. There must have been plenty of frustrated demand, because most of these buyers had to know there was an all new second-generation Corvette coming out in 1963, and with it sales soared to over 20,000 a year.

**In 1960,** both Zora Arkus-Duntov and Bill Mitchell had a car that represented their objectives for the next Corvette. Mitchell was concerned about its appearance, and Duntov, its technical content. Mitchell easily sold corporate management on the shape of his Sting Ray racer—even though its problems with front-end lift were well known—while Duntov lobbied unsuccessfully to make the new Corvette mid-engined like his Chevrolet Engineering Research Vehicle (CERV). This idea was ahead of its time, and the low-volume Corvette sales could never have paid for the transaxle tooling, but Duntov did manage to incorporate the CERV's independent rear suspension in the new chassis. The Sting Ray racer's 92-inch wheelbase was stretched to 98 inches for the new production Corvette, which was still 4 inches shorter than the existing car.

Larry Shinoda was lead designer. He painted a full-size clay mockup of XP720 in April 1960, followed (at the insistence of the sales department) by a convertible with a removable hardtop before the end of the year. The new body featured concealed headlights set into an uninterrupted razor-edged nose; they were rotated 180 degrees by electric motors and became a signature Corvette styling feature, just like the four round taillights introduced in 1961. It included ribbed aluminum rocker panel trim moldings, similar to the 1962 models with simulated vents above them on the front fenders,

and a pair of rectangular vent openings covered by grillees on the hood that were intended to be functional, but in the end didn't work. (On the Sting Ray, racer grillees in this location relieved under-hood air pressure, reducing front-end lift and improving cooling, but they didn't work on the street.)

It was discovered that heated air released through the hood grilles flowed directly into the interior's ventilation system and deposited grit from underhood vapors on the windshield. The hood grilles on 1963 Sting Rays were little but die-cast aluminum ornaments with openings simulated by black paint, but the coupe's most controversial nonfunctional styling feature was a post dividing its rear window. The "split window" gave the coupe a unity of form that Mitchell was enamored with, but it unnecessarily obscured rearward vision and outraged Duntov, who confronted Mitchell about it on Design Staff turf. Duntov was ejected and the post stayed, but only for one model year. It disappeared in 1964, along with the phony hood grilles, and many owners removed the post themselves when one-piece rear windows became available.

Mitchell envisioned the American muscle car of the future on the outside as Duntov engineered it from within. They didn't always agree, but their complete overhaul of everything from window casements to intricate engine and fuel components

Opposite page: The all-new Corvette was called the Sting Ray after Design Staff Vice President Bill Mitchell's racer that inspired its styling—from overhead especially the cars looked remarkably similar. The fact that this shape produced extreme front-end lift was not of any concern to Mitchell with his "function follows form" approach to design, even though the production cars' nonfunctional hood grilles added to the problem.
*GM Media Archive*

To keep the headlights from interrupting the Sting Ray's razor-edged nose, they were concealed with the backside of their housings completing the leading edge of the nose. Their wedged-shaped housings were rotated 180 degrees by electric motors when the lights were turned on, starting a signature Corvette styling feature that would last for the next 42 model years.
*GM Media Archive*

1963 Corvette interiors were entirely new with a dual cowl instrument panel mounting the clock and radio in a center divider—a big improvement in the placement of the gauges. The small tachometer on top of the steering column was replaced by a much larger one next to a matching speedometer, with the secondary gauges stacked diagonally on either side. *GM Media Archive*

transformed the Corvette in more ways than anyone could imagine. The Vette, though, wasn't the only thing changing—American car culture was also evolving all around them. Power accessories had become a part of American motorsport—even on sports cars with power-operated windows—and also as a part of Corvette's convertible tops since 1956. Corvette's soft tops had to be raised and lowered by hand after 1962, but the new Sting Rays still had power windows, joined by power-assisted brakes, steering, and air conditioning.

There was only one power accessory of interest to racers, however: a special version of the power brakes with a dual circuit master cylinder that was part of the Z06 racing package. Duntov had been experimenting

with power-assisted racing brakes since 1957.

The Z06 special performance equipment group was a combination of other RPOs and racing parts that weren't otherwise available and could only be ordered with the 360-hp fuel-injected L84 V-8. Buyers who planned to race their Z06-equipped Sting Rays saved a little weight and money by also ordering the C48 heater and defroster deletion credit, which took $100 off the hefty $1,818.45 price of the racing package. From early October to December 1962, the first few production Z06s were all coupes with the Racing Production Order (RPO) N03 36.5-gallon fiberglass fuel tank. It cost $202.30, and a set of five RPO P48 cast-aluminum wheels added another $322.80 to the total. Casting problems kept

the wheels from becoming available, and since the big fuel tank was unnecessary for Sports Car Club of America (SCCA) racing, both items were dropped from the Z06 option, which brought the price down to $1,293.95. A total of 15 coupes were produced prior to the changeover on December 14, 1962. During the 1963 model year, the 199 Z06 coupes and convertibles became some of the most collectible Corvettes ever.

The Z06 Corvette option was a small part of an ambitious racing program at Chevrolet coming together behind the scenes during Semone "Bunkie" Knudsen's first year as general manager in 1962. Archrival Ford publicly denounced the American Automobile Manufacturers Association (AAMA) racing ban in March with the launch of their "total performance" advertising and racing campaign, so Knudsen was gearing up to go head-to-head with them during the 1963 season. This didn't mean that GM corporate had a change of heart; they were still publicly anti-racing, but they were willing to look the other way as Knudsen used racing to help turn the beleaguered Pontiac divisions around in the late 1950s. The bottom line was that the AAMA ban was still corporate policy, but divisional general managers had the power of autonomy, and Knudsen chose to push the envelope with thinly veiled factory racing efforts in National Association for Stock Car Auto Racing (NASCAR), National Hot Rod Association (NHRA), and Federation Internationale de l'Automobile (FIA) International GT racing.

## Dreaming of Daytona

The primary objective was a second Daytona 500 win—something Ford had yet to achieve—but it was out of reach with the underperforming 409ci W-motor; however, Knudsen was not to be deterred. He had Don McPherson convince corporate that the W-motor needed to be replaced. The new big-block was designed by Dick Keinath, and only those directly involved realized that this was a dedicated NASCAR racing engine. Duntov was responsible for 409 power development, and with two Chevrolet big-blocks, he started calling the new engine a Mark II. He simplified a raised intake port head W-motor for comparison and to use as a possible backup. The ultimate W-motor quickly lost out in the Dyno room to the Mark II, but Vince Piggins crafted an effective drag-racing package for it in the Impala two-door sport coupe for 1963, named the Z11.

Early Corvette bodies had aluminum support structures weighing 48 pounds, while the new bodies' steel structure added 85 pounds; it saved weight overall by allowing the fiberglass body panels to be lighter. Nicknamed "The Bird Cage," the new body support structure was far more rigid, tying the rocker sills and door pillars into the cowl, along with supporting the top of the coupe's doors and roof.
*GM Media Archive*

Without an opening rear deck lid, the spare tire was relocated from the trunk to a fiberglass tub, with a hinged cover mounted to the underside of the frame. The fuel tank moved from this same location to the back of the storage compartment, with an exposed filler cap on the rear deck. *GM Media Archive*

Both the new convertible and coupe had fixed rear deck lids that were bonded in place and a carpeted storage compartment that was only accessible through the interior. This space was under the coupe's rear window, making it fairly roomy, but it was less useful covered by the convertible's deck lid. *GM Media Archive*

As the manufacturers steadily increased engine displacement, NASCAR and the NHRA finally capped how big they could be. The racing giants decided that a 427ci or 7-liter displacement was the limit for their 1963 seasons. Chevrolet's big-blocks both had 4.312-inch bores and 3.50-inch strokes for 409ci, and they shared the same crankshafts, which, when stroked to 3.650 inches, gave them 427ci to rival Ford's 427 FE and Chrysler's Max Wedge 426s. For Duntov, Knudsen's big racing program represented a new lease on life, and he had two proposals arrive at his desk. He chose the most tantalizing—a mid-engine GT prototype racing car capable of winning overall at Le Mans. This project started under the cover name "CERV II," but it didn't make it far off the drawing board before being shelved in favor of Duntov's other proposal, a lightweight racing Sting Ray replica during the summer of 1962.

The lightweight Corvette was officially called Grand Sport, a name later appropriated by Chevrolet R&D for the Grand Sport II experimental sports racing cars, but in 1962 and 1963 it referred to a limited-production Corvette. The FIA realigned requirements for the Manufacturers' World Championship, opening it up to production grand touring cars without any minimum weight or maximum displacement restrictions. This open invitation excited American automakers, particularly Chevrolet and Ford. Internal politics, however, prevented Chevy from producing the 100 examples necessary to homologate the Grand Sport as a production car. The plan was to build 5 pilot cars, followed by 20 more at the Chevrolet Engineering Center, with a production run of 100 additional Grand Sports turned out by an outside contractor and sold through selected Chevrolet dealers.

By 1963, front-engine sports racing and GT prototypes were at a disadvantage, but the rear-engine revolution had only reached the smaller production classes, which were dominated by cars like the Porsche. In big-block GT racing, the car to beat was the front-engine Ferrari 250 GTO, powered by a 290-hp V-12 pushing 2,300 pounds; it had a power-to-weight ratio of 7.9 lb/hp, which didn't give it an insurmountable advantage over the fuel-injected Sting Ray's torque of 8.6 lb/hp. The GTO had a solid rear axle, but it also had a five-speed transmission, efficient and effective four-wheel disc brakes, and aerodynamics that the deceptively high-drag Sting Ray would need to overcome. The Grand Sport program gave Duntov a second chance to design and build a dedicated racing Corvette, even though its goals were more modest than the SS six years earlier: an overall win at Sebring or even Le Mans might have been possible that first year.

Rochester's new second-generation Ramjet fuel injection unit was an impressive sight under the hood of a 1963 Corvette, with its removable finned plenum cover matching the aluminum rocker arm covers. This was the first year for Chevrolet's alphanumeric regular production codes, and the 360-hp fuel-injected 327 was RPO L84, with all of the engine, except for the fuel injection system carrying over from 1962.
*GM Media Archive*

Rochester's fuel injection system was completely redesigned for more precise fuel metering and increased intake air volume, becoming the L84 in 1963, with the rest of the engine carrying over from 62. Power output stayed at 360 hp that first year, but new big valve heads and a hotter cam increased it to 375 hp for 1964, which is where it stayed in 1965, the last year of production depicted in the illustration.

*General Motors*

Duntov and his team of engineers left no stone unturned in an effort to shed weight from the 3,100-pound Sting Ray coupe. They started by replacing the 260-pound perimeter boxed channel frame with a 160-pound straight-sided ladder frame made from large diameter steel tubing. The fiberglass bodies were hand laid-up from three layers of woven glass cloth instead of chopped fibers sprayed into the molds. The only hint they were something special was their fixed headlights under Plexiglas covers and one-piece rear windows. Inside, convincing replicas were made of the production instrument cluster molding and full carpeting, but in the interest of torsional rigidity, the mainframe tubes were kept straight, so the fiberglass bucket racing seats sat on top of them instead of in between them, raising the car's overall height from 49.8 inches to 51.9 inches.

Instead of steel, the Grand Sport bodies were bonded to an aluminum birdcage support structure, and additional weight was saved by using Velcro strips to raise and lower Plexiglas side windows. Duntov and Mitchell still weren't talking after a blow-up over the rear window center post, and it was left out of the Grand Sports Plexiglas rear window without consulting Mitchell on it or the opening rear deck lid below. This change allowed quick and necessary access to the FIA-required spare tire that was mounted on top of the 36.5-gallon fuel tank. The five pilot Grand Sports appeared a little racy; they were painted white with roll-on Firestone racing tires. Halibrand, magnesium, 6-inch-wide knock-off wheels and short mufflers in side exhaust pipes completed the look.

The Corvette group requested bids from American brake manufacturers, including GM's own

Chevrolet Public Relations parked this Daytona Blue convertible and Sebring Silver '63 Corvette coupe on the infield side of Riverside's Esses, within view of the Turn 6 grand stands. The occasion was the new Sting Ray's racing debut on October 13, 1962, and while Chevrolet had to keep a low profile, it never missed a chance to show off the spectacular new Corvette. *GM Media Archive*

Delco Moraine Division, for a disc brake system for the new Corvette. They didn't receive a single positive response. Girling (England) was the leading supplier, but their existing components couldn't handle the 3,100-pound Corvette; however, because the Grand Sport weighed over one-third less, it could be equipped with their off-the-shelf aluminum two-piston calipers. A vacuum booster-assisted dual-circuit master cylinder was used with a solid .50-inch thick, 11.50-inch diameter disc that had parking brakes built into the drums formed by the rear disc to mounting face hat section off-set. Because the car now weighed less than 2,000 pounds, unsprung weight became critical. Losing the heavy cast-iron brake drums was a step in the right direction, and every ounce was trimmed out of hand-fabricated control arms and links as well.

The starting point for Chevrolet's R&D team was the Grand Sport engine's strong cast-aluminum 356 alloy 327 cylinder block, equipped with cast-iron cylinder liners that were the first Chevy V-8s to have four-bolt main bearing caps. With thick bulkheads and reinforcing ribs on their exterior sidewalls, these experimental blocks were put to the test in the Grand Sports, with half-inch stroker crankshafts for a displacement of 377ci. Duntov's group designed hemispherical combustion chamber cylinder heads. They continued to use a push rod valve train for these blocks, reminiscent of his Ardun flathead Ford conversion but with two spark plugs per cylinder, which produced the most complete burn in a hemisphere. The engines breathed through downdraft fuel injection intake manifolds with eight throttle bodies with a projected output of 550 hp.

The No. 119 Daytona Blue Z06 was entered in the three-hour endurance race by Mickey Thompson, who was signed up to manage a big Corvette factory racing program in 1963. Doug Hooper drove a conservative race in the Z06 and wasn't a factor until late in the event, but after three hours, Mickey's team and the new Sting Ray won their first time out. But their victory was overshadowed by the Cobra.
*GM Media Archive*

Duntov described the 16-plug 377ci Hemi V-8 in detail to the FIA in a homologation request, but it didn't progress any further. The advanced engine was all but stillborn and never made it into a Grand Sport. Both the engine and car fell victim to Knudsen's underestimation of GM corporate's resolve to maintain the AAMA ban as standard policy. During 1962, Knudsen continued with under-the-table handouts and support to racers, and he involved the same people within Chevrolet in getting his far more ambitious 1963 racing program ready to roll. Piggins was one of the key players, as he had been since 1955, remaining almost invisible to the public; many racers mistook his product promotions group for Chevy R&D, which was the source for some of the trick parts they distributed.

Corvette racers had their own back door at Chevrolet with Duntov behind it, who, unlike Piggins, was a very public figure. In addition to the teams and drivers Piggins and Duntov worked with, Knudsen brought racers of his own. At Pontiac, Knudsen employed Mickey Thompson under contract to help him build the division's performance image in drag racing. Because Thompson attracted significant attention from the press, Knudsen signed

him up to field a team of four Z06 Corvettes in international endurance racing in 1962. The size of Thompson's speed equipment company made him a believable front man for a team of this size, and appearances were scheduled at a few Grand Sports at Sebring and Le Mans behind the wheel of a pilot-line blue Z06 air freighted to him on September 23, 1962. Doug Hooper was Thompson's first driver; he picked the car up from Flying Tigers at the Burbank, California, airport, and hauled it to Thompson's shop in Long Beach, which must have created quite a stir on the L.A. freeways.

## The Z06

The first five production ZO6s were built early in October, which didn't leave much time for three of them to be ready to compete at Riverside, California. They were convoyed from St. Louis to the West Coast by the drivers who would race them. Three were painted Ermine White and the others were Sebring Silver; one of each color was shipped to the FIA's New York office for homologation. The cars reached Thompson weeks later after Riverside, where he had entered the Daytona blue Z06 pilot car. The occasion was the *LA Times* Three Hour Invitational Endurance

Race, which ran the day before the *Times* Grand Prix, making the Endurance Race an ideal venue for the Sting Ray's racing debut, which should have been a walkover for the four Z06s. The wild card was a lone red Ford Cobra entered by Carroll Shelby, also making its racing debut after rave reviews in the car magazines.

The race's greatest irony was that Shelby had talked to Chevrolet before approaching Ford. Chevrolet turned him down because they already had the Corvette, but Shelby's Cobra was a perfect fit for Ford's "Total Performance" campaign, and they bankrolled the whole vehicle. The car he chose for a V-8 transplant was the production version of a sports racing car. It had been built by John Tojfiro in the early 1950s and had been beating up on the Jaguars in SCCA C-production racing for years with

## "The writing is on the wall."

*—Zora Duntov, after witnessing the Cobras blow by the Corvettes at Riverside in 1962*

its six-cylinder, two-liter Bristol engine, which was no longer being produced. There was room in the ACE's tubular ladder frame for Ford's new pint-sized 260ci V-8; scaled down for compact cars, it weighed 100 pounds less than a small-block Chevy motor and only a few more pounds than the six-cylinder Bristol. The version Ford supplied for the first Cobras was equipped with a hot solid-lifter cam and breathed through a 4150 two-barrel Holey carburetor on

Both the Corvette Sting Ray and Shelby Cobra made their racing debut at the *Times* Three Hour Invitational, which began with a Le Mans start across Riverside's back stretch under the foot bridge. Bob Bondurant's No. 614 Z06 Corvette was lined up ahead of Dave MacDonald's No. 00 and Jerry Grant's No. 8 Z06, which started next to Bill Krause's No. 98 Cobra, with Doug Hooper's No. 119 Z06 separated by three cars.
*GM Media Archive*

There were four Z06 Sting Rays in the race, along with numerous solid-axle Corvettes, and Dave MacDonald was the first to get away in Don Steve's white Z06, with Bill Krause in the red Cobra soon catching him up. Dave was able to keep the Cobra behind him for several laps, but after the first hour, Krause was leading by more than a mile when a rear stub axle broke ending the Cobra's impressive debut.
*GM Media Archive*

a cast-iron intake manifold and produced about 260 hp.

What made the ACE into a Cobra was the restyled aluminum body with a lower hood line, smaller grille, fender flares, and the addition of grilling four-wheel disc brakes and a small-block Ford V-8. AC's chassis was dated with a simplified form of independent suspension inspired by the Fiat Topolino, with transverse leaf springs at both ends that doubled for upper control arms and produced less than precise suspension geometry. Combined with sticker tires and more power, the frame was overstressed and flexible; Cobras were a handful, and even though the Sting Ray handled better, there was no beating a 1,100-pound weight advantage. The Cobra out-accelerated the Corvettes at Riverside, but both cars were handicapped with teething problems.

The three West Coast Chevrolet dealers that had their Z06 orders filled with an early factory delivery sponsored some of the hottest Corvette drivers in the country. Dave MacDonald drove Don Steve's white No. 00, and Jerry Grant drove Allen Green's white No. 8. Washburn Chevrolet only got their Sebring silver No. 614 on the condition that Bob Bondurant drive it. Hooper was behind the wheel of Thompson's Daytona blue No. 119. At most, there were seven or eight Z06 Corvettes, and three or four Cobras with the red No. 98 driven by Bill Krause, the second one competed leaving the track stewards with a dilemma. To race as production cars, the SCCA required at least 100 examples, but they had an out that would allow both cars to compete—the XP, or experimental production class—which let them race without scoring championship points.

The *LA Times* Three Hour Endurance Race began with the cars lined up along the edge of the backstretch under the foot bridge, and MacDonald won the foot race across the track. MacDonald was away first in the white No. 00 Corvette, followed by Krause in the red No. 98 Cobra—which was the order they had finished the 1961 race but with Krause in a Jaguar XKE. MacDonald was able to keep the Cobra behind him for several laps, but after the first hour, Krause was leading by more than a mile when a rear stub axle broke, ending the Cobra's impressive debut. All of the cars had to make at least one pit stop, and MacDonald led the field until a rear suspension failure ended his race. Grant and Bondurant went out with blown engines. Hooper drove a conservative race in Thompson's No. 119 Z06 and wasn't a factor until late in the event. After three hours, though, Thompson's team and the new Sting Ray won, but the victory was overshadowed by the Cobra's stellar performance.

In addition to the Cobra's superior power-to-weight ratio, the Z06 Corvette's drum brakes had to

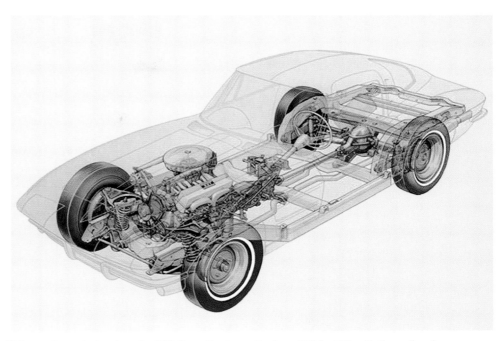

This see-through drawing of a 1963 Corvette shows the base 250-hp 327, with the optional M20 four-speed transmission mounted in the new five crossmember perimeter rail frame. The Sting Ray's independent rear suspension, with its boxed radius arms and frame-mounted axle housing, can also be seen, along with the passenger car sourced unequal length A-arm front suspension. *GM Media Archive*

It was raining at Daytona on February 16, 1963, during most of the American Challenge Cup Race, with the Mystery Motor–powered Corvettes on the front row for the pace lap. Bill Krause, in the silver No. 3 Mickey Thompson Z06, was on the pole with his teammate Rex White in the white No. 4 starting beside him, followed by Paul Goldsmith in the white No. 50 Pontiac Tempest. *GM Media Archive*

With big-block hood bulges still two years away, the Mystery Motor's Holley carburetors stuck through the 63 Corvettes' hoods, covered by rear-facing scoops taking in high-pressure air off the windshield. Rex White's No. 4 looks a lot like a Corvette-bodied Grand National car, with six stud truck hubs mounting reinforced steel wheels and rolling on huge 800/820 – 15 Firestone stock car specials.
*GM Media Archive*

stop one-third more weight than the Ford-powered British-American hybrid's disc brakes. Despite extensive testing, the Z06's brakes were terrible the first time in competition. Under maximum braking, the Corvettes jerked from side to side so violently that they couldn't enter turns on the line, having to stay in the middle of the track. Duntov was in attendance, but he couldn't do anything about the brake problem at Riverside. A crash development program in the weeks that followed revealed the finned cast-iron drums were too thin in the interest of saving unsprung weight, and with more rigid castings, Thompson proclaimed them the first "really good Corvette brakes."

Even though Duntov thought highly of Dick Guldstrand as a driver and car builder, he wasn't one of the favored few racers to get a Z06 for Riverside under Chevrolet's sales manager Joe Pike's vehicle allocations. Guldstrand ran his veteran '56 Corvette,

powered by a fuel-injected 283, and watched the Cobra blow by him on the track. Duntov witnessed its performance from the stands and commented, "The writing is on the wall." Guldstrand discussed crafting a Z06-equipped convertible, and Duntov believed that a convertible's lighter weight and lower center of gravity would more than offset the slight increase in drag and loss of torsional rigidity. Guldstrand installed a full set of the racing package components on a '63 droptop that was provided by his sponsor, Baher Chevrolet, in the weeks before this combination became available from the factory. In the meantime, and in the face of Cobra domination, Guldstrand and a few other Corvette holdouts won a few regional championships.

Chevrolet's big NASCAR and FIA racing program was scheduled to debut in the series of races at Daytona during Speed Week, but the Florida track was open to the public for preseason testing of the top-secret MK II engine, or Grand Sport Corvette. The first MK II track test was on GM's high-banked 5-mile circle at the desert proving grounds in Mesa, Arizona, during November 1962. Rex White, 1960 NASCAR champion, drove a pair of 1963 Grand National Impalas. One of these cars was powered by a full-competition MK I W motor and reached 156 mph, while the other car, with an MK II, achieved 172 mph. Both engines displaced 409ci, and in January, the same car was back running a phenomenal 177 mph powered by a 427ci MK IIS. The Corvettes, including the first Grand Sport completed, were tested at Sebring in December. Surprisingly, and considering the high-performance company, Thompson turned in the quickest lap (3:19.10) in a Z06, while Maston Gregory was fastest in the Grand Sport, lapping at 3:16.40, which was close to the overall 1962 lap record of 3:12.40.

## Meet Carroll Shelby

In the fall of 1962, Shelby American was just a small start-up company when they moved into their first permanent facility in Venice, California, establishing an assembly line and race shop in the brick building where Lance Reventlow had built Scarabs built in the late 1950s. By December 1962, about 30 street Cobras were assembled, along with a second competition car that was sold to John Eberly. Eberly and Krause both drove the car from Riverside to Nassau for Speed Week. While they didn't win anything, the cars were blindingly fast, and their performance in front of the big-money crowd netted Shelby many orders and additional international publicity. Thompson lured Krause away from Shelby with more money, along with the prospect of racing a Grand Sport at Le Mans, and Carroll replaced him with MacDonald who had been working for his sponsor Don Steve's Chevrolet as a line mechanic and was attracted by the idea of getting paid to race.

With Fords' resources behind him, Shelby fielded strong teams at both Daytona and Sebring. The Cobras hadn't yet won a race, and an SCCA Regional in January offered an opportunity for testing some new developments, as well as a rematch with the Z06 Corvettes. As the Cobra's manufacturer, Carroll had the ability to homologate and added speed equipment to his parts catalog that Corvette racers could only dream about.

Corvette was outraged by the pair of competition Cobras that showed up at Riverside. Ford didn't even have an aluminum intake manifold for the 260, but one of the Cobras mounted four 2V Weber 48mm IDA carburetors, the ultimate in 1963 technology, along with the latest in roller lifter cams and tubular

Ferrari's formidable 250 GTO was the defending FIA Manufacturer's Grand Touring Championship winner and the car to beat at Daytona, with five of them in the race. Weighing 2,300 pounds, with its 3.0-liter single overhead cam V-12 producing 290 hp and equipped with four-wheel disc brakes, Daytona would be first time GTOs came up against the new Sting Rays and Cobras. *David Kimble/ Road & Track*

*Right and below:* The Daytona Continental was the only FIA endurance event that began with a rolling start and ironically, after a wet oval race for GT cars on Saturday, it was run in good weather on the 3.81-mile road course Sunday. Paul Goldsmith's No. 50 6.9-liter Pontiac Tempest, having the largest displacement engine, started on the pole, with Bill Krause driving Mickey Thompson's No. 4 Z06 Corvette next to him. *GM Media Archive*

headers. This combination drove the power output of Ford's little V-8 up to 325 hp and gave the Cobra an overwhelming power-to weight-ratio of 6.15 lb/hp, and still there was more to come.

MacDonald was one of the most spectacular West Coast Corvette racers, and soon after signing him, Shelby also hired the transplanted Englishman Ken Miles as both a driver and development engineer. Together, they formed the nucleus of Shelby's team, and Riverside was their first race in the Cobras. MacDonald spun his No. 198 during the preliminary race on Saturday, but still managed to finish second behind Miles' No. 98 car. Third place belonged to Paul Reinhart in the No. 6 Z06 Sting Ray coupe. The Corvettes were so hopelessly off the Cobra's pace that Miles decided to pull a stunt that burned Corvette fans for months—he pulled into the pits for a drink of water from a commanding lead at the points race on Sunday. After the field roared by, Miles took off in pursuit at about half distance. He soon finished second behind MacDonald for another Cobra 1-2 punch. Guldstrand, in his Z06 convertible, finished a distant third.

Despite GM's insistence that they were "not involved in racing," Pontiac dominated NASCAR in

1961 and 1962, including back-to-back wins in the Daytona 500, and GM corporate suspected Chevrolet was going to renew their racing effort in 1963. With more rumblings of a federal antitrust action to break up the corporation from the Kennedy administration, and bad press from the Corvair rollovers, upper management decided to pull the plug before the racing season got started. On January 21, 1963, GM Chairman Frederic Donner and President John Gordon sent an internal policy letter to all divisions reinstating the AAMA ban against racing in no uncertain terms. Pontiac General Manager Elliot M. "Pete" Estes pulled over to the curb and severed all connections with his factory-supported teams, but Knudsen, with his big investment in Chevrolet's new NASCAR engine, forged ahead as planned, except for a publicity blackout.

NASCAR's president and owner of the Daytona International Speedway, "Big" Bill France, was a visionary promoter, and by 1963, he had built Daytona Speed Week into speed *month* with a variety of races at his track every weekend in February. Chevrolet and Pontiac competed in three of these events, starting with The American Challenge Cup, a short five-lap qualifier on Sunday, February 10, for an experimental race that could only have been organized by France himself. The American Challenge Cup was a 250-mile event on the full 2.5-mile tri-oval. For GT cars that would compete in the Daytona Continental on the road course, and to make it more entertaining, the cars were allowed engines up to 428ci, like NASCAR's Grand National cars. Thompson's team was divided—to compete in this unique event, two of his Z06 Sting Rays were equipped with MK IIS 427ci NASCAR engines at Smokey Yunick's shop, making them the first big-block Corvettes.

Even with handling problems, Thompson's 427 Sting Rays were the fastest other cars on the track, and Junior Johnson won the pole position qualifying race in 4:39.40. Rex White took second, and Paul Goldsmith, behind the wheel of a Pontiac Tempest, placed third.

This competition debut of Chevy's new MK IIS NASCAR racing engine was followed by decisive victories at the Daytona 500 qualifying races powered by the MK IIS. Because of the publicity blackout, the media's questions went unanswered, leading the press to dub it "the mystery motor."

Because of the publicity blackout, all the journalists' questions went unanswered, whipping up a storm of curiosity. Hidden in plain sight under the hoods of Thompson's Corvettes, the engines went unnoticed.

It was raining at Daytona on Saturday, February 16, 1963, when the American Challenge Cup was scheduled to run 100 laps around the tri-oval. NASCAR never ran in the rain, but these were GT cars, and the race started as scheduled. The wet track was the 427 Sting Ray's undoing, but Chevrolet was in trouble before even before the rain began because Thompson's team never balanced their cars' handling. The big-block engines added an additional 100 pounds to the front ends. The Corvettes were torn down in the crews' motel parking lot the night before the race to head off any developing problems, and what little progress they made in their setup was lost, particularly in Johnson's silver No. 4 car. Johnson said that with a good setup, the car was capable of lapping at 180 mph, but he had an easier time turning a lap at 164.083 mph in Ray Fox's Impala than wrestling Thompson's understeering Corvette around at 162.220. The morning of the race the Corvette handling worsened, and he bowed out.

The No. 3 Sebring silver 427 Corvette started beside White's Ermine White No. 4 from the pole but with team driver Krause behind the wheel. On the first lap, Goldsmith took the lead in his white No. 50 SD 421 Tempest. Thompson's Sting Rays were in trouble from the drop of the green flag, slogging along in the rain and taking on water. Aluminum floor pans were added for the high-speed race, and the water that entered through the vents was quickly

Getting away sideways, Bill Krause took over the lead from Paul Goldsmith when his Tempest's fuel pump broke on the 3rd lap and was out of the race 41 laps later with a blown engine in the silver No. 4 Z06. After driving the Cobra at Riverside for Carroll Shelby, Mickey Thompson lured Bill away with Chevrolet money and his big FIA endurance racing program that included Le Mans. *GM Media Archive*

Grady Davis' white No. 11 Z06 was the best finishing Corvette, with Dr. Dick Thompson coming in 3rd overall, while his teammate Don Yenko's No. 10 was out on Lap 44. Coming up from behind the dark blue No. 99 Cobra, driven by Bill Krause's replacement, Dave MacDonald was the only one to finish. Slowed by a lengthy pit stop, Dave still managed to come in 4th overall. *GM Media Archive*

turned to steam by engine and exhaust heat and fogged the windows. The front tires wore quickly and started losing grip. White brought his under-steering beast into the pits after 38 laps in a light bulb at 160 mph, and told Thompson it was unsafe to continue. Thompson took the car back out for one lap before suspension failure parked it for good. Goldsmith led every soggy lap, averaging 145.161 mph for the 250 miles. A. J. Foyt Jr. placed second driving Nickey Chevrolet's 327ci Z06, followed by Krause, who toughed it out in Mickey's 427ci Z06 for a distant third.

Ironically, after an oval race for GT cars in the rain on Saturday, many of the same cars competed in the Daytona Continental three-hour the next day, held on the 3.81-mile road course in good weather. This international race for points in the FIA's Manufacturers Grand Touring Championship

pitted Chevrolet's Z06 Corvette and Ford's AC Cobra against the defending champion Ferraris' formidable 250 GTOs for the first time. Ten Z06 Sting Ray coupes took the field, making them the most numerous entries, plus five Ferrari GTOs and a three-car Cobra team that, with new engines, were even faster than before. Ford bored out their diminutive 260 cylinders from 3.80 inches to 4.00 inches—the same as a 327 Chevy—but with a short 2.87-inch stroke; this alteration made it a 289, which would completely replace the 260 in production after the first 75 Cobras, as the 289 was rated at 271 hp with a single four-barrel carburetor.

Unlike other FIA endurance races, the Daytona Continental began from a rolling start, with Goldsmith's 6.9-liter No. 50 Pontiac Tempest on the pole with the largest engine in the field. Next were twelve 5.3-liter Corvettes, including two 1962s.

Attrition for the American cars started quickly; Robert Brown's No. 41 Z06 was out by the second lap, followed by Goldsmith's No. 50 Tempest on the third with a broken fuel pump. Meanwhile, Krause took the lead in Thompson's silver No. 4 Z06. Hooper drove Thompson's dark blue No. 3 Corvette and had to retire on Lap 14, and Krause's engine blew 30 laps later.

Only three Corvettes were still running after an hour and a half. Grady Davis' No. 10, driven by Don Yenko, bowed out on Lap 44. The Cobras were the fastest cars on the track, but they were also slowed by a variety of problems. Dan Gurney entered the race late after replacing the experimental Indy engine, which overheated in practices, only to leave the race 48 laps later with ignition failure. Skip Hudson, driving No. 97, recovered from an early pit stop to repair a broken fuel line only to crash out on Lap 54 from a blown clutch, breaking his ankle in the process. MacDonald's No. 99 Cobra was the only one to finish after a lengthy pit stop; he took fourth. Pedro Rodriguez, No. 18, was the newest and fastest of the Ferrari GTOs, and after trading the lead with

John Mecom's No. 29 GTO, driven by Roger Penske, he became the overall winner, with Penske in second and Thompson in Davis' surviving Z06 Corvette taking third.

## The Mystery Motor

The grand finale of speed month came on Sunday, February 24. The MK IIS–powered Impalas swept the qualifying races on Friday, but through a combination of bad racing luck and mechanical failures, the Daytona 500 was a disaster for them. Johnson took a commanding lead from the drop of the green flag and stretched it out until his mystery motor broke a valve spring. Three of the other four Chevys also powered by these engines led at some point in the race, but despite their speed, only two finished. To make matters worse, archrival Ford—who had never won the great race—took the first five places in the 1963 Daytona 500, and the surviving mystery motor–powered Chevys finished 9th and 14th. The results were poor but ultimately of little long-term importance when compared to the corporate fallout from Knudsen's Daytona adventure.

After three hours the overall winner of the 1963 Daytona Continental was Pedro Rodriguez in the newest and fastest of the Ferrari GTOs, No. 18, followed by John Mecom's No. 29, driven by Roger Penske. After seeing the Cobras performance at Riverside, Zora Arkus-Duntov would say, "The writing is on the wall," and he was right; the Cobras were the fastest cars on the track at Daytona while they lasted, and it wouldn't take long for them to become dominate. *GM Media Archive*

At a press conference in March, when reporters bombarded GM Chairman Donner and President Gordon with questions about the mystery motor, they were embarrassed to say they didn't know anything about it. When Knudsen was called before the executive committee to answer for his transgressions, however, he successfully defended the MK II program as a significant improvement over the existing big-block, keeping it alive to be developed as a production replacement. No one lost his job, but it was made clear that if there was any repeat of Daytona, heads would roll, and Knudsen's shenanigans prompted a restatement of the no-racing mandate in March. This time, they vowed, it would be strictly enforced.

Everyone associated with Chevrolet's racing program on the outside was out of a job, including Thompson's Corvette team, never to race again. Piggins and his product promotion group were also casualties of the situation. The Grand Sports were ordered scrapped, but Duntov hid them in deep storage where he could still complete them.

Fireworks were still erupting at Chevrolet from the performances at Daytona when the 12 Hours of Sebring began in March, and while the Grand Sports wouldn't be there, seven privately entered Z06 Corvette coupes were. A few of these cars showed evidence of Duntov's handiwork, suggesting that Chevrolet's back door wasn't completely closed—developments like hood air deflectors, fender flairs, and rear deck brake cooling scoops pointed to Duntov's meticulous abilities and vision.

With the cars lined up in numerical order for a Le Mans start, the Nos. 4 through 7 Corvettes all raced on steel wheels like at Daytona, but no matter how well prepared they were, none of them could deal with the five factory Cobras. The Vettes were separated from Shelby's snakes by a pair of front-engined Chaparrals, and farther down the line after the Jaguar XKEs came six Ferrari GTOs that had the advantage of staying power—not speed—over the rest of the field. Thompson drove the first Corvettes out of the race—Davis' white No. 1 experienced transmission failure after 14 laps, while the No. 7,

entered by Alan Green Chevrolet for Grant and Don Campbell, only lasted 32 more.

Indy car regular Jim Hurtubise shared the Nickey Chevrolet No. 5 Z06 with the 1961 500 winner, A. J. Foyt Jr., for almost six hours until their engine blew on Lap 84. The No. 4 Corvette's engine bit the dust after 120 laps. The car's demise put Ralph Salyer and Roy Kunnick out of the race, while Miles and Lew Spenser made several unscheduled pit stops for engine trouble in their No. 16 Cobra before the mounting bolts sheared on their rack-and-pinion steering. MacDonald, driving the No. 14 Cobra with NASCAR star "Fireball" Roberts, didn't last much longer; they were 8th overall when their engine's rear main oil seal let go. The mishap left Shelby with only one full competition car still in the race, No. 98, driven by Phil Hill and Gurney, while his other two entrants were essentially lightly prepared street Cobras.

Hill had won GT at Sebring in 1962 and had finished an amazing 2nd overall while co-driving a GTO in its racing debut. In 1963, the six GTOs entered were bulletproof—all of them lasted the full 12 hours, and the first three took 4th through 6th overall. After coming in 2nd at Daytona, Penske

won GT driving with Augie Pabst in John Mecom's GTO, while Hill and Gurney were joined by Miles and Spencer both driving stints in the surviving competition Cobra, which was slowed by numerous stops for engine and brake problems. They managed to finish 11th overall, good enough for a class win, while the highest-placed Corvette, No. 3, spent even more time in the pits with ignition trouble, but Delmo Johnson and Dave Morgan recovered to finish 16th overall and 2nd in class. Jeff Stevens with Johnny Allen in the No. 6 Z06 captured 17th place for 3rd in class while Davis' No. 2 was the fastest Corvette for most of the race, running as high as 5th overall before blowing a head gasket in the 10th hour. Yenko, with Duncan Black and Ed Lowther, had still completed enough laps to be scored 25th even though they weren't running at the finish.

## The USRRC

The year 1963 marked the beginning of a transition for the SCCA. After fighting to stay true to their amateur racing-for-fun origins, they started a professional series—the United States Road Racing Championship (USRRC). The USRRC was actually two championships: one for

With the course marked by cones past a huge globemaster, the No. 4 was one of seven Z06 Corvettes that started the 12-hour grind at Sebring, but it wasn't among the three that finished. Ralph Salyer and Roy Kumnick made it about halfway in the black Z06 with white graphics before its engine blew on Lap 120, but that didn't discourage Ralph, who won an SSCA A-production regional championship with the car that same year.
*GM Media Archive*

The trickiest thing about the No. 6 white Z06 were its red painted wheels; it was plain vanilla and perhaps the stockest-looking Corvette in the Sebring field, but a solid performer in the race. Johnny Allen and Jeff Steves drove a steady conservative race and finished an unremarkable 17th overall, but that was good enough for a solid 3rd in class. *GM Media Archive*

manufacturers' production cars and the other for drivers in modifieds (sports racing cars), with both championships divided into over-and-under 2-liter categories. After Sebring, Shelby's objectives were to win the SCCA National A-production championship by supporting a few privateers, while also winning the USRRC Manufacturer Championship with a factory team of three competition Cobras. These cars toured the country, competing in USRRC events, backed up by the privateers at national when there wasn't a conflict in dates.

After some initial problems, Shelby's road show became so dominant in the summer of 1963 that it became known as the "Cobra Train" because they finished 1-2-3 in practically every race they entered. McDonald, Miles, and Bob Holbert usually decided among themselves who would win before the start of even the professional USRRC races, and they sometimes entered and won the modified events as

well. When Duntov saw the Cobra run at Riverside in October 1962, he realized the only Corvette that could deal with it on equal teams was the Grand Sport he had under construction because it followed a similar approach. Both cars were based on simple tubular steel ladder frames with weight kept to a minimum; they had independent four-wheel suspension and disc brakes; they were intended primarily for racing, but with full interiors and road equipment, they could be licensed and driven on the street.

From Knudsen down to the sales team, everyone at Chevrolet was fuming about the Cobras. Because the only Corvettes that could potentially compete with Shelby's snakes were hidden away in storage, Duntov quietly loaned a couple of Grand Sports to trusted friends. Davis and Dick Doane both had close ties to Chevrolet and could be counted on to keep quiet about where the lightweight Sting Rays came from while running them in a few SCCA races, even though they would have to compete as modifieds. They competed against sports racing cars like the Scarabs and front-engine Chaparrals, but the point was to log some track time in competition before a venue was found where they could make a statement—and hopefully humiliate the Cobras.

Davis didn't waste any time getting his borrowed Grand Sport into action. He entered it along with his other Corvettes in the SCCA's first national event of the season at Marlboro, Maryland, on April 7, 1963. Thompson was delayed starting the modified race by fuel injection trouble, but once running, the Grand Sports' performances were encouraging, with lap times only four seconds slower than the winning Cooper-Climax sports racing car. At Cumberland, Maryland, on May 12, Thompson finished fifth overall, and at Elkhart Lake on June 3, he followed with a fourth overall finish. At Bridgehampton later in the month, Grady drove one of his Z06 coupes while Thompson was doing double duty defending his 1962 A-production National Championship in the second coupe. Yenko drove the Grand Sport, touring with them and defending his B-production title in a 283 Corvette.

They were collectively known as the "Grady Bunch" and usually competed in the Eastern SCCA regions, but so did Shelby-backed privateers Bob Johnson and Dan Gerber (of the baby food family), both of whom who had abandoned their Corvettes in favor of Cobras. Perhaps looking for a snake-free environment, in July, Davis entered his team in an obscure national championship race at Lake Garnett, Kansas. The prospect of such heavy hitters racing in the grain belt and generating favorable local publicity ran high. This same prospect may be what attracted Johnson, and with an off-weekend in the USRRC schedule, the Cobra Train came along with him. More than 60,000 people showed up to watch, most of them hoping to see the Cobras get whipped. Team Cobra had been using rear axle oil coolers for most of the season, but at Lake Garnett they were protested, and even though the coolers were homologated, the cars ran the short production race with them disconnected. It didn't change anything.

To the crowd's disappointment, the big-bore production race was the usual Cobra walkover. Johnson took first, followed by MacDonald and Miles, with Corvette drivers Thompson and Davis a distant fourth and fifth. The only bright spot was Don Yenko's sixth place overall for a B-production class win, but there was hope for a positive result in the modified race, even though Miles negotiated his way into the field. The track stewards didn't let Miles' production Cobra into the race until he successfully argued that disconnecting his rear axle oil cooler made his Cobra a production car, then hooking it back up turned it into a modified. Thompson was more competitive in the Grand Sport than in his Z06, but it would take months of development before Corvette was ready to take on a Cobra. The lightweight Corvette maintained second place until the rear axle let go with Miles finishing a full lap ahead of Harry Hever's front-engined Chaparral.

Doane's Grand Sport saw much less action, with the Illinois Chevrolet dealer even racing it himself a few times. Davis worked closely with Chevrolet Engineering, developing the vehicle he had through the season. After this well-raced Grand Sport returned to Chevrolet Engineering for some updates, it became more competitive. Thompson drove it to victory by winning C-modified at Watkins Glen on August 24, 1963. At the end of the season, this endurance racing Corvette was ranked fourth in the C-modified National Championship, while Thompson also placed third in the A-production

Delmo Johnson's No. 3 looked almost like a team car to Grady Davis' dark blue No. 2, equipped with all the recently developed parts from Chevrolet, including center lock aluminum wheels. Delmo and his co-driver David Morgan recovered from losing time in the pits sorting out an ignition problem to come in 16th overall, 2nd in class, with Roger Penske and Augie Pabst finishing 2nd overall in a Ferrari GTO. *GM Media Archive*

Zora Arkus-Duntov loaned out a couple of the lightweight Grand Sports for some development in competition, and Grady Davis added one to his team, with Dick Thompson driving the No. 11 in C-modified events. Thompson did double duty also defending his SCCA A-production title in a Z06, while Don Yenko successfully defended his B-production national championship in the No. 11 solid-axle 1962 283 Corvette. *GM Media Archive*

championship with Grady's Z06 Sting Ray. Yenko won the B-production title for the second year, and Carroll Shelby met all of his and Ford's objectives, winning A-production along with both the USRRC drivers' and manufacturers' championships.

## Ford's Big Idea

"Ford has a better idea" was a popular television advertising slogan of the time. While it was true of the Cobra's performance on the racetrack, it was false in the showroom, where the second-generation Corvettes' performance was equally spectacular. For the first time, Corvettes were available in two body styles. The company sold 10,919 convertibles in addition to 10,594 coupes for a total of 21,513, up almost 7,000 (about 33 percent) from 1962. The Cobra was essentially a race car that could be driven on the street, and Duntov commented that it was a shame to see the new Sting Ray beaten by a car that hardly anyone would want to buy. Only 99 Corvettes were ordered equipped with the RPO Z06 racing

package in 1963, while not many more Cobras sold that year, but Shelby considered anything over the 100 required to qualify it as a production car to be a bonus.

Publicity from the Cobras' devastating racing sessions and performance advantage over Chevrolet's Corvette put Shelby American on the map. GM corporate policy blocked Chevrolet from any direct response, but a plan came together in the fall of 1963 that would give Chevrolet a chance to demonstrate the Grand Sport's capabilities at the Cobra's expense in front of the international press. The cover was the Mecom racing team. The place was Nassau, Bahamas, and the go-between was Penske, driving for Mecom and an occasional consultant to Chevrolet R&D. John Mecom Jr. had received the Mitchell SR-2 Corvette from Ebb Rose and raced it briefly before his father found out. It led him to give up driving and start his own professional team in 1962 backed by an abundance of Houston, Texas, oil money. Mecom Jr. had a variety of first-rate racing cars, and without being aligned with any single manufacturer, he was the ideal front man for Chevrolet at Nassau.

Nassau was the only place where Grand Sport Corvettes could race Cobras on equal terms because "Captain" Red Crise, the flamboyant Speed Week organizer and promoter, generally followed FIA rules but could be persuaded to bend them if it would improve the show. In a November press release, the Captain eluded to an upcoming Ford versus Chevy confrontation, so Shelby knew Chevrolet was up to something, but with his team on a season-long roll, he had to expect better results than the Cobras achieved in 1962. Shelby American's dominant three-car Cobra team was joined by a pair of 289 Ford-powered Cooper Monaco sports racing cars hailed as "King Cobras" by the press. Even with this formidable stable, the Mecom racing team had to be intimidating. No one could have been ready for the five 1960 Cadillac Pelham blue cars that were

off-loaded from the *Bahama Star* on November 30, the day before the first race. John Mecom's team was as fast as it looked.

The field displayed three Grand Sports that appeared as if they were jacked by automobile steroids, the only Lola GT to get away from Ford when they started their GT 40 program, and the one and only mid-engined Scarab—all powered by aluminum small-block Chevys. The Lola and Scarab came from Mecom's racing headquarters at the Houston Hobby Airport, while the Grand Sports were prepared at the Chevrolet Engineering Center and shipped directly to Don Allen Chevrolet in Miami.

The Corvettes were intended to be Cobra killers, and they looked the part with dramatic fender flairs covering the big Goodyear tires and a pair of air intake nostrils on bulging hoods that fed a quartet of 58mm DCOE side-draft Weber carburetors. The

Harry Heuer would win the C-modified National Championship for a second time in 1963, but it was Dick Thompson who came across the finish line at Watkins Glen, taking the checked flag, driving a much-improved Grand Sport. This was the lightweight Corvette's first race after a rebuild at Chevrolet Engineering, and the larger of two scoops that appeared on its hood covered a new dual downdraft air meters setup that added to its newfound power. *GM Media Archive*

four-bolt main bearing cap aluminum cylinder blocks and half-inch stroker cranks were available so the engines would still displace 377ci, and while this combination couldn't produce the projected 550 hp, it was good for 485 hp, over 100 hp more than the Cobras' output. The aluminum small-block Chevys weighed about the same as the little cast-iron Ford V-8s, but the Grand Sports were a little lighter than the Cobras, with a power-to-weight ratio of 3.9 lb/hp, compared to 5.2 lb/hp for the Cobras. The new ratios shifted the balance of power solidly in the Corvettes' favor

Mecum Jr. had an all-star driver lineup with Penske, Jim Hall, and Thompson in the Grand Sport Corvettes, along with Pabst and Foyt Jr. for his Lola GT and Scarab. Racing started on December 1, 1963, with a 5-lap qualifier, followed

by the 100-lap Tourist Trophy race for production GT cars, but Crise allowed the Grand Sports and even the Lola GT into the field. This marked the first in a week-long series of humiliating defeats for Shelby's all-concurring factory Cobras. The lightweight Corvettes posted times that averaged an amazing 11 seconds per lap quicker than the snakes around the potholed 4.5-mile airport circuit. Mecom's GT cars were classified as prototypes and only allowed to race on a "just for fun" basis, but this limitation didn't trivialize their success in these nonchampionship events, which were all about publicity and bragging rights.

Pabst won the qualifier in Mecom's No. 00 Lola GT, followed by Thompson in the No. 80 Grand Sport in second and Hall with the No. 65 in third. Penske had to park the No. 50 Corvette when a rod started knocking. Following their makeover, the Grand Sports' only testing was a shakedown by Penske at Waterford Hills, north of Detroit, and their lack of development showed up in the race with both cars out after 15 laps. Mecom's Chevy-powered trio quickly pulled away from the pack with Pabst easily winning while the Corvettes suffered from extreme front-end lift but were taken out by over-heated rear axles. With five days to the next race, a Chevrolet engineer with some very heavy luggage joined the ones that were already vacationing in the Bahamas, and all three Grand Sports were ready to start the Governor's Cup race.

Duntov and his wife Elfi were also in Nassau for all eight days of the event. John Mecom provided a deep sea fishing boat for the vacationing engineers from Michigan, but they didn't have much time to use it. The Corvettes' rear-end problems were twofold, with the ring and pinion gear sets not properly broken in. Both needed pressure feed oil coolers to deal with the 377ci V-8's torque. For the 25-lap Governor's Cup Race on Friday, December 6, all three Grand Sports had oil coolers mounted below their rear windows to keep the temperatures of their new well-seasoned rear gear sets under control. The cars' other problem was familiar; with their ride height raised for clearance, the infamous Sting Ray front-end lift became so severe that the Grand Sports were almost uncontrollable at high speed, but it didn't stop them from trouncing the Cobras.

The Governor's Cup included sports racing cars, which gave Shelby's mid-engined King Cobras a chance to show what they could do against the mid-engined Chevy-powered Scarab and Chaparral 2, but they weren't any more competitive than the Cobra roadsters. The race started with a fight for the lead between Hall in his No. 66 Chaparral, Pabst who took over the No. 65 Grand Sport, Penske back in the No. 50, and Foyt Jr. driving the No. 77 Scarab. Hall was off in the weeds on Lap 19 with brake failure, leaving Foyt the winner. Foyt was followed across the finish line by Rodriguez in a Ferrari 250 P, with Penske coming in third overall and first in GT driving the highest-finishing Grand Sport, followed by Pabst in fourth and overall second in GT. Dr. Thompsons' lightweight Corvette No. 88 wasn't running at the end, but he completed enough laps to be scored sixth overall and third in GT, while the highest-finishing Cobra was eighth overall.

The police didn't get to hand out speeding tickets at the Oakes Field Airport during Speed Week, but they did maintain order, and the crown above this sergeant's Chevron was a reminder that the Bahamas were still part of the British Commonwealth. The Grand Sports were an astounding 11 seconds a lap quicker around the potholed 4.5-mile circuit than the Cobras, and being allowed to compete only on a "just for fun" basis didn't take anything away from Chevrolet's bragging rights. *GM Media Archive*

## Pushing the Limits

Speed Week's main event was the 56-lap Nassau Trophy race on Sunday, December 8, where all of the surviving cars battled it out for 252 miles. Thompson took over the No. 50 car, with John Cannon now in the No. 65, and they

were running in third and fourth overall when the high-pressure air that built up under their hoods at three-digit speeds finally broke the latches. After a series of pit stops to tape down the back edges of the cars' hoods, Thompson still managed to finish fourth overall and first in GT, with Cannon eighth overall and second in GT, and A. J. Foyt Jr. getting his second win behind Mecom's Scarab. The Cobras were shut out again for a clean sweep. Exuberant, Duntov shipped the Grand Sports back to Chevrolet for another round of modifications, wondering how far he could push the corporate racing ban in 1964.

With no immediate repercussions from Nassau, Duntov had big plans for the Grand Sports in 1964. Even racing as modifieds, he felt they could be competitive (if only for a short time) against the rapidly developing mid-engined prototypes. Their next race was the Daytona Continental, where the lightweight Corvettes' high drag and front-end lift would severely compromise their performance on the high-speed tri-oval banking, and redesigned hoods offered an improvement. The engine air intakes moved from the front to the sides of the hood bulge with a louvered duct taking their place to release air trapped underneath, reducing both lift and drag. The Grand Sports were about 2 inches taller than production coupes, and searching for a higher top speed, Duntov took the last two out of storage and cut them down into roadsters to reduce

their frontal area. All five cars were equipped with Indy car–style air jacks and a pressure fitting for adding water to speed pit stops, but with corporate intervention again bringing Duntov's plan to a screeching halt, these cars didn't make it to Daytona in 1964.

It took a while before news of Chevrolet's racing success at Nassau reached the 14th floor of the GM building, but Knudsen was called downtown before Daytona in February and told Chevrolet would sever all connections with the Mecom racing team. The Grand Sport roadsters were relinquished to storage. Mecom, Hall, and Johnson each received one of the rebuilt coupes, and while none of them made it to Daytona, they would all be at Sebring.

In contrast, Ford intended to go after the FIA Grand Touring Manufacturers' Championship in 1964, and with the Cobra's even higher drag than the Sting Ray, Shelby had a new weapon named for the track where it debuted: the Daytona coupe. Ironically, this aerodynamic fastback coupe body perched atop a production Cobra chassis was designed by Peter Brock, the same man who had penned the Q Corvette and the Sting Ray racer when he worked for Mitchell.

## Cobra Strikes

The Daytona Continental 3-hour race was lengthened to 2,000 kilometers in 1964 and took about 11 hours to run. The first Cobra Daytona coupe was allowed to compete as a production GT car covered by the roadster's homologation. The Cobra team's only real opposition came from a fleet of GTOs. In the lone Daytona coupe, MacDonald and Holbert quickly pulled away from the field; they were an amazing five laps ahead when a pit fire ended their race. The Ferrari GTO, like the Cobra Daytona coupe, was a production chassis with a more aerodynamic body. It qualified for production class GT racing under a special dispensation that Enzo Ferrari had pressured the FIA into granting but that only came back to bite him. The best Shelby American could salvage was a fourth place finish from a Cobra roadster behind three GTOs. The only consolation was that it qualified as a class win.

All three Grand Sports coupes arrived for the 12 Hours of Sebring in March. After dominating his Cobras at Nassau, Miles had something he hoped could deal with them—a 427 Cobra. The only engine Ford had that could match the 377 Chevy's 485 hp was their 427ci "side oiler" FE series big-block, and with Shelby's approval, Miles managed to squeeze one into a Cobra chassis. Unfortunately for Miles, his strategy failed. The monster motor-powered Cobra was never competitive with the old AC leaf spring chassis, and the frame was unable to cope with the added weight and torque. Though the car was blindingly fast in a straight line, it practically parked in the turns. Miles' co-driver, John Morton, described the beast as "handling more like a 48 Buick than a race car," and during the race it was plagued by a series of mechanical problems, finally retiring with a broken connecting rod.

With the largest engine in the field, the 427 Cobra was No. 1 and first in line for the Le Mans start at Sebring. The Grand Sports started 2nd through 4th, but it was Ludovico Scarfiotti in the No. 23 Ferrari 330 P who quickly took the lead. Penske, driving Jim Hall's No. 4 Grand Sport, was past him before the end of the first lap, only to start sliding back the next time around; he and Hall were fast enough to stay with the prototypes for hours. John Mecom's No. 2 lightweight Corvette was also impressive; A.J. Foyt Jr. charged from 62nd to 12th on the first lap. Paired with co-driver Cannon, he also managed to keep up with all but the fastest prototypes until bad luck caught up with both of them. Jim Hall's lightweight was the first to run into trouble—a half-shaft let go, and they dropped hopelessly out of contention.

All three Grand Sports completed the 12-hour race, but one of the five production Corvettes finished ahead of them—it was Nickey Chevrolet's No. 9 Z06, now painted purple, finishing 16th overall and driven by Grant and Hudson. Hall's Grand Sport finished best, placing 18th overall. Mecom finished 23rd. Both Hall and Mecom were contending for the lead during the race, but Johnson's lightweight Corvette never had a chance—he struggled throughout, finally finishing 32nd overall. Ferrari had dominated Grand Touring at Sebring for years, but the Cobra coupe that came so close to winning at Daytona not only won the class, but finished 4th overall, driven again by MacDonald and Holbert. The first Ferrari GTO crossed the finish line 7th overall, while the Cobras were 1st, 2nd, 3rd, 6th, and 16th in class, good enough for Ford to declare it a clean sweep.

Sebring declared Shelby superior to Ferrari in the FIA GT Manufacturers' Championship, and it was good enough for Ford to send Shelby and the Cobra team in Europe; by this time, plenty of privateers maintained Cobra's presence in the SCCA. With the professional USRRC series starting its second year, the SCCA reorganized their amateur national championship into an annual runoff between the top three finishers in each class from every region. With the ARRC held alternately on opposite coasts at Riverside and Daytona, the disproportionate number of national events held in the Eastern states was no longer an issue, making the winners true national

# G-FORCES

As racing tire technology evolved, cornering forces increased to over 1 G; most of the compliance had to be removed from the suspension and the rubber bushings replaced by nylon. The rear axle housing was mounted directly to the frame without its rubber isolator biscuits, which lowered ride height while maintaining the suspension geometry. Cut-down coil springs lowered the front end. The brake system and several other components were salvaged from the wrecked Z06, and because the SCCA allowed aftermarket wheels, it was no longer necessary to widen the stock steel ones like the kind that failed Guldstrand at Riverside. An additional 1.5 inches could be added to the factory aluminum knock-off's 6-inch width, and Guldstrand chose 7.5-inch-wide American racing equipment torque-thrust D cast-magnesium wheels, which were bolt-ons, not requiring heavy center lock adaptors.

## Shelby produced ads with tombstones inscribed "R.I.P. Sting Ray."

champions. This didn't do anything to level the playing field for the Corvettes, but in the interest of keeping the popular cars (and rivalries) returning to the races, the SCCA allowed a 2,700-pound minimum weight and limited modifications to make the races more competitive.

With a growing number of Corvette racers switching to Cobras, there were a few successful holdouts. In southern California, Guldstrand studied engineering at UCLA and possessed an exceptional ability for chassis setup and preparation. After winning the 1963 Cal Club Championship, Guldstrand's Z06-equipped Sting Ray convertible was destroyed in the third turn at Riverside—when he veered around the curve, a production steel wheel pulled off over the lug nuts and sent the car rolling and flipping. When Guldstrand was released from the hospital, his sponsor and Chevrolet dealer Hy Baher had a new 1964 Corvette convertible waiting for him. Guldstrand stripped it of every unnecessary pound the rules allowed. This now included the interior with only the seats and door trim panels having to stay in place. The underweight car allowed him to add some ballast in the right places, improving the balance and raising its weight to the required 2,700 pounds.

Guldstrand carried over his signature No. 56 to the new red Corvette convertible and continued battling the Cobras along with other holdouts. The rivalry continued off the track—no sooner did Brock design a Cobra T-shirt then a more popular mongoose Cobra killer parody hit the market. Shelby produced ads with tombstones inscribed "R.I.P. Sting Ray." The first time Guldstrand arrived at Riverside, the new Corvette track manager, Les Richter, tied a roller skate to his roll bar as a joke, prompted by all of the times he had skated along the track on his old one. Guldstrand permanently attached the skate, adopting the symbol for several years, and for good reason—he managed to successfully defend his Cal Club Championship even though Ed Leslie won the Pacific Coast Division driving a Cobra.

### American Rematch

The competition between Goodyear and Firestone had gradually accelerated racing tire development, leading both developers to a breakthrough in tire technology and construction. For decades, every Indy winner had won on Firestone tires. As chassis designers pushed for wider and lower aspect ratios, however, conventional tire construction had reached its limits, and both manufacturers took a new approach that allowed greater width without increasing cross sectional height. What emerged at the Indy Speedway were bias cross-play tires, equipped with thin sidewalls and thick, multi-ply reverse crown-modeled tread belts that changed from concave to straight when they were inflated. This type of tire gradually found its way into road racing, putting greater loads on chassis and increasing cornering speeds. The SCCA progressively allowed more modifications to production sports cars to keep up with high-performance tire technology.

Cobras won the USRRC Manufactures title for the second time, but Hall, with covert assistance from Chevrolet R&D, took the Drivers Championship in his Chaparral 2. The first runoffs for the SCCA National Championships, the American Road Race of Champions (ARRC), were held at Riverside in November, and the results in A-production were all too predictable: Johnson successfully defended his title in the new format. The only bright spots for Corvette supporters were Dick Lang's third place finish in A-production, and the 283 Corvettes ongoing dominance of B-production; Frank Dominianni defeated the two-time champ Yenko, who was second. Ford's unprecedented total performance racing program was far from all-concurring—despite the Cobra's successes in the United States, they failed to win Le Mans or the FIA Manufacturer GT Championship.

With its sensational styling and exceptional street performance, Corvette Sting Ray sales increased for both body styles from 21,513 in 1963 to 22,229 in 1964, with convertibles outselling coupes by a wider margin. For an all-around sports car that appealed to a wide range of buyers, the new Sting Ray, equipped with the right options, could be made into an effective racing car, but there was no way it could contend with a single-purpose car like the Cobra. For the 1963 and 1964 model years, only 75 260-powered Cobras and 655 289s (including Daytona coupes) were produced, and while these numbers were microscopic by Detroit standards, they relieved Shelby, whose only concern was continuing to sell 100 per year.

A Ford versus Chevy rematch took place at Nassau in 1964, but without the vacationing engineers from Michigan who arrived with direct factory support from Chevrolet, Shelby American took on more responsibility from Ford. They now ran Ford's GT 40 program along with the Cobras, and Shelby entered two of each at Speed Week, including another more radical big-block Cobra that Miles built to be a Grand Sport Corvette killer. Miles' latest creation featured ultra-lightweight bodywork and was equipped with an experimental aluminum 390ci FE series big-block that produced about 450 hp. It was still less powerful than a 427, but the car only weighed 1,600 pounds. Mecom Jr.'s team returned with five cars, but only three of them were powered by Chevrolet without any further Grand Sport developments.

The star of Speed Week was Penske, who pulled off a hat trick by winning all three races in Hall's Grand Sport and both his and Hap Sharp's Chaparral 2s. After the sweep, Penske promptly retired as a racing driver to concentrate on business. He occasionally replaced in Hall's Chaparral 2 and was his codriver at Sebring. As Hall concentrated on developing his Chaparrals, Penske took over running the Grand Sport after Sebring, maintaining it at Bill Scott's shop in New Town Square, Pennsylvania,

where he would later base his racing team. The car was completely rebuilt for Nassau—the air jacks and every other unnecessary pound were removed, and it weighed about 1,900 pounds, even though the engine now had a cast-iron cylinder block for a power to weight ratio of 4.9 lb/hp. It was impressive, but Miles' killer Cobra beat it at 3.5 lb/hp.

In the five-lap qualifier for the Tourist Trophy Race, Penske drove the No. 82 Grand Sport. He managed to use the Corvette's superior handling to keep Miles and the No. 98 Cobra behind him, rallying for a win despite Miles' superior start. When the green flag dropped, Miles couldn't be held back—he blasted off to a quarter mile lead by the end of the first lap and continued pulling away until his aluminum 390 began losing power. Penske inherited the lead as Miles regressed and soon fell out of the race, followed by another Shelby entry. Mecom's Grand Sport No. 00, driven by Jack Saunders, also bowed out. It started to rain late in the race, and the recently repaved track became so slick that the race was stopped after 23 laps. Penske finished first, while Ken Hall, in the only production Corvette at Nassau, finished 18th.

Soon, Roger arranged the sale of the Grand Sport to his friend George Wintersteen. Wintersteen changed the number to his signature 12 and drove

Speed Weeks main event was the 56-lap Nassau Trophy Race on Sunday December 8, where all of the surviving cars battled it out, and in 1963 it started with an all-Mecom racing team front row. The two remaining Grand Sports, with John Cannon now in the No. 65 and Thompson taking over the No. 50, were lined up beside Augie Pabst, driving Mecom's No. 00 Lola GT, with Thompson finishing 4th overall winning GT.
*GM Media Archive*

out, and a power antenna came with a RPO V69 AM/FM radio. A new side-mounted exhaust system was available as RPO N14, covered by dramatic fluted heat shields. New wheel covers included six simulated spokes, and for the first time in Corvette history, the tires increased in width, but the only choice remained between nylon cord blackwalls and rayon cord whitewalls. Another Corvette first was a big-block engine, which required a unique hood, with a raised center ridge flaring out into a clearance bulge and functioning air intakes on the sides.

Chevrolet's new big-block V-8 was a direct development of the Mark II mystery motor with almost identical cylinder heads, but it had an entirely new and more ridged block. The Mark III designation was unavailable from a stillborn design study conducted during the summer of 1963, so the new production engine was designated Mark IV. The heads formed semi-hemispherical combustion chambers, and this patented design gave these engines the potential for more horsepower than anything to come out of Detroit in the 1960s, except for Chrysler's King Kong motor, the second-generation 426 Hemi.

Duntov had successfully kept the W-motor out of the Corvette since its introduction in 1958 because of its weight, but he welcomed the Mark IV—even though it was just as heavy; the increasing popularity of big-block engines and the need for more power dictated a change. Chevrolet's second-generation big-block was introduced as a Corvette engine, and production didn't begin at the Tonawanda engine plant until January 1965. It was a mid–model year debut, displacing 396ci as RPO L78 and rated at 425 hp. Even though racing remained strictly off limits, it was initially developed as a 427, which was the NASCAR and NHRA displacement limit. A 396ci version was tested just to see what would happen. Corvettes were classified as mid-sized cars, limiting them to 400ci by corporate mandate, making the 396 the first of three displacements to enter production during 1965.

The Cobra Daytona coupes and roadsters narrowly missed winning the FIA Championship in 1964 while Ford promoted a fleet of GT40s that never won a single race, so they added a pair of the 40s to Shelby's team for 1965. Only 51 competition 427 Cobras were completed before the 100-production-vehicle homologation deadline, and production switched to the street versions; Ford

In March 1964, the run and jump start of the 12 Hours of Sebring was as exciting as ever but had a different look, with the field lined up by qualifying times rather than engine displacement. This put many of the red Ferrari prototypes at the front of the starting lineup, even though the cars were still numbered by engine size, with Shelby's experimental 427 Cobra getting No. 1, starting well back in the field. *GM Media Archive*

it in the two remaining races. Both Grand Sports retired from the Governor's Cup—Wintersteen was out after 12 laps, and Saunders only lasted 22 laps, leaving Ken Hall, the only Corvette, to finish in 17th. Penske won behind the wheel of Jim Hall's Chaparral.

Miles returned with the big-block Cobra for the Nassau Trophy Race on Sunday. Mecom's Grand Sport was parked, but Wintersteen's was still ready to go. The Nassau Trophy Race was the main event, and it was run entirely in the rain, making it impossible for Miles to get the Cobra's power down; he was out after 40 frustrating laps while Wintersteen spun several times, knocking off most of his Corvette's nose. He still managed to finish 23rd overall, which was good enough for 1st in GT, while Penske won again, this time in Sharp's Chaparral, completely shutting out Shelby's team for the second year in a row.

## Shelby Pulls a Fast One

The 1965 Corvettes were identified by a second round of small cosmetic changes. The recesses for the simulated grilles disappeared from the hood, and three open vertical slots replaced the faux front fender vents. The horizontal grille bars were blacked

was not interested in funding a racing program for these cars, and only one of them ran a few times as a factory entry. The 427 Cobra's racing debut was in the spring USRRC event at Riverside where two of them competed against the mid-engined sports racing cars; Miles' performance was impressive, and the cars began to sell. By mid-season, enough second-generation Cobras were racing to mitigate whatever impact the 396 Corvettes and later developments might have made, prolonging the Cobra's domination of SCCA A-production late into the decade.

The Daytona Continental in February continued as a 2,000-kilometer race in 1965, and it was a Shelby American benefit that featured a pair of Ford GT40s and four Daytona coupes. It was privateer Cobra roadsters, however, that swept the field. Shelby had the same Ford-powered armada at Sebring, but in the 12-hour race, the only class they won was production GT with Hall's Chaparral 2. It was a deluge that day, and Hall had to navigate through standing water up to 1-foot deep to claim his victory. The Grand Sport Corvette that had defeated Shelby's team at Nassau came in second overall, driven by Wintersteen and Peter Gortz. Mecom's Grand Sport was also in the race, but it was now owned by Alan Sevadisian, and

it was powered by one of Duntov's experimental Mark IV racing engines under the hood of a new Corvette convertible. The car was fast, but plagued with problems— it finished 36th overall, while Dick Boo and George Robertson finished 32nd in a production Sting Ray.

In 1964, SCCA B-production racing was still dominated by Corvettes, but that changed in 1965 when Ford revealed another "better idea." Shelby American developed a special version of the new Mustang; Fomoco wanted their hot-selling sporty four-seater to have a performance image and to be perceived as a low-cost alternative to the Corvette. By removing the back seat, Shelby was able to get the fastback Mustang homologated as a B-production sports car. The Shelby Mustangs were called GT350s, and the racing version GT350Rs, which coincidentally was about the power output of their competition-prepared 289 engines. Ken Miles developed most of these cars, and with a homologated weight of 2,550 pounds, the 1961 and early 283 Corvettes never had a chance when a well-driven GT350 Mustang was in the field.

A 396ci 427 engine was tested just to see what would happen.

Ludovico Scarfiotti in the No. 23 Ferrari 275 P got away first, followed by Pedro Rodriguez and John Surtees, No. 25 and No. 21 Ferrari 330 Ps, with Roger Penske charging to the front, driving Jim Hall's No. 4 Grand Sport. Charlie Hayes' No. 17 is the first of the Cobras, with Bob Holbert's Daytona coupe No. 10 closely following Penske, who quickly took the lead only to start falling back the second time around. *GM Media Archive*

In 1966, only 37 Corvettes were ordered with A85 shoulder belts as an option.

## Neither Wind, Nor Rain, Nor Sleet…

Corvettes were so well established as America's performance icon that sales continued gathering momentum despite Ford's onslaught, increasing from 22,229 in 1964 to 23,564 in 1965.

Estes followed the same line of succession as Knudsen when he moved from general manager of Pontiac to Chevrolet, and he was established by the debut of the 1966 Corvette. Estes supported Duntov's efforts to regain the Corvette's performance edge, and they even received help from another corporate edict that recognized the Corvette's special status as a sports car, allowing it 427ci for 1966. Exterior changes were limited to a chrome egg-crate grille, new rocker panel trim moldings, emblems, and wheel covers, along with the deletion of B-pillar vents and, with them, interior flow-through ventilation. Headrests and shoulder belts were offered as optional safety equipment, but the A85 shoulder belts were ahead of their time in an era when few drivers buckled up—only 37 Corvettes were ordered equipped with them.

As GM corporate eased up on their racing ban, Duntov directed his group to work on an all-out competition version of the 427ci Mark IV engine, as well as the chassis components needed to make the most of it. Even though Chevrolet brass squashed earlier racing developments, Duntov was irrepressible—he was determined to make RPO L88 as competitive as could be, and he submitted homologation papers to the FIA in the fall of 1965. By this time, Penske wanted to get back into racing as a team owner. Duntov felt his new Corvette racing package was ready for a discreet track test, and they worked out a deal that realized both of their goals.

Late in 1965, Penske sold a 427 Corvette to Elmer Bradley, vice president of marketing for Sun Oil, and through him was able to set up a meeting that led to a major race sponsorship deal for Daytona. Penske asked Duntov to send a set of experimental racing package parts to the St. Louis Corvette plant for installation in a red 1966 coupe. The February FIA race became a 24-hour event in 1966, and because Penske felt he needed a third driver, Duntov recommended Guldstrand, who flew from California to drive the new Corvette to Pennsylvania. In the dead of winter in a car without a heater or defroster, the assembly line workers left it to Guldstrand to start the cold-blooded beast. They wrapped him in furniture blankets and sent him on his way to make the frigid drive across the country to Bill Scott and Murph Mayberry's shop in Newtown Square.

Though Scott had prepared the Nassau-winning Grand Sport for Penske and Mayberry had continued maintaining the car for Wintersteen, it was Guldstrand who had the most experience with production Corvettes, and he took it upon himself to set up the chassis. Jerry Stahl fabricated tubular headers with side pipes to Chevy Engineering specifications that, along with American Racing bolt-on mag wheels, would eventually have factory part numbers and be available through the heavy-duty parts catalog. The production Mark IV engines were manufactured at Tonawanda, but the pair of experimental racing engines for Daytona were built at the Chevrolet Engineering Center. One was sent to St. Louis for installation in Penske's Corvette, and the other was sent to Traco. Jim "Grumpy" Travers was Reventlow's shop foreman, and Frank Coons built the Scarab engines; together, they teamed up to form Traco in Culver City, California, preparing Chevrolet-based racing engines for teams across the country, including Penske's. Traco's engine was scheduled for installation on Penske's Corvette at Daytona, but first the team had to get to Florida through the harsh Pennsylvania winter. When it was time to head south, they were snowed in, and though Sun Oil came to their rescue with snow removal equipment, Sunoco offered nothing but obstacles in lieu of sponsorship when they reached the track. Pure Oil (later Union 76) invested a lot of money in Daytona and wouldn't let Sun Oil's truck—loaded to the brim with Sunoco 260—through the entry gates. The fuel, with its 103.6 research octane rating, was essential for the 12.5:1 compression ratio engine.

Fortunately, an unorthodox compromise was reached—the fuel was transported into the garage area within several large drums in an unmarked truck—but there was still one more obstacle to deal with. The FIA wasn't happy with the Corvette's fender coverage of the wide Firestone racing tires, and aluminum flares had to be pop-riveted in place before they could get on the track for practice. After Penske drivers Wintersteen, Ben Moore, and Guldstrand all got some seat time, the Traco-built engine was installed for qualifying heats and

Dan Gurney, who co-drove the No. 11 Shelby American factory Cobra with Bob Johnson, is followed by Jo Schlesser in the No. 14 team car just after the start, with most of the field behind them. After a short troubled race in 1963, with an all-aluminum 265ci Indy V-8 in his Cobra, Dan and Bob were in third overall until a crash in the last half hour dropped them to a sixth place in GT finish. *GM Media Archive*

the 24-hour race, where they would all compete against formidable opposition. Ford's Shelby was concentrating on running the company's new GT40 Mark II with 427 power for the overall wins, but plenty of 427 Cobra roadsters were in production GT, and Penske hired Ray Fox's NASCAR pit crew to give his team an edge during pit stops.

Duntov's involvement in Penske's team was limited to arranging for the prototype engines and chassis components, making this a legitimate privateer effort, but Gib Hufstader, Duntov's clutch driveline and brakes engineer, was there on his own dime. The red No. 6 Corvette performed flawlessly during the race, pulling into the pits every two hours for fuel, tires, and driver change.

Night fell, and Guldstrand started to slow for another pit stop. The car unexpectedly swerved into the tri-oval banking from the infield and hit the wall, braking off the nose, shattering the right front fender, and damaging the radiator. Back in the pits, Bill Preston, a Sunoco engineer, had two large four-cell flashlights, and he immediately racer-taped them to the remnants of the front fenders as do-it-yourself racing headlights. Stop-leak was added to the radiator.

It wasn't pretty, but it was functional. Guldstrand returned to the race and even managed competitive lap times, trailing a Ferrari prototype. At dawn, the flashlights were removed and a replacement radiator was found in a spectator's big-block Corvette. Once installed, Penske's battered Corvette was able to continue competing as track temperatures increased during the day. Despite the mess, Penske's Corvette finished 12th overall and somehow managed a first-place finish in production GT. Penske's team and Sunoco enjoyed a well-publicized win with an unpublicized victory for Duntov's new racing package. A production 427 also did well in another 1966 Corvette coupe, No. 61, coming in 3rd in GT and 20th overall, driven by George Cornelius, Boo, and Robert Brown, but the overall winner inevitably was Miles, who shared a Ford GT40 MK II with Lloyd Ruby.

On the strength of this success, Sun Oil extended Penske's sponsorship deal to the 12 Hours of Sebring, and Duntov provided additional experimental engine parts and even offered the pair of Grand Sport roadsters to Penske. Hidden in storage since 1964, the cars' lighter weight and open bodywork minimized their well-documented

All three Grand Sports that had competed at Nassau were updated at Chevrolet Engineering and finished the 12 Hours of Sebring entered by different teams, with John Mecom Jr.'s No. 2 driven by A. J. Foyt and John Cannon. After a late start, A. J. made a spectacular charge from 62nd to 12th on the first lap and, along with John, managed to keep up with all but the fastest prototypes for most of the race until losing a wheel in the last hour. *GM Media Archive*

aerodynamic disadvantage, and Duntov believed that they could compete against the GT40s when powered by the Mark IV racing engines. Penske bought one of the Grand Sports and struck a deal for Wintersteen, his friend and fellow racer, to buy the other one. Duntov sent Guldstrand to Warren, Michigan, to pick up the vehicle he was going to drive at Sebring. The cars were secured in the basement of the Design Staff building on the GM Technical Center campus, and the technician overseeing them told Guldstrand there had been a sixth car built, which was burned for photography at the Milford proving grounds to show upper management they had been destroyed. Traco rebuilt the engines for Sebring, and Duntov sent them a set of experimental aluminum cylinder heads for the 1967 production release known as RPO L88. The big-block dropped right into the Grand Sport's tubular frame, only needing a clearance notch

in the front crossmember and the aluminum heads were tested during practice at Sebring. They saved 60 pounds over cast-iron parts, but Traco couldn't open their ports up as far, limiting airflow. Concerns about durability led to them not being used in the race. Duntov provided another cowl induction hood, and Stahl built the headers along with the side pipes. Guldstrand removed the roadster's headrest and added a front air dam to help deal with front-end lift, but with stiffer springs raising the nose, it stayed about the same.

The production coupe's temporary fender flares were blended in with brake cooling scopes under the grille, and both cars were painted Sunoco blue with yellow wheels and side pipes. The striking color scheme became the symbol of Penske racing, and with Sun Oil's continued sponsorship, their cars were impossible to miss for the next nine years.

With his experience driving a Grand Sport at Nassau, Penske hired Thompson as Guldstrand's codriver in his Grand Sport, while Wintersteen and Moore stayed with the production Corvettes at Sebring. The three-year-old lightweight Corvette competed against the latest mid-engine GT prototypes in the Ferrari 330 P2, Chaparral 2D, and Ford GT40 MK II, but it had one distinct advantage: it could blow the doors off any of them in a straight line. Nothing could beat its acceleration.

International Colors were still the rule of the day in FIA racing, although many cars were starting to be painted in their sponsors' colors. Penske's rolling Sunoco billboards, however, really stood out. The Grand Sport was impressive in the early laps of the race but after three and a half hours was 12th overall. Then a back marker forced Thompson off the track and out of the race with a bent frame. Wintersteen and Moore, in the Daytona-winning Corvette coupe, had an uneventful race, finishing 9th overall and 1st in production GT. Yenko and Morgan were 11th overall and 2nd in GT in another 1966 427 Corvette. After back-to-back wins in the two most important road races in the United States, Sun Oil continued sponsoring Penske for years, but the Corvettes were sold after Sebring, and Penske

moved up to a Lola GT 70 MK II for the rest of the season.

This distance racing success was encouraging, but it didn't improve the chances of competition-optioned Corvettes that could actually be ordered from Chevrolet dealers against the 427 Cobras in amateur SCCA events. Ford and Chevrolet's big-block A-production sports cars were numerous enough for the SCCA to reclassify the 327 Corvettes and 289 Cobras as B-production cars, but surprisingly, the GT 350 Mustangs continued to dominate the class. The SCCA added two additional professional racing series—the Trans-Am for pony cars like the Mustang and Plymouth's Barracuda, and the Can-Am for sports racing cars—to account for the USRRC cutback to the Manufacturers' Championship for production cars after 1966.

Corvette sales surged by an additional 4,156 cars for a total of 27,720 produced in 1966—17,762 were convertibles—and there were only three optional engines; the combined 10,374 orders for 427s were outstanding. The 427 engine had more impact in the showroom than on the race track in 1966, but its potential for dominant horsepower was beginning to emerge, a fury that would soon turn around the future for Corvette racing.

Four-wheel disc brakes and an optional 425-hp 396 big-block gave 1965 Corvettes more of a chance against the 289 Cobras, but "Ford had a better idea," coming out with a 427ci-powered Cobra on a new chassis that had coil spring suspension. The first '51 second-generation big-block Cobras were built as competition cars, powered by NASCAR-style FE side oiler 427s, with Halibrand knock-off wheels, a hood scoop, roll bar, and side pipes; they maintained the snake's 1,000-pound weight advantage.

*David Kimble*

David Kimble

**Regular production option L88** was the beginning of a new era in Corvette racing success. The new lower-drag body was conceived in 1967 and only 20 models were built, but it was not mass-produced until 1968. Still, the 20 development cars made an impact all their own. The second-generation Corvette was only intended to have a four-year life cycle, and Zora Arkus-Duntov saw the planning for a third generation as an opportunity to try again (as he had with the first new platform) to make a mid-engine car. Bill Mitchell didn't have any trouble selling his latest sea creature, the Mako Shark II concept car, to a conservative and cost-conscious upper management, winning the second round with Duntov. This time, however, the decision was made to not only keep the third-generation Corvette's engine in front, but to build the new car on the same chassis.

The Shark, with its exaggerated high fenders and long low nose, proved difficult to adapt to production. Duntov managed to get its introduction delayed a year to deal with development problems, but he was moved off to the side as a PR spokesman before he could get it sorted out. The third-generation Vette developed without anyone below Chief Engineer Jim Premo. He implemented the powertrain and some of the other features for the new body from the 1967 Sting Ray, along with some minor cosmetic changes. Hood script emblems and fender flags disappeared with the front fender side vents, changing from three vertical slots to five louvers, while big-block hood bulges were restyled into simulated scoops. The raised centerline ridge kept its crossed flag emblem on the nose, and 427 script was added to the sides of the hood scoop. Both the ridge and top of the scoop were painted contrasting colors, outlined with .12-inch-wide stripes.

The base steel wheel's rim width increased from 5.5 to 6.0 inches and the name changed to Rally Wheels. They featured five bean-shaped slots, a silver paint job, and chrome trim rings, along with small center hubcaps. Safety legislation had eliminated knock-off spinners, both real and simulated, so the optional cast aluminum wheels were bolted on with unique cone-shaped hubcaps covering their lug nuts. Ralph Nader's safety crusade also had an impact on the inside of the vehicle—redesigned seats had "Nader Latches" that locked their folding backs, an energy-absorbing steering column, and padded

dash. The passenger's grab handle above the glove compartment was eliminated, and the parking brake handle was moved from under the dash, emulating European-style levers between the seats.

For the 1967 model year, another General Motors (GM) corporate engine policy change banned multiple carburetion on all cars except the Corvair and Corvette, compelling Pontiac to give up the GTO's legendary tri-power option. The GTO's loss was the Corvette's gain—Holley divided their 4150's primary and secondary barrels into a pair of two-barrel carburetors and added another secondary, providing Corvette with a superior three-carb setup. Unlike a typical three two-barrel system controlled by manifold vacuum, the three-carb setup still operated with a vacuum signal, but from the primary carburetor, producing a smooth turbine-like flow of power from low rpm. Two 427s were equipped with this setup, which sat on a high-rise aluminum intake manifold under a distinctive triangular air cleaner.

There were five optional Corvette engines in 1967. The 350-hp 327ci L79 remained the only small-block, and the 390-hp 427ci L36 also carried over. Additionally, the engine could be ordered with

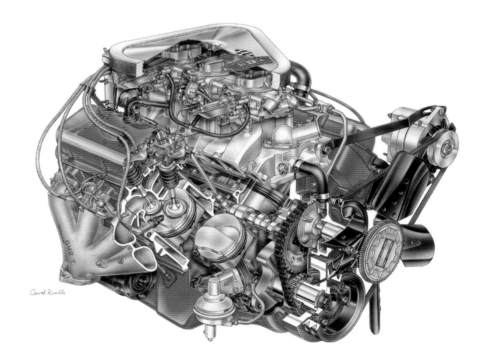

In 1967, Pontiac's GTO lost its famous tri-power carburetors by corporate mandate, and the Corvette was allowed to introduce a far superior system developed by Holley from their 41-50 four-barrel carburetor. There were two versions of the triple two-barrel 427, with the hydraulic lifter L68 rated at 400 hp, and the solid-lifter L71 shown in the illustration equipped with cast-iron L88 heads, making 435 hp. *General Motors*

## The L88 was more than an engine LPO.

triple two-barrels, making it the 400-hp L68. With an all-out racing engine on the option list, the street solid-lifter 427 was tempered with a shorter duration cam that, along with three carburetors, improved drivability of the L71 and brought a new high of 435 hp, 5 hp more than the L88 racing engine's 430-hp rating. This kind of muscle power steered casual buyers away from an engine that was totally unsuitable for casual driving and also away from the same number used for Chevrolet's last dedicated production racing engine, the 1963 Z11. Only 20 favored buyers were actually able to get an L88 in 1967, but the lightweight and costly aluminum cylinder heads could be ordered on the L71 as RPO L89, adding 368.65 to the 437.10 435-hp 427. Not surprisingly, there were only 16 takers.

### The L88

Chevrolet's ultimate weapon was constructed atop their high-performance street bottom end, with a four-bolt main bearing cap block and floating piston pins added to the forged steel connecting rods. The L88's impact extruded (forged) aluminum pistons were unique—featuring deep valve clearance reliefs and big pop-ups; the compression ratio increased from the street pistons from 11:1 to 12.5:1 with the same 106.8cc volume combustion chambers. Both aluminum and cast-iron versions of the L88 cylinder heads entered production for 1967, with the iron heads used on the L71 sharing 2.19- and 1.72-inch-diameter intake and exhaust valves. Since 1965, the same basic design of a dual-plane high-rise aluminum intake manifold had been used, but now it was tweaked; the center divider was machined out from under the carburetor, forming an open plenum.

Bill Mitchell's Mako Shark II proved to be a difficult shape to adapt to the real world as the body for the third-generation Corvette, delaying its planned introduction for a year to 1968. Unlike the production version of Mitchell's Sting Ray, which wasn't even evaluated in a wind tunnel until after its shape finalized, 1/4-scale models of the Shark were tested throughout the design process. *GM Media Archive*

These engines breathed through a large-model 4150 list No. 3418 Holley four-barrel with a whopping airflow capacity of 850cfm, and while the Holley had vacuum-operated secondaries and a choke-like street carburetor, the choke was inoperative. The required RPO K66 transistor ignition's magnetic pulse distributor also looked like the street version, but its vacuum diaphragm was nonfunctional. The L88 cam was on the wild side of earlier MK IV solid-lifter camshafts—there was so much additional lift that the rocker arms had to be given longer slots and stiffer triple valve springs with two inner dampers, along with larger diameter push rods, to compress them. This valve train was safe at engine speeds approaching 7,000 rpm. Peak horsepower was achieved at about 6,800 rpm; the 430 rating was at 5,800 rpm, with the actual output closer to 500.

The L88 was more than an engine RPO. It also included an updated version of the experimental 1966 cowl induction hood. The new simulated hood scoop opened up at the back to pick up high-pressure air from the base of the windshield. A duct was bonded to the bottom of the hood with a space for the air filter element. The air cleaner base remained on the carburetor with a foam ring in the filter's place to seal against the underside of the duct. More horsepower needed additional cooling, and the package also included a heavy-duty aluminum radiator. The fan shroud was not included in order to improve high-speed airflow through the core. Engine cooling fans weren't normally used in racing, so the shroud was redundant, but without it, the cars overheated in traffic, which was another reason to discourage their use for anything but racing.

Since 1961, a closed-loop positive crankcase ventilation system was required to register a new vehicle in California. It became standard equipment on all of GM's engines in 1963, though it wasn't legally required in the other 49 states. With concerns about internal air circulation compromising sustained high rpm lubrication, L88s had a breather cap on their right rocker arm cover and a road draft tube with an air oil separator canister on the left for an open system. They were coupled to the mandatory (and now L88-

With the new body inspired by a shark, the Sting Ray name was dropped in 1968, but the signature front fender side vents and two pairs of round taillights carried over; the coupe's roof was inspired by Porsche. Like the 911 Targa, a removable roof, which had to be a T-top on the Corvette, was supported by a fixed hoop behind the seats, with a vertical rear window similar to the Porsche 904 in a tunnel formed by a flying buttress on both sides.
*GM Media Archive*

exclusive) Muncie M22 four-speed transmission by a small-block, size 12.5-inch diameter clutch, and a 15-pound flywheel. The G81 Positraction rear axle, F41 special front and rear suspension, and J56 special heavy-duty brakes were also required.

This was the most comprehensive racing package that Chevrolet had ever offered, but unlike the Z06, it was buried in the option list, though the C48 heater and defroster also came mandatory. Any option that added weight without contributing to performance was strictly off limits and could not be ordered. Blacklisted items included the U69 AM/FM radio, power windows, and C60 air conditioning. Even though the production GT class in the 1966 24 Hours of Daytona was won by a 427 Corvette, none of the 20 built at St. Louis during 1967 were available in time for the February 4 to 5 running of the event. A lone Grand Sport coupe was entered in the prototype class by Toledo, Ohio, Chevrolet dealer Jim White. It was driven by Tony Denman and Bob Brown and powered by a 427 with a pair of four-barrel Holleys on a Cross Ram intake manifold. It was the last appearance of a Grand

Sport in international competition, and it ended after only 72 uncompetitive laps.

Don Yenko was sponsored by Sunray DX for the 1967 season. The deal was arranged by Dave Morgan, whose father was a Mid-Continent Petroleum vice president. Yenko picked up the only complete production L88 Corvette in time for Sebring in St. Louis on March 9 that year. Dave drove Mid-Continent Petroleum's new company car to Yenko Chevrolet in Canonsburg, Pennsylvania, where it was prepared for racing and painted in Sunray DX colors: white on top with dark blue sides and a red hood stinger carrying over the top as a stripe.

Sebring ran on April Fool's Day in 1967. Yenko and Morgan won GT, and finished 10th overall, even though the new Corvette suffered a complete brake failure and was stuck in a sand bank for the last 40 minutes of the race. George Wintersteen returned in Roger Penske's 1966 GT class-winning Corvette, now owned and co-driven by Joe Welsh; they fell out of an early class lead with an extended stay in the pits but found the track again, finishing in 2nd in GT.

With less head room and doors squeezed in by the Coke bottle contours, the new interior also had less shoulder room, but increasing the redesigned seats' back angle did improve the driving position. A large speedometer and tachometer remained above the steering column, with the secondary gauges moving to a panel in the center of the dash and outlets for the new flow through "Astro ventilation" in the lower corners. *GM Media Archive*

## Bumper-to-Bumper with the GT350

By 1967, Shelby American was winding down. Peyton Cramer, a Ford executive accountant turned general manager in 1964, had moved on. Ironically, he was the co-owner of a Chevy dealership. Cramer was hooked on racing after his years with Shelby, and his partner, Paul Dombrowski, ran Dana Chevrolet in South Gate, California, while he set up the Dana High Performance Center at a separate location. Cramer had been at Le Mans in 1964 with the Cobra team when they won the GT class with a Daytona coupe, and he wanted to return with one of the new L88 Corvettes. Cramer hired Dick Guldstrand to manage the High Performance Center and, through his connection with Duntov, was able to get the dealership's order for an L88 Corvette coupe approved. Dana Chevrolet eventually received two of the twenty proposed development cars.

Dana Chevrolet was also going to campaign a pair of Chevy-powered Lola T70 MK IIs in the Can-Am series, driven by Scooter Patrick and Bob Bondurant. Patrick had co-driven the winning Cobra at Le Mans in 1964, and he brought his experience to the dealership's Le Mans effort. Guldstrand naturally set

up the new Corvette, oversaw its preparation, and was one of the co-drivers. Sunray DX sponsorship brought Yenko on board as a third driver, with the car painted in their colors. Cramer found a second sponsor in Botany 500 men's clothing, but its decals couldn't share space with Sunray; publicity photos were taken with both sponsors' decals. A potentially embarrassing situation was avoided at the track, as both sponsors called the Dana Chevrolet effort their racing team because commercial advertising was not allowed on the cars at Le Mans.

Traco built two L88 engines for the trip to France, following their usual Federation Internationale de l'Automobile (FIA) endurance racing approach, except that the ACO, who presided over Le Mans, was far pickier about factory original parts, so Traco couldn't use their taper ground piston pins. The factory piston pins were straight, and Jim "Grumpy" Travers felt they wouldn't last, but with Chevrolet unwilling to homologate Traco's preferred design, the engines were limited to 6,200 rpm, improving their chances of lasting 24 hours. That was just the start of the team's problems, however—once in France, the promised truck from GM of Europe was

Even though the third generation Corvette's fiberglass bodies continued to be supported by a steel "bird cage," they were still too flexible for a removable roof panel like the all-steel Porsche 911 Targa. The windshield frame and Halo bar had to be tied together with a center support to make a removable roof possible, but it was a T-top with two panels divided by the longitudinal support. *GM Media Archive*

nowhere to be found, and the car had to be driven from Paris to Le Mans. The booming side pipes kicked up dirt along the shoulders of narrow country roads all the way. The famous ACO scrutinizers threw up the final barrier by demanding that most of the road equipment, removed to shed weight, be flown to France and put back in place, including the bumpers.

The Dana Corvette's racing weight was 3,265 pounds with the required equipment bolted back on. Though it was the heaviest car in the field by 300 pounds, that didn't slow Bondurant down. He qualified on the GT pole, breaking the class lap record by 10 seconds, and led from the start of the race, trading off driving stints with Yenko and Guldstrand, until disaster struck in the glow of dawn. Guldstrand was behind the wheel when one of the suspect piston pins let go, releasing a connecting rod through the side of the block. Even though it didn't finish, the Dana Corvette was a success—at least for Chevrolet. The lone American car led the GT class in the 1967 24 Hours of Le Mans for 11 hours, putting on a spectacular performance that brought other L88- and later ZL1-powered Corvettes back to the French race for years.

Tony De Lorenzo was among the favored few who would be able to get a 1967 L88 Corvette, which was a big step up from the D-production Corvair he raced in 1966. Tony's father was GM's vice president of public relations, positioning him to order a black convertible. It was delivered through his sponsor, Detroit Chevrolet dealer Hanley Dawson,

who also provided a matching black Suburban. He didn't have any trouble adapting to big-bore racing, winning his first time out with the car in May 1967 at Wilmot Hills, Wisconsin, and he soon teamed up with Chevrolet Engine Development Engineer Jerry Thompson. De Lorenzo and Thompson met when they were both racing Corvairs, and they did well enough in 1966 to be invited to the Sports Car Club of America (SCCA) runoffs. De Lorenzo was unable to afford to make the trip, but Thompson won the D-production championship. The two former Corvair racers started sharing the driving in distance races like the Watkins Glen 500 in August, where they finished 6th in Tony's L88 convertible.

Mid-Continent Petroleum was based in Tulsa, Oklahoma, and after Sebring, Morgan continued racing their Sunray DX L88 Corvette in the SCCA Midwestern Division, qualifying for the runoffs along with De Lorenzo. The 1967 American Road Race of Champions was at Daytona, and the combined A- and B-production race had a substantial number of A-production Corvettes for the first time since the runoffs started in 1964. Ed Lowther set fast time and led the first 11 laps of the race until he had to pit his 427 Cobra to change a flat tire. He relinquished the lead to Dick Smith, who drove another big-block Cobra, followed by De Lorenzo, who was able to hold on to 2nd. With the finishing order determining the national championship, Lowther worked his way back up to 3rd, and Morgan was 6th, while B-production was a GT 350 Mustang 1-2-3 sweep.

## German Inspiration

The year 1967 was the last for production of both the second-generation Corvettes and Cobras. Corvette sales dropped for the first time since 1955 to 22,940, but those figures were still enormous when compared to Shelby's hand-built sports cars. Only 356 427 Cobras were sold from 1965 through 1967, and with the objectives of Ford's total performance campaign long since accomplished, it meant that era was coming to an end—and Shelby American as an original equipment manufacturer (OEM) along with it. The 1967 Mustang had gained enough weight; Shelby didn't homologate it for SCCA racing, and for 1968, Ford took production of a watered-down version in house, leaving only the '65 and '66 models eligible for SCCA B-production racing. Cobra factory racing development ended in 1965, followed by losses in technical and financial support. Cobra became vulnerable to the third-generation Corvette in 1968 and was eventually overwhelmed.

Even so, the third-generation Corvette had a troubled beginning. Some of the problems that had led to the production version of Bill Mitchell's Mako Shark II were still delayed a year and

unresolved. Chevrolet Engineering reorganized during 1967; Premo transferred to Opel in March, and he was replaced by Alex Mair as chief engineer. General Manager Pete Estes consolidated all of the vehicle platform groups. On April 1st, Duntov was reassigned from his position as the Corvette's de facto engineering director to its public relations spokesman and remained only a consultant to his old group. That move left no one in charge of the new Corvette below Mair. Duntov managed to stay involved from the sidelines, until prostate surgery in New York City during May and June took him completely out of the picture.

When Duntov returned to work, his first assignment was getting a group of preproduction 1968 Chevrolets ready for the press. The first thing he discovered was that the Corvettes had many build-quality issues, and the 427 chosen for the event was overheating. This problem had slipped through the cracks, but Duntov was ready with a quick fix: he cut two long oval slots in the chin below the grille, which overhung the air dam. He extended the dam, effectively forcing air up through the slots. This saved the day, even though the car still ran a little

The chassis under 1968 Corvette's all-new fiberglass skin carried over almost unchanged, along with the powertrain lineup, but with lower intake manifolds to fit under the lower hood line. Only the L88 kept a high-rise manifold, but even it had to be equipped with an air injection reactor emission system, which can clearly be seen in this photo on a 427ci 435-hp L71.
*GM Media Archive*

Lined up for a photo finish at the conclusion of the 1968 24 Hours of Daytona, the Sunray DX Corvette team came in 1st and 2nd in GT, with the class winning 1967 L88 No. 31, driven by Dave Morgan and Jerry Grant, 10th overall. The 1968 L88's were built in St. Louis, with Tony DeLorenzo and Jerry Thompson assembling the No. 30 from parts, while Don Yenko converted a new convertible from his dealership into the No. 29 in which he finished 2nd in class. *GM Media Archive*

Dave Morgan's father was a mid-continent petroleum VP, and their racing manager picked up a new L88 convertible at St. Louis in time to prep it for Sebring, where it ran as No. 3, replacing the team's 1967 L88. Working their way up from 21st after the start, Dave Morgan and Hap Sharp of Chaparral fame won the GT class at the 1968 12 Hours of Sebring, coming in 6th overall, the highest finishing position for a Corvette ever.
*GM Media Archive*

hot; with the improved airflow through the radiator, the temperature stabilized at 210 degrees, but the journalists didn't think anything about it, and these changes were incorporated in the production cars. Other problems with the 1968 Corvette made it clear to Estes that it wasn't just another Chevrolet product, and Estes reinstated a Duntov to a position in charge of development.

In July of 1967, Duntov finally received the title most people assumed he had by 1956 or 1957— Corvette chief engineer. It made him the first one at Chevrolet for a single vehicle platform. Duntov's hands were full as he sorted out the new Corvette's problems, even though it was little more than a heavier body on the same chassis. The extended front overhang added 7.3 inches, and the Sting Ray name was dropped for 1968. The length grew, but the third-generation body was narrower and lower than its predecessors. The coupe's roof was intended to be like Porsche's 911 Targa, with a fixed halo bar behind the seats and a removable roof panel, but with the Corvette's more flexible fiberglass body, a center support had to be added to its steel birdcage. This tied the support structure's halo bar to the windshield frame, dividing the roof into two panels, making it a T-top.

Porsche's influence extended to the coupe's rear window treatment, with a near vertical window in a tunnel formed by a flying buttress on both sides akin to their 904, with the window and roof panels removable for open air motoring. There was also a droptop convertible, and it remained by far the most popular model, with a far more aerodynamic RPO C07 auxiliary hardtop available, making this combination the easy choice for endurance racing. With the side glass vent windows not carrying over, "Astro ventilation" was introduced, taking high-pressure air from the cowl and blowing it through the dash. Fresh air flowed through the interior and out a pair of grilles on the rear deck in the low-pressure area behind the window, but while it worked, Astro ventilation was only marginally effective.

Side marker lights appeared in 1968. The signature four round taillights and concealed headlights carried over, but the headlights were now popped up by vacuum instead of being rotated into view by electric motors. A vacuum-operated panel also concealed the windshield wipers, with push buttons and recessed finger grips instead of door

handles (Mako Shark features), along with pinched-in rocker panels that accentuated the Coke-bottle shape of the sides. The hood line was lower, giving even the small-block cars a slight bulge—with a functional duct in front of a more pronounced one on the 427 hoods and a seal on top of the radiator support. This change, along with larger front fender louvers, and the addition of a front air dam were part of a carefully developed aerodynamic makeover that kept Mitchell's latest sea creature from ending up as another fish in the frying pan.

Both coupe and convertible rear decks remained fixed in place; the spare tire was still stored between the frame rails, and the storage space behind the seats could be accessed only through the all-new interior. The dramatic shape didn't leave as much interior space—the doors squeezed in on the occupant's shoulders and head room left much to desired—but increasing the seat back angle did improve the driving position. A large tachometer and speedometer of equal size remained above the steering column, and secondary gauges moved to a panel in the center of the dash. The glove compartment was replaced by a lockable storage bin behind the seats. Compartments for the jack and tools occupied the right, and the battery moved from the narrow engine compartment to the rear storage area, slightly improving the weight bias.

The optional side-mounted exhaust system and cast aluminum wheels were no longer available in 1968, leaving only the steel Rally Wheels. Their rim widths increased from 6 to 7 inches for F70 X 15 tires. Firestone introduced 70-series tires with the

The 1969 Corvettes were almost identical to the '68s, but with improved build quality, along with some minor appearance changes, including a blacked-out grille and the reappearance of the Stingray name, which was on the front fenders as one word. This Monza Red 1969 coupe has the optional P17 F-70X 15 nylon cord, white stripe tires mounted on base wheels, with the chrome TJ2 front fender louver trim, which was only available that year. *GM Media Archive*

wide oval in 1966 at a time when anything under a 90-percent aspect ratio was considered low profile, and the third-generation Corvette's chassis received some changes to get the most out of them. The new wheels had more positive offset, increasing front track from 56.8 to 58.7 inches and the rear from 57.6 to 59.4 inches, with the rear roll center lowered from 7.56 to 4.71 inches for a shallower roll axis. Despite being promoted as a luxury sports car, ride harshness actually increased due to stiffer springs at both ends and wider wheels and tires. This design paid big dividends on the skid pad, however, as lateral acceleration increased from .75 to .84 G.

Specifications for the 1968 engine lineup didn't change, but some differences came with the four-barrel Holleys on every engine except the L88, which was replaced by Rochester Quadrajet carburetors. The Q-jets sat on top of shorter high-rise intake manifolds to clear the new body's lower hoods, and all of the engines, including the L88, had to comply with new federal emissions

regulations. Both a positive crankcase ventilation system and a device to purify the exhaust were needed to register a new car in 1968. L88 Corvettes had to be street legal to qualify for production class racing, and new safety regulations also required a heater and defroster. Radios, along with air conditioning, were still off limits, and none of this stuff would reach the racetrack.

Regular production of 1968 L88 Corvettes didn't start until April, but three Le Mans blue L88 hardtop-equipped convertibles rolled off the St. Louis assembly line on a central office production order in late November 1967. These special cars were built for the American International Racing team, which was started by Bondurant, former Shelby PR guy Don Rabbitt, and Sandy Sandin. Actor Jim Garner added his name for publicity. Garner was more than a front man, though, and helped arrange the team's Goodyear sponsorship. Rabbitt managed the business, while Guldstrand, who got involved about the same time as Garner, oversaw the cars'

After disappearing from the 1968 option list, the N14 side-mounted exhaust system was back for a one year encore in 1969, sculptured to match the curved rocker panels of the new body. The car in this photo is also equipped with P02 deluxe wheel covers, and the Stingray script can be seen above unadorned fender louvers without the optional chrome inserts.
*GM Media Archive*

preparation and managed the team on the track. Bondurant and Guldstrand met Garner during the filming of *Grand Prix,* but Bondurant had been injured in a crash at Watkins Glen and wasn't able to take an active part when the team got started.

Guldstrand flew to St. Louis, and after following the American International Racing (AIR) Corvettes through final assembly, he was joined by AIR Chief Mechanic Bob McDonald and Perry Moore to convoy the cars to the team's shop in Culver City, California. One of the new L88 Corvettes was registered for the street and used for promotion, while the other two were stripped and retooled as racing cars, with nothing left of their interiors but the door trim panels. Even the dash was cut away. The tachometer was clamped to the steering column and a vertical row of fuses installed for the simplified electrical system in the center, along with a switch panel for everything from the starter to the windshield wipers. There were fully supportive racing seats in front of a diagonally braced roll bar, and a fire extinguisher was clamped to the right front brace. The driver was restrained by a five-point harness.

With the use of fuel cells being encouraged by both the FIA and SCCA, the 36.5-gallon fiberglass tank was discontinued. Chevrolet Engineering recommended suppliers for racing fuel cells. The AIR Corvettes had steel 42.5-gallon tanks behind their roll bars, each of which contained open-cell, foam-filled, rubber fuel bladders. These were no lightweights—they featured FIA-approved fixed headlights, tubular headers, and side pipes, along with bolt-on American mags that could now be 8.5 inches wide; however, they still weighed in at 3,210 pounds. The L88 engines were prepared by Traco, and with a 2:73:1 rear axle ratio and the lower-drag bodies, speeds approaching 200 mph were expected. Concerned about overstressing the car while banking, McDonald ran the cars on NASCAR-style steel wheels at Daytona.

A three-car L88 Corvette Sunray DX team showed up at the 1968 24 Hours of Daytona, with their 1967 Sebring-winning coupe joined by two 1968 convertible hardtops. Yenko custom-built one of these cars. He started with a new '68 convertible from his dealership, while the other one was assembled from service replacement parts by De Lorenzo and Thompson. De Lorenzo's sponsor, Hanley Dawson Chevrolet, had tried to get him

## POWERGLIDE AND HYDRA-MATIC

The two-speed Powerglide automatic transmission was never very popular, with only 2,324 buyers opting for it in 1967, but with the introduction of the three-speed Turbo Hydra-Matic, that number more than doubled in 1968 to 5,063. An up-to-date automatic widened the Corvette's appeal, and the dramatic new styling drew attention away from the poor build quality, but it received a fair amount of criticism from the automotive press. The third-generation body was an improvement in both drag and aerodynamic balance. The convertible's lower center of gravity and lighter weight made third-generation droptops the most popular choice for competition, and they were usually equipped with a hardtop for GT racing and ran topless in the SCCA.

a production '68 L88, but with none available for months, he and Thompson had to use their connections to get the parts and had the car put together in time for Daytona. Thompson met Yenko while he was racing a Yenko Stinger Corvair in which he had won his D-production championship, and it was Yenko who invited De Lorenzo and Thompson to become part of the Sunray DX team on a two-race deal.

All these cars were painted in Sunray DX colors, even though De Lorenzo's primary sponsor was still Hanley Dawson with Mid-Continent Petroleum covering little more than the cost of fuel and tires. Garner's American International Racing team also had a distinctive paint job—white graphics were added to their Le Mans blue Corvettes, including large Goodyear decals in front of their doors. They had the giant tire company's full sponsorship and dominated qualifying with the No. 44 car, driven by Guldstrand, Ed Leslie, and Herb Caplan on the GT pole, followed by their No. 45 with Davey Jordan and Patrick. The race started at 3 p.m., and the AIR Corvettes led the GT field until about midnight, occasionally split by Yenko and Peter Revson in the Sunray DX No. 29 Corvette, which slipped into second place at times during the pit stop rotation.

The No. 45 AIR Corvette was in the GT class lead with Jordan behind the wheel when the engine began to overheat. A stripped head bolt loosed its clamping

For a company that wasn't officially involved in racing, Chevrolet wasn't shy about keeping the automotive press up to date on their latest high-performance developments, like the all-aluminum ZL1 427ci big-block. In this widely used publicity photo a ZL1, with its emission system removed, and equipped with tubular headers like it would be for racing, appears to be running with its fan spun by a special effect.
*GM Media Archive*

track and the load on the steering linkage and wheel bearings. The relay rod was reinforced with a piece of angle iron, but wheel bearings became one of the car's recurring chassis problems during the race. The No. 30 car spent so much time in the pits that it didn't complete enough laps to even be classified. This gave the Mid-State racing team the opportunity to form up for a sponsor's dream—all three cars took the checkered flag in formation 24 hours after the race began.

## Racer to Roadster

The AIR Corvettes were dominant while they lasted, but the team didn't come away from Daytona with anything to show for it, and this

pressure on the head gasket, and it wasn't long before AIR's No. 44 car was also in trouble, making several pit stops to repair an overheated rear axle. All the team's spare parts ran out, ending Guldstrand, Leslie, and Caplan's race. When the AIR team stumbled, Yenko took the GT class lead in the No. 29 Sunray DX Corvette, which after dawn was still running 1st in GT and 8th overall, when the car was slowed by a series of stops to deal with rear axle and wheel bearing problems. Yenko and Revson still managed to finish 2nd in GT, 25th overall, while the Sunray DX 1967 L88 coupe, driven by Grant and Morgan, took the class win, coming in 10th overall.

De Lorenzo and Thompson started having problems with the 1968 L88 Corvette they assembled in Thompson's garage during practice. The steering linkage relay rod bent then broke. De Lorenzo used 8.5-inch-wide aluminum Ansen sprint front wheels, with even more positive offset than the new 7-inch-wide Rally Wheels, which increased the front

would be the only time they raced them. Dan Rabbitt, the team's business manager, had his sights set on overall victories, and with Goodyear's support, he lined up a pair of Chevy-powered Lola GT70 MK III coupes before leaving Daytona. Even though the 1968 Corvette was on essentially the same chassis, the car's performance at Daytona showed weaknesses that hadn't showed up in normal development. Gib Hufstader, who was still the Corvette's driveline and brake engineer, kept track of the part failures. Duntov called in Jerry Thompson, a Chevrolet engine development engineer, and Tony De Lorenzo for a debriefing when they returned to Michigan. His directives to them were to redesign the faulty parts in time for the next race at Sebring.

Bill Morrison, Mid-State Petroleum's racing manager, picked up a new 1968 L88 convertible ordered through Don Yenko at St. Louis and drove it to Yenko's Pennsylvania dealership for racing preparation in time for Sebring. This car replaced the oil company's 1967 coupe, and the Sunray DX team was made up of the only 1968 L88s at Sebring, joined in the starting field by a couple of 67s. Yenko continued driving his No. 29 car from Daytona, now No. 2, and managed to sign Pedro Rodriguez as his co-driver in a one-race deal. Morgan moved to the new car No. 3 with his friend Hap Sharp as co-driver. Long before Sharp was Jim Hall's partner in starting Chaparral cars, Sharp and Morgan, who were both from Tulsa, Oklahoma, had bought a new Corvette together when they started racing.

Rodriguez was spectacular in Yenko's Corvette. He qualified it on the pole, broke the GT class record by 10 seconds, and led the class from the start. He even lapped faster than he qualified. Rodriguez was keeping pace with most of the prototypes when the L88 engine let go after 43 laps, followed 5 laps later by the engine of De Lorenzo and Thompson's Sunray DX sponsored No. 41. The Corvette's driveshaft and rear axle problems weren't yet fully resolved, and those issues took the No. 41 out of the race. Morgan and Sharp worked their way up from 21st to 1st in GT and 6th overall, the highest finishing position ever for a Corvette. Mid-State Petroleum had co-sponsored the Dana Chevrolet Corvette Le Mans in 1967, and with their Sunray DX teams' wins at Daytona and Sebring, they were one race away from

the triple crown of endurance racing. The only thing left was Le Mans.

## French Fury

All was not well in France. Civil unrest and a national strike delayed the 24 Hour Race from June to September, and by that time, Sun Oil was in the process of buying Sunray DX, and while they never made it back to France, Sunray was able to continue racing in the United States for quite some time. The Watkins Glen 6 Hour Race in July was added to the FIA championship in 1968, and Yenko entered with Sunray DX sponsorship and managed to get Rodriguez back as his co-driver. The only other Corvette in the field was a brand new British green convertible owned by Doug

In order to qualify for production class racing, ZL1s had to be street legal when they left the factory, which meant equipping them with Chevy's air injection reaction emissions system. To make preparing these engines for racing easier, the water pump pulley was split so the front single groove pulley could be removed, along with the rest of the smog system and the cast-iron exhaust manifolds. *GM Media Archive*

# RACING TO PRODUCTION

**There was never a better example of how racing improves the breed. Most of the upgraded parts reaching production, including the 2.73:1 rear axle gears, became standard equipment for 427 Corvettes equipped with automatic transmissions. The wheel bearings were upgraded, with the spindles, stub axles, and driveshaft welds shot-peened to improve durability, while universal joint U-bolts were replaced by bolt-on bearing caps. A heavier forged relay rod was introduced. The second-generation Corvettes had gotten by with sheet metal scoops mounted to the bottom of their rear axle housings for cooling, but Daytona made it clear that with wider tires and more weight, something more was needed. Hufstader made sure that a Harrison rear axle cooler and pump were homologated and available for Sebring, but on the bumpy airport circuit, Corvette's problems weren't completely solved.**

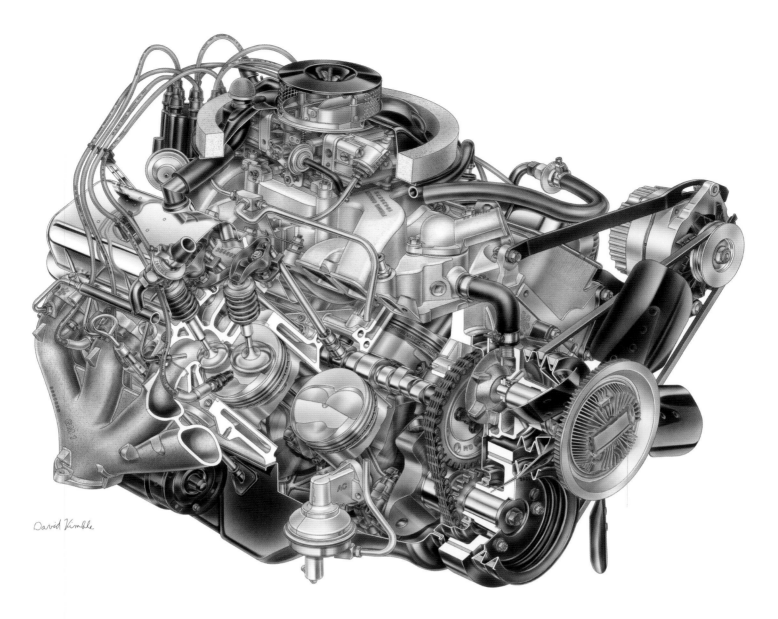

David Kimble

Speculation was that the ZR-1 would be an L88 with an aluminum block, but it turned out to be a lot more, with a new "dual feeder" Holley four-barrel, a hotter cam, and open chamber heads that flowed 30 percent more air. The 1969 L88s were also equipped with the new carburetor and heads, making them a ZL1 with an iron block, producing 475 to 480 hp when they left the factory, while ZL1's made as much as 525 hp. *General Motors*

Bergen and driven by two Bob Johnsons, both from Ohio. Columbus Bob Johnson qualified the car on the GT pole, breaking the class record, and they finished 1st in GT, 11th overall, while Yenko and Rodriguez crashed out. Victory went to John Wyer's Ford GT 40s in a 1-2 finish.

De Lorenzo still had his 1967 L88 Corvette as well as the '68 he and Thompson had assembled, giving him the basis of a two-car team. He searched for big-time corporate sponsorship and wrote a proposal to Owens-Corning, Chevrolet's fiberglass supplier for Corvette bodies. GM President Ed Cole's wife, Dolly, personally delivered the message, and it wasn't long before he received a much-welcomed phone call. GM Stylist Randy Whitten managed to repaint the '68 in a red and white color scheme he designed for the fiberglass giant's racing team, but the '67 was still black for their debut at Mid Ohio in August. De Lorenzo drove the '68 with Thompson in the old

car, but the race was dominated by "Marietta" Bob Johnson in Bergen's 1968 L88 convertible.

Four Corvettes entered the 1968 24 Hours of Le Mans, but with the race delayed three months, the Sunray DX team was no longer able to make the trip, leaving the two red 1968 L88 T-top coupes from Scudera Filpinetti. Bob Lutz was working at Opel and had a hand in getting the accomplished Swiss racing team the pair of Corvettes and arranging for French rally driver Henri Greder to drive one of them at Le Mans. One car raced as No. 3, with the inexperienced Greder teamed with that year's Targa Floro winner, Umberto Maglioli. The other car raced as No. 4 and was driven by Sylvain Garant with Jean-Michel Giorgi as co-driver. Maglioli shattered the Dana Corvette's 1967 GT qualifying time and raised the class speed record from 172 to195 mph on the Mulsanne Straight. He pulled away from the GT field at the start of the race, but the No. 3 Corvette blew a head gasket during the 5th hour. The No. 4 Corvette inherited the GT lead and stayed in front until the 14th hour when rain slicked the track. Giorgi lost control on the Dunlap curve and knocked both ends off his car.

Not long after forming the Owens-Corning racing team, De Lorenzo and Thompson stopped racing each other in A-production. With a 327 installed in the '67, Thompson continued driving it in B-production. By November they had both accumulated enough points to be invited to the SCCA runoffs at Riverside, where they competed against Yenko and David Dooley in the Sunray DX L88 Corvettes, along with several formidable Cobras and GT 350 Mustangs. The defending national champion, Smith, took the initial lead in the 30-minute race, but the 427 Ford in his No. 1 Cobra went flat on the back stretch, handing the lead to Yenko's No. 9 with De Lorenzo's No. 4 pushing past him on the 5th lap. Pete Consiglio in the No. 19 427 Cobra came through the field and caught up to De Lorenzo, getting by underbraking just three laps from the finish, so he and Thompson both came up one position short as Don Robert won B-production in a GT 350 Mustang.

## Summer of '69

With the new third-generation, Corvette sales started increasing again after dropping to 22,940 in 1967; they were up by 5,826 to 28,566, of which 80 were equipped with the L88 engine package. Duntov was back in charge of Corvette engineering by the time the 1968 model-year production started, but it would take another year to get the problems under control. To keep up with demand, Pete Estes made a third shift at St. Louis, where an unprecedented 32,473 Corvettes were turned out in 1968, making it impossible to improve build quality. Poor panel fit, rippled body surfaces, and sloppy assembly characterized the '68s. It didn't discourage many buyers, but it did draw criticism in the automotive press.

The 1969 Corvettes were almost identical to the '68s, but they boasted an improved build quality and some minor appearance changes, including a blacked-out grille and a reappearance of the Sting Ray name, which now appeared on the front fenders as one word. The backup lights moved to the centers of the inboard taillights, with the push buttons that unlatched the '68 doors relegated to only lock cylinders. The doors were released by squeezing down the flush covers over the finger grip recesses. The RPO N14 side-mounted exhaust was back for a one-year encore coupled with TJ2 front fender louver chrome inserts (also available only in 1969). The search for more room in the cramped interior led to redesigned door panels, increasing shoulder room. Designers reduced the steering wheel diameter from 16 to 15 inches, moved the ignition switch from the dash to the steering column, and added map pockets to the passenger's side dash.

In its first 14 years, the Corvette's base steel wheel's rim width

The ZL1 cylinder block was a new design that benefited from durability testing Chevy R&D aluminum blocks in the Can-Am Racing series and weighed about 40 pounds less than the production iron castings it was interchangeable with. Main bearing bulkheads, cylinder walls, and block decks were thicker than on previous aluminum blocks, with numerous reinforcement webs, gussets, and core supports, which were closed-off with large-threaded pipe plugs.
*GM Media Archive*

only increased 1 inch, but it gained an additional inch in both 1968 and 1969, reaching 8 inches, which was the optimum width for the low-profile F70X15: nylon cord tires. With increased tire grip, the frame needed additional tortional rigidity, so it was stamped from heavier gauge steel while the goose necks at the front end of the main frame rails were reshaped and diagonal braces were added to the rear frame rails. These braces tied the crossmember between the frame rail kickups to the rails themselves. Together all of these upgrades took most of the shake out of the body, giving '69s a more solid feel and a quieter ride. With independent suspension at all four corners and racing tires continuing to develop more cornering power, the importance of this more stable platform would be magnified on the track, making the 1969 Corvette a better racing car.

Chevrolet introduced a 350ci version of the small-block V-8 in 1967, which retained the 327's 4.00-inch bore with its 3.25-inch stroke, increased to 3.48 inches, adding the additional 23ci as well as speculation about its long-term durability. This increase was less radical than the 377ci racing engine's

After a disastrous Daytona, the Owens-Corning Corvettes looked immaculate at Sebring in March 1969, with the No. 2's raised hood showing off the team's red hesitation stripe. Corvette engineer Gib Hufstader filled in as Dick Lang's co-driver in this car, and with all of the Corvettes in the 12-hour race having trouble, the No. 2's 2nd in GT, 14th overall, made it the best finishing one. *GM Media Archive*

Corvettes first got the 350 in 1969, which was a 327 stroked from 3.25 to 3.48 inches in 1969, and the first solid-lifter small-block since 1965, RPO LT1, a 370-hp 350-inch 1970. The 1965 fuel-injected L84 still held the title as the most powerful small-block with 37 5hp, but the LT1, with its larger displacement, had more torque, producing 380 ft/lb compared with the L84's 352 ft/lb. *GM Media Archive*

3.75-inch stroke, but for tens of thousands of miles on the street, it was on the edge, and the production 350 started cautiously as a 295-hp hydraulic lifter engine, exclusive to the new Camaro. The cylinder block had to be modified to make room for the longer stroke, and main bearing diameter increased from 3.25 to 3.48 inches, running in thicker bulkheads with four-bolt main bearing caps coming along in 1969 for the 302 and solid-lifter LT5 in 1970. The 350 equivalent of the popular hydraulic lifter 350-hp 327ci L79 was the L46, which also was rated at 350 hp, but with 20 ft/lb of additional torque. This engine brought the 350 to the Corvette—along with the base engine also becoming a 350—but still rated at 300 hp like the 327 it replaced.

During 1968, research was already underway on lowering emissions. Chevrolet followed suit by producing a new combustion chamber for the MK IV engine, with the secondary squash area scooped out around the spark plug, forming an open chamber. It was thought this change would produce a cleaner burn, which would also lead to additional power, and when a set of open-chamber L88 type experimental heads were sent down to Tom Langdon in the Dyno lab, he tried them without having corresponding pistons. Langdon had been in charge of solid-lifter big-block power development since 1967, and he installed the new 118cc combustion chamber heads on an L88 with the earlier closed 106.8cc chamber heads, which lowered the compression ratio to about 11:1, but it still produced as much power. This discovery led to redesigned design aluminum heads for 1969, with reconfigured ports that, along with larger 1.88-inch exhaust valves, increased airflow about 30 percent, unleashing even more power.

Chevrolet R&D started experimenting with aluminum MK IV cylinder blocks and heads during 1965. By 1967, Chevy was supplying Hall with them for his Chaparrals, while Vince Piggins provided similar engines to the other Can-Am competitors in 1968. Piggins also lobbied for a production aluminum 427 engine with Duntov's enthusiastic support, and it was manufactured as RPO ZL1 at Chevrolet's Tonawanda engine plant like the other big-blocks. Fred Frincke, from Duntov's original group, was the project engineer, and with lessons learned from extreme durability testing in the Can-Am racing series, the blocks were redesigned with thicker decks, cylinder walls, and main bearing bulkheads. These aluminum blocks had iron cylinder liners, and ZL1s shared the second design aluminum heads with the L88, which was the same engine except for an iron block and milder camshaft in 1969.

Both engines breathed through a new version of Holley's 850 cfm four-barrel, a "dual feeder double pumper" with individual fuel lines and accelerator pumps for both float bowls, allowing enough initial fuel flow to use a mechanical secondary linkage. The open-chamber pistons produced a lower 12:1 compression ratio, down from 12.5:1, and they were linked to the forged SAE 5140 steel crankshafts by third design high-performance connecting rods. The early L88 rod problems were only a bad memory. Forged steel SAE 4340 connecting rods employed a thicker lower beam section and smooth shank 7/16-inch bolts, replacing the marginal 3/8-inch knurled shank rod bolts. Even though both of these

special engines were produced at Tonawonda, their manufacturing processes were very different; L88s were produced on the assembly line while the ZL1s were hand-assembled in the "white room" and hot-tested before leaving the plant.

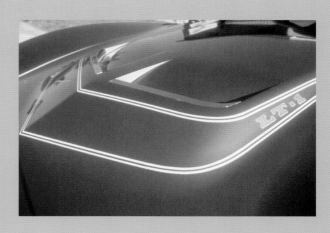

The L88 continued to be rated at 430 hp. ZL1s were given the same rating, even though internal factory Dyno sheets showed about 475 hp from the L88 and 525 hp for the ZL1's cast-iron exhaust manifolds. These manifolds' rectangular runners weren't reshaped to match the second design heads' round exhaust ports, making them even more restrictive than on earlier L88s, and bolting on tubular headers added about 100 hp. Only 116 L88-equipped Corvettes rolled off the St. Louis assembly line, but only 2 ZL1-powered Corvettes and 69 ZL1 Camaros were assembled as COPOs at Norwood, Ohio. Chevrolet's crate motor program began with the L88 in 1967, and this would be how all of the aluminum 427s that were road raced in the early 1970s found their way into Corvettes.

## A Fabulous Finish

Early production 1969 L88 Corvette engines still had closed chamber cylinder heads, but with the right connections, it was possible to get an engine built with open chamber heads, and one man had those connections—De Lorenzo.

De Lorenzo's '67 L88 had raced at Riverside in the runoffs with a 327 engine. His car featured curious *For Sale* signs on its rear fenders, and they worked—the car was bought by California racer Doug Hooper, who had driven a Sting Ray to its first race win at Riverside in 1962. The team's 1968 Corvette was completely rebuilt on a new frame to race alongside the new '69 L88 convertible in the season-opening events at Daytona and Sebring, running on the extra-wide wheels and tires allowed by the FIA. This meant fender flares had to be built, and Corvette engineer Gib Hufstader made paper patterns of what was needed. Randy Whitten at Design Staff sculpted them so they could be molded in fiberglass.

Corvettes equipped with the LT1 engine were identified by a special domed hood with outline LT-1 lettering surrounded by pin striping, and if the ZR-1 package was ordered, cowl induction. RPO ZL1 was a racing package very similar in content to the L88 that included a lot more of the same components like the M22 close ratio, heavy duty four-speed manual transmission, and stiffer shocks and springs.
*GM Media Archive*

Big-block hood bulges in 1970 were styled like the LT1's hood, with 454 on the sides of their dome in anticipation of dramatically lower compression ratios starting in 1971. This displacement increase partially compensated for the loss of horsepower, with the MK IV's stroke lengthened for the first time, going from the 427's 3.760 to 4.000 inches, giving the 454ci L55 390 hp.
*GM Media Archive*

Randy painted both of the Owens-Corning Corvettes in a new version of the racing team's red and white color scheme. The new '69 No. 66 was driven by De Lorenzo and Dick Lang, while Jerry Thompson took over the 1968 No. 67. The early laps of the 24 Hours of Daytona went well for the Owens-Corning team, until De Lorenzo blew a tire on the banking and brought the No. 66 into the pits trailing gas from a broken fuel line. The fuel lit up and damaged the '69 L88 enough to take it out of the race. All four of the team's drivers traded stints in the No. 67 car, until De Lorenzo had more bad luck with a tire on the tri-oval during the night. The steering became heavy on the east banking and prevented the car from properly turning. It hit the wall and climbed the fence on Lap 230, joining Robert Esseks' only other 1969 L88 Corvette as a DNF. Lucky for Chevrolet, it was still a Corvette that took the GT honors—the highly improbable 1967 327, driven by Smokey Drolent and John Tremblay.

The Owens-Corning team Corvettes showed up at Sebring in March, looking immaculate again and with no evidence of the mayhem they experienced at Daytona. Because Dick Harrell was not able to

drive, his place was taken by Hufstader. Thompson and Lang traded seats, meaning a Chevrolet engineer was available in both cars. The De Lorenzo/Thompson team drove the No. 1 1969 Corvette, and the Lang/Hufstader team was behind the wheel of a resurrected 1968 No. 2. Financier Esseks was back for another try at big-league endurance racing with experienced co-drivers: Frank Dominianni and Lowther shared his burgundy '69 L88, and Or Costanzo added a Daytona Yellow L88 convertible to the field. Costanzo was the sales manager of Ferman Chevrolet in Tampa, Florida, and his car was delivered to the dealership in January to replace his 1966 427. Dave Heinz was still named co-driver.

Pedro Rodriquez shattered the GT qualifying record in 1968, driving Yenko's Sunray DX L88 Corvette. At Sebring, however, with a lap time of 3:00.30, Tony De Lorenzo lowered it another 2 seconds in his Owens-Corning L88 convertible. All of the Corvettes in the 12 Hours experienced problems, but only Esseks/Lowther/Dominianni in the burgundy No. 3 were unable to finish. Their left rear suspension failed on Lap 55. De Lorenzo and Thompson made several unscheduled pit stops for oil cooler and brake problems in the No. 1 Owens-Corning Corvette and *still* managed to finish fourth in GT, while Costanzo and Heinz finished third in class. Their Daytona Yellow No.4 was slowed by ignition problems, while the Owens-Corning No. 2 with Hufstader and Lang had the fewest problems; at second in GT, it was the best finishing Corvette. Yenko won the class, but he drove a Camaro at Daytona and Sebring in 1969, with best photo sponsorship from one of his customers, Mike Summers, and aluminum 427ci ZL1 power. His co-driver in the 12-hour race was Bob Grossman.

The Scudera Filipinetti 1968 L88 coupes were the only Corvettes entered in the 24 Hours of Le Mans in 1969, but one of them was withdrawn in favor of a Lola GT 70 coupe. Greder, who raced in the 1968 Le Mans, returned to pilot the Corvette once more.

Because he and co-driver Reine Wisell needed to conserve the brakes, they chose to downshift a high rpm, which produced better lap times than backing off early. Despite their precautions, the transmission failed after 15 hours, ending their race. After a less than stellar performance at Le Mans, Greder decided he wasn't finished with the year-old red Corvette and bought it from Georges Filipinetti; it was soon repainted in his team colors, white with a flat black hood. His shop in Dissy, Les Moulineaux, with assistance from Chevrolet, prepared the car for a unique event—the Tour de France—which was the triathlon of motorsports.

Greder was a champion rally driver, and while the tour was virtually unheard of in the United States, it was a very big deal in Europe. It played to Greder's skill set, and his was the first Corvette

The 1970 Corvette bodies received a facelift, with flared fenders that were a better fit for the wide F70 tires and reduced paint damage from debris thrown up from the road. There were also new front fender side vents, covered by egg crate grilles replacing the '68 and '69s four vertical louvers for a new look.
*GM Media Archive*

New rectangular exhaust tips were recessed into the lower rear fascia, with both LT1 and MK IV–powered 1970 Corvettes getting the same big 2.5-inch exhaust pipe system. The backup lights moved from below the split rear bumper to the inner pair of the four round taillights in 1969, which received further detail refinements for 1970. *GM Media Archive*

ever entered. The tour was spread over 20 stages in 9 days, with races on famous circuits like SPA-Francorchamps and Le Mans mixed with hill climbs. The competitors traveled between venues in a timed road rally, which also counted for points. Began in 1899, the four-wheeled Tour de France was considered an even more grueling test of automotive endurance than the Monte Carlo rally, and Greder, along with co-driver Andre Vigneron, almost won all of the marbles. Even slowed by numerous mechanical problems along the way, their 1968 L88 Corvette won the GT class and finished an unbelievable second overall.

## Plastic Power

Big-bore SCCA racing saw Corvettes return to dominance in 1969, winning most of the A- and B-production regional championships while the aging first- and second generation Cobras and GT 350 Mustangs were relegated to back markers. Many St. Louis–assembled L88 Corvettes raced in the SCCA, along with those built up by racers, but none of them were prepared or maintained to the level of the Owens-Corning team cars. With major corporate sponsorship and direct ties to Chevrolet Engineering, De Lorenzo and Jerry Thompson won 22 races in a row, including 14 one-two finishes, often deciding before the start whose turn it was to win. In both SCAA and FIA racing,

Chevrolet offered most of the parts needed to take advantage of and comply with the rules for both series, even though they still couldn't be directly involved. It was a racing blowout.

Through 1969, the SCCA continued to allow a 1.5-inch increase in stock rim widths. Even with a 1-inch positive offset, the '69 Corvettes' 9.5-inch-wide wheels required notches in the rear radius arms for clearance. American Racing mag wheels were an almost universal choice, and teams usually mounted Firestone 5.25 x 10.4 x 15 and 8.00 x 11.50 x 15 racing tires, which fit within the stock fenders. Flairs weren't permitted by the SCCA; however, dispensations were sometimes granted, so cars running both series didn't have to tear up their fenders. Distance racing fixed headlights had to be replaced with stock covers. Almost all the Corvettes competing in both series were convertibles, and they typically ran with hardtops in FIA races. Hardtops and windshields were usually removed for SCCA events.

After a few months of steamrolling the competition in a string of SCCA nationals, the Owens-Corning team was back in FIA trim for the Watkins Glen 6 Hours of Endurance in July 1969. The team's '69 Corvette was No. 14, and Lang was De Lorenzo's codriver. Jerry Thompson's '68 Vette ran as No. 15, and he was teamed with Bill Morrison, but Morrison never got a chance to drive in the race. During the third lap, Thompson slipped on some dirt kicked onto the track by another car and ended up in a copse of trees. The frame was bent, and spectators made off with most of the bodywork even before the car could be recovered. Robert Esseks finally had some good luck; he drove with John Paul, who usually ran his own 427 Cobra Roberts 1969 L88 Corvette. They finished second in GT, and De Lorenzo/Lang brought home the Owens-Corning teams' first FIA victory.

The SCCA's American Road Race of Champions returned to Daytona in November 1969, and the all-concurring Owens-Corning team had plenty of competition, but this year the A- and B-production national championships was decided between Corvettes. Only two Cobras even made it to the runoffs, and they were hopelessly uncompetitive in the combined A- and B-production race. Jerry Thompson drove the Owens-Corning No. 7, starting from the pole. Gerry Gregory started beside Thompson in one of the former AIR Corvettes as No. 2, De Lorenzo's car No. 1, qualifying third behind his teammate, was in the second row beside Don Yenko's No. 91 Sunray DX Corvette. The balance of power was shifting, however, and a sign came when, John Paul, owner of a 427 Cobra, bought Esseks' 1969 L88 Corvette after he co-drove to a second place finish at Watkins Glen.

The 30-minute race was 18 laps around the combined tri-oval and infield road course. Thompson led the field, followed closely by Yenko as they flashed by the start-finish line on Lap 2. Yenko stayed with Thompson as they under-braked for the turn into the infield, but he ran wide and collided with cones, shattering the right front corner of his Corvette's nose. De Lorenzo wasn't able to avoid some of the sharp fragments of fiberglass, and they slashed one of his tires, taking him out of contention. Thompson led from wire-to-wire for his second national championship and Owens-Corning's first. Yenko was able to recover and finished second. Herb Caplan took third followed by Morrison in fourth. All drove C3 L88 Corvettes. Alan Barker won B-production in a 1964 example of the plastic sports car.

### Nixon, the EPA, and the End of an Era

Chevrolet couldn't build 1969 Corvettes fast enough. The plant ran three shifts but was interrupted by a two-month strike early in the year and couldn't keep up with demand. A huge backlog of orders lingered into the model year changeover, and new general manager John Z. De Lorean decided to extend production of '69s into the winter for a 16-month model year. His decision inflated production numbers to an unprecedented 38,762 Corvettes—116 were L88s. The balance had shifted in favor of coupes, and for the first time they outnumbered convertibles—by 5,496. The 250,000th Corvette rolled off the St. Louis assembly line on November 7, 1969, and the Apollo 12 astronauts Pet Conrad, Dick Gordon, and Al Bean all received complementary big-block, gold-painted Corvette coupes.

On New Year's Day 1970, President Nixon signed the National Environment Policy Act, forever changing the automotive industry and,

## Chevrolet couldn't build 1969 Corvettes fast enough.

Parking lights went from round to square in 1970, with the lens missing from this one in the corner of the new egg-crate grille that matched the front fender side vent treatment. One of the oval slots cut in the overhang above the short air dam, added by Zora Arkus-Duntov to get the '68's overheating problem under control, can be seen below the grille. *GM Media Archive*

Quite a few Mako Shark II features made it into production, but the recessed door opening mechanism was only simulated in 1968, with the doors unlatched by push button lock cylinders. For 1969 the recessed door latches were functional, and in 1970 the continuing search for more interior room led to redesigned seats, adding an additional inch of head room, complemented by a 1-inch smaller-diameter steering wheel. *GM Media Archive*

combined with increasing safety regulations, making production cars progressively less suitable for competition. This law mandated a 90 percent reduction from pre-1968 emission levels by 1975. The EPA opened for business late in the year, primarily to oversee the auto industry's compliance with this seemingly impossible demand. Congress didn't specify how this miracle was to be accomplished, but both the industry and the feds were looking at catalytic converters as the only solution, which meant tetraethyl lead would have to disappear from the nation's gasoline supply. Lead would poison the catalyst, and with its gradual removal from pump gas starting in 1971, octane numbers began falling and compression ratios along with them, stifling engine performance.

## The Swingin' 70s

Corvettes started the 1970s with flared fenders that were a better fit for the wide F70 tires, square parking lights in the corners of an egg-crate grille that matched the front fenders' side vent styling, and rectangular exhaust pipe tips. In the continuing search for more interior space, the seats were redesigned, adding 1 inch of headroom. Back release latches were relocated for easier access to the slightly roomier storage compartment. The substantial increase in the Corvette's base price—from $4,781 to $5,192 for a coupe—and its new deluxe interior marked the car's new position as a luxury sports. Optional genuine leather seats had been offered since 1963, but they were now only available as part of the custom interior trim package, which also included cut-pile carpeting, along with woodgrain trim on the doors and console.

A higher base price brought some added content, and the M20 four-speed became standard equipment (it was still possible to substitute the M21 close-ratio four-speed or M40 Turbo Hydra-Matic at no additional charge). Positraction also became standard equipment, and the 300-hp, 350ci base engine carried over, along with the 350-hp L46, which also had hydraulic lifters. It was joined by a third 350 with solid-lifters: the 370-hp LT1. As the only Corvette engine equipped with a Holley four-barrel or four-bolt main bearing caps in 1970, it holds the distinction of being the most powerful carbureted production small-block Chevy of all time. Detroit's first performance era was about to end, but with only 103-plus octane super premium missing from the gas pumps, which limited the new cars' compression ratios to about 11.5:1, things stayed pretty much as they were for one more year.

In anticipation of dramatically lower compression ratios starting in1971, the 427s were stroked from 3.76 inches to 4.00 inches, increasing displacement to 454ci to compensated for the loss of power output per cubic inch. Two 454s were planned for the 1970 Corvette—a 390-hp hydraulic lifter LS5 breathing through a Rochester Q-jet four-barrel and the 465-hp solid-lifter LS7 equipped with a Holley carburetor—but it didn't work out that way. Problems validating the LS7 for production caused it to miss the model year cut off, relegating it to a crate motor and leaving the Corvette without a solid-lifter big-block. Racing packages were also planned for both solid-lifter engines, the ZR-1 and ZR2, but because LS7 didn't make it into the Corvette, only the ZR-1 actually became available. It included the same suspension and brakes as the L88.

The Owens-Corning team debuted a new predominantly black and white paint scheme at the 1970 24 Hours of Daytona, with Jerry Thompson and John Mahler not only winning GT but finishing sixth overall in the team's No. 7 Corvette. Despite this success, their sponsor wasn't happy about the team abandoning the red and white colors of their logotype for black upper surfaces, with red limited to a hesitation stripe on the car's hood, and the black was gone at Sebring.
*GM Media Archive*

For the 1970 season, De Lorenzo and Randy Whitten decided to redesign the red and white Owens-Corning color scheme without consulting their sponsor. De Lorenzo favored black, similar to his '67 L88, so they repainted the cars with black upper surfaces and white sides. Their sponsor's red was confined to a centerline hesitation stripe composed of a series of blocks and to Owens-Corning logotypes in large rectangles on the sides of the front fenders. The cars were meticulously rebuilt for the coming season in the team's Madison Heights, Michigan, shop and competed at Daytona as Nos. 6 and 7. Dick Lang returned as co-driver with De Lorenzo in the No. 6. John Mahler teamed with Jerry Thompson. Doug Bergen sold his green '68 L88 to Jim Greendyke, who joined the Bob Johnsons as a third driver for Bergen's new black 1969 L88 No. 8.

Don Yenko returned with his Camaro, running as No. 9 with Bob Grossman as co-driver. Costanzo's yellow L88 Corvette was No. 90, with Dave Heinz continuing as his co-driver. No. 91 was a T-top C3 L88 Corvette entered and driven by Daytona rookie John Greenwood, a Woodward Avenue street racer from Detroit and professional engine builder. Alan Barker, who had won B-production in the American Road Race of Champions (ARRC) at Daytona several months earlier, was one of Greenwood's customers and, along with Richard Hoffman, was there to back him up with the driving. Cliff Gottlob had been one of the lucky few to get a factory '67 L88 Corvette, and he had been racing it with a 327 engine in Kansas. For Daytona, he updated the 427 with new rods.

There's plenty of time for things to go wrong in a 24-hour race, and the first casualty among the Corvettes was John Greenwood's red and white No. 91. He crashed out on Lap 101. Doug Bergen's black No. 8 Corvette led the GT field for hours, with the Johnsons and Greendyke trading off stints until their race abruptly came to an end during Lap 475 when the crank broke. Costanzo's No. 90 had a slightly less-than-fatal disaster after about 12 hours when a crossmember broke loose. The frame had to be held together with a chain until a welder could be located, costing him and Heinz several laps. They

<h2>There's plenty of time for things to go wrong in a 24-hour race.</h2>

still managed to complete 521 laps for fifth in GT. De Lorenzo and Lang in the Owens-Corning No. 6 were also delayed by unscheduled pit stops and finished fourth in class following Yenko and Gossman's third-place Camaro.

The surprise of the event was Cliff Gottlob. Driving his white No. 89 C2 L88 Corvette with Dave Dooley for a second place finish in GT, they loaded up and drove the car back to Kansas after the 24-hour race. The race couldn't have gone better for the Owens-Corning No. 7 Corvette driven by Jerry Thompson and John Mahler. They completed 608 laps to not only win the GT class, but also finish sixth overall—the highest position ever for a Corvette. Despite the win, Owens-Corning was less than pleased, and De Lorenzo was summoned to their corporate headquarters in Toledo, Ohio, to answer for the new paint scheme. Jim Murphy made it clear that black wasn't used in the company's logo, and when the cars appeared at Sebring, they had to be red and white again if the fiberglass company was going to continue paying the bills.

The Corvette contingent was back in Florida for Sebring in March 1970 with the same car and driver lineup, except for Gottlob, who didn't make the trip from Kansas. Don Yenko was there with Bob Grossman in last year's winning ZL1-powered Camaro, and a Le Mans blue L88 T-top driven by Bill Schumacher and Bill Petree made its first appearance at the Florida track. De Lorenzo picked up an associate sponsor, Marathon Oil Decals.

With five-point driver restraints now mandatory, Sebring started from a roll. Thompson qualified on the pole in the Owens-Corning No. 2 L88 convertible, but it was Greenwood in his No. 4 L88 T-top that pulled away from the start to an early GT class lead. Schumacher and Petree's blue No. 5 was the first Corvette to get into trouble—it hit a course marker pylon and was knocked out on the track. The collision damaged the oil pan, which began leaking and ended their race on Lap 39. The No. 2 Owens-Corning Corvette spent an agonizing 40 minutes in the pits replacing a broken steering box, taking Johnson and Mahler out of contention. Greenwood and Barker spanked the GT field, however, leading by five laps at halfway, but during this amazing run, the clutch housing bolts had been backing out on Greenwood's No. 4 car. This malfunction led to a late race clutch failure. Costanzo and Heinz' No. 8 Corvette lasted a little longer, breaking its crankshaft in the 11th hour. The Owens-Corning team's winning streak continued—De Lorenzo and Lang finished first in GT ahead of Bergen's No. 8 Corvette.

Greder had a new Corvette at Le Mans in 1970. It was a 1969 engineering car that Duntov had equipped with a ZL1 engine and shipped to France, just in time to be prepared for the June race. This last minute workup gave Greder the benefit of all the latest developments, and he ran the car as it arrived, still painted Daytona Yellow with a black vinyl-covered hardtop. He equipped it with English minilite eight-spoke magnesium wheels. Jean Claude Aubriet bought the 1968 L88 T-top coupe that Greder had codriven for two years at Le Mans and in which he won the GT class in the Tour de France and entered it as No. 1, still painted white with a flat black hood. The '68 was more balanced than the new Corvette, and in qualifying, Aubriet was 3.3 seconds faster per lap than Greder; however, Aubriet and codriver Joseph Bourdon struggled in the race. For the first time, Le Mans started with the drivers strapped in their cars, and most of the 24-hour race was run in the rain, adding to the No. 1 Corvette's problems with brake and ignition trouble and already dropping it down through the running order. Aubriet and Bourdon lasted until the 19th hour when the car slid off the wet track at Tertre Rouge, planting itself in the banking. This end was in stark contrast to Greder's race, which couldn't have gone better. Teamed with Jean-Pierre Rougets in Greder's new ZL1-powered '69 Corvette No. 2, they finished first in GT and sixth overall. Powered by Chevrolet's Corvette with wins at Daytona and Sebring, America had achieved the coveted triple crown of endurance racing—or did it? The ACO had some quirky rules, including a formula that determined how far a car of a given displacement had to travel in 24 hours to be scored as a class winner. Upon this discrepancy, Porsche was awarded the GT victory at Le Mans.

## Winning Combinations

As a team, the Owens-Corning Corvettes won every event they chose to enter in 1969 and early 1970. They took on the challenge of the professional Trans-Am series while continuing to race the Corvettes on off weekends. De Lorenzo and Thompson started the Trans-Am season with a pair of Bud Moore–built, ex-Ford factory Mustangs, filling in until their Camaros could be prepared for racing and painted Owens-Corning team colors. Maintaining four racing cars stretched the team's resources to its limits, but they remained as immaculate as ever, and despite

Still painted Daytona Yellow, with a black vinyl–covered hardtop, Zora Arkus-Duntov got the results he was hoping for by having a ZL1 installed in this 1969 Corvette and shipping it to Henri Greder in time for Le Mans. With Jean Pierre Rouget as Henri's co-driver, the No. 2 achieved an identical finish to the Owens-Corning team's No. 7 at Daytona, winning GT and coming in sixth overall, the highest finish for a Corvette ever in both 24-hour races. *GM Media Archive*

Even though Corvette Stingrays were handicapped by their short 98-inch wheelbase and independent rear suspension, they were still popular for drag racing. This 1966 coupe is a regular competitor. With its rear window and rocker panels covered with sponsors and supplier's decals, it's winding up a pair of wrinkle wall slicks with their beads screwed to steel wheels coming off the line.
*GM Media Archive*

their commitment to the Trans-Am, De Lorenzo and Thompson scored enough points with the Corvettes to make the runoffs.

GM Stylist Randy Whitten continued to handle the expanded Owens-Corning's color scheme design, paint, and bodywork, but he also designed the paint schemes of their Detroit rival John Greenwood. Greenwood's racing season was going well until he suffered a major setback at the Gratten road course in Michigan. Greenwood let a local racer and potential customer try out his Corvette, and he totaled it. Greenwood already had enough points to be invited to the runoffs, but had to piece together a replacement in time. The car had been a T-top coupe, but it was resurrected as a convertible with the help of Art Jerome. Jerome was the Owens-Corning team's full-time mechanic, and the car appeared at the runoffs in the first version of Greenwood's American flag paint scheme designed by Randy Whitten.

After alternating between coasts for its first six years, the ARRC found a permanent home at the new Road Atlanta circuit where it would stay for

many years. The combined A- and B-production race looked like a Corvette owners' club event—there was just one lone Cobra in the field.

Greenwood's No. 48 car stood out for more than its star-spangled paint job. Greenwood became known as an innovator, often introducing new ideas, and for this race he equipped minilite eight-spoke mag wheels with air extractor wheel covers on the fronts for better brake cooling at Road Atlanta. The Owens-Corning Corvettes, Nos. 11 and 12, sported new Whitten paint jobs that moved their sponsors' logotypes from the front fenders to the doors. Extended red hesitation stripe blocks reached their noses.

The national championship races continued to be 30 minutes in length at this new venue, and Greenwood led from start to finish, winning his first A-production championship in only his second year of SCCA racing. Jerry Thompson in the Owens-Corning No. 12 was a close second. Hot on his tail in the No. 11 Corvette was De Lorenzo until a fuse jarred loose, bringing him to a stop on the course. Like most well-prepared Corvettes, the No. 11's fuse panel was in the

center of the dash, and the car restarted when Tony brushed his glove across it, but he would have to work his way back up through most of the field. Thompson stayed in contact with Greenwood for most of the race and finished second. De Lorenzo was third, followed by Herb Caplan in fourth. The first seven finishers were Corvettes, and it was Alan Barker in seventh who took first in B-production, giving him back-to-back titles.

## A Short Year

A scant 8-month model year marked 1970. Chevy produced 1969 Corvettes into December, and the 1971 model year changeover occurred in August with the new models on sale in September. The 1970 Corvettes weren't even introduced until February 1970, which was reflected in sales numbers that dropped by 21,446. That's almost as many as were sold in 1963, and production totaled only 17,316.

The year 1970 was the quiet before the storm; federal regulations started reshaping new cars that could be sold in the United States, but on the streets and in showrooms across America, things would seem as they had been for just one more year. One hundred octane pump gasoline was still available, so high-performance engines for the street could still be sold, but the performance era was over. Detroit was about to descend into the dark decade of the 1970s.

Corvette production returned to a normal 12-month cycle in August 1970 without any noticeable changes to the appearance of the body or interior for the 1971 model year. GM President Ed Cole had spent years as Chevrolet's chief engineer and general manager. He knew how to bypass corporate mandates to keep his division in racing, but now he was the one making the mandates per the federal government, and there was no getting around them. Cole decreed early in 1970 that all of GM's cars had to be able to run on 91-octane low-lead fuel in 1971 and that both gross and net horsepower numbers be published; he also instituted a deproliferation policy to reduce the number of options. The compression ratios of all the corporation's engines were dropped to 8.5:1 or less, except for Chevrolet's pair of solid-lifter V-8s, which were on the ragged edge at 9:1. Even so, they still suffered a dramatic blow to power output.

The LS7 solid-lifter 454 missed its only chance to be under the hood of a production Corvette when it didn't make the 1970 model year cut off, turning the usual powertrain pecking order upside down—instead of a Corvette, Chevrolet's most powerful engine, the 450-hp LS6, was found beneath the hood of a Chevelle. The 454ci LS6 was equipped with aluminum heads for 1971 and moved from the Chevelle to the Corvette, but the loss of the LS7 for 1970 had reduced the Corvette to three optional engines, and deproliferation didn't allow one to be added. The 350ci L46 was moved out of the way on the Corvette's option list to make room for the LS6, giving it two hydraulic lifter engines, counting the base 350 with the solid-lifter LT1's power output falling from 370 to 330 gross hp. With a slightly higher compression ratio, the LS6 lost a little less power, dropping from 450 to 425 gross hp. Customers could order a racing package (RPO ZR2), but there were only 12 takers.

## American Muscle

After full sponsorship of two Corvettes and a pair of Camaros in FIA and SCCA racing for the full 1970 season, Owens-Corning was winding down their involvement in motorsports while Marathon was increasing their presence. The oil company had decals on many of the cars at Daytona in 1971, including Greenwood's Corvettes. De Lorenzo gave Owens-Corning equal billing on his cars, complete with a new paint scheme designed for the transition. Greenwood's Corvette was still painted like the American flag while Costanzo's Daytona Yellow '69 had orange graphics. During qualifying, De Lorenzo and Thompson outperformed Greenwood, taking both first and second; it was their first rematch since the runoffs in November.

The 1970 24 Hours of Daytona ran January 30 to 31. It started at 3 p.m. with the Owens-Corning Marathon Corvettes leading the early laps until Jerry Thompson's car No. 12 broke its timing chain on Lap 83. Greenwood's No. 50 assumed the GT class lead and stayed in front for hours, but his Corvette dropped back in the running order after several pit stops to deal with transmission problems. Costanzo and Heinz in No. 57 were slowed by an electrical fire. With De Lorenzo's No.12 car out of the race early, he and his co-driver Don Yenko were joined by John Mahler in the surviving No. 11 team car. They traded stints between pit stops to change out two alternators and a battery while lapping fast enough to finish a stellar fourth overall, and first in the GT class. They were followed by Costanzo's No. 57 in second and

# Corvettes dominated IMSA's GTO class in its first year.

John Greenwood's No. 50 in third. It was a 1-2-3 Corvette sweep.

At Sebring, De Lorenzo's cars were Marathon Corvettes. Greenwood continued to receive some support from the oil company, and he entered two Corvettes in the 12-hour race, both with American flag paint jobs. Even though a ZL1-powered Camaro won the GT class in 1969 and most of the racers were using its hot cam, Greenwood was one of the first to take advantage of the lightweight engine's potential with aluminum blocks in both of his cars. Greenwood recruited a celebrity racer, comedian Dick Smothers, as his co-driver in the No. 48 car. Yenko moved over to the new No. 50 Corvette and teamed with Eugene Harrington. Costanzo kept his No. 57 and acknowledged some financial help from the Tri-City Corvette Club on his front fenders. He and Heinz were joined by Bob Johnson with Cliff Gottlob's '67, making six Corvettes total in the starting field.

## The Beginning of the IMSA

The American Automobile Manufacturers Association (AAMA) ban had faded away by 1971, but Chevrolet still didn't race. Zora Duntov had to take vacation time to come to Sebring, giving advice and support to the half dozen Corvettes in the race. In a repeat of Daytona, De Lorenzo qualified his No. 11 Marathon Corvette on the GT pole. Jerry Thompson, in the No. 12 car, was out of the race after only 42 laps with another engine failure. Greenwood's No. 50 car lost its engine a few laps later while De Lorenzo and Thompson in the No. 11 weren't able to repeat their victory at Sebring. Slowed by a myriad of problems, they finished without completing enough laps to be classified. Costanzo, Heinz, and Bob Johnson also had a terrible race in the No. 57 Corvette; they dropped a cylinder after about six hours, limping around in fourth gear for the last two laps. Somehow, they managed to finish an amazing second in GT, while Greenwood and Dick Smothers won the class.

Winning at Le Mans remained the ultimate goal of most Corvette racers competing in the U.S. FIA long-distance races. In 1971, however, the only Corvettes in the 24-hour race were French entries. This was the fourth consecutive appearance of Aubriet's 1968 T-top L88 coupe, and it competed in the new GTS class as car No. 1. It still had a flat black hood, but the rest of it was repainted blue gray. Greder was also back—his 1969 ZL1-powered hardtop-equipped convertible was painted in his new sponsor's colors (white with a red hood for Craven-A Cigarette). Greder's co-driver, Marie-Claude Beaumont, attracted a lot of attention from the press for his team—she was the first woman to drive at Le Mans in 20 years, and she did well while they lasted.

Grossman was driving at Le Mans in 1971, but in a Ferrari Daytona GTB/4, not a Corvette. He was Luigi Chinetti Jr.'s co-driver of the North American Racing Team's No. 58, and they finished fifth overall. The Porsche 911S was by far the most numerous car in GTS—18 in the class—but they were no match for the Corvettes, save for longevity. Both of the big American cars ran into trouble, though; Aubriet in his No. 1 Corvette out-qualified Greder and led GTS through the night until his transmission failed during the morning hours. After the disappointment of having his 1970 class victory taken away by a technicality, Greder had another bad year in 1971. His ZL1 Corvette was slowed by a drive shaft replacement and taken out by a blown motor after 15 hours.

The SCCA had a rival in 1971—it was founded by John Bishop, former executive director of the SCCA and called the International Motorsports Association (IMSA). In 1969, IMSA was small, and it took a few years for the strictly professional road racing series to find its way. But with the establishment of two production-based GT classes in 1971, John Bishop's "Racing with a Difference" really took off. The difference was that without any affiliation with other racing sanctioning organizations, the rules governing car preparation were very liberal and drivers could make a few bucks to help offset the tremendous cost of competition. Grand Touring Over (GTO) was a good fit for the 427 Corvettes, while Datsun's popular 240Z was in Grand Touring Under (GTU). Porsche 911s were the most numerous cars in both classes, with the dividing line over and under 2.5 liters.

Another factor that made IMSA attractive to Corvette team's running the long-distance races was that their cars could compete with FIA wheel, tire, and bodywork packages still in place. Corvettes dominated IMSA's GTO class in its first year, and Costanzo joined the series about a month after his 1969 L88s second-place finish at Sebring. The

Florida-based car had a controversial new overall red paint job with white borders and stars on blue stripes that formed a X on the roof—it had become a rolling rebel flag. Costanzo was able to keep his signature No. 57 in IMSA, and with Heinz as his co-driver, they won their first time in the series at Virginia International Raceway.

The IMSA ran many of their races on combined oval and road courses. Costanzo and Heinz won on the Talladega and Charlotte rovels in May before Costanzo decided to sell his veteran '69 Corvette and quit spending his weekends at the track. Costanzo's team manager, Toye English, bought the car, and together with his son Dana quickly organized the Race Enterprises and Development (RED) Team, with Heinz as their lead driver. The new RED team was ready for the big summer FIA race at Watkins Glen in July. Don Yenko signed on as a co-driver for the rest of the season. At Watkins Glen, they competed against four Corvettes as well as a gaggle of Porsche 911s. Greenwood brought both of his star-spangled Corvettes. The No. 49 car was co-driven by Bob Johnson, and the team car No. 50 was driven by Richard Hoffman and Frank Cipelle.

Greenwood's No. 50 team car was the first Corvette out of the six-hour race; its suspension failed after just six laps. The only other car not to finish was the No. 64 driven by Bob Baechle, Michael Summers, and Fred Kepler. Radiator damage ended their race on Lap 91 while Schumaker's 1969 T-top L88 finished third in GT and eighth overall. Co-drivers McClure and Kiefer finished behind the new RED team's No. 57 Corvette. Heinz and Yenko were seventh overall and second in GT. Greenwood and Johnson were a in a class by themselves—they had an eight-lap lead when the checkered flag fell over Greenwood's No. 59 Corvette. Four GT protypes flashed across the finish line ahead of them. An Alfa Romeo T33/3 was the overall winner, followed by two Porsche 917s and a Ferrari 512. The Corvettes easily beat the rest of the international field.

### The Rise of B. F. Goodrich

Since the 1950s, Goodyear and Firestone competed head-to-head in a racing tire war. In the 1970s, however, Firestone ran into financial trouble, and B.F. Goodrich emerged as Goodyear's new rival. B.F.G. started manufacturing radial tires before the larger U.S. tire companies and decided to promote the advantages of their American-made, high-performance radials by racing them shaved to half their new tread depth. They competed with their lifesaver radial T/As against other manufacturers' dedicated racing tires, and did so well that Goodyear was compelled to start manufacturing a street radial of their own. B.F.G. worked its way into IMSA, supporting small sedans and making a one-race deal with Greenwood to run their Lifesaver T/As on his Corvette in 1971.

The event was an IMSA endurance race on the Michigan International Speedway rovel. Teamed with Johnson, Greenwood won the GT class on Lifesaver T/A's street tires—and the tire company's sponsorship along with it. While Greenwood defended his SCCA national championship in Michigan, the RED Corvette team was on its way to winning IMSA's GTO title but suffered a setback at Summit Point Speedway in West Virginia—after qualifying on the pole and leading the first half of the race, a light rain fell and Yenko couldn't avoid T-boning a Porsche 914-6 that spun directly in front of his Corvette, putting the team in crisis mode. The No. 57 was still painted like a Confederate flag, with a new front clip at IMSA's season finale "The 200 miles of Daytona Beach," and a happy accident in bonding the new nose on too low gave it less drag and front-end lift. In qualifying, Yenko broke the class speed record on the tri-oval at 201.4 mph. Yenko and Bob Johnson easily won the race and the GTO Championship on November 21.

A week after Yenko and Johnson drove the RED 1969 L88 Corvette to victory at IMSA's 1971 GTO Championship at Daytona, Greenwood won his second SCCA A-production national championship at Road Atlanta on November 28 in his 1969 ZL1 Corvette. Alan Baker also successfully defended his B-production title in the same event for the third time behind Doug Bergen's old L88 Corvette.

Soon after, 1971 returned to a normal 12-month model year and sales leveled out at 21,801. Coupes outsold convertibles two to one, and an unprecedented 10,060 buyers chose the three-speed Turbo Hydra-Matic transmission. John De Lorean, Chevrolet's general manager, took advantage of the lower volume to push for improved build quality and started overcoming the Corvette's shoddy reputation acquired during 1968 and 1969.

**Even from under the hood,** the appearance of 1972 Corvettes remained almost unchanged from 1971. Because the LS6 had been cancelled, only two optional engines remained. Horsepower continued to fall, but an industry-wide change from SAE gross-to-net testing standards made the power output of the 1972 engines seem even feebler than it really was. The advertised 270 gross hp of Corvette's base 350s dropped to 200 net, while the 454ci LS5 dropped from 365 gross in 1971 to 270 net in 1972. The 350ci LT1 was GM's only remaining solid-lifter V-8 in 1972. After losing 40 gross hp in 1971, its 330 rating plummeted in 1972 to 255 net.

SAE gross horsepower was all that could be coaxed out of an engine with optimized timing and fuel mixture that was running on a dynamometer without air cleaner or mufflers or driving its own accessories. This testing standard was favored by the industry because it produced impressive results for advertising, but it was deceptive, inflating the numbers by about 20 percent over the engine's actual power output. SAE net horsepower is just that: the amount of power actually going to the rear wheels

with the timing and fuel mixture set to production specifications and the air cleaner exhaust system in place. Engines also were required to run their belt-driven accessories. Despite various loopholes that have closed over the years, the testing criteria and standards for SAE net horsepower remains in place to this day.

After one year, the ZR2 racing package and the 454ci solid-lifter LS6 were canceled, leaving the ZR-1 package. It could only be ordered with GM's sole solid-lifter V-8, the 350ci LT1. Because most racers continued to operate Corvettes from 1969 and earlier, neither of these special purpose engine packages sold very well. Only 12 ZR2s were ordered in 1971, and a paltry 53 ZR-1s were built between 1970 and 1973. While a few ZR-1s and ZR2s were raced, the 1969 L88s were recognized as the high-water mark of Corvette racing development and continued to be the weapon of choice for most of the next decade. As new production Corvettes became progressively less suitable for competition, these cars were repaired and additional ones built from service replacement parts and wrecks.

Opposite page: John Greenwood is standing behind his struggling No. 50 convertible, which had finished sixth in GT at Sebring, while it's taking on some fuel during practice; it also failed to qualify at the Glen. Fortunately John had entered his old T-top coupe as No. 29 and managed to get it into the race, but his co-driver Dick Smothers never got behind the wheel, with John hardly getting started before retiring. *GM Media Archive*

Race Engineering Development's 1969 Corvette finished an all-time high fourth overall at Sebring in March, but after four years of competition, it had been repaired so many times it would have never passed scrutineering at Le Mans. The new car had been painted like a NART Ferrari in France, but both of the Florida-based teams' Corvettes had rebel flag paint schemes at the Glen, with Old Scrappy renumbered from 57 to 54. *GM Media Archive*

With full sponsorship from B. F. Goodrich, John Greenwood built a pair of new race cars for 1972 from recycled 1969 Corvette convertibles, powered by aluminum ZL1 engines, they were on English minilite 8-spoke mag wheels. Randy Whitten from GM Design Staff did a beautiful new take on his American flag paint scheme, but after qualifying sixth at Sebring, good looks couldn't give the No. 48 the speed it needed to make the field at Watkins Glen. *GM Media Archive*

## The Tire Wars

By 1971, Goodyear was by far the largest U.S. tire manufacturer and had overwhelmed Firestone in their ongoing racing tire war. In 1972, however, they started another war with B. F. Goodrich over radial tires. B.F.G. was the first American tire company to manufacture radial tires, and it promoted the advantages of its street radials by competing against other manufacturers' dedicated racing tires in International Motorsports Association (IMSA) and other series, starting with the small sedans. With B.F.G.'s tread shaved to half its new depth to prevent chunking, its tires proved surprisingly competitive. B.F.G. persuaded John Greenwood to try the tires on his Corvette in an IMSA endurance race at Michigan International Speedway during 1971. Driving with "Marietta Bob" Johnson, Greenwood won the race, and B.F.G. made the most of it; the tire company launched a major advertising campaign and signed him to run a two-Corvette team on their tires for the 1972 season.

In 1972, the FIA shortened the North American season opener—no longer would Daytona be a 24-hour race. It was shortened to 6 hours, and Goodyear was ready to challenge B. F. Goodrich with a "street radial" of its own, even though these tires weren't really in production. Goodyear was just starting to manufacture radials, and the tires it was supplying for racing amounted to DOT-legal racing tires, which gave Goodyear an advantage over the regular

production B.F.G. Lifesaver radial T/As. With his major corporate sponsorship, John Greenwood built a pair of new race cars from recycled 1969 Corvettes, and Randy Whittin designed a new B.F. Goodrich stars-and-stripes paint scheme for them. Goodyear supplied several Corvette teams with their tires and fully sponsored the Race Enterprises and Development (RED) team, which continued to run the 1969 L88 that Costanzo had debuted at Sebring that year, thoroughly rebuilt for its fourth year of competition.

RED didn't have the only racing veteran Corvette in the field; the previous year's winner was now owned and co-driven by Bobby Rinzler and entered as No. 88, with most of its Owens-Corning paint scheme still in place. The No. 53 Corvette, which Don Yenko had built it up from a new L71-powered convertible, had been in competition since Daytona in 1968. It was still in Sunray DX colors for the 1972 race and was entered and driven by Robert Luebbe. Some of the best known Corvette drivers were also in new rides: former Owens-Corning teammates Tony DeLorenzo and Jerry Thompson co-drove Ron Weaver's white No. 11 1969 L88 convertible, running the usual hardtop. Even though Yenko had driven for the RED team in 1971 and won the last IMSA race of the season at Daytona, B.F.G. was giving Greenwood the chance to race at Le Mans, and Yenko chose to be lead driver of Greenwood's second car.

With all of Chevrolet's engineering resources committed to meeting federal emission and safety regulations, what little power development that could be done was carried out at McLaren Engines in Livonia, Michigan. Alex Mair was still Chevrolet's chief engineer, and his son, Steven, was a partner in the L88 Corvette that De Lorenzo and Thompson were going to drive at Daytona. Corvette racers had always speculated about how fast their cars would be if they were powered by an 800-plus-hp, big-inch Chevy Can-Am motor, and McLaren built the beastly engine for them. While the white Corvette was being prepared for the six-hour race, a black box containing one of these monster motors showed up, and in the spirit of experimentation and good fun, it found its way into the L88's engine compartment.

Some of the Corvette teams had been running 4-inch stroke cranks with shorter compression height pistons in their L88s and ZL1s, increasing their displacement to 454ci, but the monster motor was a Reynolds 510, which was way over the top. The

McLaren big-block Chevy came ready to drop into a Can-Am car, built up on a Reynolds 390 alloy, high-silicone aluminum cylinder block, which didn't require the ZL1's iron cylinder liners and allowed larger diameter bores. The 427/454's 4.251 cylinders could be opened up to 4.376 inches that, with a 4.25-inch stroke crankshaft, gave it a 511ci displacement and, like most Can-Am engines, breathed through a eight vertical throttle body, Lucas-metered, fuel injection manifold. Eight velocity stacks sticking out of the Corvette's hood would have been a little obvious, so an L88/ZL1 open plenum intake manifold with an 850cfm Holley double pumper took its place, but they were still protested before the end of practice.

Restraint was exercised with the 510's power until Jerry Thompson finally jammed his right foot down all the way around the tri-oval, blowing by one of the Ferraris at over 200 mph, passing it as if the Italian car were parked at a local strip mall. The white Corvette soon found itself in the pits with an overheated monster motor; however, after a protest from the Ferrari team manager, a couple officials were brought over for a look. The team was lucky to only have to change engines, and officials also made clear that the big cubic-inch beast wouldn't be seen again under the hood of a Corvette. Pulling the switch was a moot point, though, because the engine overheated when the crank pulley broke and suffered fatal damage. Current production sheet metal pulleys were prone to failure, and its installation went unnoticed during preparation. It should have been replaced by a '68 or earlier-model cast-iron pulley.

The No. 11 wasn't the only Corvette that had to change engines before starting the Daytona 6 Hour. The RED team's No. 57 broke its ZL1 engine's crank while leading the midnight challenge the night before. With only 30 minutes to spare before the start of the race, they managed to replace the aluminum big-block with an iron-block L88, but the No. 11 Corvette took the GT lead and held the lead for the first hour. No. 11 was on the new Goodyear street radials, just like the RED Corvette, but it ran out of luck when a right rear tire failure careened the white Corvette into the tri-oval wall, ending De Lorenzo and Thompson's race after 21 laps. The next casualty among the Corvettes was the ex-Owens-Corning No. 88, driven by Bobby Rinzler and Charlie Kemp. It was out after 36 laps, followed by Robert Luebbe

and Michael Oleyar's former Sunray DX No. 53 in another 21 laps.

In FIA endurance racing, engines with starter problems have to be shut off during pit stops. This rule cost Greenwood's No. 48 B.F.G. Corvette the GT lead. He was soon disqualified, however, when his co-driver, Tony Adamowicz, backed the car up on pit road. This thrust Yenko and John Cordt's No. 50 B.F.G. Corvette into the lead on Lap 114, only to have their ZL1 engine lose oil pressure 21 minutes from the finish. Now the GT lead was handed to the No. 57 RED Corvette. By this point in the race, it was only running on seven cylinders, but it was still fast enough to maintain eighth overall and finish first in GT. It was driven by Dave Heinz, and "Marietta" Bob Johnson had replaced Yenko, giving Goodyear a win in the first round. The competing Corvette teams were from Michigan and Florida, and they were painted like the Yankee and Confederate flags. It was the Civil War revisited at Daytona, fought at over 200 mph.

Goodyear didn't waste any time publicizing their victory—the company bought a full-page ad in the next edition of the *Wall Street Journal* and began preparing for Sebring by renting the track a couple of weeks before the race for a tire test. The American tire giant extended the RED team's sponsorship to Sebring and also supplied Rinzler with new radial tires for the former Owens-Corning Corvette, which

The 6 Hours of Watkins Glen on July 22, 1972, was an FIA event that attracted 44 cars. That total included 12 Corvettes, with 6 of them making the 30-car starting field, including the RED team's No. 57. This car was a product of the tire war between B. F. Goodrich and Goodyear, with B.F.G. backing John Greenwood's team at Le Mans; Goodyear money built this new racing Corvette from a wrecked '68 convertible to take the tire battle to France.
*GM Media Archive*

During the 1972 racing season, 1968 and 1969 Corvettes continued to be the best choice for competition, but in FIA events they were coming under threat from newer foreign competition. The RED team's No. 57 was a 1968 body on the improved 1969 frame, but there were still earlier Corvettes racing on a budget, like the No. 28 '67 L88 on heavy but inexpensive Anson aluminum wheels.
*GM Media Archive*

was now No. 23 and painted orange. Oscar Koveleki replaced Rinzler as Charlie Kemp's co-driver and qualified on the GT pole, breaking Tony DeLorenzo's two-year-old lap record. Koveleki raced to an early GT class lead, which Kemp maintained for the first hour and a half. The No. 23 Corvette lost the lead when Kemp spun in someone else's oil and planted the car in a sand bank, doing too much damage to continue. The GT lead was relinquished to the No. 57 RED Corvette.

Although both of Greenwood's Corvettes were in a position to win Daytona, they both faltered due to mechanical failure. At Sebring, they never had a chance—their B. F. Goodrich Lifesaver radial T/As were unable to grip the bumpy airport circuit. Once in the lead, Heinz and Johnson kept the No. 57 Corvette in front of the GT field for the remaining 9 1/2 hours of the race, while Greenwood's No. 48 Corvette, with Dick Smothers, only qualified sixth in GT, steadily losing ground with tire trouble during the race. They were 42 laps behind when a cracked oil pan parked the B.F.G Corvette. The No. 50 team car, driven by Yenko and John Cordt, finished sixth in GT; they were 58 laps down. Three very fast Ferrari 365 GTB/4 Daytonas finished second through fourth in GT. A local Corvette driven by Bob Gray and Terry Keller placed fifth.

### The Tire War in France
The No. 57 RED Corvette's fourth place overall finish in the 1972 12 Hours of Sebring was the highest ever

for a Corvette, notching Goodyear two victories in the radial tire war. B.F.G. sponsored Greenwood at Le Mans, so Goodyear asked the RED team's owner, Troy English, to take the radial tire war to France with their full support. Two problems had to be overcome, however. First, their 1969 Corvette was in its fourth year of competition. It had been rebuilt and repaired so many times that the team called it *Old Scrappy*; there was no way it would pass the ACO's scrutinizing at Le Mans. Second, by March, the starting field for the 1972 24 Hours of Le Mans was full, but Goodyear's Larry Truesdale managed to pressure the North American Racing Team (NART) to let the Corvette take one of their four entries.

To compete in France, the RED team built a new racing car from a wrecked 1968 convertible and a new '69 frame and suspension components (complements of Chevrolet Engineering), then painted it to match the NART Ferraris. TWA provided transportation for the team and all of their gear to France and back to the States, with their logotypes joining the Ferrari prancing horses and plenty of Goodyear decals on the red Corvette. Both Corvette-racing Bob Johnsons were on the team— "Marietta Bob" continued as Yenko's co-driver, while "Columbus Bob" was the team manager and had to deal with the fallout from a three car pile-up that the RED No. 4 was involved in during practice. A new nose was needed, but with none available, a neat duct tape job satisfied ACO officials. One of the other cars in the crash burned, though, and that spooked TWA,

# amazon.com

## A gift from Harvey C Drake

---

# amazon.com

**Gift from**
Harvey C Drake

**Shipping Address**
**Harvey C Drake**
29 Dannah Drive
Carlisle, PA 17015
United States

SDXvfKiBjR

**Returns Are Easy!**
Most items can be refunded, exchanged, or replaced when returned in original and unopened condition. Visit
http://www.amazon.com/returns to start your return, or http://www.amazon.com/help for more information on
return policies.

### Your order of May 7, 2013 (Order ID 105-7934273-5671402)

| Qty. | Item |
|------|------|

**Suzanne Somers Thigh Master**
Misc.
(** P-1-E568A440 **) B00578Q5ZO
Suzanne Thigh Master FBA 608866850946 **(Sold by River Rat Store)**

/DXvfKiBjR/-1 of 1-//SP-PHAZ/sss-us/6280617/0508-16:00/0508-01:24

**P4**

which asked to be removed from the car. The airline was still willing to fly the team home but didn't want to risk being associated with any more wrecks. TWA struck a deal with British Petroleum to cover up the TWA decals with some from BP.

The B. F. Goodrich Lifesaver radials were as fast as the Goodyear's at Le Mans, but they didn't keep Greenwood's second car, entered as No. 72, from blowing its ZL1 engine after nine hours, ejecting Alan Cudini and Bernard Darniche from the race. Greenwood set the fastest GT lap of the race before his engine blew an hour later, parking his No. 28 Corvette with co-driver TV comedian Dick Smothers. The main casualty among the five Corvettes didn't occur until the 19th hour, when Le Mans veteran Jean Claude Aubriet's No. 71 retired with a blown head gasket, followed soon after by the No.29 Corvette, again driven by Henri Greder and Marie Claude Beaumont, who crashed out in the 21st hour.

The RED No. 4 was the only Corvette to survive 24 hours to the finish, although not to glorious fanfare: Yenko and "Marietta Bob" finished 15th overall, 7th in GT, after being slowed by electrical problems. Back in the United States, the RED Team rebuilt their Le Mans Corvette and *Old Scrappy* to compete in selected Federation Internationale de l'Automobile (FIA) and IMSA events as a two-car team, with matching stars-and-bars paint jobs. The new car featured the team's signature No. 57, while *Old Scrappy* raced as either No. 56 or 54, and Dana English became the team's principal, taking over from his father, Troy. Greenwood entered a few races after Le Mans with B.F.G. sponsorship, appearing at the 6 Hours of Watkins Glen race with three Corvettes. He was only able to qualify one, and Greenwood never won another race on B. F. Goodrich street radials after Michigan in 1971.

With sponsorship from R. J. Reynolds Tobacco Company, the IMSA GT Professional Racing Series became the Camel GT Challenge. It was promoted by a major nationwide advertising campaign, with IMSA racing hyped everywhere by a cigarette-smoking Camel cartoon character. As the professional Trans-Am and Can-Am Racing Series from the Sports Car Club of American (SCCA) faded, IMSA gained momentum, but many of the well-known Corvette drivers continued to compete in enough SCCA nationals to make the runoffs. The SCCA's American Road Race of Champions continued to be held at Road Atlanta

in 1972 on November 26, and the combined A- and B-production race looked like a Corvette Club event. Jerry Hanson, driving an ex–Jerry Thompson Owens-Corning Corvette, won the A-production championship, with Alan Barker taking the B-production title in a 350ci LT1-powered Corvette for an unprecedented fourth year in a row.

## The End of an Era

With the end of the 1972 model year, GM's last solid-lifter V-8, the LT1, was history, and along with it, the last vestiges of Detroit's first performance era. These were also the last Corvettes to feature chrome bumpers at both ends, a bright egg-crate grille, egg-crate side fender vents, and a removable rear window for the coupe. Despite the industry-wide loss of horsepower, 1972 Corvettes continued to impress automotive journalists and buyers with their performance, and sales increased from a total of 21,801 in 1971 to 27,004 for 1972. Only 6,508 of these were convertibles—even fewer than the 7,121 sold in 1971. Since its introduction in 1968, the Turbo Hydra-Matic three-speed automatic transmission had grown steadily in popularity, climbing in sales from 5,063 in 1968 to 14,543 in 1972.

The push to comply with new federal safety regulations while reducing manufacturing costs brought some of the most dramatic changes to the appearance of the Corvette's body since 1968. For the 1973 model year, the nose had to be able to withstand a 5-mile per hour impact with a solid object without damaging the lighting or safety

No. 57 was competitive while it lasted at the Glen, but sustained some battle damage, popping off one of its Plexiglas FIA headlight covers and requiring some duct tape to patch up the left front corner. A new Goodyear "street radial" is going on, with the American mag wheel's lug nuts being tightened before replacing the brake cooling fan lying beside the tire changer.
*GM Media Archive*

Wearing his helmet, Bob Johnson is about to jump into the No. 57 with co-driver Dave Heinz holding the shoulder belts out of the way while assisting the rear tire changer. There was a lot of attrition at Watkins Glen, with only 12 of the 30 car starting field completing the race, including 2 Corvettes, but the No. 57 wasn't among them, with the throttle linkage breaking after 102 laps.
*GM Media Archive*

equipment, which was accomplished by replacing the chromed steel front bumper with a molded urethane front pad painted in the body's color. The interior and exterior changes added 2.1 inches to the nose and 35 pounds to the front end, and it was accompanied by corrugated steel side impact barriers inside the doors to tie the birdcage latch supports to the A-pillars. The coupe's rear window was fixed in place, which helped offset the weight of the added safety features and opened up a little more room. A new hood eliminated the troublesome vacuum-operated hinged panel that had covered the windshield wipers and included an air duct bonded to the underside for cowl induction, similar to the L88 and ZR-1 package hoods. High-pressure air was picked up from the base of the windshield and reached the carburetor through an open-topped air cleaner sealed to the underside of the duct and was standard equipment, even on the base engine. Front fenders with simple vents replaced the grilles, giving the 1973 Corvette an up-to-date look that further boosted sales despite declining performance.

The publicity Corvette enjoyed after successful races on B.F.G. and Goodyear street radials raised the awareness of radial tires in the United States, so much so that they became original equipment on a number of American cars in 1973. Most of the U.S. tire companies, including Firestone, had started manufacturing radials, and the Corvette's F70 X 15 wide-oval bias ply tires were replaced by wider GR70 X 15 Firestone steel-belted radials. Cast-aluminum wheels made a comeback in 1973, after not being

available since 1967. They were not only beautiful, but also 8 pounds lighter than the steel Riley wheels of the same rim width. Unfortunately, first few sets were quickly recalled because the castings were too porous to hold air, similar to Corvette's first aluminum wheels when they were introduced in 1963.

For the first time in the Corvette's 20-year history, a solid-lifter engine was not included in its power train lineup, and for the second year, customers were limited to a base and two optional V-8s. All three engines breathed through Rochester Q-jet carburetors. The base 350 lost 10 hp, dropping it to 190, while the optional 350ci L82 was rated at 250 hp, only 5 hp less than the solid-lifter LT1 that had been equipped with a Holly carburetor. The only bright spot was that the 454ci LS5 boasted 275 hp, 5 more than the LS4 it replaced in 1973. Unfortunately the ZR-1 racing package was canceled, along with the LT1 engine and the Muncie "Rock Crusher" close-ratio, heavy-duty four-speed transmission. Special heavy-duty brakes and suspension were available for the first time since 1970 as RPO Z07.

Without the clatter of solid-lifters, the rumpity-rump cadence of a long duration cam, or the rush of brutal acceleration, the Corvette's personality diminished, and only the luxury sports car remained. The squeaks, rattles, and road noise that had always been its downside were exacerbated by the radial tires and could no longer be tolerated as part of the plastic sports car's new image. Zora Duntov put Walt Zetye, who was still his chassis man, and body engineer, Bob Vogelei, on the problem. They developed an extensive NVH (noise vibration and harshness) package that included rubber-cushioned body mounts. Inner panels were deadened with an asphalt compound, that along with an underhood blanket, prevented drumming, and additional acoustic insulation was stuffed in every nook and cranny, all contributing to the sound of silence.

## The FIA Hits the Road

The year 1973 brought sweeping changes to the face of American professional road racing. The FIA pulled out of the United States, and IMSA's Camel GT Challenge took over their events, including Daytona and Sebring. The IMSA also had an impact on the SCCA's Trans-Am series, which all but died in 1972—it was reorganized with a rules package that closely resembled IMSA's GTO class in 1973, opening up the strictly pony car series to everything from Porches to Corvettes. The lid was taken off the 5-liter displacement limit, along with restrictions on wheel and tire widths, with more liberal body modification rules allowing wild fender flairs; the Trans-Am roared back to life and flourished for a second time. Ultimately, the open Can-Am, along with Formula 5000, the SCCA's other professional series at the time, faded away, but the Trans-Am was reinvented several times and survived into the new millennium.

The racing radial tire war between Goodyear and B. F. Goodrich quickly made its point to domestic manufacturers, and radials were supplied as original equipment on a number of American cars in 1973. B.F.G. felt it still had unfinished business; because Greenwood's Corvettes remained winless on their Lifesaver radial T/As for the entire 1973 season, the first American radial tire manufacturer was still looking for a high-visibility victory in a major international event. B.F.G. continued to sponsor Greenwood at Daytona and Sebring, along with another chance to race at Le Mans, but the introduction of slick dry-track racing tires made the chances of another win on street radials extremely remote. Midgets and sprint cars had been racing on paved ovals with slick tires for years, while the tread on Indy and road racing tires had faded away, gradually finally disappearing during the 1973 season and widening the performance gap with any street tire.

John Bishop returned the February distance race at Daytona to 24 hours as an IMSA event, with most of the familiar Corvettes and drivers that had competed there in recent years in the field, along with a few new additions. Since 1969, De Lorenzo and Jerry Thompson were in every Daytona 24 Hour as the lead drivers of a two-Corvette team owned by De Lorenzo and sponsored by Owens-Corning. Their last drive together was the 1972 Daytona 6 Hour. For the 1973 race, both built their own new 1969 L88 Corvette race car. De Lorenzo kept the No. 11 with its iron-block L88, 4-inch stroke crank, and a .060 overbore for 467ci, which was just fine with IMSA. His codriver was Mo Carter with sponsorship from Marathon Oil and the Bud Company, an automotive supplier.

Thompson built his new race car primarily from service parts in his garage, as he and De Lorenzo had done in 1968 for the first Owens-Corning C3 L88. He enjoyed sponsorship from Union 76 for his No. 34 Corvette. Thompson signed Ike Knupp and Mike Murray to trade stints with him in the 24-hour race, while Greenwood had no less than six drivers for his pair of B.F. Goodrich ZL1-powered Corvettes, still painted like American flags. Greenwood drove his usual No. 48 with Ron Grable as co-driver, while his No. 49 was shared by Yenko, Bob Johnson, and Denny Long, with Jim Greendyke in relief for either car. The RED team had sold *Old Scrappy* in the fall of 1972 and entered the Le Mans car under Goodyear sponsorship and a conventional paint job, which

Most Corvette convertibles ran endurance races with the removable hardtop, but there was nothing in the rules about not going topless, like the No. 66, which has a Goodyear tire deal. Only the RED team had full sponsorship from Goodyear, but there were usually several other teams at major events competing on their "street radials," which were really legal racing tires. *GM Media Archive*

replaced the rebel flag carrying No. 5. It was driven by Dave Heinz, Bob McClure, and Dana English.

The Daytona starting field looked odd without the "European" factory prototypes, but Corvettes remained the dominant GT cars. De Lorenzo's big cubic-inch L88 helped him to qualify his No. 11 Bud Corvette on the GTO pole. De Lorenzo and Carter contended for the early race lead against the No. 5 Corvette. The rest of the GT field was unable to match their pace. Greenwood's bad luck continued when tire trouble forced him to pit after only 7 laps, and his No. 48 Corvette's race ended when it slipped off the jack and damaged its radiator. The next casualty among the Corvettes was Thompson's No. 34, out after 50 laps with an ailing L88 that sidelined Thompson, Knupp, and Murray. Heinz, McClure, and English's No. 5 was overheating, losing 3 laps in the pits while the crew changed its water pump.

The third and last DNF among the Corvettes was front runner De Lorenzo's No. 11 car, whose clutch failed on Lap 101. The way was clear for the RED Corvette to assume the GTO class lead. The No. 5 had enough of a lead that its early morning stop to replace a broken rocker arm only dropped one position overall for Heinz, McClure, and English. They finished 3rd overall, 1st in GTO, having completed 644 laps in 24 hours. The only other Corvette to finish was Greenwood's team car No. 49, driven by Yenko, Johnson, and Long. At 150 laps behind the class winner, they took 15th overall.

## Sebring 1973

Attendance had dwindled at Sebring to the point that John Bishop considered not continuing with the 12-hour race, but with promotional and financial help from Greenwood and R. J. Reynolds Tobacco, he held the race anyway and even drew larger crowds than he had in years. Porsche had taken IMSA seriously from the beginning of the GT series, and the development of their wild 911 Carrera RSR's ultra-wide tires and huge fender flares were inspired by the liberal rules. These cars didn't have the Corvette's pace, but their lower fuel consumption allowed fewer pit stops, and along with bullet-proof reliability, they began to show in greater numbers and became a threat to the plastic sports car supremacy. A record number of Corvettes dotted the starting field, including most of the cars that had been at Daytona. Greenwood brought a three-Corvette team, all on B. F. Goodrich street radials, hoping for better results than in 1972.

The Bud Co. and secondary sponsors Marathon Oil and Camel Cigarettes continued to sponsor De Lorenzo's No. 11, while Goodyear and Marathon Oil supported the RED team's No. 5 Corvette. Some reshuffling changed the top Corvette's driver lineup from Daytona. Instead of entering his Corvette at Sebring, Thompson co-drove the RED No. 5 with Heinz. De Lorenzo also had a new co-driver, Steve Durst, who qualified De Lorenzo's No. 11 on the GTO pole. Greenwood kept Bob Johnson in the No. 49 while he moved Yenko over to his No. 48 and replaced him with Greendyke. Ron Grable, Greenwood's co-driver at Daytona, was in his third Corvette, No.50, with Mike Brockman. The No. 50 car was the only B. F. Goodrich car to finish.

B.F.G.'s Lifesaver radial T/A street tires couldn't grip the bumpy track surface at Sebring the previous year, but despite advancements in dedicated racing tires in 1973, these street legal tires competed nonetheless. This gain in performance didn't improve Greenwood's luck, as his No. 48 was the first of the front-running Corvettes out of the race, but his No. 49 and 50 team cars were the only ones to finish. Greenwood and co-driver Yenko's race ended on Lap 105 with a blown engine, followed by the RED team's No. 5 only 5 laps later, coming into the pits with an overheated engine.

While the fastest Corvettes were falling out of the race, a couple of Porsche 911 Carrera RSRs had caught and passed the survivors, with their less frequent pit stops overcoming the aging American sports cars' speed advantage. Both of Greenwood's team cars stayed in the top 10 for the first 6 hours of the race, until the No. 4 driven by Bob Johnson and Greendyke, slowed and eventually left the race on Lap 219. Grable and Mike Brockman were joined by Greenwood behind the wheel of the No. 50. They had completed 219 laps in 12 hours when the checkered flag fell—3rd overall—and the highest finishing position to date for a Corvette at Sebring.

## Le Mans 1973

The only American Corvette entries in the 1973 24 Hours of Le Mans were Greenwood's pair of B. F. Goodrich team cars. Bob Johnson and Jim Greendyke co-drove the No. 29 with Greenwood, while Don Yenko and Ron Grable were in his No. 68. Five-time Le Mans veteran Jean-Claude Aubriet was back with his 1968 T-top L88 Corvette coupe, entered as No. 69. "Depnic" returned as his co-driver. Marie-Claude Beaumont teamed again with Henri Greder in his 1969 ZL1-powered convertible hardtop, No. 30. Practice was even more disastrous than it had been for the RED team in 1972; Greenwood's second Corvette was seriously damaged in a crash and was forced to withdraw before the race even started.

In 1973, both perennial French Corvette entries at Le Mans not only finished the 24-hour race, but placed 1st and 2nd in over-5-liter GT, giving Greder his second class win in the same Corvette. However, unlike 1970, it wasn't taken away as a technicality. Greder's No. 30 was 12th overall, followed by Aubriet's No. 69 in 18th overall. John Greenwood's No. 29 B.F.G Corvette was in trouble from the start, slowed by numerous pit stops for tire trouble. For Greenwood, his ill luck was a blessing in disguise. On Lap 37, a loose connecting rod brought the B. F. Goodrich Corvette into the pits and out of the race, and the tire company decided to end their sponsorship afterward. Though Greenwood's team had benefited from their financial support, they hadn't won another race on B.F.G. tires since 1971.

## Sales Versus Performance

With both IMSA's GTO class and the SCCA's Trans-Am series open to Corvettes, Greenwood, like a lot of professional Corvette racers, raced selected events in both series. The foreign competition was catching up with the aging Corvettes—wild Capri RSs from Ford of Germany and the pesky Porsche 911 Carrera RSRs started gaining the upper hand. Corvettes still dominated SCCA and series racing, and the best of them even had speed advantages over the German cars on short runs, but the longer the event, the more of a challenge it became for American muscle to compete with European engineering.

Corvette production exceeded 30,000 units for the first time in a regular 12-month model year, and the coupes continued to rise in popularity. But increased sales numbers at the cost of performance was contrary to everything Zora Duntov believed in.

Joe Pike, Chevrolet's sales manager, changed tactics to attract a different kind of buyer. Pike recognized that most Corvette owners would hold on to their better performing older cars for a few years, while many new customers would buy new ones for their looks, automatic transmissions, power windows, and air conditioning. At first,

demand had slackened for the progressively more lethargic 1971 and later Corvettes, but Pike made them available to dealers that had never been able to get one before, and sales climbed for the remainder of the decade.

The first model year in which F. James McDonald called the shots as Chevrolet's general manager was 1974. Production in 1973 was already locked in and well underway when he took over the division on October 1, 1972. McDonald had worked as a manufacturing engineer at Chevrolet prior to being chosen as John De Lorean's successor and worked as a Pontiac general manager for a three-year stint prior to managing GM's largest division. Pike continued to sell all of the Corvettes that could be built, and McDonald waited to take advantage of the unfilled demand, ordering the St. Louis plant to produce one additional car per hour, from eight to nine. This modest increase didn't push the assembly lines' pace to the point of risking a return to 1968's build-quality problems, and the additional cars in the pipeline allowed dealers to finally stock them, further increasing sales.

Another federal safety regulation reshaped the 1974 Corvette body's back end; this time, cars not only had to be able to run forward into a wall at 5 mph without damaging lighting or safety equipment, but also in reverse. The two-piece chrome rear bumper was replaced by a soft urethane end cap, molded in two pieces and joined on the car's centerline. The whole rear end was backed up by a box section aluminum bumper beam mounted to the frame on slider brackets equipped with energy-absorbing Omark bolts.

The Corvette's powertrain lineup carried over. The base 350 gained 5 hp for 195 total, while the optional 454ci LS4 lost 5 hp, bringing it down to 270. The 350ci L82's output stayed at 250 hp. The only improvement under the hood was to the cooling package; a new radiator design featured louvered fins better able to keep engine temperature down at low speeds. In keeping with its more sedate personality, new resonators tuned out most of the remaining rumble from the low compression V-8's exhaust, although several options were available for enthusiast drivers. The M21 close-ratio four-speed was still available and a must-have for anyone looking for challenging corners by equipping a new Corvette with the Z07 off-road suspension and brake package.

## Corvettes were crowd favorites everywhere they raced.

### Oil and OPEC and Nixon, Oh My!

An oil embargo by the twelve members of OPEC began in October 1973, and long lines of cars waiting to buy rationed amounts of gasoline were seen across the country. On January 4, 1974, President Nixon signed the Emergency Highway Energy Conservation Act into law, mandating a 55 mph national speed limit. Meanwhile, the 24 Hours of Daytona and 12 Hours of Sebring races were canceled, delaying the start of IMSA's season until April. But the energy crisis wasn't John Bishop's only problem—the popular five-year-old Corvettes were starting to become uncompetitive, and he had to find a way to keep them in the show. Bishop created a new class, All American GT, to give America's sports cars a chance to always win something, and also to possibly attract other suitable U.S. cars, like Chevrolet's new Monza.

### Wide-Body Changes

Corvettes were crowd favorites everywhere they raced, and IMSA wasn't the only sanctioning organization wanting to extend the aging plastic-bodied sports car's competition life—the FIA and SCCA also were willing accommodate the aging American sports cars. In 1973, Duntov asked Randy Whittin at GM Design Staff to create a prototype of a Corvette wide-body, something that Greenwood had suggested to Duntov after winning a Trans-Am race at Road America. The wide-body incorporated a stylized interpretation of the 1973-and-later production Corvette nose and front fenders, swooping down in front and flaring out into huge pontoon fenders front and rear; only the removable hardtop and L88 hood were unaltered. After Duntov directed Diversified Glass to make several sets of parts and assigned them factory part numbers, Greenwood contracted with Diversified to make permanent molds and started selling body kits.

This body, complemented by an adjustable rear wing, undertray, and rear diffuser, constituted an effective aero package that generated a lot of downforce, and it even had room under its pontoon fenders for 20-inch-wide rear tires. Greenwood and race car builder Bob Riley designed a radical GT racing Corvette that capitalized on the more liberal rules, and it was first shown at the Detroit Auto Show in November 1973 with the new wide-body fiberglass. This car featured a revised anti-dive front along with anti-squat rear suspension, and was the first step toward a surface-plate, tubular frame Corvette.

Like the SCCA's Can-Am series, Corvettes in IMSA had no limit on engine displacement, and Greenwood Racing bought the L&M Lola Can-Am cars that Jackie Stewart raced in 1971. Greenwood wanted to explore the possibility of using something like Lola's big cubic-inch Chevy's Lacus Fuel Injection system on his Corvettes, but their downdraft throttle bodies wouldn't fit under the homolugated L88 hood bulge. Gib Hufstader and Duntov provided the only assistance Greenwood received from Chevrolet, and Hufstader loaned Greenwood a Cross-Ram side-draft fuel-injection intake manifold that was developed for the Chaparral 2H by Chevy R&D. John Greenwood Racing designed its own Cross-Ram manifold, and an aluminum prototype was fabricated by Charlie Selix and Gary Pratt. Steve Kinsler supplied Lacus throttle plates and fuel injectors and the fuel-management system.

### Racing in the USA

The fuel injection system wasn't ready for competition until late in 1974, but Greenwood debuted the wide-body Corvette with a carbureted engine at Road Atlanta in April at IMSA's first race of the season. As the current production cars became completely unsuitable for racing, John Greenwood Racing carried on Corvette development with a growing product line of suspension engine and body parts, and his wasn't the only wide-body at Road Atlanta. Jerry Thompson was there with the Corvette racing car he had put together for the 1973 24 Hours of Daytona, rebuilt as a wide-body with an aerodynamic setup that did Greenwood one better with a front splitter.

At Road Atlanta, the pair of updated Corvettes still weren't able to deal with the foreign competition, but they sure looked and sounded intimidating. The Greenwood/Brockman car was Greenwood's familiar No. 48 (with yet another American flag paint job) while the Thompson/ Gimondo No. 17 was overall red. Greenwood led the first two laps of the race ahead of a gaggle of Porsches before his engine went flat, dropping the

No. 48 Corvette back through the field, until he finally retired it on Lap 17. Thompson's red No. 17 Corvette was never exceedingly fast, but it did finish, covering 188 laps for a lackluster 17th overall, making it all too obvious that the super Corvettes needed further development.

For IMSA's 5-hour race in Ohio in June, the front end of Greenwood's No. 48 was painted black, and both wide-body Corvettes were competitive, easily making the field. For the race, Greenwood signed Sam Posey as his co-driver. Thompson had Corvette veteran Yenko co-driving his No. 15, and again Thompson had better luck with Greenwood out after 76 laps; he and Yenko finished a respectable 4th behind the usual Porsche parade. Also in June, and despite the cancellation of Daytona and Sebring, the 24 Hours of Le Mans was run as usual. Henri Greder entered the only Corvette in the field, bringing back his ZL1-powered 69 for the 4th time, but it was plagued with mechanical problems. Marie-Claude Beaumont reprised her role as Greder's co-driver, backed up by Alain Cudini. The ignition, battery, water pump, and brakes all gave them fits before losing 1st and 2nd gears, and it was a miracle that they finished 18th overall.

The first win for one of Greenwood's racing wide-bodies came at the Bama 200 at Talladega. Ironically, it was Milt Minter behind the wheel of the No. 48—not Greenwood—but he would soon get his chance. At Road America in Elkhart Lake, Wisconsin, during August, Greenwood spanked the field after months of development, setting a new lap record in qualifying on the pole and winning the race. For IMSA's finale, the Daytona 250 in November 1974, Greenwood's wide-body Corvette sported a new overall white paint scheme with red and blue graphics, proclaiming it the *Spirit of Sebring 75*, which was also the car number. His signature American flag was confined to the hood, while the rest of the car promoted the return of the 12-hour race in March, which he had contracted to publicize and finance for five years from 1972 to 1977.

Given their success, the number of wide-body Corvettes was growing, and Dave Heinz was still driving the RED team's No. 57, which had been transformed into a wide-body. Tony De Lorenzo was also at Daytona for IMSA's final, driving the Lendon Blackwell racing team's red and yellow No. 94 wide-body Corvette. Most of these cars' trick components were developed and sold by John Greenwood Racing, but the No. 75 Corvette still had an advantage with its new fuel injection system. A cast-magnesium Cross Ram intake manifold, equipped with Lucas fuel injection components, sat atop a 467ci aluminum ZL1, improving both power and throttle response. In Greenwood's words, it was "awesome," and he qualified on the pole, winning the race one full lap ahead of the second place Porsche Carrera RSR.

## A Legend Retires

Zora Duntov retired on January 1st, 1975, after 21 years and 7 months at GM. He was on the Daytona 250 podium to help Greenwood celebrate his victory. After only 2 years and 2 months, another major change at Chevrolet was the replacement of General Manager James McDonald by Robert D. Lund. Lund was transplanted from the same position at Cadillac. Despite complaints about poor performance and build quality, Corvette production actually increased, and Chevrolet continued to sell every one they could build.

A letter from Don McPherson, Chevrolet's engineering director, dated December 19, 1974, announced David R. McLellon's promotion to chief engineer at Corvette five months after McLellon had returned to Chevrolet with a master of science in management from MIT. McLellon was first assigned to Duntov and later promoted to staff engineer, with the added responsibility of seeing that the new catalytic converters installed in all of GM's 1975 cars were safe. In order to be able to continue selling new cars in 1975, the industry had the seemingly impossible goal of complying with the 1970 federal mandate to lower exhaust emissions by 90 percent from pre-1968 levels. The EPA certification tests were both time-consuming and expensive, resulting in the 454 being dropped from the Corvette's option list after failing the 50,000-mile durability test for emissions.

The 1975 Corvette's only identifying external feature was a pair of black impact pads on both front and rear soft bumpers, which were completely redesigned under their urethane plastic skin. Bumpers in 1975 not only had to be able to run undamaged into walls at 5 mph, but they also had to withstand a pendulum impact test. To meet the requirements, he front bumper cover was now backed up by a molded plastic matrix, much

## The Corvette racing veterans put on a great show, passing the Porsches on the banking like they were parked.

like a giant ice tray, eliminating the Omark bolts. At the rear, the bumper cover was one piece, and these energy-absorbing bolts were replaced by Delco's new hydraulic enersorbers. To meet federal fuel tank impact rules, a new steel tank contained a rubber bladder like a racing fuel cell. This assembly was isolated from the interior of the car by a "hat" in the rear floor, and unleaded fuel was required to avoid poisoning the converter's catalyst.

The Corvette's remaining pair of 350ci V-8 engines were choked by a single catalytic converter under the passenger's seat, with dual exhaust pipes converging in front of it and Y-ing out under the back, giving the impression of true dual exhaust. The base engine was down to 165 net hp, while the optional "performance" L82 was rated at a whopping 205 hp. Both engines were equipped with a new magnetic triggering high-energy ignition. With any kind of real performance only a memory, the demand for four-speed transmissions was fading. Chevrolet and other GM divisions started phasing out the Muncie in favor of Borg-Warner. This started with the introduction of the Super T10 in 1974, and by the end of the decade, it no longer made sense for the competition to continue manufacturing their own.

### Night of the Porsches

From its beginning in 1971, Porsche dominated IMSA's GTO class. Even though Corvettes won the 1971 and 1972 Manufacturers' Championships, the big American sports cars proved too thirsty and fragile to win many of the longer races. BMW wanted to increase their market share in the United States, and after winning the European Touring Car Championship in 1974 with their 3.0-liter CSL, they decided to take on IMSA in 1975. Their team manager was ex-Porsche driver Jochen Neerpasch. Neerpasch had led the Ford and BMW teams to ECT championships before coming to the United States, running the Bavarian Motor Works team. Their pair of CSLs was about as close to production as the wide-body Corvettes and every bit as wild. Neerpasch

signed Hans Stuck and Sam Posey for his lead drivers, and the cars were tested and further developed for weeks before Daytona.

The much-anticipated return of the 24 Hours of Daytona was on February 1, 1975, and the factory-backed Porsche Carerra RSRs were threatened by BMW's full factory CSL team and the latest wide-body Corvettes, led by Greenwood. By 1975, John Greenwood Racing shops in Troy and Dearborn, Michigan, were building 800-plus hp ZL1-type big-block Chevys and GT racing Corvettes, with enough tire area and downforce to harness all of those ponies. Bob Riley designed a full tubular space frame that was integrated with the roll cage, stiffening the production ladder frame, and extensively revised the rear suspension with coil-overs taking the place of the leaf spring. Upper and lower A-arms replaced the radius arms that squatted the back of the car under acceleration.

The wide-bodies were built at Greenwood's Dearborn facility, and most of the fabrication was done by Charlie Selix. Selix worked with Gary Pratt, who would eventually build the most successful Corvette endurance racing cars of all time. Jim Kinsler supplied the cars' fuel injection systems for the first few years of the program. He had been involved with the Chaparral injection system when he was an engineer at Chevy R&D before starting his own fuel injection business. Kinsler Fuel Injection was little more than a Lucas dealer when Greenwood started his fuel injection project, but by 1975 he was equipped to machine and assemble Greenwood's Cross Ram fuel injection manifolds, which were good for an additional 100 hp. This was an unprecedented amount of power for a GT racing car, and to help deliver it, the car's balance was optimized for the track by repositioning the engine.

Greenwood's *Sebring 75* led the 24-hour race's 51-car field from the 3 p.m. start, followed by the pair of factory BMW CSLs and Jerry Thompson in his No. 18 wide-body Corvette in fourth. It surprised everyone when the Ronnie Peterson/Brian Redman BMW suffered a connecting rod failure, thrusting Thompson and Yenko's No. 18 into third. Greenwood had to pit on Lap 27 to deal with an overheating engine, handing the lead to the Posey/Stuck BMW. Thompson's No. 18 Corvette moved into 2nd, and Greenwood's No. 75 rejoined the race 25 minutes later.

Greenwood's Corvette continued falling through the running order, making numerous unscheduled pit stops, trying to find the cause of the overheating. It was finally resolved, only to have the car crash out early in the morning. Co-driver Carl Schafer was behind the wheel when he was squeezed into the wall coming off the banking, ending their race, followed minutes later by the surviving BMW CSL. Posey and Stuck's car threw a rod, leaving Thompson and Yenko's No. 18 Corvette to deal with the snarling pack of Porsche Carrera RSRs. Thompson's white home-built, wide-body was still fast, but he was hopelessly behind after recovering from brake failure and replacing the radiator not long after dawn. The Corvette racing veterans put on a great show, passing the Porsches on the banking like they were parked. They made up laps until about three hours from the finish, when their big-inch L88 finally blew up. The Peter Gregg/Hurley Haywood Porsche team won after 24 hours.

## '69 in '75

Greenwood Racing continued to honor their contract with Sebring and IMSA to finance and promote the 12-hour race, and with the event's return in 1975, Greenwood's promotional obligations were a major distraction. Unable to focus his attention on the race, Greenwood managed to sign Thompson to take over as lead driver of his No. 75 Corvette, with Greenwood himself as codriver. Thompson hadn't been able to garner enough sponsorship to bring his own wide-body Corvette to Sebring and jumped at the chance to race Greenwood's factory car, which he found faster than any Corvette he had ever driven. Even so, the best they could do in qualifying was third behind a factory BMW CSL on the pole and a factory-backed Porsche Carerra RSR. Thompson was confident, though, they would be able to get by the German cars in the race.

Thompson started the race and easily kept pace in third position behind the factory BMW team cars, until he turned the No. 75 car over to Greenwood at the first scheduled pit stop. Greenwood was determined to put on a show of American muscle, and wasted no time, quickly taking the lead and pulling away from the field. Despite the bravado, his beefed-up but overstressed Muncie M22 transmission failed. BMW also had early trouble with CSL braking, but their team car driven by Redman and Allan Moffat bolted across the finish line, winning the 12 Hours of Sebring. The Corvette presence at Le Mans had dwindled down to a single

car in 1975. Greder brought his '69 back for its sixth and final appearance in the 24-hour race; he was out on the second lap.

## Can-American Brawn

As the regular IMSA season got underway, the German cars were getting faster, and even when Greenwood finished, he wasn't winning—until a Canadian customer with very deep pockets came calling. Rudy Braun bought the ex–B.F.G. No. 50 from Greenwood and was determined to use it as the SCCA's Trans-Am series had become a rival to IMSA's highly successful Camel GT Challenge. Greenwood updated the car to current Trans-Am specifications. He and Greenwood worked out a deal to campaign the car in the 1975 Trans-Am series, with Greenwood driving and maintaining the Corvette at his shop while Braun provided financial support along with a mechanic at the events. For most of the season, the car had an unusual paint job, with a red nose that faded in a series of steps through yellow to white, just forward of the doors, which carried big red 5s, and that's how it looked when Greenwood won the 1975 Trans-Am Championship.

Braun's racing aspirations extended beyond the Trans-Am. He made a similar deal with Greenwood to run the *Sebring 75* car in IMSA races on a limited schedule. It became the first wide-body in IMSA, appearing as No. 48 in April 1974 and now re-bodied with the latest very wide bodywork. Braun's friend, Paul Smith, christened it with a new identity: *Old Blue*. The car remained No. 75 but featured a primarily blue paint scheme, dominated by a large *Old Blue* logotype on its hood and nose and hound dog caricatures on the rear fenders. It was used as a development car, practicing and qualifying, but not racing. New Corvette racing cars were built for a full IMSA program in 1976, but pressure from his business interest forced Braun to pull the plug, bringing the deal to an end.

Braun's *Old Blue* racing team was shaping up to be a major player in North America, but even with Duntov as a technical consultant, the program didn't make it into competition. The cars built for it, though, gave Greenwood back his edge, if only briefly. Greenwood brought one of these cars to the IMSA final in November. He had painted it overall white with promotions for the upcoming 12 Hours of Sebring with a patriotic twist, tying it to the 1976 bicentennial as the *Spirit of Sebring 1976*. Greenwood accomplished a hat trick at Daytona, qualifying on the pole, setting fastest lap of the race, and winning for the second year in a row; he also introduced a new project from John Greenwood Racing. The look of the Greenwood Corvettes created a sensation—some fantasy racers even bought his body kits for their street Corvettes.

Despite their anemic performance, a sulphur fragrance from its catalytic converter, and a substantial price hike from $6,001.50 for the base coupe to $6,810.00, 1975 Corvettes still outsold the '74s by a modest 963 cars. With only 4,629 convertibles of the 38,465 Corvettes built, they were no longer profitable and the accounting department canceled them, leaving the 1976 models with only one body style for the first time since 1962 when all Corvettes were convertibles. In all fairness to Chevrolet Engineering, these cars were no worse than other 1975 models, suffering from the ravages of federal regulation. It would ultimately benefit consumers, but it would take 10 years before the industry started to recover.

The 1976 Corvette didn't give automotive journalists much to write about. It came in five new colors, and the long-awaited optional aluminum wheels (RPO YJ8) finally became available three years after they were introduced. The cowl induction intake on the back edge of the hood made a satisfying moan at full throttle—but there weren't many performance enthusiasts left to appreciate it—and intake air from the front of the car was silently ducted over the radiator. With the federal emissions mandate met in 1975, a little additional power was coaxed out of the catalytic converter–equipped engines in 1976, bringing the optional L82 up to 210 hp—a pickup of 5—while the base L84 was the big winner, picking up 15 hp for 180 total.

This was of special importance to the 3,527 California who that bought 1976 Corvettes, because the base 350ci 180-hp V-8 with an M40 automatic transmission was the only powertrain combination available in their state. The owners of all 1975 and 1976 Corvettes had to be careful where they parked their catalytic converter–equipped cars to avoid

A letter from Don McPherson, Chevrolet's engineering director, dated December 19, 1974, announced David R. McLellan's promotion to chief engineer at Corvette effective January 1, 1975. This was also Zora Arkus-Duntov's retirement date after 21 years and 7 months at GM, with 10 years as the Corvette's de facto chief engineer, followed by his last 8 as Corvette's first official chief engineer. *GM Media Archive*

starting fires, and their fiberglass floors had to be shielded from the converter's intense heat. With a partial undertray added to the frame protected the floor and helped isolate the interior from the heat, Corvettes lost their Astro ventilation system (it never worked well anyway) along with the interior air outlets on the rear deck. With 99 percent of 1976 coupes equipped with air conditioning, Astro ventilation was hardly missed, but another cost-cutting makeover, the use of the four-spoke, modeled vinyl Vega econo box steering wheel on Chevrolet's flag ship, didn't go over so well.

With Porsche and BMW competing head to head and gunning for IMSA's Camel GT Championship in 1976, the pace of both manufacturers' development was intense, but Greenwood's *Spirit of Sebring 76* only qualified eighth for the 1976 24 Hours of Daytona. His co-driver, Brockman, started the race and quickly moved up to 2nd place behind the pole-winning factory-backed Buno's BMW CSL driven by Peter Gregg and Redman. Brockman came into the pits on Lap 39 with transmission trouble, which kept the Corvette sidelined for 40 laps. It was replaced by Greenwood, who rejoined the race in 28th position with his car back up to speed. By Lap 200, the *Spirit of Sebring* was in 14th, but unfortunately, the rear axle began to fail, ending his race on Lap 298.

Brockman continued as Greenwood's co-driver at the 12 Hours of Sebring. Things were looking up as the wide-body Corvette qualified on the pole and set the fastest lap of the race early in the event. Greenwood maintained a torrid pace until he tangled with a slow back marker at the end of the first hour, taking the car out of contention for a win, but not out of the race. The race was lost on Lap 36 when the clutch blew after Brockman took the patched-up car back on the track, but he managed to finish fourth in the same car the next month at Road Atlanta. The first two finishing positions went to a pair of Chevrolet's new subcompact Monzas that had made their IMSA debut a year earlier and had been dominating AA/GT in 1976.

## Le Mans 1976

Corvettes were extremely popular with the crowds at Le Mans, just like they were at IMSA events in the United States. With their numbers dwindling at the 24-hour French race, the organizers took steps to maintain the American cars' presence. After Greenwood competed in the 1972 and 1973 races

with B. F. Goodrich sponsorship, Greder entered the only Corvette at Le Mans in 1974 and 1975, running the same car in six consecutive races. Even though Greenwood wasn't winning many races, he was building the most spectacular Corvettes on the planet, and he received not only an invitation to enter the race, but enough money to be sure he showed up.

The first of the new generation Greenwood Corvettes was designated customer car #001, and after debuting at IMSA's 1975 final, it was used in every event run by the team until Le Mans, when it was replaced by #007. This car was built to take advantage of the liberal FIA group's rules, which allowed cars to be even more radical than IMSA AA/GT, except that engine displacement was limited to 7 liters (427ci). This car had the same basic bicentennial paint scheme as #001, but with "Spirit of Le Mans 76" emblazoned across its hood and nose. Support from Goodyear was acknowledged by several decals. Greenwood brought his brother Burt along as a co-driver, and they were joined by Bernard Darniche. Despite a terminal speed of 209 mph on the Mulsanne, the car raced better than it qualified. Greenwood drove the first stint, charging from 9th place to the front of the pack almost immediately, staying with the front runners. The cockpit ventilation systems of the No. 76 Corvettes began failing, and soon their pace was soon slowed by several flat tires. One finally cracked the fuel cell, ending John Greenwood Racing's last appearance at the Circuit La Sarthe.

It would be 18 years before another Corvette was entered in the 24 Hours of Le Mans. Greenwood's brief appearance in the 1976 race certainly gave the organizers their money's worth—at least as long as his car lasted. Time had finally caught up with the Corvette's 8-year-old body and 13-year-old chassis, and no amount of modification to the existing platform could make it competitive enough to match the latest European technology at the highest levels of international racing. Corvettes still dominated the SCCA's A- and B-production classes and held their own in the Trans-Am series, but it would take a new platform to bring them back to world-class status, and that wasn't going to happen any time soon—not so long as Chevrolet could sell every one of the plastic sports cars they could build. In 1976, St. Louis turned out an amazing 46,558 vehicles, an increase of over 20 percent since the previous year.

**Changes to the 1977 Corvette** were limited to a few interior details and a new engine color. A new center console housed heater and air conditioning controls, located on a new center console that was even deep enough to allow the use of a standard size Delco radio. A shorter steering column moved the wheel 2 inches closer to the instrument panel, improving the driving position and making it easier to get in and out of the cramped interior. The RPO V54 roof panel rack allowed a little more room in the luggage space behind the seats when the T-tops were removed and stored on top of the rear deck. Glass roof panels (RPO CC1) also appeared on early options lists but were delayed by a dispute with the supplier and didn't appear until 1978.

Speed control was added to the 1977 Corvettes' option list as RPO K30 and could only be ordered along with the M40 Turbo Hydra-Matic automatic transmission, but that didn't limit the car's popularity. Also that year, 84 percent of new Corvettes were equipped with automatics. This early form of vacuum-operated cruise control helped drivers stay under the tedious 55 mile-per-hour national speed limit on the highway. Chevrolet's V-8s were painted red in 1955 and 1956 and orange in 1957. For the 1977 model year, the Corvette's V-8 engines returned to blue like the "blue flame six" of 1953 and 1954.

Corvettes were mid-pack cars at best by the end of the 1976 season in IMSA, and in a further effort to prevent them showing up for Camel GT Races and other IMSA events, John Bishop made an adjustment in the AA/GT regulations. He instituted a loose interpretation of FIA Group 5 rules in which only a production GT car's profile and general mechanical layout had to be retained. In response, Bob Riley designed an entirely new GT racing Corvette for Greenwood. It was finally possible to replace the 260-pound production frame with a much lighter and more rigid three-dimensional space frame, fabricated primarily from 2-inch diameter tubing.

The new rules required only that the "original suspension principles" be followed, and Riley designed a 5-link rear suspension complete with cast-magnesium hub carriers. He also relocated the suspension control arm, mounting points inboard on the new frame so the wheels could be moved inward, narrowing the wide-body Corvette's fenders. The Porsche factory had also moved into Group 5 during 1976, developing their street 930 Turbo into the 700-hp 935 GT racing car. In the 1977 season, Greenwood first contended with them in the United States with a production frame wide-body Vette.

Tubular frame racing cars built on surface plates with bodies that resembled production cars were the wave of the future in 1977 when Gary Pratt and Charlie Selix built Greenwood's super Corvette. Greenwood's answer to Porsche's 935 wouldn't be ready for months, leaving his wide-body customer

Opposite page: With only the coupe remaining in production, Corvettes had an entirely new skin that started to evolve in 1973 and ended in 1980 with restyled front fenders and a soft body color front fascia over a 5-mph bumper. This red 1980 Corvette is equipped with the N90 aluminum wheels that became available in 1976, mounting QGB Goodyear white letter tires, and has CC1 removable glass roof panels introduced in 1979. *GM Media Archive*

A soft rear fascia in 1974 completed the transition to 5-mph bumpers, with the optional front air dam and rear spoiler from 1979 integrated into new 1980 soft endcap holdings. The fastback rear window didn't open, but it was inspired by a hatchback Zora Arkus-Duntov had prototyped earlier in the decade and was introduced in 1978 for the Corvette's 25th anniversary, improving aerodynamics. *GM Media Archive*

series Corvettes to face the turbocharged Porsches with their unprecedented 2.85 lbs/hp at Daytona and Sebring. Rick Mancuso maintained Greenwood's racing presence at the 24 Hours of Daytona with sponsorship from Mancuso Chevrolet, entering a white wide-body No. 77 with Burt Greenwood, John Cargill, and Dave Heinz as co-drivers. The car performed well, but it was hopeless on the high-speed circuit; the best they could do after qualifying 23rd was to finish 19th, a discouraging distance behind the winning Porsche 935.

Rick Mancuso entered the former *Spirit of Sebring '76* in the 1977 12-hour race with most of its original paint scheme still intact, but the Chicago skyline replaced a patriotic scene on its hood. John Greenwood joined his brother Burt as Mancuso's co-drivers in the car Greenwood had qualified 2nd the previous year and managed an impressive 3rd against intense opposition. It was reliable but didn't have the pace to keep up with the turbocharged German cars and finished 23rd, 67 laps down. The new AA/GT rules offered the aging Corvettes a second chance to remain competitive at the highest level, but it would take time and money to develop a new version that could take on the Porsche and BMW factory racing cars.

## 8-Track Upgrade

Despite not having any direct links to Chevrolet, when Greenwood's radial tube-frame Corvette GT racing car debuted at Brainerd International Raceway in June 1977, its fastback roofline and large fixed rear window were a preview of the 1978 production Corvette. The new body included a far more advanced aero package with a front splitter, complemented by a large Group 5–style rear wing designed by Bob Riley. The No. 77 Corvette was on BBS modular wheels with deep-dish turbo fan wheel covers to help control brake temperatures.

Greenwood's new weapon had a power-to-weight ratio of about 3.2 lbs/hp. It was a big step in the right direction, but still fell short of the 935's 2.85; however, it was close enough that superior braking and cornering could make the difference. With his fuel-injected, big-inch Chevy V-8s producing more torque than the Corvette's production-based driveline could reliably handle, Greenwood developed a Turbo 400 Hydra-Matic transmission for road racing to ease the strain. Unfortunately, this idea had been tried unsuccessfully by Ford for their "J Car" in the late 1960s, and Greenwood couldn't make it work either. His tube frame No.77 faltered when he accelerated off of the corners, and he was out in 24 laps. After Brainerd, the No. 77 car's next appearance was in the Paul Revere 250 at Daytona on the 4th of July weekend. Greenwood qualified it on the pole with a manual Muncie M22 four-speed transmission, but the clutch let go at the drop of the green flag.

Greenwood's next try was the Watkins Glen 6 Hours of Endurance on July 9, and he managed to get Dick Smothers back as his co-driver. The car was fast, but a Porsche 935 qualified on the pole, followed by a turbocharged BMW 320i and another 935. The tube frame Corvette started fourth, and it took everything Greenwood and Smothers had just to keep up. After driving 10-10ths for 92 laps, pushing the big-block Chevy to its absolute limits, a valve train failure ended the No. 77's race. The old

## TESTING THE *SPIRIT OF SEBRING*

The March 1976 issue of *Road & Track* magazine featured a track test of John Greenwood's *Spirit of Sebring 76* at Daytona and included a comparison with a four-speed, L82 V-8 equipped 1976 Corvette, also driven by Greenwood. The test was conducted in November 1975 at IMSA's finale, and Greenwood's qualifying time set a new course record: 1 minute, 55.05 seconds. He had never driven a street Corvette on a racetrack but was pleasantly surprised with both the car's handling and brakes. He completed a lap in 2 minutes, 36.2 seconds, averaging 88.6 mph despite its lack of power. Straight-line acceleration was no longer a Corvette strong point; with a power-to-weight ratio of 17.2 lb/hp, it took 23.6 seconds to reach 100 mph from a standing start.

Even though Greenwood's new wide-body racing car's low speed acceleration was handicapped by a 2.73:1 rear axle ratio, it was still able to reach 100 mph in just 9.8 seconds. *Road & Track* also ran both cars around a skid pad, with the 3,610-pound street Corvette generating .748 G of lateral acceleration. The 2,885-pound race car pulled 1.20 Gs at 64.8 mph. This force increased considerably at high speed, and the car's aero package was capable of producing over 1,000 pounds of downforce; however, it still couldn't match the 2,000-pound Porsche Carrera RSR's 1.45 Gs of cornering power. When the 3.0-liter RSRs started racing in the United States in 1974, they only had about 300 hp for a power-to-weight ratio of 6.6 lb/hp.

No. 76, still sponsored by Mancuso Chevrolet, raced past. With Greenwood starting to wind down his Michigan operations, the No. 76's engine was built by Pro Motor Engineering, and even though Buzz Fyhrie codrove with Paul De Pirro and ran in the middle of the pack, the No. 76 car sputtered and failed after 120 laps.

Late in 1977, John Greenwood Racing's business emphasis changed and he relocated to Sanford, Florida, southwest of Daytona Beach, while Pratt and Selix started Protofab in Michigan. Pratt and Selix continued their working relationship with Greenwood for some time and went on to build successful GTO, Trans-Am, and eventually an IMSA GTP car for some impressive clients, including Chevrolet. At its high point in Michigan, John Greenwood Racing produced 12 wide-body Corvettes in its customer series in addition to numerous one-offs, suspension, and body kits and racing engines. The manufacture of custom vehicles and components diminished, though, and Greenwood planned to manufacture a limited-production "Greenwood Corvette" for the street to be sold through select Chevrolet dealerships. The plan never succeeded, but Eckler's Corvette parts and accessories handled the body kits for years, making these the last "Greenwood Corvettes."

The cancellation of the convertible allowed a more efficient assembly process of Corvette coupes at the St. Louis plant. Output increased from 38,465 combined coupes and convertibles in 1975 to 46,558 coupes in 1976. Another increase in 1977 brought production up to 49,213. Though the price increased almost $1,000, every Corvette sold. Despite the positive sales numbers, Chevrolet was convinced that the Corvette was actually losing money and walking a tightrope by pushing the price up year by year, increasing profitability while risking lost sales. There was one notable option offered for the first time—the latest wonder in mobile entertainment technology, an 8-track tape player (RPO UM2) combined with an AM/FM stereo radio. Together, they cost $414.

## Corvette Turns 25

Corvette celebrated its 25th anniversary in 1978, and Dave McClellan's engineering team devised a cost-effective way to mark this seminal event with a major styling change. Before his retirement, Zora Duntov tested a prototype glass hatchback Corvette, but Chevrolet's financial department didn't let it progress any further because of the investment cost of putting it into production. By securing the rear window hatch in place, the 1978 Corvette was able to have the fastback roofline at a fraction of the cost, which dramatically increased luggage space behind the seats and included a sliding security cover. A session in the GM Tech Center wind tunnel capitalized on the new roofline's aerodynamic improvement, exploring strategies that would reduce both lift and drag. The addition of a front air dam and rear deck spoiler brought the drag coefficient from 0.50 down to 0.42, while improving front-to-rear balance.

Corvette was chosen as the 1978 Indy Pace Car, giving it the double distinction of being the

The Shark's 1980 and later soft nose increased cooling airflow to the radiator by about 50 percent through a pair of deeply recessed intakes with horizontal grilles while its air dam added a little downforce. This new fascia's injection molded skin was backed up by a deformable urethane egg crate mounted to the frame by a redesigned support structure that took a little weight off the front end. *GM Media Archive*

first two-seater to pace the famous 500-mile race plus the only car to not require modifications to meet the performance requirements. This led to another Corvette first—a limited-edition RPO 1YZ87/78 Indy Pace Car replica, which became a subject of major controversy within Chevrolet about how many should be produced. Handled by Chevrolet's legal department, it was decided that the only way to avoid possible litigation was to offer a pace car to every Chevrolet dealership in the United States and Canada. To accommodate every dealership, 6,502 special cars were produced and the market for them collapsed. Though initial speculators drove the selling price to over $20,000, the surplus destroyed the demand, and the last of the pace cars sold at discount after the Indy 500.

In addition to 25th anniversary badging, 1978 Corvettes featured a silver anniversary paint scheme designed by Jerry Palmer and available as RPO B27 for $399. The 1978 interior also had a new look, with a redesigned speedometer and tachometer on a flat rectangular panel in front of the driver and opposite a glove box added on the passenger's side. The center console introduced in 1977 carried over, but the door trim panels were all new with separately molded armrests held in place by screws. Whitewall tires had been a Corvette option since 1954, joined by goldwalls and other cosmetic options in 1965, and in 1978, a wider lower-aspect ratio tire also became available.

Firestone was Corvette's dominant tire supplier from the beginning, but after moving into the steel-belted radial age in 1973, Firestone ran into a processing problem with the steel wire that ultimately led to the recall of all their steel-belted radial tires. This recall weakened the company to the point that Japanese tire giant, Bridgestone, was eventually able to acquire them, opening the door for Goodyear. In 1978, Goodyear began supplying Corvette with its own radials in new metric sizes. The lower aspect ratios of Goodyear's tires added more width with approximately the same diameter, but Corvettes ordered with them still had to have their fenders trimmed for clearance.

The car magazines proclaimed the 25th edition of the Corvette a significant improvement over the lackluster emissions-choked examples of the last few years. Road testers, their senses numbed by years of evaluating the emasculated cars of the 1970s, were favorably impressed with the 1978 Corvette, writing

that the Chevy's plastic two-seater had come back to life. The base 350ci L48 V-8 had an additional 5 hp, bringing it up to 185, which was enough to push the lower-drag sport coupe from 0 to 60 mph in 7.8 seconds with a top speed of 123 mph. The optional L82 engine received a 10 hp boost for a total 220 hp, giving the Corvette a top speed of 133 mph and, coupled to the RPO M21 four-speed manual transmission, made it the fastest accelerating American car sold in 1978.

## Trans-Am Champs

After setting a closed-course speed record on the Daytona tri-oval with his tube-frame Corvette, Greenwood sold the car to Jerry Hansen, who in turn sold it to Greg Pickett. Pickett went on to win the Sports Car Club of America's (SCCA's) 1978 Trans-Am Championship in this car with sponsorship from George Foltz and technical assistance from the car's designer, Riley. Riley worked with Protofab, guiding them in building a second tube-frame Corvette for John Paul, who had been impressed with the performance of Greenwood's example while he campaigned his Porsche 935 during the 1977 season. Greenwood convinced him that a tube-frame Corvette would not only cost less, but also be a faster alternative to his Porsche, but it wasn't ready until after Sebring and ultimately proved to be a fast but fragile disappointment.

John Paul entered his Porsche 935, with Dick Barber as co-driver, in both IMSA's season-opening 24 Hours of Daytona in February and in the 12 Hours of Sebring in March, where only a few hopelessly outclassed Corvettes were entered. The best of them was the No. 3 wide-body driven by Cliff Gottlob and Danny Terrill, which finished 11th overall and 3rd in class. Unfortunately, Paul's new tube-frame Corvette wasn't able to do much better in this league. He did manage a few podium finishes (amidst many more DNFs), but he gave up and sold the car to a Mexican racer named Juan Carlos Bolanos. Bolanos would enter the tube-frame Vette in the last Trans-Am race of the season. Greenwood had won the title three years earlier, driving one of his customer series cars, and in 1978, Pickett was just as dominant in the last Corvette GT racing car Greenwood built in Michigan.

The Pickett Racing Team's updated Greenwood Corvette was white and carried the No. 6 with a red-to-yellow fade on top of the radiator exhaust

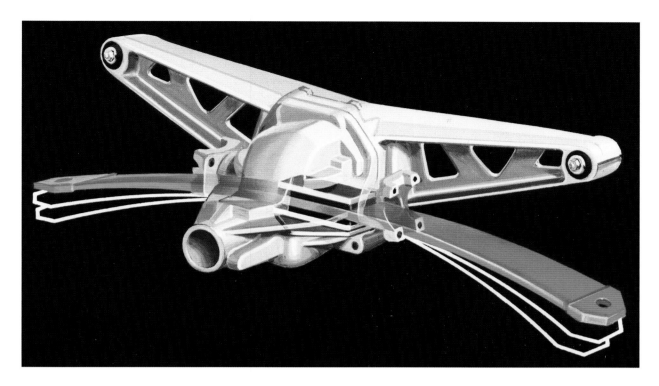

With planning for the long overdue fourth-generation Corvette underway, a new rear axle with an aluminum housing was one of several components for the new platform put into production early. Starting in 1980, Dana supplied their model 44 rear axle in an aluminum Corvette housing to Chevrolet, which included the across the car mount that had bolted on to the cast-iron unit.
*GM Media Archive*

duct bulge that took the place of cowl induction on fuel injection hoods. This fade was repeated on the body, from the forward edge of the fastback rear window with red, orange, and yellow transverse stripes extending the full width of the wing-end plate supports. Pickett rocketed away to a great start in first race of the Trans-Am Series, setting a new lap record, qualifying on the pole at Sears Point Raceway, and winning the season opener with an impressive 1 minute 30 second lead. In the second event at Vancouver, Pickett again qualified on the pole with a new lap record, but after leading the early laps, he finished the race in 3rd, starting a run of bad luck that would extend through the next four races.

Pickett's second win came at Mosport, followed by Road America, where the Trans-Am race was run in two heats, and he dominated both of them with decisive wins. The ninth race in the series was at Laguna Seca, and Pickett's tube-frame Corvette continued to shatter lap records in qualifying, and despite some damage in practice, he led the race from wire to wire. The final race of the season was at Mexico City, and with Pickett in contention for the championship, he met some unexpected competition for the race win: Juan Carlos Bolanos behind the wheel of John Paul's tube-frame Corvette. Pickett easily led the early laps, until he had to pit with a sticking throttle. Meanwhile, Bolanos worked his way up to third. When Pickett returned to the race

after removing a pebble from his Cross-Ram fuel injection system's throttle linkage, he was behind Bolanos. Bolanos faded, however, and Pickett finished second—good enough to win the 1978 Trans-Am Championship.

## Trans-Am Champs, Take Two

Of the Corvettes still racing, the most recent model was 9 years old. Though Greenwood's developments had extended their competitive life spans at the highest levels of GT racing, they had become dinosaurs by 1978. America's sports car did remain competitive in the SCCA Racing Series where it continued to dominate the amateur A- and B-production classes until they were phased out in the 1980s.

Gene Bothello won the 1979 Trans-Am Championship with an L88-based Corvette 10 years after the last of these cars rolled off the assembly line. It was a last hurrah for big-block Corvettes in road racing. With big-block engines disappearing from most production cars after 1975, the National Association for Stock Car Auto Racing (NASCAR) saw them as no longer relevant and banned them that year, lowering their displacement limit from 427ci to 358ci. The SCCA followed at the beginning of the 1980s, returning their Trans-Am Series to its original 5-liter or 305ci displacement limit, eliminating A-production and big-block engines. A

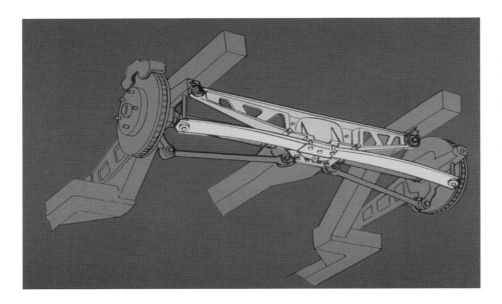

For 1981, GM's inland division came up with a 7-pound fiberglass spring that could take the place of the current Corvette's 48-pound steel rear leaf spring and would be used on both ends of the C4. This illustration shows the second- and third-generation Corvette rear suspension with the monoleaf plastic spring mounted to the underside of the aluminum rear axle housing. *GM Media Archive*

few of the Greenwood Corvettes and their derivatives continued racing into the 1980s with small-block engines, but time had finally caught up with them.

## A New Model

In 1979, Dave McLellan's Corvette Engineering Group finally received the green light to start defining the long overdue, all-new, fourth-generation Corvette, but the plastic sports car would have to enter the new decade with a familiar face. The 1980 Corvettes did look slightly different, with new front and rear bumper cover "end caps" that integrated the rear spoiler and front air dam, and a new nose that improved cooling airflow by about 50 percent. The 1980 crossed-flag Corvette emblem was new, and inside behind the seats, the battery remained on the driver side in its own compartment, but the center and passengers' side storage compartments were combined under a single lid. Federally mandated 85 mile-per-hour speedometers were phased in during 1979, so anyone adventurous enough to blaze into socially irresponsible and illegal three-digit speeds had to extrapolate their velocity from the tachometer.

The state of California led the entire country in vehicle emissions regulations, and after the federal Environmental Protection Agency (EPA) opened for business in the fall of 1970, the Sunshine State's requirements were more demanding. This new tact led to Chevrolet again offering engines in two displacements for Corvettes, even though they were both small blocks. The base 350 engine lost 5 hp, bringing it down to 190, while the L82 gained 5 for 230 hp. A 305ci V-8 was the only engine available

for Corvettes sold in California, and it had to be equipped with automatic transmissions (RPO LG4). The California 305 was a passenger car engine that filled in for one year only, but it was also a preview of future technology with its "computer command control."

Corvettes steadily gained weight during the 1970s because of the incremental addition of government-mandated safety features and increased use of acoustic insulation and other sound deadeners. With a new platform still several years away, an effort was made to lighten the aging two-seater for the new decade. The thickness of fiberglass body panels was reduced. The base L48 engine got an aluminum intake manifold from the optional L82 and a new rear axle housing also of aluminum. These few components, among others, were designed for the next generation Corvette and were put into production early to gain manufacturing experience. Chevrolet's Warren plant sought to discontinue making the cast-iron models.

Most of the Corvette's chassis components, including its rear axle, had been in production since the 1963 model year, and the high-volume parts they were based on no longer had any other application. A Dana Model 44 8 1/2-inch rear axle was chosen for a replacement, and they were asked to cast a Corvette housing in aluminum instead of cast iron, which was a new approach for both them and Chevrolet. The across-the car mount that suspended the housing below the crossmember was incorporated in the aluminum casting, saving even more weight. This early introduction gave Corvette engineers experience with aluminum castings in a high-stress, high-corrosion environment, serving as an important step in using much more aluminum in the C4.

The year 1980 marked the biggest increase yet in the price of a base sport coupe, which went up $2,920.01 at the beginning of the model year. After four additional price hikes, it finished the year costing an additional $4,125.01 over the 1979 price. Most of the popular options were made standard equipment, including RPO A31 power windows, C60 air conditioning, and N37 tilt-telescopic steering column, pushing the final price up to $14,345.24 at the end of the model year. Along with the unprecedented price hike, there was an equally unprecedented drop in sales, with demand down by 13,191 Corvettes. The year's total, however, was still an impressive 40,606. Even though the stiff

price increase undoubtedly affected sales, the bottom didn't fall out, so profit increased, and the higher numbers kept customers from experiencing sticker shock when they saw the price of the new Corvette.

## Corvette's Old Kentucky Home

After 26 years of providing Chevrolet's racers with the technical support and the special parts they needed to successfully compete, Vince Piggins retired in 1981. Racers often confused Piggins' product promotion engineering group with Chevy R&D, which did occasionally develop parts for them, but as Piggins' support vanished from the pits and offices of Chevrolet, Herb Fishel assumed this role.

Fishel eventually crafted a factory Corvette racing program that was bigger than anything Duntov and Ed Cole could have imagined before theirs was shut down by the American Automobile Manufacturers Association (AAMA) in 1957. The Corvettes on which Fishel based his GT racing cars were not manufactured in St. Louis; production moved to a larger plant in Bowling Green, Kentucky, during 1981.

The General Motors Assembly Division (GMAD) started in the early 1960s. Over the next two decades, it gradually took over the assembly of most cars for the entire corporation, including the St. Louis Corvette plant in 1971. By the late 1970s, the St. Louis paint shop could no longer meet tightening EPA emissions' regulations, and with the plant in a built-up area, establishing a temporary paint shop to keep the line moving while the old one was updated was impossible. To get around this dilemma, GMAD found an empty 550,000-square-foot factory in Bowling Green, Kentucky, that had been used by Chrysler's Air Temp Division to make air conditioners. GMAD expanded it to 1,000,000 square feet. This building was the Corvette's new home, and with the assembly line installed, the first one rolled off the line on June 1, 1981. Production continued in St. Louis for two more months, and the last Corvette rolled off that line on August 1.

## Patience Is a Virtue

In 1981, the EPA continued to tighten emissions standards. The new regulations required an even

By the late 1970s, the St. Louis assembly plant had become too small, and its paint shop could no longer meet EPA regulations, so GMAD found an empty factory in Bowling Green, Kentucky, for the Corvette's new home. The year 1981 was the first and only that Corvettes were built in two locations, with the first one rolling off the Bowling Green assembly line on June 1, while production continued in St. Louis for two more months. *GM Media Archive*

The 1982 Corvette was a car in transition between the third and fourth generations, with the new platforms, twin throttle body, fuel-injected L82 350 and upgraded four-speed 700 R4 automatic transmission. The electronic "cross fire injection" was a far cry from the earlier mechanical port fuel injection, but its single plane Cross ram intake manifold was based on the common plenum cross ram developed for Trans-Am racing in the 1960s. *GM Media Archive*

more restrictive dual-bed catalytic converter, and the electronic carburetor from the 1980 305 for all 50 states. For the first time since 1954, there was only one Corvette engine—a 350ci 190-hp V-8—dubbed L81—which was available with four-speed manual and automatic transmissions, even in California. These engines were embellished with cast-magnesium rocker arm covers and stainless-steel tubular exhaust manifolds equipped with oxygen sensors as part of the "computer command control" system. The carburetor was a hybrid mixture of old vacuum injection and new digital fuel injection technology. The exhaust manifold's oxygen sensors measured residual oxygen in the exhaust, and the computer adjusted the fuel flow through a single pulsed injector.

The "optional performance engine's" power output climbed steadily from 1977 until they were no longer available in 1981. The L81 performed poorly everywhere but California. The 1981 car was the slowest Corvette since the mid-1950s, and its single primeval fuel injector was the only thing that allowed it to be sold at all. The basis of that technology, however, is what prompted Corvette's long climb back to relevance. After the second energy crisis

in 1979, the EPA started setting standards for something it referred to as corporate average fuel economy (CAFA). Manufacturers who failed to meet it were fined, and buyers had to pay a "gas guzzler tax."

The St. Louis assembly line continued operating until Bowling Green came up to speed, and there wasn't any shortage of 1981 Corvettes; demand remained strong despite another hefty price increase. Production leveled off at 40,606 for 1981 (just eight coupes less than in 1980), and the base priced increased by $3,118.28, driving the price of the Corvette to $16,258.52, which had to make Chevrolet Financial happy. Relocating Corvette production to the new and larger facility garnered numerous benefits in addition to satisfying EPA emissions regulations: a modern paint shop and line speed of 15 cars per hour, besting the St. Louis line by 5. Both build and paint quality improved with a switch from lacquer to enamel basecoats, followed by clear topcoats, producing a superior mirror-like finish.

When the third-generation Corvette reached the last year of production in 1982, its body had been freshened many times, but it already dated back 15 model years while the chassis it was mounted on had been around for 20. It was truly the end of an era, and Chevrolet offered a special collector's edition Corvette with an opening glass hatchback and exclusive cast-aluminum wheels—reminiscent of the 1967 optional "bolt-ons"—to commemorate it. The package also included a unique silver-beige paint scheme with graduated hood and side body decals, multi-tone silver-beige leather seats and door trim, a leather-wrapped steering wheel and horn cap, and luxury carpeting. Both interior and exterior cloisonné emblems proclaimed this car's special status and added to its exclusivity. The 6,759 Collector Edition Hatchbacks were the first Corvettes to cost more than $20,000.

The 1982 Corvette transitioned between the third and fourth generations, which along with the fiberglass rear spring and Dana 44 rear axle with its aluminum housing, had the C4's engine and transmission. The new L83 engine was an incremental development of the 1981 L81, featuring a more advanced "computer command control" system and a cross-fire fuel injection system. Its single-plane intake manifold was inspired by late 1960s Z28 Camaro common plenum Cross-

Ram equipped with a pair of four-barrel Holley carburetors on Trans-Am racing 302 engines. This manifold's racing heritage was pointed out as the reason for the L83's 10-hp gain, but most of it really came from the new low back-pressure monolith catalytic converter.

The 1982 Corvette's performance was also improved by the new 700 R4 four-speed automatic transmission, which had lock-up clutches on the top three gears and a lower first gear for a better launch. The timing of this far more effective automatic was fortunate because Corvettes wouldn't feature manual four-speed transmissions for about the next year and a half. Chevrolet was Borg-Warner's last customer for their T-10 four-speed manual transmission vehicles, and the volume became so low by 1980 that Borg-Warner decided to stop supplying their manual transmissions to Chevrolet after 1981. Until a replacement could be found, this announcement left the Corvette back where it started, with nothing but an automatic transmission available. For buyers, at least the four-speed 700 R4 was a huge improvement beyond the clunky two-speed Powerglide that Corvettes started with.

By the beginning of the 1980s, most Corvette enthusiasts were sure an all-new Corvette must be in the works, and by 1982, there were plenty of rumors as well as a few hard facts published in the automotive press. The C3's continued sales success lulled upper management into waiting almost too long, and the third generation's sale numbers finally

## CORVETTE'S WEIGHT LOSS PROGRAM

In future years, fuel injection played a key role in improving both performance and fuel economy, but weight reduction also made a difference, and GM's Inland Division introduced an important innovation. They built a 7-pound fiberglass spring that replaced the current Corvette's 48-pound steel rear leaf spring and could also be used on both ends of the C4. This idea saved more weight than any alteration since the all-aluminum 427ci ZL1 engine, and it was soon installed on 1981 Corvettes with automatic transmissions and standard suspensions. These fiberglass monoleaf springs were made from laminated graphite filaments and demonstrated dramatically better fatigue life than the steel springs they replaced; in fact, they wore out Inland's testing machines without failing.

bottomed out in 1980 and 1981. Another price hike for the 1981 base coupe priced the car at $16,258.52 and $18,290.07 for 1982. The collector group price was $22,537.59, but most potential buyers were waiting because they believed the new Corvette was close at hand. For 1982, the final production numbers totaled 18,648 coupes and 6,759 collector coupes, for a total of 25,407—a 15,199 car decline from 1981. The demand was there, but Corvette enthusiasts would have to exercise patience a little while longer.

GM performance parts had this customized late '70s Corvette built up to showcase their products in car shows and at drag strips across the country, with this photo taken in January of 2004. In addition to modern speed equipment and current high performance crate motors, they continue to offer the classic GEN 1 small blocks and MK IV big-blocks, including the aluminum ZL1.
*GM Media Archive*

# 7 1983-1989
# THE ALL-NEW FOURTH GENERATION

Design of the first entirely new Corvette in two decades revived the controversy over which end the engine should be in, while emission and fuel economy regulations added what type of engine it should be. If GM's rotary engine had been successful, the fourth-generation Corvette might well have had a four-rotor Wankel behind its seats. The styling team built a prototype, but the rotary engine program was eventually cancelled, ending Chevrolet's development. Design Staff proposed that the new Corvette be powered by GM's politically correct 2.8-liter V-6 in the same location. Chevrolet turned the approach down, but that idea became the Pontiac Fiero instead. Even though the Corvette was created by styling and Design Staff usually got its way with corporate, they couldn't sell them on a mid-engine Corvette in any form, so the new one had to be a fresh, but recognizable, front-engine car.

For the first time, Design Staff was able to work with Corvette Engineering instead of dictating to them. Bill Mitchell retired in 1977, and his successor, Irv Ribicki, discontinued Mitchell's iron-handed rule. Jerry Palmer was in charge of Chevy Studio 3 and worked closely with Dave McClellan on the third-generation Corvette, making it easier for them to pick up where they left off. McClellan felt that the four-rotor Corvette was the most

pleasing interpretation of Chevrolet's sports car he had ever seen, and Palmer moved it into the studio for inspiration while the production car took shape. Palmer was determined not to repeat the mistakes made with past Corvette bodies—bodies that were styled without a thought to aerodynamics—and only tested in a wind tunnel after the design was finalized.

Aerodynamic testing of the new Corvette's body began as soon as it progressed from sketches to clay. One-quarter-scale models were evaluated, and the most effective shapes were incorporated into a full-scale wind tunnel armature. Palmer, along with his team of modelers and aerodynamicists, traveled to Lockheed's subsonic wind tunnel in Marietta, Georgia, where they conducted more than 100 tests. Once they analyzed the results, they were able to bring the C4's coefficient of drag down to 0.34, compared to the C3's stodgy 0.42. The new body also had less lift with better overall aero balance, and for the first time, the body wrapped around the frame instead of sitting on top of it and the bird cage body support structure was integrated with the frame. The new primary structure met many conflicting requirements, like increasing rigidity but losing weight and occupying less interior room. It also had to meet new federal crash worthiness standards.

Opposite page: The third and fourth generations looked dramatically different but were both recognizable as Corvettes, with the 1982 Collector Edition in the background, featuring an opening rear window like the C4. The Shark's Coke-bottle shape was in stark contrast to the new car's straight sides, divided by a circumferential trim molding, with a clamshell hood that pivoted forward from the windshield like an E-type Jaguar.
*GM Media Archive*

Jerry Palmer was in charge of Chevy Studio 3 where the "F" and "Y" cars were styled, and his idealized sketch of the first new Corvette in 14 years established a styling theme that translated well into production. After having the Sting Ray—and Mako Shark II—based bodies handed off to Corvette Engineering already finalized by Bill Mitchell, the C4 would be a cooperative effort between Jerry and Dave McLellan.
*GM Media Archive*

While McLellan's small Corvette Engineering Group concentrated on the new car's powertrain, Brian Decker was recruited from Chevrolet R&D's analysis group to build a chassis design team. Decker also developed a concept for the new frame, starting with GM's research laboratories and using newly developed techniques to establish the structure's minimum size and weight. A virtual, finite element model that included all of the local cross sections, along with gauges of steel, was constructed from GMR's findings, and the Grumman Aircraft Company tackled the crash worthiness problem. The finished design incorporated a pair of front rails that transitioned into rocker sills at the hinge pillars then back into rear rails at the latch supports with a T-bar between the windshield frame and halo bar on top. This structure achieved its objectives, until Chevrolet General Manager Lloyd Reuss decided that the new Corvette should have a one-piece lift-off Targa roof, but it was too late for a fix to be worked out without delaying production. This meant deleting the T-bar, which undid most of the work put into improving the new frame. The design team made the tapered rocker sills the same height from front to back, which helped a little but made entering and exiting the vehicle more difficult.

The fourth-generation Corvette was compared to European cars, and several were evaluated to see which matched the closest. The most relevant was Porsche's front-engine V-8 powered 928, introduced in 1978. At 3,700 pounds, the 928 was overweight but still an excellent touring car, and several of its features were either incorporated in the new design or in future generations. The front-engine Porsche's rear-mounted transaxle and torque tube driveshaft both improved weight distribution and opened up interior room, but developing a transaxle for the Corvette had to wait a generation. It was possible to adapt the torque tube by the simple expedient of adding an open C-channel to the right side of the driveshaft, eliminating the need for a transmission-mounting crossmember.

Pirelli's revolutionary new P7 low-profile high-performance tires were introduced along with the 928 as P225/50VR16s, offering unprecedented handling at the cost of rapid tire wear. Goodyear developed a similar tire for the 1983 Corvette featuring a distinctive tread pattern taken from its Formula 1 rain tires that gave them the nickname "Gatorbacks." These new steel-belted radials were P255/VR16s and had not only amazing grip, but also extended tread life. After a one-year exclusive deal on the Corvette, they became the OEM tires on the Ferrari Testa Rossa, among others.

The fourth-generation Corvette chassis was the first to not have its suspension design compromised

The new body wrapped around the frame instead of sitting on top of it, with the bird cage body support structure integrated into a perimeter frame forming a more rigid three-dimensional structure. This uniframe was designed with a T-bar, which added a lot of rigidity, but Chevrolet's general manager, Lloyd Reuss, insisted that the new Corvette have a liftoff, one-piece roof eliminating the T-bar, somewhat compromising its integrity.
*GM Media Archive*

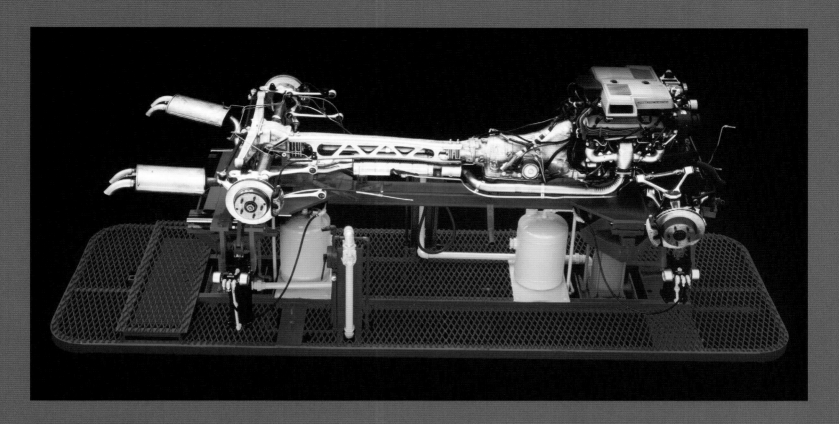

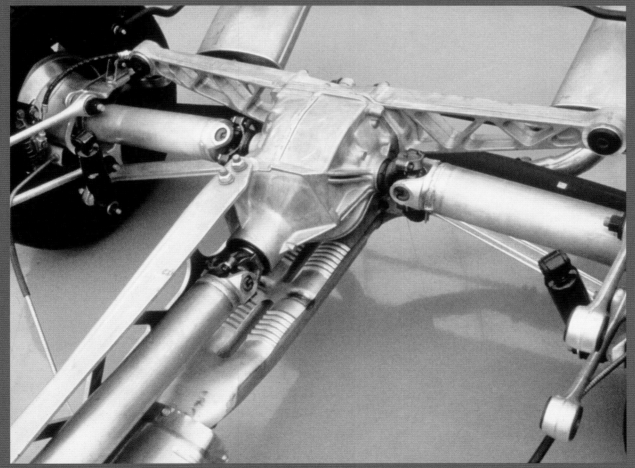

The fourth-generation engine and automatic transmission introduced a year early would be linked to the Dana rear axle's aluminum housing by a torque tube driveshaft for the new Corvette. This simple torque tube had a C-channel with a lattice pattern of punched-out triangular openings to the right of the driveshaft, making the driveline into an assembly that was raised into the car as a unit along with the suspension. *GM Media Archive*

This was the first Corvette platform to not have its suspension design compromised by the use of high-volume components, which were limited to bearings and ball joints this time around. The new five-link independent rear suspension was similar to Bob Riley's tube frame Corvette's, except for the fiberglass mono leafspring and the continued use of stressed half-shafts as the upper control links. *GM Media Archive*

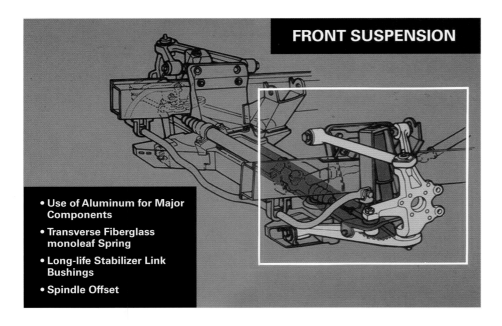

## FRONT SUSPENSION

- Use of Aluminum for Major Components
- Transverse Fiberglass monoleaf Spring
- Long-life Stabilizer Link Bushings
- Spindle Offset

The new independent front suspension stayed with conventional unequal length A-arms, but they, along with the uprights, were aluminum, which was an industry first. The fiberglass mono leafsprings at both ends also broke new ground, while the C4's rack-and-pinion steering was a production Corvette first.
*GM Media Archive*

by the use of high-volume production parts, which were limited to bearings and ball joints this time around. The aluminum rear axle housing, introduced in 1980, was joined by aluminum lower-rear suspension control links in 1982, followed by all of the other links, control arms, and uprights on the new Corvettes. The wide new tires needed the car to stay nearly flat in the turns, and a roll stiffness of 3.5 degrees per G was achieved with stiff fiberglass leaf

springs and anti-roll bars at both ends, despite low roll centers. The car was also stiff in pitch, with anti-dive front and anti-squat rear geometry built into the suspension linkages, very much like Bob Riley's tube-frame racing Corvettes.

The new Corvette was equipped with rack-and-pinion steering and had a five-link independent rear suspension, which differed from Riley's by retaining the C3's stressed half-shafts as upper links. Design Staff wanted the new sports car to be lower than its predecessor but with a higher ground clearance line. The engine was moved farther to the rear and inclined slightly down at the front, with the starter ring gear on the ground clearance line. The transmission tunnel, which was widened to make room for a small monolith catalytic converter and similar that used in the Porsche 928, was located between the seats. The driveshaft and longitudinal C channel were placed above it for a dramatically low center of gravity.

In the 1965 model year, Corvettes had become the first American-made production cars to be equipped with four-wheel disc brakes, and now, 16 years later, the cast-iron four-piston calipers were essentially unchanged. To minimize pedal travel, coil springs behind the pistons created drag by holding the pads in slight contact with the vented brake rotors. The

# HIGH-TECH SPECS

Inspiration for the C4's digital dash in front of the driver came from Corvette's interior design chief, Bill Scott, while the "loaf of bread" in front of the passenger was to comply with pending safety legislation. This large rectangular pad was part of a passive restraint system that was later dropped by the Reagan administration but remained part of the production interior, which was new but otherwise fairly conventional. The tall rocker sills made necessary by the one-piece lift-off roof were awkward to step over, but because the wider transmission tunnel squeezed the parking brake lever out of the way, it found a new location up against the driver's side sill.

One optional interior feature every bit as high tech as the LCD instrument displays was universally appreciated by everyone who heard it: the revolutionary RPO UU8 Delco Bose stereo system. This high-performance automotive sound system arrived via a proposal from Dr. Amar Bose, an MIT professor of electronics and a leader in the development of home-theatre sound systems. When McLellan heard that this advanced sound system was being developed in conjunction with Delco Electronics, he told Delco that the new Corvette had to be the first car equipped with it. Despite adding $895 to the C4 Corvette's $21,800 base price, 43,607 of the 51, 547 sold by the end of 1984 were equipped with the Bose audio system, and it became impossible for dealers to sell a Corvette that didn't have one.

drag became a serious problem as the designers tried to make the most of minimal horsepower, but fuel economy mandates had to be met. With a lighter car, it was also important to minimize unsprung weight, and a new design developed by an Australian joint venture between Girling and Lockheed offered a solution to both problems: the Girling calipers had only a single piston in a finned aluminum cylinder housing that slid on sealed greased pins within a cast-iron frame bolted to the upright, and the pads only made contact when the brakes were applied.

Like the Porsche 928's chassis, the Corvette's 4.5-liter single overhead cam V-8 engine and 5-speed manual transmission set some benchmarks for the new Corvette. The feature that would have done helped the most in the struggle for power and mileage was the Porsche's Bosch port-fuel injection, but it was off limits at the time because of a dispute over Cadillac's disastrous 4-6-8 fuel injection system. A small 5-hp gain was made by developing an in-house version of the 928's monolith catalytic converter, which was smaller and less restrictive than GM's bead-type converter, giving the 350ci cross fire V-8 a total of 205 hp. Chevrolet needed a five-speed transmission but lacked a supplier for even a four-speed manual transmission. Fortunately, Corvette Engineering was able to resolve this dilemma with a novel solution in 1984.

The Environmental Protection Agency (EPA) had set minimum speeds for manual transmissions, and cars equipped with them were required to stay in each gear during their fuel mileage testing cycle—so there was more to Chevrolet's problem than just finding another source for manual transmissions The L82's cross fire fuel-injection system was extremely thirsty. It was equipped with the 700 R4 four-speed automatic, and it barely stayed above the gas guzzler threshold during the EPA's mileage test; with a four-speed manual, there was no way. Doug Nash Inc. was developing an overdrive that could potentially be added to a four-speed manual transmission, allowing the new Corvette to offer one as an option without being branded as a gas guzzler—and to forego the accompanying fine. Chevrolet contracted Nash to start manufacturing four-speed manual transmissions using Borg-Warner's tooling, and a highly modified version of their overdrive unit for the C4 Corvette.

This combination was called a 4+3 four-speed manual transmission, but the overdrive unit had all

of the elements of an automatic transmission, with a planetary gear set, clutches, a hydraulic pump, and electrohydraulic control system. When the driver shifted the 4+3 transmission at the EPA minimum speeds of 15, 25, and 40 mph, the overdrive was automatically engaged in second, third, and fourth gears, improving mileage in the EPA test cycle by 1.5 miles per gallon—just enough to squeak by. When the overdrive was engaged in any of the top three gears, flooring the accelerator pedal automatically downshifted it until the car reached about 120 mph. At that speed it automatically re-engaged, giving the C4 a top speed of over 140 mph. This shifting strategy was scorned by many drivers, especially magazine road testers who found it confusing. But for those who chose to accept it, the 4+3 transmission worked very well.

For the 1965 model year, Corvettes became the first American production cars to be equipped with four-wheel disc brakes, and until the introduction of the C4, their cast-iron four-piston calipers remained unchanged. The new design had much lighter aluminum single piston calipers that slid on sealed greased pins developed by Girlock, an Australian joint venture between Girling and Lockheed. *GM Media Archive*

Another controversial feature of the fourth-generation Corvette was a complete abandonment of traditional analog gauges in favor of a digital liquid crystal display with easy-to-read graphs. This approach came from the Corvette group's work with Grumman's engineers, and led to a look at their F14A Tom Cat, including its cockpit, which was loaded with similar LCD displays that could be read in a millisecond while making violent combat maneuvers. It was a big leap from a Navy jet to the new Corvette's instrument panel, but like the F14, all of the pertinent information was displayed on a backlit glass panel, color-coded for clarity, and featured bar graphs and large numbers. Given a little time, most owners came to appreciate the "video arcade display," but the automotive journalists never let up, and about the time digital instruments began appearing in Formula 1 cars, Corvettes returned to analog gauges.

Many consumers hoped that the C4 would be a somewhat smaller car. Its wheelbase was reduced, and the new body was 8.7 inches shorter than the old. Its height was also reduced, but packaging wider tires increased the width from 69 to 71 inches. The fourth-generation Corvette didn't quite achieve its design goals, but it came close, missing its 3,000-pound weight objective by 7 percent with a curb weight of 3,192 pounds. It was 150 pounds lighter than the C3. While still a big car, the C4 was shorter and lower than its predecessor, and it was generally agreed to be the right size with the shortest wheelbase in Corvette history.

The new styling was a hit and met its objectives of being both fresh and yet easily recognizable as a Corvette. The C4 retained the signature concealed headlights and dual pairs of round taillights, now on a clipped-off "kamm" tail. Directional cast-aluminum 16-inch wheels reminiscent of the brake cooling wheel covers popular on 1970s endurance racing Corvettes were part of the new look and came standard. The windshield was racked back at a record 65-degree angle, and the rear window hatch was the largest compound-contoured piece of glass on any American car. An ongoing production problem dating back to 1953 was hand-finishing exposed body-bonding seams, and a rib molding in a groove extending all of the way around the new Corvette covered them up and became a memorable C4 styling clue.

This parting line groove that divided the body into upper and lower halves was contributed by John Cafaro, who was new to Jerry Palmer's Studio 3. He also contributed the integrated hood and front fenders that pivoted from the front, just like a Jaguar XKE. Lifting the dramatic clamshell hood gave a clear view of the wide Goodyear Gatorback tires and

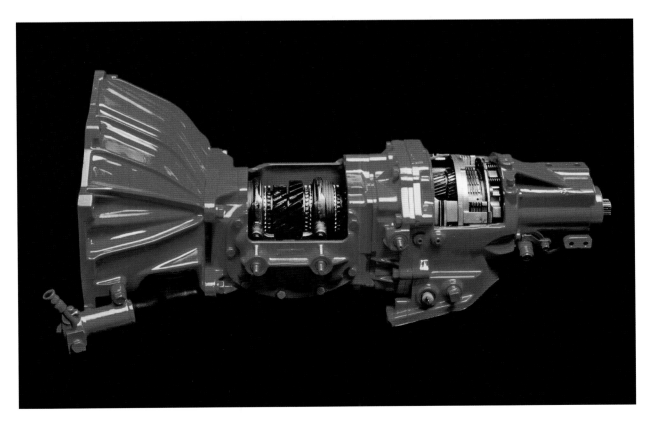

Borg Warner discontinued their four-speed manual transmission in 1981, leaving '82 Corvettes with only an automatic, which was actually a moot point because the new Corvette would have been branded a gas-guzzler with that transmission. Doug Nash was contracted to produce four-speed manuals from the Borg Warner tooling, combined with their automatic overdrive unit, making it a hybrid 4+3 transmission, which satisfied the EPA, keeping the C4 above the gas-guzzler threshold. *GM Media Archive*

slender aluminum upper control arms, framing the setback 350ci cross fire injection V-8. The engine color was now black, and the 1982 version's multiple V-belt accessory drive was replaced by another exclusive Corvette innovation: a single, flat, grooved "serpentine" belt that ran everything.

To help customers enjoy their fourth-generation Corvettes, metal parts were leaned slightly toward the sky or the ground to lower their signature on police radar. Corvettes were bottom breathers that picked up cooling and intake air off of the road, with wind tunnel testing revealing that the maximum airflow through the radiator was, with it tilted forward, 15 degrees. This helped minimize the car's radar signature, and while the radiator still had an aluminum core, it featured new design plastic tanks and a fan shroud for a thermostatically controlled electric fan. Even though the standard Corvette

suspension offered exceptional handling, it became clear during development that if it were stiffer and kept the tires almost upright, it would be possible to corner at over 1G of lateral acceleration. The RPO Z51 performance handling package that came out of this development program was the most effective option of this type ever, and beyond stiffer springs, shocks, anti-roll bars, and bushings, it included quick-ratio power steering, along with an engine oil cooler.

After decades of hand fitting, the C4 was intended to be assembled with a level of precision only possible by using a three-dimensional axis system with gauge holes and fixtures, assuring the dimensional accuracy of the uniframe. The same gauging and fixture system was intended to be used for assembling the plastic body panels but was lost on the toolmakers, turning the early weeks of production into a nightmare. This was in January 1983, and with the new Corvette not available nationwide until March, Chevrolet's General Manager Robert Stemple, after much debate, made the decision to skip the 1983 model year. The car met all of the federal emissions and crash worthiness requirements for 1984, and its emissions certificate was only good for one January 1 date, so the 1984 model year lasted an unprecedented 17 months.

## The C4 Arrives

The first new Corvette in 20 years created a sensation in the automotive press. Enthusiastic reviews proclaimed it a world-class performer, creating a feeding frenzy among speed-hungry customers. The press introduction started in southern California in the fall of 1982 at Riverside International Speedway, where Corvettes amazed journalists (the Z51-equipped cars in particular) with their race car–like handling.

The new Corvette was a natural for showroom stock racing, which had been growing in popularity since the late 1970s, and Kim Baker proved it by winning the Sports Car Club of America (SCCA) SSGT National Championship with his manual transmission–equipped 1984 Corvette and its superior handling and brakes. Despite less raw power than the favored Nissan 300ZX Turbos, Corvette

Engineering was encouraged to become more deeply involved in 1985. A hefty $3,509.98 increase in the base price brought the total up to $21,800.00, but that didn't stop many potential buyers because a near record 51,547 Corvettes were sold in 1984. Even though this number was inflated by the 17-month model year, it was still impressive and came close to the all-time Corvette sales record set in 1979 of 53,807 when Vettes cost less than half as much. Sales of the plastic-bodied sports cars would only top 50,000 in these two years, but demand remained strong for the C4's 14-year production run. The RPO MM4 four-speed manual transmission took a long time to reach production and only 6,443 cars were equipped with this no-cost option, but it was ready in time for the 1984 racing season, allowing Corvette to start reestablishing its reputation.

## Return to Racing

In 1985, the C4 got what it needed most—more horsepower. Thanks to the return of port fuel injection after 20 years, this time the injection system featured eight Bosch electronic fuel injectors that sprayed measured pulses instead of the Rochester system's constant flow nozzles. The 1965 L84 Ramjet 327 had made approximately 315 net hp at 6,200 rpm before federal emissions and fuel economy regulations, which limited the 1985 L98 tuned-port

This styling mockup of the new interior clearly shows the rectangular "video arcade instrument display" in front of the driver and the equally rectangular "loaf of bread" passive restraint in front of the passenger. This pad was part of a passive restraint system that was federally mandated when the interior was finalized, but later dropped by the Reagan Administration; however, it remained part of the C4 interior until 1990.
*GM Media Archive*

350 to 230 net hp at 4,000 rpm. This figure sounds underwhelming, but it was a 25 hp gain over 1984 and, more importantly, added 40 net ft/lb of torque, for a total of 330 at 3,200 rpm, which beat the 1965 L84's approximately 300 net ft/lb at 4,600 rpm. While lacking the excitement of a high winding 65 "Fuely," a manual transmission 1985 Corvette demonstrated comparable performance in a *Car & Driver* road test, covering the standing quarter mile in 14.4 seconds at 97 mph.

With the C4's advanced aerodynamics, the L98's 230 hp was enough to push the new Corvette to a record 150 mph, and it looked impressive with a cast-aluminum plenum standing above the block valley on eight tubular, tuned-length ram pipes. Once Chevrolet was able to develop a port fuel injection system, they chose to combine Bosch's electronic pulse-width injectors and new LH electronic, hot wire air meter with AC Delco's computer-controlled, high-energy ignition and sensors. The L98 was still a low-revving engine without much horsepower, but was the first step in the long climb back to the industry's second performance era.

The 1984 Corvette's handling was universally praised, but even the base suspension received some criticism for its harsh ride. Development

engineer John Heinricy (also an accomplished racer) undertook a testing program to improve it. Heinricy determined that the base suspension's spring rates could be reduced by 25 percent, while the Z51's spring rates could be lowered by 16 percent in front and 25 percent in back without losing cornering power. The 1985 optional performance handling package included larger diameter anti-roll bars at both ends, and from mid-year 1984, Delco Bilstein monotube high-pressure gas shocks and heavy-duty cooling options were also available. The Bilstein shocks improved the base suspension's ride isolation as much as the Z51's, and they were made available as RPO FG3, along with the Z51's heavy-duty cooling as RPO V08.

## Renewed Dominance

In 1984, the SCCA started a Playboy-sponsored Manufacturer's Championship for showroom stock cars, with secondary sponsorship from the Escort Police Radar Detector Company. A new Super Sports Division was added for the 1985 season. The Corvette Engineering Group learned that this high-visibility series would be open to the Corvette, Porsche 944, and Nissan 300 ZX Turbo in 1985, and that several racing teams were preparing

Corvettes. It was decided that Corvette Engineering should provide technical support with development manager Doug Robinson as the point man. With the entire product team behind him, they would provide support for powertrain, chassis, electrical, and body. Robinson's approach was to work directly with the Tommy Morrison, Jim Cook, and Dick Guldstrand team. He felt they had the most potential, and that they might share the results of their development with all of the other Corvette teams.

The Morrison, Cook, and Guldstrand team was supplied with a 1985 manual transmission Corvette equipped with Z51 suspension. It was first tested in a simulated 24-hour race and not entered in competition until all of the problems that surfaced were sorted out. Chevrolet could finally race out in the open, and Dick Guldstrand was contracted to drive and help develop the 1985 Corvette. Some of the testing was carried out at the Milford, Michigan, proving grounds, as he worked with Jim "Jingles" Ingle. Both he and Guldstrand contributed to Corvette development for years behind Guldstrand Motorsports, preparing Corvettes for racing both on the track and on the street and for special versions. The Corvette Engineering Group also managed the relationship with the SCCA, designing special parts when weaknesses appeared and releasing them to the racers when they were approved. Many parts, such as stronger wheel bearings, eventually reached production.

The preparation of 1985 SCCA showroom stock racing Corvettes was similar to production class

Cross Fire injection with a pair of single injector throttle bodies marked a return to fuel injection, but it was only an interim step, with the 1985 tuned port system giving the C4 what it needed most. That was more horsepower, and the new L98 with eight port fuel injectors for the first time since 1965 gained 25 hp, along with 40 ft/lb of torque over 1984 for a total of 230 hp and 330 ft/lb of torque. *GM Media Archive*

The L98 had a cast-aluminum intake plenum standing above the block valley on eight tubular tuned length runners, with air entering through a twin plate throttle body. Fuel was delivered to Bosch electronic fuel injectors by a separate rail for each cylinder bank, with the injectors spraying measured pulses directly into the ports. *GM Media Archive*

sports cars 20 years earlier, except that they were required to use street tires, and Goodyear developed an "S"-designated sport compound version of its Gatorback. The C4's brake supplier, Girlock, also supported the competition program. Girlock produced racing compound brake pads, along with a quick-change system for replacing hot, worn-out pads during pit stops in long-distance races. Upwards of 275 hp was coaxed out of the slow-revving L98 with open exhaust, and rubber suspension bushings were replaced with hard plastic, allowing more precise camber-and-toe settings to be maintained within the production specifications required by the rules. The interior had to remain

complete and unaltered, except for the addition of a tubular roll cage, a five- or six-point safety harness for the driver, and a fire extinguisher, which looked awfully out of place in the plush surroundings.

The professional Playboy United States Endurance Cup Series consisted of six races between 3 and 24 hours in length, spanning the country with a season-opening 24 Hour Race at Riverside International Raceway in southern California. Morrison-Cook's preseason testing, working with Corvette Engineering, gave Corvette a head start on the other teams, and the engineers didn't miss a beat preparing for the Playboy Series. They developed a refueling rig and endlessly practiced pit stops. The

Morrison-Cook team entered three cars to finish first and second and win the race overall. The third car was slowed by problems during the night but still able to finish the race. The other Corvette teams also finished well, but even after this performance, no one could have guessed how dominant Corvette would become: Corvette completely shut out Porsche and Nissan and won every race, including the season finale at Road Atlanta.

## Chevy Antes Up

Herb Fishel's Product Performance Group managed Chevrolet's other racing programs in addition to the showroom stock Corvette effort (including NASCAR), and Fishel imagined a new mid-engine racing car that would resurrect an old dream. For the first time since Zora Duntov's 1957 Corvette SS, Chevrolet engineered an endurance racing car that could potentially win Daytona and Sebring overall in the United States and also conquer Le Mans in France. This project was inspired by the success of the small-block Chevy-powered mid-engine Lola T-600 radical ground-effects coupe that had dominated International Motorsports Association's (IMSA's) top class grand touring prototype since 1981, and Lola was contracted to build an updated version for Chevrolet. It was designated the T-710 by Lola, and with styling clues added by Design Staff, the GTP Corvette became a test bed to develop the divisions turbocharged 90-degree V-6 engine.

Rick Hendrick Motorsports was contracted to race the GTP Corvette, and Ryan Falconer was contracted to develop and build the turbocharged V-6 racing engines based on Chevrolet's cast-iron 90-degree block. To give this central cam pushrod 229ci engine a more favorable oversquare bore-to-stroke relationship and maximum piston area, its bore and stroke was increased and the stroke for a displacement of 209ci. Equipped with over-the-counter Chevrolet aluminum heads and a Warner-Ishi model RX9-L turbocharger, power output eventually reached 900 hp at 7,000 rpm, driving the 1,950-pound GTP Corvette through a Hewland VG5 transaxle. Fishel said that the reason for using the GTP Corvette as a rolling test bed was for grooming Chevrolet's V-6 to carry on the winning tradition of the small-block V-8.

Hendrick's people didn't have any experience racing in IMSA, so they hired Ken Howes, whose GTP team had lost its sponsorship to manage the program. When the car finally appeared to be competitive, they entered it in a few races late in 1985. The GTP Corvette made its first appearance at Road America in August, where it qualified reasonably well but suffered from engine trouble during the race, which remained a problem for the rest of the season. By IMSA's finale in December at Daytona, the car was ultracompetitive and blindingly fast—while it lasted. Even though it had picked up even more power from its original 750 hp, the V-6 still wasn't reliable. Overall, the car performed well enough to encourage Chevrolet, and Chevy got serious about 1986, committing to have Hendrick run it for the full IMSA season with Goodwrench sponsorship.

## A Convertible from a Coupe

Corvette production returned to a normal 12-month model year in 1985. Sales continued to gather momentum, undeterred by a $2,603 price increase that raised the cost for a base coupe to $24,403. The 1985 Corvette offered world-class performance that could only be matched or exceeded by a few far more expensive and low-volume European exotics, and an impartial comparison test by the United States Automobile Club made the point. All three Porsche models were represented, along with a Ferrari, Lotus, and Lamborghini Countach, which, in an Olympic point system, was the only car to come close, scoring 18 points against the Corvette's 24.

Corvette introduced Bosch's new anti-lock brake system, ABS-2, as standard equipment in 1986 and continued to be America's technology leader—despite the 10 percent base-price increase from that important safety innovation. The system's sensors read the rotational speed of each tire from a 72-tooth wheel located behind the brake discs, and the ABS computer calculated the deceleration rate as the brakes were applied. When the brakes neared lock-up, the computer released hydraulic pressure through a solenoid valve to the brake calipers, then reintroduced hydraulic pressure through the master cylinder, starting the cycle over again until the brakes were released. The system managed each corner individually to maintain maximum braking performance and to fully maintain directional stability, which proved to be valuable to racers and nonprofessional drivers alike.

Another expensive addition to the 1986 Corvette's standard equipment was Chevrolet's first production

The C4's clamshell hood pivoted up from behind the front bumper cover, taking the upper half of the front wheelhouses with it for an almost unobstructed view. The L98 engine was an impressive sight, with its tubular intake runners flanked by the wide Goodyear P255/50VR16 Gatorback tires, but this tilt-up hood was both heavy and a headache for insurance companies. *GM Media Archive*

aluminum small-block cylinder heads, which not only saved weight, but with redesigned ports, also added 5 hp, bringing the L98 up to 235 hp. Unfortunately, even at this late date, Chevrolet still had problems casting aluminum cylinder heads, and their introduction was delayed until mid-year by cracking around their mounting bosses. The 1986's exterior appearance remained almost unchanged, except that the aluminum wheel's black center recesses were left unpainted and an additional stoplight adorned the roof. The center high-mounted stoplight (CHMSL) was added to the coupe's fixed halo bar ahead of the rear window hatch to comply with a new federal regulation.

In anticipation of the drop in sales that usually followed the introduction of a new model after a year or two, Reuss had the American Sunroof Corporation build a convertible out of a 1984 Corvette coupe. There hadn't been a production Corvette convertible since 1975, and Reuss wanted to reintroduce one before sales started to sag, which meant dramatically shortening the three years it normally took to release a new model. Chevrolet no longer had anyone with experience designing a drop-top, but ASC did, and an 18-month program was worked out with the American Sunroof Corporation. ASC contracted to do the engineering, while the structural development work was handled at the Milford proving grounds. Removing the Corvette roof's halo bar made the frame far too flexible, and a package of reinforcements, including an under-floor X-member similar to the original Corvette frame, was designed to make up the deficiencies.

The entire back end of the coupe body had to be redone for the convertible, with the exception of the rear fascia, which had a center high-mounted stoplight added above the license plate recesses. Like the two previous generations of Corvette drop-tops, the rear deck was fixed in place with a hinged panel behind the seats to conceal the soft top when it was folded down. Production didn't start until the spring, and Chevrolet drew attention to the first Corvette convertible in 11 years by making it the 1986 Indianapolis Pace Car. But it wasn't just the car that drew attention—World War II fighter ace and test pilot Chuck Yeager was the celebrity driver. The actual pace cars were yellow, but all mid-year 1986 convertibles sold were considered pace car replicas, and they even included a decal package regardless of color.

The SCCA's professional showroom stock racing series changed title sponsors in 1986. Instead of Playboy logos around the course, Escort took over, and placed the Porsches, Nissans, and Corvettes into a new GT class by themselves. This gave the other competitors an opportunity for class wins, and the SCCA hoped that Porsche and Nissan, companies showcasing newer and faster cars than ever before (the Porsche 944 Turbo and Nissan 300 ZX Turbo, for example), would solve the series' larger problem—Corvette domination.

Corvette Engineering continued to support the major teams and encouraged the use of anti-lock braking systems (ABS) on their race cars, even though it was untried in competition and some of the drivers were opposed to it. John Powell drove an SS/GT Corvette and had a driving school at Mosport Raceway, helped to fine tune the system, and conducted ABS classes before every race early in the season. The racers found an advantage, especially on wet tracks and in emergency situations.

For the 1986 season, Porsche returned much more confident. Its turbocharged 944s were driven by big name international endurance racing stars that were often faster than the Corvettes, and Porsche was confident it could push its racing engines and drivers farther and faster. Nissan was far behind, and Porsches and Corvettes were so closely matched that they often raced wheel-to-wheel to the checkered flag, sometimes even taking each other out, even though the Escort series was composed of endurance races.

The German cars out-qualified the Corvettes several times, starting from the pole and leading a number of races, but their turbocharged engines were thirsty, requiring them to make more pit stops. As determined as the Porsche team was to win, the additional stops for fuel kept Porsche from victory for a second year in a row. Corvette repeated its sweep.

The GTP Corvette sported a new look for the 1986 season. A black and silver paint job advertised

A fourth-generation convertible was still a year away in 1985, but this bright red coupe with a matching interior could really be opened up with its one-piece roof panel removed. The base roof panel was painted body color but a CC3 transparent roof was also available offering the effect of rear open-top motoring in any weather. *GM Media Archive*

GM Design Staff restyled a mid-engined Lola T-600 IMSA GTP body to resemble a Corvette for Herb Fishel's product performance group who managed all of Chevrolet's racing programs. This project was inspired by the success of these radical ground effects coupes that had dominated IMSA's top class since 1981, powered by small-block Chevys. *GM Media Archive*

its Goodwrench sponsorship, and Rick Hendrick stayed with Ken Howes as the team manager. The much-improved car set a new lap record, qualifying on the pole for the 24 Hours of Daytona, driven by "Doc" Bundy and Sarel Van Der Merwe, but like the IMSA finale in December, it failed to finish. The turbocharged bullet's first win came at Road Atlanta on April 6, where it qualified on the pole and raised the race's average speed record on its way to victory, breaking a string of 16 Porsche wins. Van Der Merwe had a string of his own going, qualifying the GTP Corvette on the pole 7 times in a row, with another race win at the Grand Prix of Palm Beach. Engine reliability remained a problem, though, and if they didn't win, the car was usually broken.

Corvette sales slowed in 1986, dropping by 4,620 from 1985, but at 35,109, sales figures were still strong for a two-seater sports car and they were bolstered by the arrival of the convertible. The base convertible, RPO 1YY67, was the first Corvette to cost over $30,000, with a retail price of $32,032. Even though it was available for less than half of the 1986 model year, 7,315 were sold. As America's sports car moved up in the market, it became an increasingly popular target for car thieves, and an electronic vehicle anti-theft system was included in 1986. A resistor embedded in the ignition key was installed that was read by a sensor in the lock cylinder that only allowed the car to start if the correct programmed resistance was met.

The 16-inch cast-aluminum wheels carried over unchanged for 1987, except for the black interior of the openings and the argent gray recessed centers. The wheels showed the only exterior difference

from 1986 to 1987, but interior changes were made as well. The aluminum cylinder heads were now readily available, and all of the engines were equipped with them. The L98 also had a new roller lifter camshaft, which added 5 hp to the 1986 rating, with aluminum heads bringing it up to 240 hp with 350 ft/lbs of torque, making it even stronger off the line. In response to lessons learned in showroom stock racing, the convertible's forward frame reinforcements were added to coupes equipped with the Z51 package, along with a finned power steering fluid cooler.

RPO Z51 springs were too stiff for the convertible, which limited their availability to coupes. For 1987, the performance handling package was further restricted to coupes equipped with manual transmissions. For convertible buyers not satisfied with the base suspension, a Z52 handling package was added to the 1987 coupe's option list and could also be ordered with either manual or automatic transmission. This RPO combined the softer base springs with a larger diameter front anti-roll bar, the Z51's Bilstein shocks, ultra quick 13:1 steering, and a heavy-duty radiator including the booster fan and engine oil cooler. This package proved to be extremely popular in 1987; a combined total of 12,662 were purchased for convertibles and coupes, equipped with the $470 option, while only 1,596 coupes had the extreme Z51 package, which cost $795.

Corvette performance was returning by the mid-1980s, thanks primarily to port fuel injection and electronic engine management, but the Corvette's normally aspirated 350ci push rod V-8 was still limited to 240 hp in 1987. The search for more power within the constraints of emission and fuel economy regulations led Corvette engineers to look at two possible approaches: four valves per cylinder head and turbocharging. Both would be expensive, limiting them to extra cost options, but turbocharging the existing engine was the simplest to prototype, so it was tried first in 1985 and produced 400 hp and 500 ft/lb of torque. Reuss was elated with the turbo V-8's performance, but he wanted something that would be considered high-tech for the Corvette's premier high-performance engine, and Lotus in England had been acquired by GM.

Lotus' technical director, Tony Rudd, met with Reuss, as well as two guys from powertrain, Russ Gee and Roy Midgley, to discuss designing a double overhead cam four-valve cylinder head for the Corvette short-block. It was estimated that these heads would add about 100 hp, and Rudd pointed out that it would take an entirely new engine with piston cooling and better control of cylinder wall temperature to match the turbo V-8's 400 hp. Lotus just happened to have an engine design team that had been assembled for a Formula I project that

was canceled, and Reuss gave them the go-ahead to start work on a 4-cam 32-valve V-8 for the Corvette. This put the turbo V-8 on the shelf at Chevrolet, but Don Runkle, head of market planning, suggested that it be turned over to Callaway Cars in Old Lyme, Connecticut.

Reeves Callaway had engineered several turbocharged aftermarket conversions of small foreign cars and successfully taken them through EPA certification into low-volume production. Chevrolet wanted him to do no less for the Corvette—the 4-cam V-8 was going to take several years to reach production, and a turbo system being built outside the factory might give customers the performance boost they desired in half the time, so Corvette Engineering opened their doors to Callaway and offered him every assistance. The stock engine was left alone (except for strengthening the bottom end), which left its EPA approval in effect. That decision simplified the certification process, but at the price of leaving some horsepower on the table. Chevrolet's prototypes made 400 hp and 500 ft/lb of torque, while the Callaway system was good for 345 hp with 465 ft/lb of torque. In the end, the 1987 Corvettes equipped with Callaway's system were

For this publicity photo of the first GTP Corvette, the IMSA prototype racing car shows off its long, low, and wide proportions, pulled up close to an '85 production coupe. Herb Fishel commissioned Lola to build an updated version of their T600, the T710, with Corvette styling clues incorporated into the body; these cars were available to customers. *GM Media Archive*

Hendrick Motorsports was contracted to race the GTP Corvette with sponsorship from Mr. Goodwrench, and it made its first appearance at Road America in August 1985 in their black and silver paint scheme. Herb Fishel used the Lola as a test bead to develop a turbocharged racing version of Chevrolet's 90 degree V-6 with Ryan Falconer building the engines, which would eventually reach 900 hp but were never reliable.
*GM Media Archive*

still the most powerful production cars sold in the United States.

Chevrolet made the Callaway twin-turbo package a regular production option, even though it was actually a conversion. Completed cars were drop-shipped from the Bowling Green, Kentucky, Corvette plant to Callaway Cars in Old Lyme, Connecticut. Both coupe and convertible could be equipped with RPO B2K—the Callaway twin-turbo system that could be combined with any other option—but it required a manual transmission and was not available in California. The system was a tight squeeze with the turbos sandwiched between the engine and the frame rails, which doubled as air ducts with a pair of air-to-air intercoolers flanking the intake manifold plenum on top. RPO B2K was expensive—it added $19,995 to the $27,999 price of a base coupe, and Reeves expected to only build about 50 of them, but there were enough power-hungry Corvette buyers to sell 188 models that first year.

Escort continued sponsoring the SCCA's professional showroom stock racing series with more liberal rules, allowing limited modifications, in hopes of bringing an end to Corvette domination. Porsche developed a racing package for its three-car 944 turbo team based on experimental parts that developed from race to race. Corvette Engineering responded with the early release of improved 1988 chassis components, including larger front brakes. The teams were also supplied with ZF 6-speed manual transmissions late in the season, which

at least equaled Porsche's gain in performance, and both cars surged even farther ahead of the competition. The German cars consistently out-qualified America's sports car early in the season, but mechanical failures and bad racing luck kept Porsche out of victory circle. That didn't stop the SCCA from banning both Porsche and Corvette from the series at the end of the season.

### The C4 and Corvette's 35th Anniversary

Herb Fishel's Chevrolet Special Products Group contracted with Hendrick Motorsports to campaign the GTP Corvette in the IMSA series for a second full season with continued Goodwrench sponsorship. Bundy crashed the first GTP Corvette early in 1986, relegating it to a patched-up show car, and the team started the new season with an updated T-710 they received from Lola in June 1986. Chevrolet developed an electronic engine management system for the V-6 over the winter, and with qualifying boost, it was up to 900 hp, but the system was unreliable and contributed to more DNFs in 1987. Despite increasing competition from a growing number of Porsche 962s, the GTP Corvette qualified on the Daytona 24 Hour pole for the second year in a row, which was the first of four during the season, but it didn't lead to a single win.

In its first full year of production, over 30 percent of 1987 Corvettes were convertibles, including 65 of the 188 Callaway twin-turbo conversions—an increase of 3,310 over 1986. Coupe sales dropped, but the base price only increased by a modest $972. The droptops shot up $2,788 for a new high of $34,082. The fourth-generation Corvette's good press continued in 1987; *Car & Driver* magazine picked it as one of the world's "top ten" best cars, and it also won the 70 to 0 mph braking award. In *Motortrend*'s "domestic dynamite" comparison, the Corvette came out on top, winning top speed, braking, and skidpad categories, which by this time wasn't a surprise to anyone.

In 1988, the C4's fifth year of production, it received a number of updates to ready the chassis for more power in anticipation of the 4-cam V-8 expected to be introduced in 1989. Brakes were upgraded with dual-piston front calipers, and single-piston rear calipers now doubled as parking brakes, eliminating the small internal drums that had been used in Corvette disc brakes since their first appearance in 1965. The RPO Z51 package included larger diameter 12.9-inch front and 11.9-inch rear brake rotors with 17 X 9.5-chin aluminum wheels, which it shared with the Z52 suspension-mounting P275/40ZR-17 tires.

All 1988 Corvettes equipped with the base suspension continued to feature the 255mm-wide 50 percent aspect ratio 16-inch Gatorbacks. These wheels offered a Z speed rating on a 16 x 8.5-inch aluminum wheel with similar styling, but without the dividing ring or hubcaps. Along with the addition of anti-lock brakes in 1986, the front caster was increased from 3.8 to 6 degrees, improving directional stability, and for 1988, the steering scrub radius was reduced to zero to take full advantage of the ABS system. The L98 was still rated at 240 hp, but it was possible to add another 5 hp for the coupe by adding RPO G92 (performance axle ratio 3.07:1), which included less restrictive mufflers that were too loud for the convertible or coupe with 2.59:1 rear axles. Two interior refinements were also made in 1988: the easily-scuffed vinyl covers that covered the frame rails above the door sills were carpeted and the parking brake lever up against the driver's frame rail was moved down and to the rear.

Callaway continued to develop his twin-turbo conversion, and RPO B2K was up to 382 hp with 582 ft/lb of torque for 1988. To broaden the package's appeal, it was available with an automatic transmission; this truck Turbo Hydra-Matic 400 was modified to handle the additional 232 ft/lb of torque, adding an additional $6,500 to the $25,895 package, and was covered by Callaway's 12-month or 12,000-mile warranty. RPO Z01 commemorated the Corvette's 35th anniversary with a special edition that was only available as a coupe, which featured a black halo bar and everything else (including the wheels) painted white. The package also included white leather-covered seats and steering wheel with an anniversary plaque on the console and special emblems.

## The Corvette Challenge

When the SCCA banned Corvettes from the Escort showroom stock racing series, their action left the dominant teams without any place to race, so former series competitor John Powell organized the Corvette Challenge. The one-hour sprint races ran in conjunction with the SCCA's Trans-Am events and typically featured 15 to 20 identical Corvettes banging fenders in an all-out wheel-to-wheel competition. Corvette Development Manager Doug Robinson supported the idea, and with the approval of Chevrolet General Manager Robert Berger, 56 street-legal 1988 Corvettes were built for the racing series. The engines were stock, but their power output was equalized, and they were sealed at Flint V-8 before being shipped to the Bowling Green assembly plant.

The Corvette Challenge cars were assembled with all of the base equipment, including air conditioning, and Powell arranged for 50 of them to be shipped to Protofab Engineering in Wixon, Michigan, for preparation. Protofab became a Chevrolet special products group contractor in 1987, and it removed the catalytic converters while leaving the rest of the stock exhaust system in place and installing a pair of racing seats. Protofab added a full roll cage, fire extinguisher system, and a five-point safety harness for the driver, along with a set of Dimag magnesium wheels, which had become popular once they were allowed in the Escort series. The completed cars were warehoused by Powell Motorsports in Wixon, where racers picked them up for $15,000, which included their entry fee for the season.

Sponsorship for the Corvette Challenge series came from a Corvette accessory manufacturer, Mid America Designs, along with Goodyear and Exxon. By mid-season, though, the otherwise successful Corvette Challenge was still in financial trouble. Even though Chevrolet had made it clear that it wouldn't be putting any money into the series, Divisions Marketing Manager Mike Goodman felt it was worth propping up for the remainder of the season. Powell managed to attract a number of well-known drivers, including Indy car stars Johnny Rutherford, Jeff Andretti, and Jimmy Vasser, along with some of the best professional endurance racers. The first event was run on May 1, 1988, supporting the Grand Prix of Dallas, and ten races later the championship was won by Stu Hayner.

Technology moved quickly in IMSA's grand touring prototype class. By 1988, the Porsche 962 prototypes began losing to the more advanced Walkinshaw Jaguars. The GTP Corvette's Lola T-710 chassis was based on an earlier design, and only the explosive power of their turbocharged 3.4-liter V-6s allowed them to remain competitive. Unfortunately, explosive was the operative word—the black and silver Goodwrench cars rarely finished due to mechanical failure, but their power advantage kept

**By 1988, Corvette's reputation as America's premier high-performance car was firmly reestablished.**

them out in front while they lasted. For IMSA's 1988 season, a change in rules took this advantage away by putting restrictions on turbocharged engines, dropping the V-6s to about 700 hp. The V-6s were soon replaced by normally aspirated V-8s.

The small-block V-8 was capable of about 680 hp and seemed like a good trade-off with less complexity, no turbo lag, and a much broader power band, leading to a car being assembled with a V-8 over the winter of 1987–1988. Howes continued to manage the team for Hendricks, and he tried running a car with each engine, but neither worked very well. A second V-8 powered car was built, with the V-6 was set aside for the remainder of the season. Chevrolet had a new generation two electronic engine management system which, unlike the earlier version, proved to be very reliable, and concentrating on the V-8s, the GTP Corvettes showed a lot of promise. Unfortunately, even though they were as much as three seconds a lap faster than the V-6 powered cars had been, the season ended without a single win or even a pole, and the program was cancelled.

The collaboration between engineer Riley and Protofab had produced the Greenwood tube-frame Corvettes before they were both contracted by Jack Rousch to design and build the Motorcraft Ford factory Mustangs for IMSA's GTO class. After becoming Roush Protofab between 1983 and 1985, they didn't build another Corvette racing car until 1987, and a Protofab Corvette designed by Riley and sponsored by Polyvoltac was entered in the 1988 24 Hours of Daytona in February. This racing program was initiated and managed by GM MTG, and the car driven by Greg Pickett, Tommy Riggins, and John Jones was impressive but failed to finish both there and at Sebring in March. John Jones joined Wally Dallendach Jr. in a second Protofab Corvette for the 12-hour race, and they won the GTO class, finishing sixth overall, while Pickett and Jack Balwin finished second overall at mid-Ohio in June.

By 1988, the Corvette's reputation as America's premier high-performance car was firmly

reestablished and backed up by competition success; it was taken seriously by both sports car enthusiasts and the automotive press. The 1988 Vettes came with only a moderate increase in price: $1,490 was added to the base coupe, bringing it up to $29,489, while convertibles saw an additional $1,648 increase for a total of $34,820. Callaway twin-turbos rose the most, with a retail price of $25,895 ($5,900 more expensive than the previous model), but sales only fell by 63. Overall sales dropped by 7,843 Corvettes, back to about the 1982 level, but after almost six years of strong production, this drop was not alarming.

Chevrolet's RPO ZR-1 special performance package featuring the LT5 4-cam V-8 was finally revealed to the press after months of rumors and just in time to appear on the covers of the October 1988 car magazines. What the journalists saw were preproduction 1989 ZR-1s that, like the 1983 Corvettes, were built on the Bowling Green assembly line but never released for sale. The 1989 chassis was ready for the ZR-1 package; however, there were development problems with the LT5 engine, and dealers were notified in April 1989 that the option wasn't going to be available until 1990. The 1989 version featured wheel bearings, along with revised rear suspension geometry, selective ride control, Bilstein shocks, and a six-speed manual transmission rated at 450 ft/lb of torque, replacing the unloved 4+3.

The base 16 x 8.5-inch aluminum wheels were cancelled for 1989, and 17 x 9.5-inch wheels and their P275/40ZR-17 tires became standard equipment. Inside, the seats were restyled, but the choices of cloth and leather upholstery remained the same. RPO FX3—the electronic selective ride and handling package—could only be ordered along with RPO Z51 featuring the aluminum wheels. The Z52 option was cancelled, but its softer springs and anti-roll bars, except on Challenge cars, were used for a wider range of adjustability. The Bilstein shock absorbers had three ride modes, selected by a switch on the center console to the rear of the new RPO MN6 ZF six-speed's shifter boot. The gearing strategy of this no-cost option improved both acceleration and fuel mileage, but it was still necessary to add a computer added gear shift (CAGS) from first to fourth to satisfy the EPA.

The Corvette Challenge racing series reached its second and final year, which was supported by Chevrolet marketing and televised on ESPN, in 1989.

Throughout the year, Bowling Green built 60 1989 Challenge cars. Thirty of these cars were shipped to Powell Development America in Wixom, Michigan, for installation of special high-performance engines, roll cages, racing seats, and fire extinguisher systems, along with Dimag magnesium wheels. The 1989 series didn't have a title sponsor, and the SCCA revised their rules, allowing entrants to find their own sponsors. The SCCA also allowed Corvette Engineering to open up the exhaust systems so spectators could hear the cars on the track. After a second season of close racing, Bill Cooper won the championship, and the cars were returned to Powell Development to have their original matching engines reinstalled.

## Out in the Open

On Thursday, March 16, 1989, at an off-site meeting, the name of Fishel's special products group was changed to the Chevrolet Engineering race shop, now that they could support racing out in the open. In NASCAR, the group worked with Hendrick's three teams and Richard Childress' Goodwrench car while also providing technical support to Chevrolet teams in National Hot Rod Association (NHRA) drag racing, continuing development of its Ilmor Indy V-8. Protofab also changed names in 1989 to

Pratt & Miller after Jim Miller rented one of their Camaros for a Trans-Am race and subsequently bought out Gary Pratt's partner, Charlie Selix. Pratt & Miller continued to build successful Camaros and Corvettes for IMSA GTO along with SCCA Trans-Am racing. In a decade, Pratt & Miller would start building the all-concerning C5R, and later the C6R, endurance racing Corvettes.

The fourth-generation Corvette closed out the decade with a 3,623 car sales increase over the previous year, divided between 16,663 coupes and 9,749 convertibles. The coupe's base price increased by $2,056 and the convertible's increased by $1,965. Even though the $25,895 retail price of the Callaway twin-turbo conversion didn't increase, 67 fewer Callaway cars were sold. The excitement over RPO B2K's extra power had cooled off enough after 3 years that only 58 customers felt compelled to add more than the cost of a 1985 base coupe to their new Corvette for an additional 137 hp. The RPO NM6 was the first six-speed transmission available on an American production car, and a big improvement over the RPO NM4 four-speed it replaced. Surprisingly, only about 15 percent of 1989 Corvettes were equipped with them, compared to 18 percent of 1988's with the four-speed, both of which were no-cost options.

Tommy Morrison ran this production-based Corvette in the IMSA Camel GT Series, competing against dedicated tubular frame racing cars, with technical support from Corvette Engineering in 1987. The No. 2's Mobil 1 paint scheme was identical to the Morrison-Baker showroom stock Corvettes that won 14 of 16 SCCA Escort races that year. *GM Media Archive*

The most anticipated sales introduction in Corvette history was for the ZR-1, which finally reached Chevrolet showrooms in 1990, a year after its planned release for sale. RPO ZR-1 transformed an ordinary Corvette into "The King of the Hill," a nickname it acquired during development because this option was intended to make America's sports car the fastest production car in the world. The heart of this special performance package was not only the first new Chevrolet V-8 since the MK IV in 1965, but also the first double overhead cam American production V-8 ever. This world-class powerplant was designated LT5 and designed by Lotus in Heathel, England, based on the architecture of its 4.0-liter 4-valve-per cylinder double overhead cam Etna V-8, developed by Roy Midgley and his CPC V-8 design group in Warren, Michigan.

Unlike all other Corvette engines before and since, the LT5 was unique and not based on a high volume family of powerplants used in a variety of other cars and trucks, which made manufacturing it a problem. There was no way to produce a highly complex specialized engine at the miniscule rate of about 25 per day in a typical GM engine plant, and Roy Midgley discovered that Mercury Marine in Stillwater, Oklahoma, was a good fit. Mercury Marine was already remanufacturing GM four-, six-, and eight-cylinder engines at a fairly low volume for inboard-outboard drives and had computer-controlled machining centers along with an understanding of statistical process control. They were contracted to machine and assemble the LT5 engines, and the first prototypes were completed in May 1987 for durability testing at Lotus.

Opposite page: The most anticipated sales introduction, at least up to that time in Corvette history, was the ZR-1, which reached showrooms in 1990, powered by the first double overhead cam American production V-8. The world-class 5.7-liter LT5 was designed by Lotus in Heathel, England, based on their 4.0-liter four-valve per cylinder DOHC Etna V-8, working with Roy Midgley and his CPC V-8 group in Warren, Michigan.
*GM Media Archive*

Unlike all other Corvette engines before and since, the LT5 was unique instead of being based on a high-volume family of powerplants used in a variety of Chevrolet's other cars and trucks. Featuring 4 cams, 32 valves, and 16 fuel injectors, a 3-phase induction system allowed the LT5 to produce 375hp, while meeting federal emissions standards and staying above the gas guzzler threshold.
*David Kimble*

**171**

A double overhead cam V-8 is a lot wider and a little taller than one with a central cam pushrod valve train like the base L98, making the LT5 a tight squeeze in the C4's engine compartment. The new engine's underhood appearance was styled by Design Staff making some real eye candy, with a massive oval intake duct feeding air to the 32 intake valves through individual runners. *GM Media Archive*

By 1990, automakers' searches for more horsepower led to all kinds of computer-controlled devices being added to their high-performance engines. For the LT5, this took the form of a three-phase induction system, with the engine breathing through a single throttle plate the size of a quarter and feeding air to one intake valve per cylinder below 3,000 rpm for the Environmental Protection Agency (EPA) testing cycle. These valves were operated by a conservative cam profile, with the second set of intake valves run by a more aggressive one that only came online along with a pair of larger throttle plates when a removable "power key" was turned. The key opened eight port throttles and activated an additional set of fuel injectors, increasing power output from 210 to 375 hp with fuel mileage that stayed above the gas guzzler tax threshold.

Even though the LT5 missed its original goal of 400 hp, the 32-valve 16-fuel injector 4-cam V-8 was still impressive, and no one, including the automotive press, was disappointed with its performance. Goodyear developed P315/35ZR-17 rear tires, which were wider than the base 275s to increase the LT5's additional 130 hp to the pavement. The change meant the package necessitated fender flares or wider rear bodywork. Design Staff and Corvette Engineering decided it was worth the investment in tooling to flare the body. They started at the front of the doors and kept the fender contours uninterrupted, which required a new rear bumper cover. Both ends of the 1991 Corvette were restyled, and the ZR-1 received a widened version of the new convex rear cap, which featured squared-off taillights and a small ZR-1 badge on the lower right corner.

Few visual clues separated "The King of the Hill" from mortal Corvettes, and even fewer identified the 1990 model year. Exterior changes were limited to removing the small hubcaps and revealing the lug nuts. The interior featured a redesigned instrument panel that reverted to analog gauges, save for a digital LCD speedometer. (Ironically, Formula 1 cars were starting to use similar digital instruments.) The steering wheel was also new, and it mounted the Corvette's first air bag with a glove box, replacing the "bread loaf" passive restraint in front of the passenger; the seats remained unchanged. Two Delco-Bose stereo systems were available for the first time with the premium RPO UIF and also featured a compact disc player protected by an anti-theft device for an additional $396.

By 1990, the L98 engine was five years old and near the end of its production life, but the search for more power never stopped, leading to a new intake air speed density control system. It took this development, along with a revised camshaft and a higher compression ratio, to squeeze the last 5 hp out of the 350ci V-8, bringing the horsepower up to 250 in coupes equipped with 3.07:1 rear axle ratios. Even though both the optional 4-cam ZR-1 and Callaway twin-turbo V-8s were far more powerful Corvettes, the base L98 continued to power production-based Sports Car Club of America (SCCA) racing. This included the Corvette Challenge package, which continued to be available in the early months of the 1990 model year as merchandizing code R9G.

## The World Challenge

The million-dollar Corvette Challenge had proved to be popular support events for the Trans-Am series, and SCCA pro racing replaced them with the World Challenge for the 1990 season. This new challenge remained basically a showroom stock series, allowing only limited modifications, and 23 of the R9G Corvettes were sold, along with some of the Flint-built V-8 racing engines. A wide variety of high-performance cars were eligible to compete, and though there was eventually a diverse field of cars in the series, most of the entries that first year were Corvettes. A few Camaros, Saleen Mustangs, and Nissan 300 ZXs added a little variety, but none of these cars were competitive. The season ended like the Escort series—with Corvettes winning every race.

ZR-1s didn't reach competition during 1990, but racer Tommy Morrison collaborated with the Corvette Engineering Group in making an attempt on the Federation Internationale de l'Automobile (FIA) 24-hour world endurance record with a ZR-1. For this unofficial effort, Morrison had to find outside sponsorship with only material provided by Chevrolet. He built both a ZR-1 and an L98-powered Corvette, set-up like showroom stock endurance racing cars. Firestone's 7.7-mile oval test track in Fort Stockton, Texas, was chosen for the record run, which started at 10:00 a.m. on March 1, 1990. The L98-powered backup set the first six FIA records, and the ZR-1 scored seven more. The principal goal was to beat the existing 161.180-mph average speed record for 24 hours, and after John Heinricy hit 196 mph on a trial run in the ZR-1, it was decided that a 175 mph average was realistic, which meant running 180 mph between stops. After 24 hours, drivers Tommy Morrison, John Heinricy, Jim Minneker, Scott Legasse, Scott Allman, Kim Baker, and Stu

Hayner had all taken a turn behind the wheel of the ZR-1 and averaged 175.885 mph. They did it.

## ZR-1 Frenzy

When the ZR-1 finally went on sale in the fall of 1989 at $60,000, it was the most expensive regular production American car ever. The hefty price tag, however, didn't stop power-starved buyers from starting a feeding frenzy. $60,000 was still a bargain compared to European cars that could approach this level of performance, and some ruthless dealers that were allocated early ZR-1s took advantage, selling these coveted cars for more than twice their MSRP. Even the last of the 3,049 ZR-1s produced that first year were sold to eager buyers for slightly above their manufacturer's suggested retail prices, even though overall Corvette sales declined by 2,766 cars to 23,646.

Nineteen ninety-one Corvettes had a new face that featured extended parking and cornering fog lights wrapping around wider radius front corners.

Lotus wasn't the only international engineering group Chevrolet collaborated with to create the ZR-1 Corvette, with its six-speed manual transmission coming from ZF in Germany. Like the LT5 engine, this was a joint effort, but it was introduced a year ahead of the ZR-1, which was pushed back to a 1990 release because of emissions and sound issues. *GM Media Archive*

The few visual clues that separated the "King of the Hill," as it had been nicknamed, from mortal Corvettes were only visible from the back with a restyled rear bumper cover. To accommodate wider rear tires, the body started flaring out at the front of the doors 1.58 inch per side, and the new end cap incorporated the squared off taillights and convex profile that would appear on 1991 base Corvettes. *GM Media Archive*

Three horizontal front fender vents replaced the two vertical louvers behind the front wheels. ZR-1s still had flared doors and wider rear fenders, but they lost their most distinctive styling clue—the convex rear fascia and squared-off taillights, which they now shared with the base Corvettes. The center high-mounted stoplights on their roofs became an identifying feature, with the base coupes CHMSL moving to the rear fascia like the convertible. All '91s had a wider body color perimeter molding. The cast-aluminum 17-inch wheels were also restyled, with eight slots separated by directionally curved spokes that added to the Corvette's new looks.

The finned power steering cooler that had been part of the ZR-1 package became standard equipment, while the other components were combined with the FX3 electronic selective ride and handling to become RPO Z07. If both of these options were ordered in 1990, the base springs were included, allowing a wider range of adjustment from soft to firm; the Z07, however, used the Z51 springs, limiting the selection from firm to very firm. This mix of

suspension components was available earlier in the RG9 Corvette Challenge package, which also required the rigidity of the coupes uniframe. While a manual transmission was specified, 169 of the 733 Z07s were equipped with automatics. The mufflers were redesigned with increased cross-sectional area to reduce back pressure while improving the exhaust note and power output, but for its last year of production, the L98 continued to be rated at 245 to 250 hp.

The 1991 SCCA World Challenge GT series remained popular with race fans, but not with competitors driving anything but a Corvette. America's sports car continued to dominate for a second year. The fields didn't look all that different from the Corvette Challenge, with many of the same teams and drivers switching over to this series.

The 1991 championship was won by Shawn Hendricks, driving a Baker racing Corvette. Doug Robinson continued to manage Corvette Engineering's technical support of the C4s in this new challenge as he had since the Playboy series in

1985 when the Corvette group first became involved in showroom stock racing. Robinson had his own budget and managed production-based Corvette racing independently, all the while following the guidelines of Herb Fishel's Chevrolet race shop, which handled the dedicated racing cars like the Protofab Corvettes.

## Back to IMSA

When Corvette Engineering became involved in showroom stock racing, Robinson worked directly with the Morrison and Jim Cook and continued to support them in running a production-based Corvette in the International Motorsports Association (IMSA), starting during 1987. Robinson supplied Morrison with a pair of ZR-1s to campaign in IMSA during the 1991 season, starting with the 24 Hours of Daytona in February and the 12

Hours of Sebring in March. To compete at this level against purpose-built racing cars, these production Corvettes had to lose weight while gaining power, chassis rigidity, and aerodynamic downforce. A fully triangulated tubular space frame was added to the stock uniframes within the gutted interiors, and Corvette stylist John Cafaro designed racing bodywork molded in carbon fiber. Powered by highly modified LT5 engines producing over 500 hp, the Morrison ZR-1s were slowed by fuel system problems in their first outing at Daytona but still managed to finish 12th and 21st overall, but the rest of the season they did not fare much better.

The 500th Callaway twin-turbo conversion was completed on September 26, 1991, followed by nine more before this supplier-installed option was pulled from production, along with the L98 engine. Even though sales of RPO BZK increased, the turbo

The 1990 interior had a new look, with a redesigned instrument panel that reverted to analog gauges, except for a digital LCD speedometer, ironically as digital instruments were appearing in racing cars. The steering wheel was also new and featured the Corvette's first air bag, with a glove box taking the "bread loaf" passive restraint's place in front of the passenger.
*GM Media Archive*

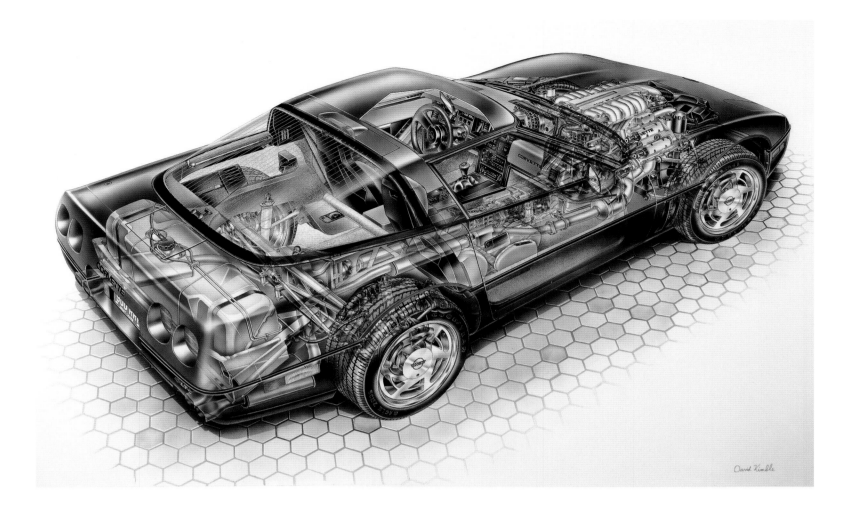

This cutaway illustration of a ZR-1 was done by the author for Chevrolet, along with the LT5 engine's technical press release, in anticipation of the "King of the Hill" going on sale as a 1989 model. With power-hungry Corvette enthusiasts around the world having to wait an additional year to get their hands on one when the ZR-1's introduction was pushed back to 1990, it ran in over 90 publications. *GM Media Archive*

system had to be redesigned for the new engine, and it was mutually agreed that 500 cars in 5 years was a good place to stop. This ended Callaway's relationship with Chevrolet as an OEM supplier, but Callaway would return to the scene in 1994 with aftermarket contributions. This bodywork was developed for the one-off sledgehammer that was officially timed at 254.6 mph around the TRC oval in Ohio, making it the fastest street-driven car in the world.

Chevy sold 14,967 Corvette coupes and 5,672 convertibles in the 1991 model year—3,007 less than in 1990 despite the restyled body and wheels. In its second year, the ZR-1 had also cooled off, with sales dropping by almost a third to 2,044. Only the Callaway twin-turbo picked up sales, but its production was only in two-digit numbers. The coupe's retail price increased by a modest $476 to $32,455, while convertibles cost an additional $1,506, bringing them up to $38,770. Both low-volume, high-performance options endured big price hikes. A base coupe equipped with RPO ZR-1 and no other options cost $65,455, which was a whopping $6,460

increase, while a Callaway conversion added $5,264 for a total of $64,138.

## 1992 Changes

After an interior makeover in 1990, followed by an exterior facelift in 1991, the '92 Corvette's appearance remained unchanged except for rectangular exhaust outlets and the addition of front fender badges on ZR-1s. Also new were Goodyear GS-C tires with an asymmetrical version of their directional Gatorback tread pattern that, like the original Gatorbacks, were a one-year Corvette exclusive. Another introductory one-year exclusive was the LT1 base engine, which replaced the L98 after 7 years of production and represented the first architectural redesign of the 36-year-old small-block Chevy V-8. The original LT1 of 1970 through 1972 was the high-water mark of carbureted small-block performance, and when this famous RPO was resurrected, it was the first Corvette engine to be rated at 300 or more net horsepower since 1971.

The engine's fuel and ignition systems also received attention, with new high-pressure fuel rails feeding Rochester Multech fuel injectors that featured a more precise spray pattern with complete digital control. The new ignition system was also digitally controlled, as the distributor moved from behind the intake plenum to a new die-cast aluminum timing cover, where it was driven by a shaft from the cam sprocket. A sensor reading a stainless-steel shutter wheel transmitted 360 pulses of light per engine revolution to the engine management computer, making this optical distributor the most precise to date and improving power and fuel mileage. These revisions were so extensive that the LT1 was designated the "Generation II" small-block V-8, and with 300 hp at 5,000 rpm and 330 ft/lb of torque at 4,000 rpm, it produced 20 percent more power than the L98 while improving fuel mileage.

The new LT1 engine was filled at the factory with Mobil 1 synthetic oil, and Chevrolet recommended that owners continue using the synthetic, which eliminated the need for oil cooler. Electronic traction control was another technological innovation added to the 1992 Corvette's list of standard equipment; it was developed by Bosch as part of the anti-lock braking system (ABS). While ABS prevents tire lock-up during braking, traction control keeps the rear tires from being overwhelmed during acceleration, limiting wheel spin with a combination of applying the rear brakes, retarding the ignition timing, and closing the throttle. Traction control was actually a misnomer; the system was called acceleration slip regulation, and it required a much larger computer, along with a complete redesign of the ABS system.

## One Million Corvettes

After two seasons of Corvette domination, the SCCA started allowing liberal modifications to the slower GT-class cars eligible for their World Challenge racing series while handicapping the faster ones. It didn't take much of a shift in the balance of power for the second-generation Nissan 300 ZXs to start winning races; Eliot Forbes Robinson drove one to the 1992 World Challenge. With a wider range of cars (including four-door sport sedans invited to compete with sports and GT cars in professional production-based road racing), Corvettes were put at an increasing disadvantage. Doug Robinson continued to coordinate the efforts of the Corvette Engineering Group to help them keep up, but at times America's sports car became uncompetitive.

Two notable events in Corvette history took place during 1992: the millionth Corvette (a white

ZR-1s didn't reach competition during 1990, but racer Tommy Morrison collaborated with Corvette Engineering in making an attempt on the FIA 24 Hour World Endurance Speed Record at Fort Stockton, Texas, in March. At Chevrolet's request, Morrison also built the white L98-powered Corvette in the photo with both cars set up for showroom stock endurance racing; it set six FIA speed records followed by the ZR-1 going for the big one. *GM Media Archive*

approach that would never threaten Corvette sales, even as it stole magazine publicity on and off the racetracks of the world.

Viper production stabilized at about 1,500 to 1,800 cars per year after some concessions made in response to owner feedback. Power windows replaced side curtains, and air conditioning improved the car's livability. The 1992 C4 Corvette sales slipped from the previous year to a low point of 20,479, which was equal to more than 12 years of Viper production. Despite being the first Corvette with a base price over $40,000, the popularity of the 1992 convertible increased even though overall sales were down and the bottom fell out of demand for the ZR-1 package.

For a second year, the Corvette's exterior appearance remained unchanged, with only a subtle switch from a powder-coat finish to a machine finish of the aluminum wheels. There was also a new base wheel and tire package: 8.5-inch-wide front wheels mounted P255/45ZR-17 tires while the rear rims remained 9.5 inches wide but mounted P285/40ZR-17 tires on 9.5-inch-wide wheels. The ZR-1 special performance package also kept its 275mm-wide front and 315mm-wide rear tires. Equipped with the RPO Z25 40th anniversary package, only the 6,749 1993s with their distinctive ruby red metallic paint jobs and wheel centers stood out as something new.

The base LT1 engine was quieter in 1993, with the original one-piece exhaust manifold heat shields replaced by self-damping two-layer stampings and the addition of thermoset resin rocker arm covers. The engines were still rated at 300 hp, but continued camshaft development yielded an additional 10 ft/lb torque for a total of 340 at 3,600 rpm. The 4-cam 32-valve LT5 also received some attention with refined ports and valves, raising its output up from 375 hp to 405 hp and exceeding its original goal by 5.

With only material and technical support from Chevrolet, the red ZR-1 was emblazoned with logos from Tommy Morrison's regular sponsor, Mobil 1, and several of the ZR-1's suppliers to pay the bills. The existing FIA record was an average speed of 161.180 mph for 24 hours, and the Morrison ZR-1 lapped Firestone's 7.7-mile oval test track at a 175.885 mph average for a new record. *GM Media Archive*

convertible) rolled off the Bowling Green assembly lines on July 2. Engineering Director Dave McLellan officially retired on August 31, but he agreed to stay on until the end of the year for an orderly transition to his yet-to-be-named successor. There were two logical candidates in the Corvette group—John Heinricy and Earl Werner—but upper management chose Dave Hill from Cadillac, who had been chief engineer of the two-seater Allante. McLellan was only the second Corvette engineering director in its 39-year history, and he held the position for 17 years, by far the longest of any in his position. His predecessor, Zora Duntov, held the official title for 9 years.

## Corvette Versus Viper

After four decades as America's only sports car, the Corvette met its domestic rival in 1992 from Dodge. Named the Viper, it was Dodge's nod to Cobra, the legendary Ford V-8-powered, British-built roadster from the 1960s. Dodge's snake was a back-to-basics sports car, with minimal electronics and creature comforts, featuring the biggest engine they could devise from the MOPAR parts bin. It was an all-aluminum version of Dodge's 8.0-liter V-10 truck engine rated at 400 hp, which made the Viper more than a match for the ZR-1 Corvette. Like Ford's Cobra, though, the sales appeal of this hard-edged car was limited. Chrysler's president, Bob Lutz, characterized Dodge's Viper as "yestertech," a fun

The only new-for-1993 standard feature was the passive keyless entry (PKE) system with a key fob transmitter that automatically locked or unlocked the doors as the fob moved into or out of range of the receiver. This bit of techno gadgetry and the other minor updates probably didn't have much to do with the sales increase, but sales did grow from the low point of the previous year to 21,590. Despite this overall gain, convertibles continued to lose ground; 183 fewer buyers chose droptops, and ZR-1 sales also dropped to a miniscule 448. The retail price of RPO ZR-1 remained unchanged at $31,683 for the third year, but with the cost of a base coupe rising by $960 to $34,595, the out-the-door price of the special performance coupe rose by the same amount.

## Fifth Generation

The year 1994 marked the 4th generation and Corvette's 10th model year, but because the cars actually went on sale in March 1983, it was their 11th year of production, and a 5th generation was in the works. No distinguishing exterior features set the '94 Corvettes apart from the previous year, but 2 new colors became available—admiral blue and copper metallic—which were limited to 116 cars. On the other hand, 1994 ZR-1s' special performance package, with distinctively styled wheels with 5 tapered spokes that were only available as part of the special performance package, gave them a stronger identity. An important feature of the coming 5th generation was developed by Goodyear and introduced as an option in 1994—extended mobility tires that could travel some distance without air. They became standard equipment in 1997.

Despite only having three remaining years of production, numerous changes and upgrades were made to the 1994 interior, including the addition of a passenger's side air bag in place of the glove compartment. A new two-spoke steering wheel was designed around an air bag compartment, and new instrument graphics changed from white to tangerine at night. Leather upholstery was included with the base seats while cloth was no longer available, and all seats (including the optional sport seats) were restyled with less prominent bolsters, improving entry and exit. Door trim panels also had a new look, and the driver's power window had an express "down feature" while convertibles got a ridged glass rear window that included a defogger grid.

A powertrain control module replaced the ECM to manage a new electronic version of the four-speed automatic transmission, the 4L60E, along with the LT1 engine. This transmission offered seamless gear changes with more precise shift points and included

The 1991 Corvettes had a new face with extended parking, cornering, and fog lights wrapping around larger radius front corners, and three horizontal front fender vents replacing the two vertical louvers. ZR-1s still had flared doors and wider rear fenders but lost their most distinctive styling clues with the convex rear fascia and squared-off taillights now shared with the base Corvettes.
*GM Media Archive*

a "safety interlock" that required applying the brakes to shift out of park. The LT1 was still rated at 300 hp, even though it also received some significant upgrades that improved throttle response, with a smoother idle and lower exhaust emissions. These gains resulted from a new sequential port fuel injection system that sprayed precise amounts of fuel, determined by a mass airflow sensor into the individual ports, timed to match the high energy ignitions firing order.

The Callaway twin-turbo conversion disappeared from the Corvette's option list in 1992 with the introduction of the LT1 engine, ending Callaway's years as a Chevrolet supplier, but not their association with the Corvette. In 1994, following up the twin-turbo now as an aftermarket tuner, Callaway's successor was normally aspirated, relying on internal modifications instead of force-feeding to produce a similar increase in horsepower. These engines were called supernatural, and they were carefully engineered to offer increased performance while complying with emissions standards and maintaining extended durability for road use. Supernatural versions of both the pushrod LT1 and double overhead cam LT5 were initially rated at 400 and 475 hp, respectively, and the LT1 eventually reached 450 hp.

Reeves Callaway took a step towards producing his own unique Corvette-based sports car with the 1992 introduction of the partially rebodied Callaway C6, which was based on a highly modified Corvette chassis. From the front, a C6 resembled a late 1960s Ferrari 275 GTB4, but it was still a Corvette, and in 1994, it became the first one to be entered in the 24 Hours of Le Mans in 18 years. Reeves had the car prepared for GT1 class racing at his facility in Germany where European orders for his products were filled. Their principal rival at the Circuit de la Sarthe, Porsche, was a neighbor. The Callaway C6R proved to be very competitive. Driven by Boris Said, Michel Maisonneuve, and Frank Jelinski, the car ran well until about halfway through the race when it was disqualified for receiving improper assistance on the course.

Corvette sales continued to increase for a third year in a row, reaching 23,330 in 1994. In 1990, the 3,049 ZR-1-equipped Corvette coupes that were sold exceeded expectations, but after sales fell to 502 in 1992, the expensive option was phased out and availability was limited to 448 cars a year. The ZR-1's retail price was lowered by $425 after it had leveled off at $31,258 for the past three years, bringing it down to $31,258, but this was more than offset by a $2,086 increase in the base price of a coupe. This increased the retail price of a stripper ZR-1 coupe without any other options to $67,443, but the convertible wasn't that far behind—its base price was $42,960.

After being kicked out of the Escort Series for overachieving, and with the Corvette Challenge ending in 1989, a lot of Corvette teams found their way into the SCCA World Challenge. With sponsorship from major auto industry supplier, Dieline, Corvette tuner Doug Rippie's new 1991 was the car to beat for most of the season, driven by Bill Cooper. *GM Media Archive*

After the Corvette's exterior styling was freshened up for the 1991 model year, its appearance remained unchanged until 1995 when the front fender side vents were redesigned. These vents evolved from a pair of vertical louvers in 1990 to four horizontal slots, which were integrated into a single recess divided by four short strakes behind a raised forward lip. After a single year, copper metallic paint disappeared from the option list and a new color, dark purple metallic, became available. The 527 dark purple convertibles were built as RPO ZAZ Indy 500 Pace Car replicas. This was the third time a Corvette had been chosen for this honor, and the 1995 pace cars stood out with ZR-1 style five-spoke wheels and a distinctive paint job—white below the perimeter molding with red graphics.

## Preparing for the C5

After three years as Corvette's engineering director, Hill was also named its vehicle line executive (VLE) in 1995, making him the first VLE to also be chief engineer. Even though the all-new fifth-generation Corvette was nearing production, Hill continued to refine the C4, adding numerous Velcro straps to reduce squeaks and rattles, along with a more rigid radio mount. The LT1 engine also received some refinements, with redesigned connecting rods forged from powdered metal introduced late in 1994 and fuel injectors that could deal with bio fuel blends and didn't dribble after shutdown. The 4.0-liter 6OE four-speed automatic transmission was equipped with improved clutches for smoother shifting, aided by a lighter but stronger torque converter.

The final year for RPO ZR-1 was 1995, and an event to commemorate the completion of the last car equipped with this option was held in May at the National Corvette Museum in Bowling Green, Kentucky. The museum is located directly across Interstate 65 from the Corvette assembly plant, and even though it had no direct ties to GM, many Chevrolet luminaries—from Chevrolet's general manager Jim Perkins to Zora Duntov—attended. The ultra-expensive 4-cam LT5 engine that was the heart of the ZR-1 had been doomed to extinction since 1993 when its production was wrapped up at Mercury Marine in November. All LT5 tooling belonging to GM was removed from the Stillwater, Oklahoma, plant, while they continued to do internal warranty work on LT5 engines until the end of the year.

Up to the optional LT5, Corvettes had always been powered by derivatives of regular passenger car engines, which was still true of the base LT1 V-8. The LT5's double overhead cam heads made it wider

Tommy Morrison built a pair of used ZR-1s into IMSA GT cars with lightweight carbon fiber bodies and tubular space frames fabricated at Chuck Mallet's shop in Brea, Ohio. Competing against dedicated racing cars at Daytona in February of 1991, the No. 92 finished a rain soaked 24-hour race 12th overall and 4th in IMSA's GTO class, while the team's No. 91 came in 21st overall delayed by an off-road excursion.
*GM Media Archive*

The 1992 Corvettes had a new base engine designated LT1 after the famous 1970 to 1972 solid-lifter 350, which produced 300 net hp thanks to the small-block V-8's first architectural redesign since its inception. The second-generation small block was the subject for the author's first engine illustration for Chevrolet, and at their request, it's shown on a simulated "Blue Print" of the Corvette's first V-8, the 1955 265. *GM Media Archive*

and taller than the pushrod LT1, and the GEN III small-block V-8 under development was still more compact, even though it shared the same 350ci displacement. When it was decided to design the fifth-generation Corvette around the GEN III engine, the ZR-1 option was phased out, along with the LT5 after six model years. This program remains unique in Corvette history, and while it was never quite the fastest production car in the world, it offered the most bang for the buck, even though they were very big bucks.

Goodyear's extended mobility tires (EMTs) were part of the plan for the next Corvette platform, and offering them as an option was both a realistic test and accustomed buyers to the idea. These "run flats" stiff sidewalls could support the car without air pressure, but only for about 50 miles at speeds under 55 miles per hour, and the RPO VJ6 low tire-pressure warning system was required as well. Corvettes equipped with EMTs no longer needed a

spare, and starting in 1995, it was possible to delete it with RPO N84 and receive a $100 credit. Even this close to the end of C4 production, the list of standard equipment was still growing, with the addition of the Z07 and ZR-1's big brake package, along with other refinements.

## The World Stage

For the 1995 IMSA season, Morrison's team was back with several production-based Corvette racing cars, including a pair of ZR-1s competing for the last year with backing from Chevrolet. These cars' uniframes were fabricated from special lightweight stampings that, wrapped in carbon fiber bodywork, reduced their weight to 2,375 pounds despite the heavy LT5 engine, making them reasonably competitive. The Morrison team's No. 96 Corvette, driven by Don Knowles, Hayner, and Heinricy, finished 10th overall and 1st in GTS at the 24 Hours of Daytona in February. Rippie also built a production-based

endurance racing ZR-1, but his objective was much higher: the Holy Grail of endurance racing—the 24 Hours of Le Mans in June.

Among their other accomplishments, Doug Rippe Motorsports won the 1989 Corvette World Challenge Championship, but the ZR-1 was built for a customer who wanted to race at Le Mans, and that was a stretch. Even though the promised financial support never materialized, Rippe believed Corvettes should be racing on the world stage and moved forward with another Corvette tuner and friend, Jim Van Dorn, as team manager. The effort was underfinanced and underprepared, but not underpowered with a pair of 600-hp LT5s stroked to 385ci: one for the lengthy day and night practice sessions and the other for the race. The practice engine succumbed to overheating before James Mero, Chris Dougall, and John Paul Jr. could get enough track time, so the race engine had to be installed early, ominously hot.

The race started badly for ZR-1 Corvette Team USA, with their second engine only lasting 3 ½ laps before the car limped back to the pits with terminal overheating. It was possible to continue in the 24-hour marathon if the original crank and block stayed

in place, and Van Dorn mounted a desperate effort to get the ZR-1 back out on the track. Powered by an LT5 assembled from both engines' best surviving parts, the car reentered the race after a 13-hour, 50-minute pit stop. It performed reasonably well, lasting until about noon, when it was parked for good. After this out-of-pocket adventure, Rippe was able to arrange a meeting with the Corvette team at Chevrolet, where he and Van Dorn made a half-hour presentation that turned into a two-hour discussion. Their point was that if Corvettes were going to be called world class, Chevrolet should be racing them, and they proposed a program to start doing just that.

A factory Corvette joined the starting field at the 1995 Le Mans for the second year in a row, but it was a C6R entered by the Callaway factory in Germany and its performance in the 1994 race attracted a customer: the Agusta Racing Team from La Provence, South Africa. The Agusta team entered two C6Rs as Nos. 75 and 76, with the No. 75 car competing in several other FIA endurance races that season. Driven by Richard Agusta, Robin Donovan, and Eugene O'Brien, they finished 11th overall and 3rd in GT2 at Le Mans, while the team's No. 76, with Patrick Bourdais, Almo Coppelli, and Thorkild

Two notable events in Corvette history took place during 1992, with the one millionth Corvette, a white convertible, rolling off the Bowling Green assembly line on July 2, and engineering director, Dave McLellan, retiring on August 31. This was Dave's official retirement date because it was the last day in his early retirement window, but he agreed to stay on until the end of the year for an orderly transition to his yet to be named successor.
*GM Media Archive*

After four decades as America's only sports car, the Corvette had a domestic rival in 1992 from Dodge, named the Viper as a pseudonym for Cobra, the British American hybrid of the 1960s. The Viper was a back-to-basics sports car like the Cobra with minimal electronics and creature comforts, powered by the biggest engine that could be devised from the corporate parts bin. *David Kimble*

Dodge did the second-generation Cobra's cast-iron 7-liter Ford V-8 one better with an aluminum version of their 8-liter V-10 truck engine initially rated at 400 hp. This "Monster Motor" was based on the Chrysler Corporation's 360ci V-8, with an additional pair of cylinders and a 72-degree crankshaft breathing through a twin throttle body cross ram intake manifold. *Chrysler Corporation*

Thyrring behind the wheel, crashed out on Lap 82. The Callaway entry No. 73 came close to a class win, finishing 11th overall and 2nd in GT2, driven by Johnny Unser, Enrico Betaggia, and Frank Bertaggia. Porsche took the victory.

Fourth-generation Corvette sales fluctuated in the 1990s. Sales fell in 1991, rebounded in 1993, and started falling again in 1995. For the third and last year of its six-year production run, 448 ZR-1s closed out the Corvette's most expensive option. Base retail prices climbed steadily during the decade; the coupe cost an additional $600 for a total of $36,785, while $750 was added to the convertible, bringing it up to

Below: Tommy Morrison continued bucking the odds, competing with production-ased Corvettes against ground-up racing cars in IMSA's GTO class, with backing from Corvette Engineering to further develop the C4 chassis. His No. 93 was in its third year of racing at Watkins Glen in 1993, with Mobil 1 remaining the primary sponsor for his racing ventures. *Dr. Peter Gimenez*

There was a factory Corvette in the 1995 starting field at Le Mans for the second year in a row, but it was a C6R entered by the Callaway factory in Germany, and their performance in the 1994 race attracted a customer. This was the Agusta Racing Team from La Provence, South Africa, and they had a pair of red C6Rs numbered 75 and 76, with the No. 75 driven by Richard Agusta, Robin Donovan, and Eugene O'Brien finishing 11th overall, 3rd in GT. *Dr. Peter Gimenez*

RPO LT4 was part of the Grand Sport package along with the MN6 six-speed manual transmission, but this combination was also available in base Corvettes in place of their standard LT1, equipped with the four-speed automatic transmission. The LT4 had a distinctive underhood appearance, with its aluminum intake manifold painted red and a higher 10.8:1 compression ratio, along with a more aggressive cam; crane roller rocker arms increased output from 300 to 330 hp. *General Motors*

$43,665 in 1995. After leveling off at $31,683 in 1991, the ZR-1 package was marked down to $31,258 for 1994 and 1995, but with the price increases of the base coupes, they still cost a minimum of $68,043 for the last king of the hills.

## Road to Retirement

The year 1996 was the thirteenth model year and fourteenth year of production for the fourth-generation Corvette; it was also the aging platform's last year of production before its long overdue replacement. With excitement and expectations building over the upcoming fifth-generation Corvette, a number of new options were available for the outgoing platform's final year—including a hopped-up engine: RPO LT4. The LT4 featured freer flowing cylinder heads with an increased compression ratio and a more aggressive camshaft and crane roller rocker arms. This made for a freer revving engine, and the red line moved from the

LT1's 5,700 to 6,300 rpm, requiring LT4-powered cars to replace the base 6,000 gauges with equipped with 8,000 rpm tachometers. The LT1's only upgrade was a new throttle body it shared with the LT4. RPO LT4 didn't raise the horsepower, which was still rated at 330 hp.

The LT4's aluminum intake manifold was painted red and along with a Grand Sport logotype on top of the throttle body, also in red, gave the optional engine a distinctive underhood appearance. The Grand Sport package RPO Z16 included the LT4, but this engine was available with any combination of options, and the logotype stayed regardless. The only restriction was that the LT4 could only be ordered with the RPO MN6 six-speed manual transmission while the LT1 engine had to be paired with the four-speed automatic. This was the first time the fabled Grand Sport name from 1963 was given to a production Corvette, and availability was limited to 1,000 cars.

The 1996 version was primarily an appearance package, with a broad arctic white centerline stripe running from end to end over admiral blue that was accented by three torch-red hash marks over the left front wheel well. Grand Sport coupes rode on the ZR-1's P275/40 ZR-17 front and P315/35ZR-17 rear tires, while the more flexible convertibles were equipped with P255/45ZR-17 front and P285/40ZR-17 rear ties. Both the coupe and convertible came with five-spoke ZR-1 style wheels painted black, and interior color choices were limited to black or a black and red combination. These special cars had their own serial number sequences. Even with add-on fender flares instead of the ZR-1's wide rear bodywork, at $3,250, RPO Z16 was by far the 1996 Corvette's most expensive option; ordered with a convertible, it did reduce the option's price to $2,880.

A collector's edition, available as RPO Z15, marked the fourth-generation Corvette's last year. It included again the ZR-1 style 5-stroke wheels, but these were painted silver. All of these cars were on the P255/45ZR-17 front and P285/40ZR-17 rear tires and came in Sebring silver with either black, red, or gray interiors that included perforated leather sport seats with "collector edition" embroidery. At $1,250, this appearance package was relatively affordable, compared to the $3,250 Grand Sport package, and it attracted 5,412 buyers; more than 4,000 chose the coupe.

After being replaced by the RPO Z07 adjustable suspension package in 1991, the famous Z51 performance handling package was back on the option list, taking the Z07's place for 1996. As before, it featured stiffer suspension bushings, anti-roll bars, springs with damping by Bilstein shocks, and P275/40ZR-17 tires (only available with the coupe). The other suspension option, FX3, had been available since 1989, and was both high-tech and expensive;

it boasted electronically controlled shock absorbers that could be set for three levels of firmness. RPO F45 selective real-time damping was the far more sophisticated replacement for FX3; it used data from ride height sensors and the powertrain control module to calculate the individual shock damping rate every 10 to 15 milliseconds.

As the enticing technical details of the literally all-new 1997 Corvette filled the car magazines, sales of the outgoing fourth generation remained strong, actually improving slightly over 1995. Coupe sales increased to 17,167, which more than offset the 602 decline in convertibles. Convertibles sales hit 4,369, continuing a downward trend that had started in 1993. Retail prices also continued to climb for the last year of the old platform: the base coupe rose a modest $440 to $37,225. The droptop's base price received a much larger $1,395 hike to $45,060, which with a few popular accessories, could easily exceed $50,000 once delivered to the customer.

The legendary Grand Sport name was given to a production Corvette for the first time since 1996 to fill the void left by cancellation of the ZR-1 for the C4's final year of production. There were only five tubular frame Grand Sport GT racing cars built in 1963, and while the 1996 version was an RPO, its availability was limited to 1,000 cars featuring special paint, ZR-1 rear tires, and a hopped-up engine.
*GM Media Archive*

David Kimble

**The "all new" 1997 Corvette** was the most completely overhauled new Corvette since its beginning in 1953 when the powertrain and most of the chassis was adapted from the Chevrolet's parts bin. The fifth generation not only featured a unique chassis layout with a record number of dedicated parts, but it also featured a new platform and engine in tandem. This third-generation, small-block V-8 kept a central cam pushrod valve train and the original small-block's 4.40-inch cylinder bore centers but still managed to be lighter and more compact. All of its major castings were aluminum, including the cylinder block.

GM's small-block V-8 required a complete redesign to reach the LT5's 405 hp and beyond. The redesign included a stronger bottom end with 4-bolt main bearing caps cross-bolted through deep side skirts. The new cylinder heads had freer flowing ports that were equally spaced, abandoning the book-fold arrangement that paired the intakes at the ends and placed the middle exhaust ports together in the center. This asymmetry, along with the previous V-8's 90-degree firing order, led to a slight imbalance that, with the new design's revised firing order, was smoothed out. It also allowed more even air distribution through a nylon six-plastic intake manifold that saved weight and stayed cooler, contributing to an initial power output of 345 hp at 5,600 rpm, with a 6,000 rpm red line.

Designated LS1, the new V-8 was 44 pounds lighter than the LT1 and had 8 individual ignition coils flanking its plastic intake manifold, giving it a distinctive appearance. The LS1 no longer had a distributor, and the coils, like the fuel injectors, were digitally controlled by the engine management computer, with the firing order changed from 1-8-4-3-6-5-7-2 to 1-8-7-2-6-5-4-3. The LS1's separate block valley cover under the intake manifolds included a pair of knock sensors that were part of an expended digital controls package. Throttle by wire used a stepping motor to move the single throttle plate in response to the driver's right foot, with the pedal hooked to a rheostat.

Decorative engine covers became popular on most manufacturers' premium cars in the early 1990s, and Corvettes were no exception, producing engine covers alongside the LT1 V-8 in 1992. Many engines were completely shrouded in stylized plastic, but in keeping with the Corvette's sporting nature, its black plastic covers only concealed the fuel rails

and sides of the intake manifold plenum. The LS1 engine covers were larger, extending from the fuel rails to the lower edge of the ignition coils, leaving only the bottom of the rocker arm covers exposed. The fifth-generation Corvette bodies saved weight and made insurance companies happy by returning to fixed front fenders, and the LS1 was surrounded by complementary styled plastic moldings.

The new driveline was unlike any previous Corvette. It featured a rear-mounted transaxle, which drove the back wheels through splined half shafts, and CV joints at both ends replaced the earlier U-joints. Power reached the back of the car through a driveshaft running in an 8-inch diameter torque tube that rigidly mounted the engine to the transaxle through torque bells at both ends. Dave McLellan wanted a transaxle for the C4, but found that impossible because no suitable, adaptable high-volume components were available from GM's parts bin. A manual transmission wouldn't have been a problem, but automatics made up about 75 percent of Corvette sales, and GM's hydramatic

Opposite page: The "all new" 1997 Corvette was the most completely all-new Corvette ever, with almost nothing from the previous generation carrying over to its unique chassis and powertrain. Going all the way back to the plastic sports car's introduction in 1953, Corvettes had always been based on high-volume components, but for this go around, the high-volume cars and trucks would borrow components from it. *General Motors*

The third-generation small-block V-8, the LS1, stayed with the 1955 Chevy V-8's 4.40-inch cylinder bore centers and central cam location, with a pushrod valve train, but was lighter and more compact. Every other aspect of the third-generation small-block was entirely new, from its aluminum major castings to a new firing order, which changed from 1-8-4-3-6-5-7-2 to a smoother 1-8-7-2-6-5-4-3. *GM Media Archive*

LS1s had rock-solid bottom ends with massive steel main bearing caps held in place by four bolts through the bottom and a pair of cross bolts through the aluminum block's deep side skirts. The new aluminum heads departed from the earlier book fold port arrangement, with all of the valves at the same ends of the combustion chambers allowing equal length ports, and they were topped by a plastic intake manifold. *General Motors*

division didn't have a suitable housing in the works at that time.

Despite its success, the Corvette Engineering Group had never been very happy with the C4's primary structure, which was compromised by having to remove the roof's reinforcing T-bar. They wanted to at least bring the new uniframe up to the rigidity of competing vehicles, so they evaluated nine other relevant cars for noise and vibration-related characteristics. Their first torsional frequency ranged from 17 hz for European luxury cars to 11 hz for the American sports category. The ZR-1, without its roof panel, measured 13 hz. Their goal for the new structure was for it to be both lighter and more ridged—at least equaling the best European sports cars—and for it to be as good a convertible as it was a coupe.

The new uniframe was based on a sheet metal central backbone tunnel, made possible by moving the transmission to the rear of the car, flanked by hydroformed steel side rails. Water pressure was used to reshape prebent round seamless tubing into a rectangular cross section in a steel mold cavity, which was an automotive industry first. Early C5 coupes built on these uniframes tested at an unprecedented 23 hz during development, making them the most rigid removable top vehicles of the time. This layout increased foot room and allowed easier entry and exit, as the driver and passenger no longer had to step over the top of the frame rails.

The C5 didn't come with a spare tire, but instead relied on Goodyear's extended mobility tires (EMTs), which had been an option since 1994 and were now

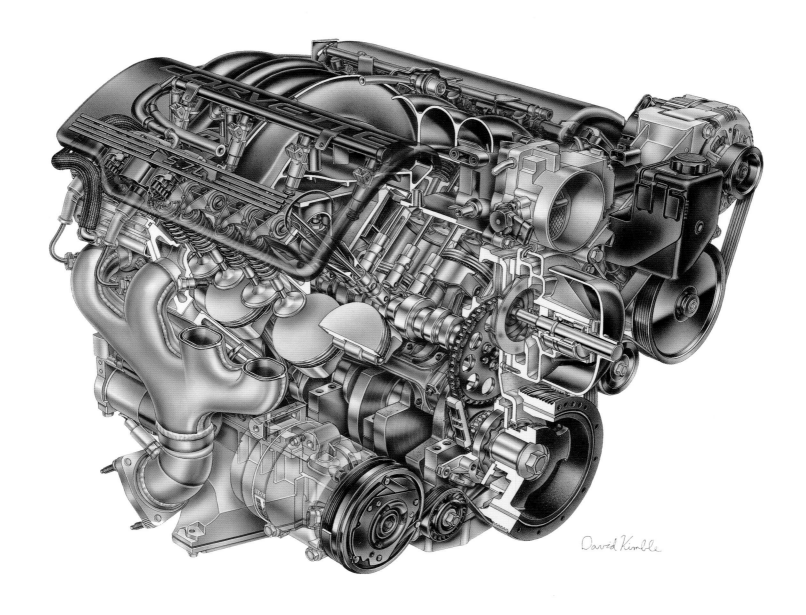

standard equipment along with the low tire pressure warning system. The new five-spoke aluminum wheels featured different front and rear rim widths as well as different diameters. The fifth-generation suspension was similar at both ends of the car, with transverse fiberglass leaf springs, tubular shock absorbers, and anti-roll all attaching to the lower control arms. Upper A-arms were added to the rear suspension and stub axles replaced the front spindles, allowing left- and right-hand versions of the same uprights to be used at all four corners.

The chassis was as innovative as it was unique; the engine, torque tube, and transaxle assembly was mounted on cast-aluminum subframes at both ends, which also mounted the lower suspension components. These "cradles" were in turn attached to the underside of the hydroformed steel frame rails by through-bolts with shock absorbers and upper control arms mounted to the rails' sides. The driveline was equally unique—the torque tubes' end bells were mounted to the engine, which was empty except for the flex plate and the driveshaft on cars

equipped with automatic transmissions. The torque converter was at the back of the driveshaft in the transaxles, while the flywheel and clutch on manual transmission cars stayed at the front with the engine.

It was the transaxle that made this unique arrangement possible, and it was the tooling cost of a special housing for the automatic transmission that had put this approach out of reach for the C4. Luckily, Hydra-matic was engineering a new case with a bolt-on converter housing that would also work on the Corvette, and GM's full-size truck group was covering most of the cost. With this new housing assembled into a transaxle, the electronically controlled four-speed automatic was the only part of the driveline to carry over. Borg-Warner's T-6 replaced the ZF six-speed manual transmission.

## New Style

John Cafaro's Chevy Studio 3 started sketching ideas for the fifth-generation Corvette's styling in 1988, surviving an undisclosed shootout orchestrated by GM's Vice President of Design Chuck Jordon

Decorative engine covers appeared on most premium cars in the early 1990s and were introduced under the Corvette's hood in 1992 on the LT1 engine only concealing the fuel rails and the sides of the intake manifold. The LS1's covers were larger, extending from the fuel rails to the lower edge of the ignition coils, and surrounded by highly styled plastic moldings between the C5's fixed front fenders. *GM Media Archive*

The new driveline was unlike any previous Corvette's, with a rear-mounted transaxle driving the back wheels through sliding spline half shafts and with CV joints at both ends replacing the earlier V-joints. Power reached the transaxle through a rigid driveshaft running in an 8-inch-diameter aluminum torque tube that mounted the engine to the transmission through torque belles at both ends. *General Motors*

The new uniframe was a backbone structure based on a sheet steel central tunnel made possible by moving the transmission out of the way to the rear, combined with one-piece hydroformed frame rails. These rails were an industry first with prebent round seamless tubing reshaped into a rectangular cross-section by water pressure in a steel mold. The earlier coupe uniframes tested at 23 hz, making them the most rigid removable top structure up to that time. *General Motors*

with two other design staff studios. This was typical
of "the Chrome Cobra's" management style, and
even though Jordon retired before the C5 reached
production, his influence could still be seen. The new
plastic bodywork that wrapped around the fifth-
generation's innovative chassis featured the rounded
look of the 1990s and had a .293 coefficient of drag,
the lowest of any regular production car at that time.
The signature concealed headlights were back but
now popped up instead of rotating into view, and the
four round taillights in pairs also carried over, except
they were stretched into horizontal ovals.

In 1997, complete analog gauges returned after
a 15-year absence, with a large round speedometer
overlapping an equally sized tachometer and two
pairs of secondary gauges off to the sides. The only
remaining digital displays appeared on a small
LCD screen located directly above the steering
column called the Driver's Information Center,
where a variety of readouts could be selected. The
Lear Corporation continued to supply both the
base optional sport seats, which, like the rest of the
interior, were completely redesigned, making the C5
as new inside as it was out.

The F45 electronic real time damping suspension
option carried over to the C5, along with the Z51
performance handling package, making this platform
the most race worthy Corvette ever. In the fall of
1996, as the new Corvette approached its sales
debut, the time at Chevrolet was right to tap into this
potential with the first full factory Corvette racing
program since 1957. Herb Fishel's Chevrolet Race
Shop had become GM Motorsports by this time,
and his company managed this program while also
handling the racing activities of the corporation's
other divisions. It had been 40 years since Chevrolet
had rushed the Corvette SS sports racing car into
competition at Sebring, and the results had been
disastrous. Chevrolet vowed to not make the same
mistake twice.

## A New Plan for Old Races

This time, Chevrolet followed a plan devised by Doug
Fehan and supported by Herb Fishel. It involved two
years of development before entering a single race
with the new Corvette. It was also part of the plan
to not offer any technical support for independent
efforts to compete with the fifth-generation Corvettes
until everything was in place to assure they would
be competitive. Corporate money was going to be

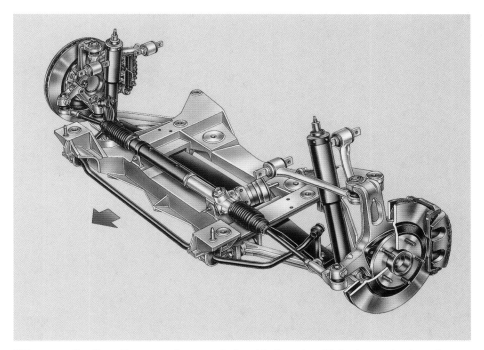

Fifth-generation Corvette suspension was similar at both ends, with the lower aluminum A-arms
mounted to cast-aluminum subframes called cradles. The monoleaf fiberglass springs and
anti-roll bars were attached to the undersides with the rack-and-pinion steering and engine
mounted to the top of the front cradle. *General Motors*

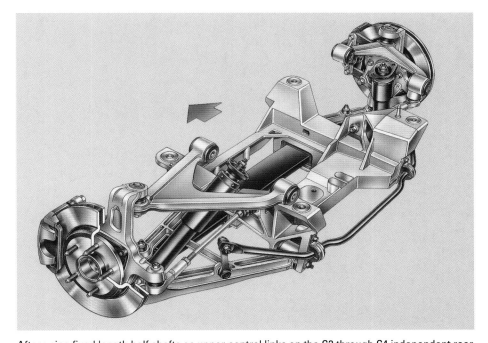

After using fixed length half shafts as upper control links on the C2 through C4 independent rear
suspension, the fifth generation featured upper rear A-arms. Left and right versions of the same
aluminum uprights with stub axles replacing fixed front spindles used at all four corners, with
the transaxles mounted to the rear cradle. *General Motors*

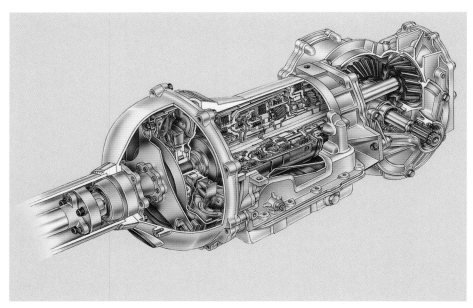

It was the transaxle that made the C5's unique chassis layout possible, and it was the tooling cost of a special case for the automatic transmission, which was by far the most popular, that kept a transaxle out of the C4. By a coincidence of fate, the truck group was tooling a new case for the four-speed automatic while the C5 was being designed that could be assembled into a transaxle covering most of the cost. *General Motors*

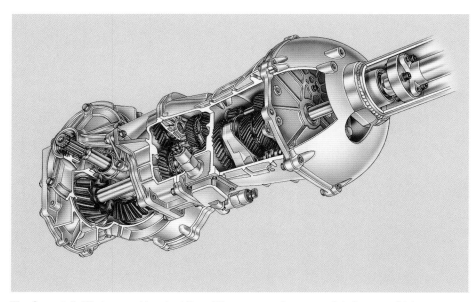

The Corvette's ZF six-speed inspired Borg Warner to produce one of their own, which was introduced in the Dodge Viper and picked up by GM in 1993 for the Camaro and Firebird, followed by the C5 Corvette in 97. Borg Warner's T-6 took the place of ZF's six-speed manual transmission, sandwiched between a torque bell and the same Getrag rear axle used with automatic-equipped C5 Corvettes. *General Motors*

spent on a secret racing program over an extended period of time. This method differed dramatically from the way GM had developed its racers in the past, and with a go-ahead from Chevrolet's General Manager John Middlebrook, it became the longest-lived and most successful racing program in the corporation's history.

The fourth-generation Corvettes had dominated showroom stock racing, campaigned by independent teams with technical support from Corvette Engineering, but the objectives of the fifth-generation program were far more ambitious. Chevrolet wanted the new Corvette to compete at the highest level of production-based international endurance racing, and winning the 24 Hours of Le Mans was the ultimate goal. GM Racing contracted the competition development of the new Corvette to Pratt & Miller in Wixom, Michigan, and the management of the program to Fehan. Pratt & Miller received its first C5 early in 1997 and began testing later in the year. Chris Kneifel was the first development driver.

Initial production problems kept the fifth-generation Corvettes in short supply for most of the 1997 model year; many dealers sold the few examples they acquired well above MSRP. Pressured to not repeat the 1982 delay in producing saleable fourth-generation Corvettes, the C5s weren't completely ready when they started rolling off the assembly line. Bowling Green Plant Manager Will Cooksey was an enthusiastic Corvette customer, and when he wasn't satisfied with the quality of the newest edition, he stopped production until the issues were resolved.

The C5 was the most raceable Corvette yet, and even though the cars were in short supply and fetching premium prices, Jeff Cauley turned the first model his family's dealership received into a race car. The new 1997 Corvette was shipped from Cauley Chevrolet in West Bloomfield, Michigan, to Mallett Cars in Bera, Ohio. The Mallett brothers had worked on Tommy Morrison's ZR-1s, and were doing contract work for Corvette Engineering. Employing them was the next best thing to technical support from Chevrolet, and Cauley successfully competed with the car in local events. No doubt a few other cars found their way onto racetracks, but the new Corvette wouldn't have an impact on any of the major series until Chevrolet became directly involved.

It took five months to get past the fifth-generation's initial build quality and detail development problems, limiting 1997 production to 9,752 coupes compared to 17,167 C4 coupes turned out in 1996. The new Corvette's price only increased $270 to $37,495, which remained unchanged for 1998, and with plenty of cars available, sales almost doubled.

One of the primary objectives of the fifth-generation Corvette's innovative chassis structure was to make as solid a platform for a convertible as it was for a coupe. This goal was realized in 1998 with the introduction of a fifth-generation convertible that weighed 114 pounds less than the 1996 fourth-generation droptop, with four times the torsional rigidity. None of the supplemental bracing needed by the fourth-generation's uniframe was added, and the new convertible was rock solid. It was never possible to offer the ultra-stiff Z51 suspension package with the C4 convertible, but the C5 version only gave up 10 percent of the coupe's torsional rigidity and handled it easily.

This was the first Corvette convertible since 1962 to have an opening rear deck lid, providing outside access to the trunk's 11.2cf of cargo space, more than any other drop top two-seater of the time. When it

was folded, the convertible top was concealed under a hard tonneau cover, and it was joined by a body color divider between the seat (a feature not seen since the first generation). The new tight-fitting top featured a glass rear window with a heated defroster grid, and the top was exceptionally low-drag.

In 1998, the fifth-generation Vette was chosen as the Indy 500 Pace Car and had a very distinctive paint job. The purple body and yellow accented base wheels held limited appeal, which is probably why only 1,163 packages were sold. At $5,039 with an automatic and $5,804 with a manual transmission, RPO Z4Z was an expensive option, even though it included the full list of equipment, except for mag wheels, a 12-disc CD changer, and front license plate bracket.

Corvettes were the first American production cars to be equipped with electronic driver aids. It began with anti-lock brakes in 1986, followed by traction control in 1992. In 1998, the next step was RPO JR4, an electronic safety net for adventurous drivers that could cancel out excessive under- or oversteer by individually applying the brakes. Corvette called it *active handling,* and it was the first step toward the

The new plastic bodywork that wrapped around the C5's ultra-rigid uniframe was designed in John Cafaro's Chevy Studio 3 with the rounded look of the 1990s. Its .293 coefficient of drag was the lowest to date, and the Corvette's signature concealed headlights now popped up instead of rotating into view with the two pairs of round taillights stretched into ovals.
*General Motors*

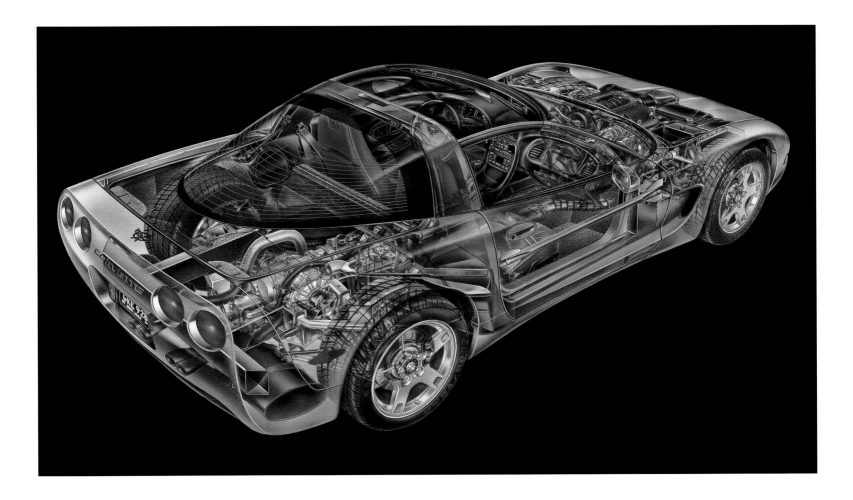

A full set of analog gauges returned to the roomier interior in the fifth generation after a 15-year absence, with digital readouts of all the car's vital signs still available through the driver's information center. A large speedometer and tachometer over the steering column were flanked by the secondary gauges, with illumination through "black" lighting and a small LCD screen below the instruments displaying digital information.
*GM Media Archive*

advanced stability control systems of the next decade. Even the most skilled drivers found JL4 helpful in learning unfamiliar twisty roads and new tracks, and they were able to switch the system off once they gained confidence.

## A Return to Glory

In November 1998, Middlebrook announced that Chevrolet was going to enter a team of Corvettes in international endurance racing. After almost two years of intensive development, Doug Fehan and everyone else involved were confident the cars and drivers (Ron Fellows and Chris Kneifel) were ready. Chevrolet hadn't raced publicly since 1957, and it was planning to compete in GTS, the Federation Internationale de l'Automobile's (FIA's) highest class for production-based cars, and the opposition was formidable. The program started cautiously, but a long-term commitment led to unparalleled success.

With initial quality problems overcome, 1998 was the first year of full production for the fifth-generation Corvette, and pent-up demand created an unprecedented surge in sales. Coupes alone almost doubled in volume to 19,235, and the new convertibles added another 11,849, for a production total of 31,084 Corvettes—the most since 1986. The

fourth-generation droptops best year was 1987 when 10,625 of them were sold, but by 1996, the last year of production, their popularity had dwindled to the point that there were only 4,396 buyers. Not only was the 1998 a better convertible, but at $44,425 it was also $635 less expensive and was the best-selling drop top since 1969.

The fifth introduction of a new generation Corvette was stretched out over three years, with a coupe in '97, followed by a convertible in '98, and finally a hardtop in 1999. The original plan was for this "notch back" to be what General Manager Jim Perkins characterized as a "Billy Bob Corvette," a featureless stripper on smaller wheels and tires, but fortunately it didn't happen. Its body style was essentially a convertible with a coupe's halo bar under a fixed fiberglass roof instead of the soft droptop, and it was the least expensive version to produce. This unprecedented third model was also lighter and stiffer than the coupe.

It was decided that an econo-Vette was not what customers were looking for. A segment of the population wanted more emphasis on performance, and they got it with the hardtop. RPO 1YY37, the base hardtop, was only available with a $825 MN6 six-speed manual transmission and a $350

Z51 performance handling package as standard equipment. The only interior color available was black, and black leather base seats and exterior color choices were limited to five of eight hues on the Corvette's palette. The hardtop's top speed was less than the coupe, but it was also 80 pounds lighter, giving it better acceleration and a cheaper price tag at $400. In short, it was a performance bargain.

An innovative driver's aid, RPO UV6 head-up display, was added to the 1999 option list, which projected digital readouts from the gauges on the windshield in the driver's line of sight. Road speed, engine rpm, oil pressure, water temperature, fuel level, and the turn indicators were normally displayed, but using a page switch, drivers could select any combination without taking their eyes off the road. The other new options were RPO T82, a power telescoping steering column, and RPO T8Z called "Twilight Sentinel," which had a light level sensor that prompted the headlight pods to automatically raise and lower, turning the lights on and off as needed.

## The Factory Racer

Chevrolet's first openly factory-backed production-based Corvette racing program debuted at the 1999 24 Hours of Daytona, with a second appearance scheduled for the 12 Hours of Sebring. Entering the untried two-car team of modified Corvettes in these high visibility events ensured garnering the most attention from the press. Initially, only these two races were scheduled, and the results would determine where (and what) the team would do from there. Fortunately, the cars showed enough promise for a go-ahead to race several American Le Mans Series (ALMS) events that season. After Daytona, which was now part of a rival racing series, Team Corvette concentrated on the American Le Mans Series, with the big French 24-hour race as its ultimate goal.

The coupe body was chosen over the hardtop for endurance racing because of its lower drag glass rear hatch and was essentially duplicated in carbon fiber for the C5R Corvettes. ALMS racing car classifications and preparation rules were compatible

For the C5R racing program, Chevrolet followed a plan worked out by Doug Fehan to ensure success by doing two years of behind the scenes testing before entering competition. Pratt & Miller was contracted to build and run the cars at the track with Chris Kneifel as the first test driver, later joined by Ron Fellows; the C5R was taking shape by 1998. *Richard Prince*

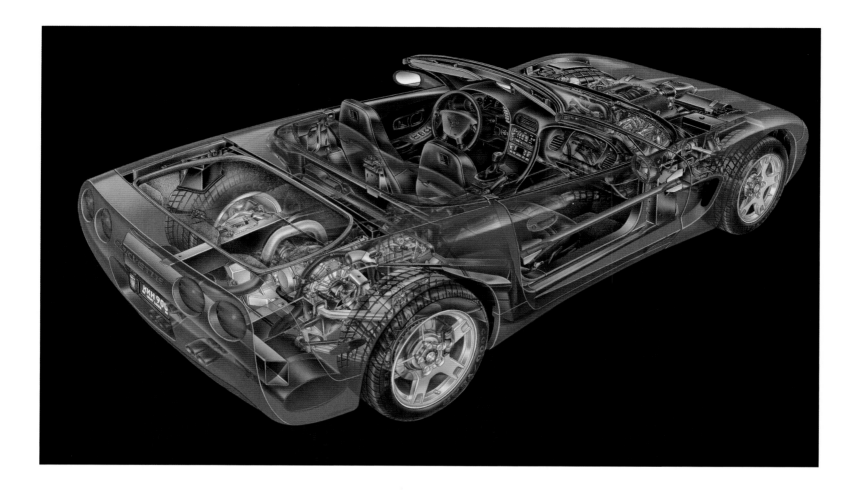

One of the primary objectives of the fifth-generation Corvette's chassis structure was for it to make as solid a convertible as it was a coupe, and that goal was realized in 1998. This was the first Corvette convertible since 1962 to have an opening rear deck lid, providing outside access to the trunk's 11.2 cubic feet of cargo space, more than any other droptop two-seater of the time. *General Motors*

with FIA requirements, so cars competing in the American series could also race in Europe, and the C5Rs were prepared to GTS class rules. This was the highest category for production-based cars, and liberal modifications were allowed to both the engine and chassis, which only had to retain a minimum of stock parts and stay with the same mechanical layout. The C5Rs greatly exceeded these requirements, utilizing far more production components than their competitors did, including the signature hydroformed steel frame rails.

The C5Rs were powered by an endurance racing version of the Corvette LS1 V-8, developed and built by Katech of Clinton Township, Michigan, working with GM Motorsports. The production cylinder block heads, water and power steering pumps, and the rack-and-pinionpinion steering were all stock components used in the racing cars' engine compartments. Even though the GTS class displacement limit was a whopping 8.0 liters, Katech started conservatively, only increasing the LS1's displacement from 5.6 to 6.0 liters for that first racing season. With these big engines, GTS cars could potentially outrun the prototypes, so the FIA

limited their output to about 600 hp, with intake air restrictors making the modest displacement increase enough to do the job.

Even though the C5R engines were production based, they didn't look it. They were topped by a Kinsler port fuel injection system with a down draft throttle body for each cylinder. The racing ignition system also changed the appearance of these engines; eight production ignition coils sat atop the rocker arm covers, were consolidated into a pair of modules, and were mounted on a shelf above the pulleys. Internally, the cylinder head ports were enlarged, while both the rotating group and valve train were made up of dedicated racing components, with the compression ratio raised from 10.5 to 12.5:1. Like most racing engines, the lubrication system was dry sump. Oil collected but was not stored in the pan; instead it was pumped through a cooler into a remote tank before returning to the engine.

Like the Corvette Grand Sports that appeared at Nassau in 1963, the C5Rs appeared pumped up on steroids when they arrived at Daytona in 1999, riding on massive 18-inch Goodyear Racing Slicks. The stock pop-up headlights were replaced by frog-eyed fairings over fixed headlights that, along with louvers on top of the front fenders and hood, added to these cars' aggressive looks. The GTP Corvettes had raced in black and silver Mr. Goodwrench colors in the 1980s, and when Goodwrench returned as the C5R's sponsor, and the cars were painted in a new version of the old color scheme.

Pratt & Miller not only built the C5Rs, but they were also contracted to race them. Doug Fehan managed the team, and their main opposition wasn't Ferrari or Porsche, but Chrysler. After introducing the Dodge Viper two-seater roadster in 1992, Chrysler brought out the GTS coupe in 1996, named after the FIA GT class it was intended to race in. They wisely hired the successful French endurance racing team Oreca not only to develop and campaign a team of factory GTS coupes, but also, once they were winning, to build customer cars for privateers. By 1999, the red Oreca Vipers had won at Daytona, Sebring, and Le Mans; they were so dominant that Porsche had given up on the GTS class, making the Vipers a formidable challenge for the Corvettes.

## More Exposure, More Pressure

With a tremendous expansion in the number of cable and satellite television channels during the 1990s, including specialized channels like Speedvision, coverage of motorsports increased exponentially. The additional exposure attracted more corporate money, changing the sport's financial climate, and a major road racing series changed hands. The International Motorsports Association (IMSA) became PSCR late in the decade and was sold to Dr. Don Pnoz

in time for him to organize the AMLS' first season in 1999, which started at Sebring in March. The C5Rs were built primarily to compete in the new ALMS, but they got a head start a month earlier at the traditional endurance racing season opener in Daytona.

In 1999, the 24 Hours of Daytona was a United States Road Racing Championship (USRRC) event where the C5Rs could be entered in the GT2 class with only minor changes, which included substituting cast iron for their carbon brake disc. The pair of silver Corvettes, with a black swept-back checked flag pattern on their sides, wouldn't be unopposed in GT2 because Chrysler's Team Oreca red Vipers had dominated the class for a couple of years. The Ron Fellows, Chris Kneifel, and John Paul Jr. Corvette No. 20 qualified on the GT2 pole, putting

This display features The Big Corvette News for 1999, with one of the C5R endurance racing team cars and a GTP Corvette from the 1980s in front of a huge photo of the new hardtop. This unprecedented third model with a fixed notch back roof capitalized on being the lightest and most rigid version of the C5 by being only available with a six-speed manual and Z51 suspension. *GM Media Archive*

The coupe body was chosen over the hardtop for endurance racing because of its lower drag glass rear hatch and was essentially duplicated in carbon fiber for the C5R Corvettes. Painted in a black and silver Goodwrench paint scheme, only its pin drive BBS wheels, splitter, side skirts, and rear wing set this C5R apart from the 1999 production coupe next to it. *GM Media Archive*

Even though the C5Rs were built to compete in the new ALMS Series that started at Sebring in March, the C5Rs made an early racing debut in February 1999 at the 24 Hours of Daytona, which was a USRRC event. The No. 2 driven by Ron Fellows, Chris Kneifel, and John Paul Jr. qualified on the GT2 pole and finished third in class despite teething problems, which led to the No. 4 team car's retirement a half distance. *Richard Prince*

them in the 16th starting position, with the Andy Pilgrim, Scott Sharp, and John Heinricy C5R starting 20th overall. In the race, both Corvettes were slowed by teething problems, and the No. 4 retired at half distance, while No. 2 hung on for an 18th overall finish and 3rd in GT2.

For the 12 Hours of Sebring in March, the Corvette's numbers were different, but their driver lineups stayed the same, except that Kelly Collins took Heinricy's place in the second team car. Entered as Nos. 3 and 4, Fellows again qualified on the class pole, this time breaking the GTS lap record for the 26th starting position, while Andy Pilgrim qualified No.4, 29th overall. Andy also broke the existing class lap record, but the No. 4 Corvette crashed out midrace, while the best the No. 3 car could manage was a 4th in the GTS class behind three Vipers and 23rd overall. This was the first of eight races in the inaugural ALMS season, and Team Corvette selected four additional events to compete in, but they needed more torque to beat the Vipers.

After skipping races at Road Atlanta and Mosport, the No. 3 Corvette resurfaced at Series Point, where Fellows and Kneifel, competing as a single-car team, finished second in class. Combined with another second place at Laguna Seca in September, these were the C5R Corvette's best finishes of the year, and they were good enough to attract positive attention from the press and develop a huge fan base. For their

season finale, the series returned to Road Atlanta for a 9-hour endurance race, the Petit Le Mans. Team Corvette returned to full strength for this event, with the full roster of drivers from Sebring. The best finisher was No. 4, driven by Pilgrim, Sharp, and Collins, coming in fourth in class, with No. 3 in fifth.

**Corvettes in a Box**

Along with the C5Rs, GM Motorsports also had a program for independent racers, assisting them in preparing and competing with fifth-generation Corvettes in series like the Speed World Challenge. For this and a number of other high-visibility production car road racing series, the rules were a long way from showroom stock, and what racers needed were "bodies in white" as a starting point to build up their cars. The chassis for these racing kit cars were assembled at the Bowling Green Corvette plant primarily on weekends by volunteers and were shipped with their hardtop bodies in boxes.

This program lasted three years, and 20 "Corvettes in a box" were produced in 1999, followed by 10 more in 2000 and 12 in 2001. Gib Hufstader came out of retirement to offer technical support. Hufstader had been part of Zora Duntov's Corvette Group and was an accomplished racer both on and off the track; he attended every Speed World Challenge event as a GM Motorsports contractor. The first Corvette kit went to Jim Van Dorn's

Pirate Racing Team, and the second one to Danny Kellermyer's DJ Race Enterprises, but they weren't ready in time to have much of an impact on the 1999 season. Pirate Racing's C5 reached the track mid-season, and Bill Cooper qualified it on the pole at Mosport. Kellermyer's new car only made the final three races, with Heinricy winning at Pike's Peak.

## Duntov's Vision Realized

Duntov's dream of a full factory-backed Corvette racing program was about to be realized in 2000 on the strength of the C5R's limited first steps in 1999. The partially assembled "Corvettes in a box" were also a success, giving the C5s more press in several series that required cars closer to production. Overall sales improved, and the fifth-generation Corvette earned rave reviews—*Car & Driver* selected it as one of the 10 best cars, while *Autoweek* readers picked it as America's *best* car.

With the start of the new decade, all of the doomsayers' speculation about the millennium bug crashing every computer was proven wrong. Y2K brought nothing with it but a change of dates, which was especially good news for owners of Corvettes and other high-tech cars that relied on multiple computers. The only noticeable change for 2000 was restyled thin spoke forged aluminum wheels. Two new colors were available—dark Bowling Green metallic and Millennium Yellow.

Millennium Yellow became Team Corvette's new racing color for 2000. A pair of second-generation C5Rs with a wider track for improved stability was under construction at Pratt & Miller. Thanks to Team Oreca, Chrysler's French connection, the FIA's GTS class displacement limit was 8.0 liters, which coincidentally, was the size of the Viper V-10. Even though both engines were restricted to about 600 hp, more displacement means more torque, and the Corvette 6.0-liter V-8's deficit was cut in half, with a displacement increase to 7.0 liters.

Both the AMLS and the Corvette C5R racing program had a successful first season, leading the ALMS to add 3 more events to their 2000 schedule for a total of 11. While still not running every race, Team Corvette extended its schedule, competing in 6 ALMS events in addition to the 24 Hours of

Along with the C5Rs, GM Motorsports also had a program for independent races to assist them in preparing fifth-generation Corvettes for racing series like The Speed World Challenge by providing partially assembled kit cars. The rules for this and other production-based racing series allowed extensive modifications, and 20 assembled rolling chassis with hardtop bodies and other components in boxes were made available as a starting point for racing cars in 1999.
*General Motors*

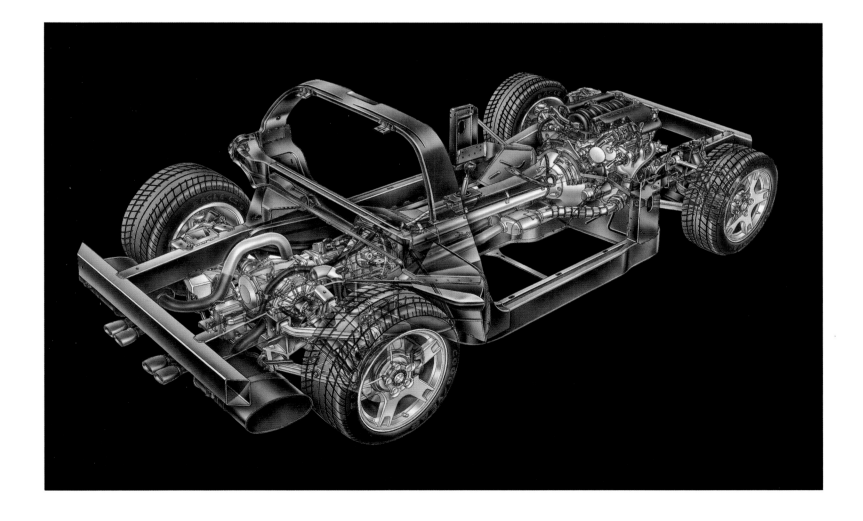

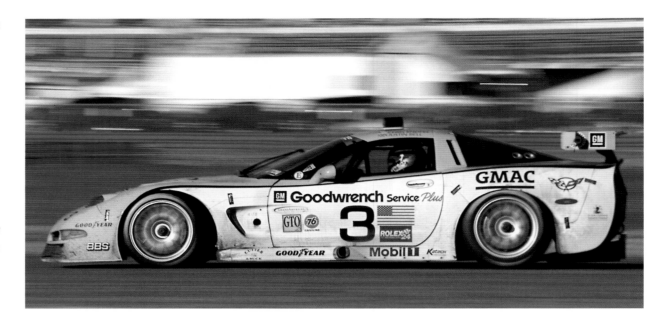

The C5Rs arrived at Daytona in February 2000 with their engine displacement increased from 6 to 7 liters to help them deal with the dominant 8-liter Vipers. Ron Fellows qualified the No. 3 on the GTO/GTS pole, and with all of the fragile prototypes dropping out, the No. 3 Corvette came in second overall, co-driven by Justin Bell and Chris Kneifel behind the winning Viper.
*Richard Prince*

Daytona, as well as the big one, the 24 Hours of Le Mans. In 2000, the 24-hour race at Daytona was part of the new Grand-Am Series, which was affiliated with NASCAR but at first followed FIA classifications and car preparation rules. This meant Team Corvettes could compete in the same configuration for all of the events on its calendar in the GTS class.

In February 2000, the Corvette team arrived for the 24 Hours of Daytona with 7.0-liter power and new predominantly yellow paint jobs to compete head-to-head with the Vipers on a more level playing field. The cars continued to use their 1999 ALMS numbers, and Fellows qualified the now No. 3 Corvette on the GTS class pole for the second year in a row. Fellows' codrivers were Justin Bell and Kneifel. Pilgrim, Collins, and Frank Freon shared the No. 4 car, which again experienced bad racing luck and failed to finish. World Sports Car was the top prototype class, and most of these fast-but-fragile cars fell out of the race, leaving first overall to a Viper and second overall to the No. 3 C5R Corvette.

At Sebring, it was déjà vu with the same driver lineup as Daytona and Fellows again setting fast time in GTS, but this time it was the No. 3 car that ran into engine trouble, failing to finish. Surprisingly, the slower-revving 8.0-liter Viper V-10s were getting better fuel mileage than the Corvette 7.0-liter V-8s, forcing the surviving Corvette to make more frequent pit stops. Driven by Pilgrim, Collins, and Freon, the best the No. 4 C5R could manage was a 16th-place finish overall and 5th in GTS, behind a parade of 4 GTS R Vipers.

## Corvette Versus Viper, Again

In April 2000 when the C5R team arrived in France for Le Mans practice and prequalifying, they were the first Corvettes to be entered in the French 24-hour race since 1995. This was GM's first direct involvement in this famous race, and GM Motorsports entered two teams: the C5R Corvettes and a pair of short-lived Cadillac LMPs. Fellows got off to a promising start, setting the fastest GTS lap time around the 8.45-mile circuit on the first day of the practice, and by the end of the session, the Corvettes were fourth and fifth behind three Vipers. After prequalifying, the Corvette team concentrated on preparing to compete against the Oreca Vipers in June on their home turf—Le Mans—passing up three ALMS events.

GM made a grand entrance at Le Mans in 2000, introducing the Cadillac LMP and Corvette teams with a lot of corporate hoopla and fanfare. The Corvette guys first donned cowboy hats and then berets for their official team photos, making them a crowd favorite.

The yellow C5Rs, Nos. 63 and 64, led a pair of red Vipers in the early laps of the race. The No. 63 car was driven by Fellows, Bell, and Kneifel, followed by Pilgrim, Collins, and Freon in the 64. Fellows turned the fastest GTS class lap of the race, but the Corvettes' poor fuel mileage forced them to make more frequent stops than the Vipers. The No. 64 lost an additional 10 minutes in the pits to replace a bad starter. This dropped them completely out of contention, but the No.

63 Corvette managed to finish a respectable 4th in GTS and 11th overall.

Back in the United States, the Corvette team ran a single car, the No. 3, driven by fellows and Pilgrim, in the next few ALMS events. As the Corvettes continued developing, the Vipers were becoming vulnerable. Oreca's lone entry finished 5th overall and 2nd in GTS at Mosport in August. Then it finally happened in September at Texas Motor Speedway: Corvette beat Viper to the checkered flag. It was Fellows and Pilgrim, and they celebrated the C5R Corvette's first class victory from the top step of the podium. For Petit Le Mans later in the month at Road Atlanta, both C5Rs were entered, and it was the No. 4 driven by Pilgrim, Collins, and Freon that scored the team's second GTS win.

After four model years of production, with only minor updates, fifth-generation Corvette sales remained strong. Sales were divided between the three-body lineup, and coupes remained the most popular, followed by the convertible. Droptops saw the most dramatic increase while sales of hardtops—despite being the least expensive choice—fell.

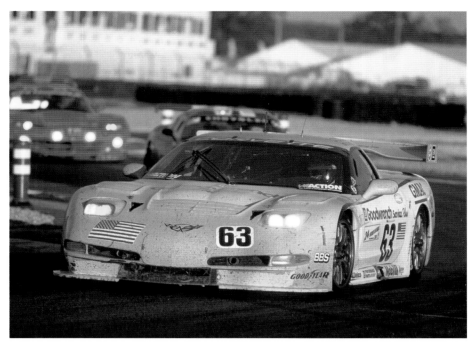

GM made a grand entrance at Le Mans in 2000 introducing their Cadillac LMP and Corvette teams with the yellow C5Rs numbered 63 and 64; they lead a pair of the red ORECA Vipers in the early laps of the race. Surprisingly the Vipers 8-liter V-10s got better fuel mileage than the Corvette's 7-liter V-8s, forcing the Vettes to make more pit stops, but the No. 63 driven by Fellows, Bell, and Kneifel still finished 4th in GTS, 11th overall. *Richard Prince*

Back in the United States, the No. 3 ran alone in the next few ALMS events with dramatic new black and white graphics on its nose, driven by Ron Fellows and Andy Pilgrim, while Pratt & Miller continued development. The Vipers were becoming vulnerable by the time they reached Texas Motor Speedway in September, and the yellow C5R finally broke through to its first class win, with Fellows and Pilgrim on the top step of the podium. *Richard Prince*

For Petit Le Mans, the ALMS season finale at Road Atlanta later in September, the C5Rs were back to a two-car team with new overall yellow paint jobs, and the No. 4 got the team its second GTS class win. Driven by Andy Pilgrim, Kelly Collins, and Franck Freon, the No. 4 Corvette C5R finished ninth overall and won the GTS class, with the No. 3 coming in third in class. *Richard Prince*

Millennium Yellow was not only the Corvette racing color but also the lead color for an unprecedented high-performance model that transformed the slow-selling hardtop into the fastest accelerating Corvette ever. The famous Z06 RPO from 1963 was resurrected as a name for this new model, which went much further than the original that only lasted one year, and with a well-published racing program, it was here to stay. *GM Media Archive*

## Classic Components Return

For 2001, the famous Z06 RPO was resurrected as the name of an unprecedented high-performance model that transformed the slow-selling hardtop into the fastest accelerating, best handling Corvette ever. The original 1963 Z06 was a racing package for the new Corvette Sting Ray coupe that combined all of the high-performance options, along with a few special parts under a single RPO. This option was cancelled after one year in a resurgence of the corporate ban on racing, but with the well-publicized Corvette racing program, the new Z06 was here to stay. This package was no longer a regular production option but rather the Corvette's first separate model, and it developed the Corvette much further than the original version.

Hardtops were the lightest C5 Corvettes, and the comprehensive Z06 package further reduced their mass in a myriad of small ways, including thinner glass and a titanium exhaust system. They even had smaller batteries and a fixed-mast radio

antenna, which reduced the weight by another 100 pounds, bringing their curb weight down to 3,115 pounds compared to the coupes 3,298 pounds. This body style was also the most rigid version of the C5, allowing it to handle the Z06 specific FE4 suspension, which was even stiffer than the RPO Z51 performance suspension package. The EMTs were replaced in favor of wider P265/40ZR-17 front and P295/35ZR-18 rear Goodyear Eagle F1 Supercars, which not only improved grip but also saved 23.4 pounds over the "run flats."

Another feature that separated Z06s from lesser Corvettes was brake cooling air ducts. Stainless-steel mesh grilles were added to the simulated openings in the nose to take in air for the front brakes, while openings had to be added to cool the rears. These highly styled black plastic scoops surrounded stainless mesh, like the front intakes, and followed the radius of the lower rear corners of the doors.

Z06 interiors had plenty of special graphs to remind occupants of how special these Corvettes

Hardtops were already the lightest C5s, and the comprehensive Z06 package further reduced their mass in a myriad of small ways, including thinner glass and a titanium exhaust system, altogether taking off 100 pounds. This body style was also the most rigid, allowing it to handle the Z06 specific FE4 suspension, which was even stiffer than the RPO Z51 performance handling package, making it best handling Corvette up to this time. *General Motors*

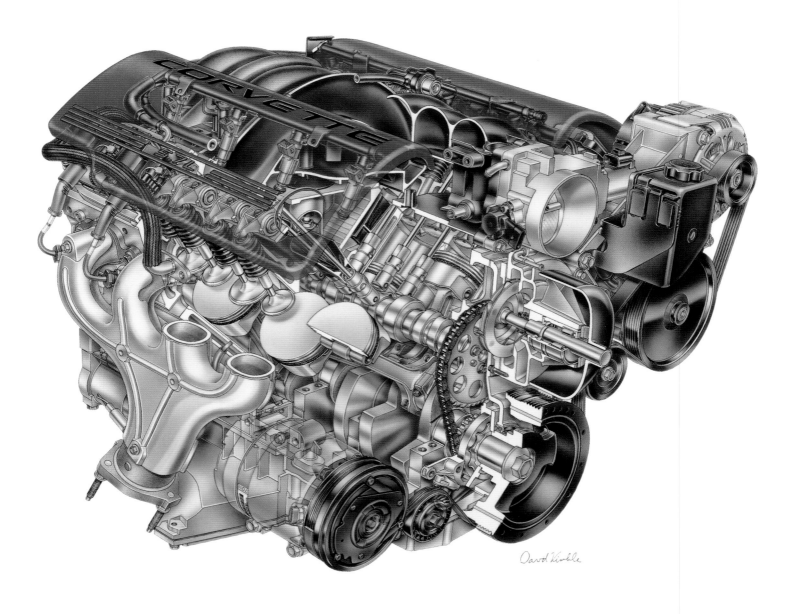

Unlike the original 1963 Z06, which was only available with the 375-gross hp 327ci fuel-injected L84, the 2001 version was powered by the exclusive LS6, which produced an additional 40 hp over the base LS1, bringing it up to 385 net hp. Despite extensive internal modifications, the LS6's external appearance didn't change, so to give it some underhood recognition, its plastic engine covers were molded in red instead of the LS1's black. *General Motors*

were. Z06 logotypes were embroidered on the seats' headrests in either red or black thread. The seats were a special lightweight design, with dual-density side bolster foam, upholstered with leather facings. Like the rest of the interior, they were only available in two colors: black or a black and red combination with the embroidery in the opposite color from the seat facings. Exterior colors were almost as limited, with only five to choose from. The gauge faces featured Z06 logotypes, italicized numerals on a checkered background, and 6,500 rpm red lines on their tachometers (up from 6,000).

Unlike the original 1963 Z06, which was only available with the RPO L84 fuel-injected 327 (rated at 375 gross hp), the new and improved 2001 version was powered by the exclusive LS6. This engine had the same 346ci displacement as the base LS1 it was

developed from, but it produced an additional 40 hp, bringing its output up to 385 net hp.

Since the Z06's early introduction in mid-2000, the automotive press repeatedly raved about its performance, along with the growing success of the C5R endurance racing Corvettes. The second-generation C5Rs had also gotten an early start on 2001, dominating GTS in the last few races of the 2000 ALMS season. The new Pratt & Miller Corvette racing cars featured tubular steel upper and lower A-arms that added 1.5 inches to track over the production-based aluminum arms they replaced, increasing the car's overall width by 3 inches and improving stability at the cost of additional drag. Combined with a re-engineered EMCO five-speed Indy car, these new features made the cars a little quicker.

After five years on top of International GT endurance racing, the Oreca Viper GTS Rs struggled to keep up with the latest Pratt & Miller Corvette C5Rs. Chrysler realized that it was going to take a second-generation Viper race car to remain competitive, so one was designed; but the company decided the program had fulfilled its mission and pulled the plug instead. There would still be plenty of independent Vipers to fill out the GTS fields, but the Corvette teams' only real competition came from a new threat: the mid-engined Saleen S7R.

The year 2001 was the last the factory Corvette's racing season started in February at the 24 Hours of Daytona; 2002 marked the start of the Grand-Am car classifications change, making the cars incompatible after their final appearance in this classic event. The team's six regular endurance racing drivers were joined by the Earnhardts of NASCAR fame. The lead Corvette became No. 2 for this one event, with Fellows, Kneifel, Freon, and Johnny O'Connell, making room for Dale Earnhardt, along with Dale Earnhardt Jr., in what was now the No. 3. Fellows was true to form and set both the fastest lap in qualifying and the race for the GTS class, while the

Earnhardts impressed everyone on the team with their willingness to learn about endurance racing. The race finish was as improbable as 2000—most of the prototypes dropped out. A GTS car won overall again, and this year it was the No. 2 Corvette, and Fellows, Kneifel, Freon, and O'Connell crowded on the top step of the podium.

Early in March, the AMLS stopped at Texas Motor Speedway on the way to Sebring, and the Corvette's team's lone entry returned to its usual No.3 and two drivers: Fellows and O'Connell. The No. 3 Corvette didn't win overall, but Fellows again pulled off the trifecta, taking the GTS pole and setting the fastest lap of the race on the big yellow Corvette's way to its second win of the season. At Sebring later in the month, the Corvette team was back to full strength with both cars, but the bumpy central Florida track remained a problem, and the aluminum Ford V-8-powered Saleen SR7 won the GTS class. The Saleen was driven by Terry Borcheller and Oliver Gavin, followed by the No. 4 C5R, driven by Pilgrim, Collins, and Freon, finishing 7th overall and 2nd in GTS, ahead of the No. 3's 11th overall and 3rd in class.

With the Grand Am Series changing its rules, 2001 would be the Corvette team's last appearance in the 24 Hours of Daytona, and their six regular drivers were joined by a pair of NASCAR luminaries. The Corvettes were renumbered so that Dale Earnhardt and Dale Jr. could be in the signature No. 3, even though they drove the No. 4, which retained its identifying black stripe at the top of the windshield. *Richard Prince*

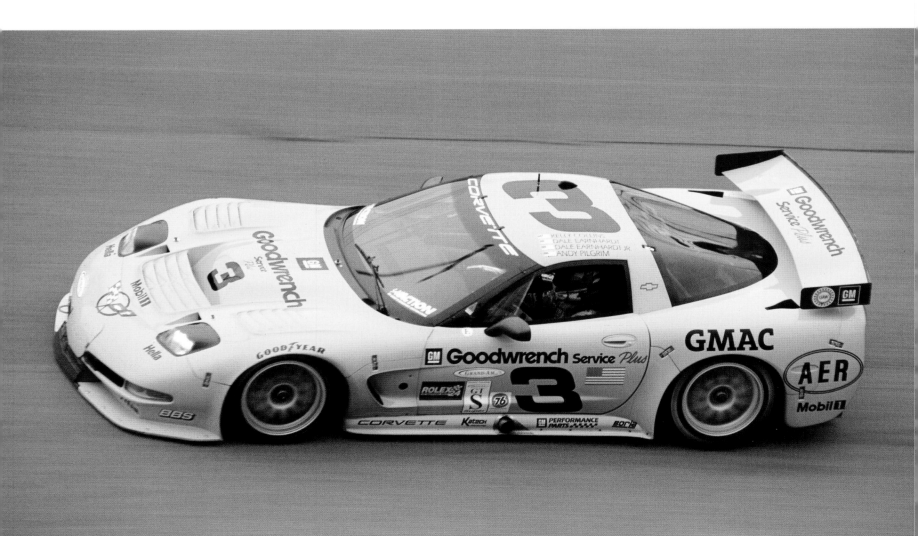

### Return to Le Mans

A far more experienced Corvette team returned to Le Mans in June 2001 with a new engine management system that improved mileage and a revised refueling setup to speed pit stops. The second-generation C5Rs scored a 1-2 sweep of the GTS class, crossing the start/finish line side by side. The winning No. 63 was driven by Fellows, Scott Pruett, and O'Connell, and finished 8th overall. Pilgrim, Collins, and Frank finished 14th overall in the No. 64 Corvette, overcoming several off-track excursions. As the Corvette's last competition withdrew from the race at about the 22-hour mark, the Vettes spent a controversial hour in their garage. The surviving LMP Cadillac passed them, leading to speculation about corporate intervention.

The Corvette C5Rs ran the remainder of the AMLS as a two-car team, winning every event they entered against strong opposition from the Saleens and Vipers. At Sears Point, Fellows and O'Connell finished fifth overall and first in GTS, followed by Pilgrim and Collins at second in GTS and sixth overall—for another 1-2 sweep. After finishing the same way at Portland, Mosport was more challenging for the Corvette team; Saleen finished second in GTS. At Mid-Ohio in August things were back to normal, and the No. 3 Corvette, driven by Fellows and O'Connell, finished first in GTS, followed by Pilgrim and Collins second in class, with Saleen in third.

For Petit Le Mans at Road Atlanta in October 2011, the Corvettes featured special paint jobs with American flags on their hoods extending over their roofs to honor those who fell on 9/11. This tribute extended to the cars' noses, with FDNY and NYPD decals above their license plate covers. Fellows was in line to win the ALMS Driver's Championship, but the No. 3 Corvette only completed two laps before retiring, taking him out of contention for the title. The Pilgrim, Collins No. 4 C5R, saved the day, finishing sixth overall for another class win, helping to secure both the Corvette's first ALMS manufacturers and team championships.

Corvette sales continued to grow in 2001, and the mix was changing: the coupe lost popularity, while the hardtop made the biggest gain. As the least expensive Corvette, with a base price of $38,900, the lowly hardtop's sales had dropped by half in its second year, but performance-hungry enthusiasts flocked to it in droves as the Z06. This transformation made the hardtop into the most expensive version of the 2001 Corvette, going for $500 more than the $47,000

After returning from a 1-2 GTS class win at Le Mans, the C5Rs were on a roll and ran as a two-car team for the remainder of the ALMS season, winning every event they entered. With strong opposition from the Saleens and Vipers at Sears Point, Ron Fellows and Johnny O'Connell drove the No. 3 to fifth overall, first in GTS while the No. 4 Corvette with Pilgrim and Collins was second in class.
*Richard Prince*

There were normally three drivers assigned to each C5R for 24-hour races, but to make room for the Earnhardts, this was increased to four, with Andy Pilgrim and Kelly Collins staying with the car. Both Dales performed well in the event and impressed the team with their willingness to learn about endurance racing; their Corvette came in fourth overall. *Richard Prince*

The race finish at Daytona was as improbable as 2000 with most of the prototypes dropping out; the overall winner was a GTS car again, and this year it was the No. 2 Corvette that had qualified on the class pole. It was a spectacular victory for Team Corvette with Ron Fellows, Chris Kneifel, Franck Freon, and Johnny O'Connell, along with the crew, all crowded on the top step of the podium. *Richard Prince*

For Petit Le Mans at Road Atlanta in October 2001, the Corvette team had special paint jobs to honor those who fell on 9/11, with American flags on their hoods that extended over the cars' roofs. The No. 3 car completed only two laps before retiring, leaving it to the No. 4 to save the day. Andy Pilgrim and Kelly Collins finished 6th overall, for another class win securing the GTS championship.
*Richard Prince*

convertible, but compared to the 1995 $68,043 ZR-1, the Z06 was still a bargain.

## Benchmarks of Horsepower

Few upgrades were made to the 2002 Corvette base coupes and convertibles, but the Z06 received enough improvements to excite the car magazines all over again. The biggest news was the package's LS6 engine—it gained 20 hp, equaling the legendary ZR-1's mega buck, double-overhead cam LT5's 405 net hp and beating the original 1971 425-hp 454 LS6's actual power output. Testing standards for advertised horsepower changed from gross to net in 1972, which reduced ratings by about 15 percent. It would have dropped the 454 to about 360 hp. Bragging rights on 405 hp were a big deal in 2002, and the LS6's power rating was proudly added to the Z06's front fender badges for the remainder of its production run.

When the 385-hp LS6 was released for 2001 production, it was a work in progress, with continuing power development—a more aggressive camshaft with more lift than any previous small-block was ready for 2002. Along with additional power, the 2002 Z06 received a number of less exciting but worthwhile upgrades, including adding the heads-up instrument display to the package's standard equipment. All Z06s and convertibles equipped with heads-up displays featured thinner windshields and a change from forged to spin-cast wheels. The FE4 suspension got a stiffer front anti-roll bar, with lighter aluminum drop-links, and revised rear-shock valving improved both traction and the ride over rough surfaces.

## Long Awaited Victories

Now that Grand-Am series' rules were no longer compatible with FIA car classifications, the 24 Hours of Daytona was off their calendar and the Corvette Racing Team's 2002 season started at Sebring. March 16, 2002, was the 50th running of the 12 Hours of Sebring, and after three previous attempts at victory, the Corvette team finally found the checkered flag that eluded them. The team's car numbers and driver line-ups remained unchanged from 2001, except that GTS class numerals were now green instead of black—and Gavin replaced Kneifel in the No. 3 car. Gavie had codriven last year's GTS class-winning Saleen SR7, and as one of the No. 3 C5R's drivers, he was a back-to-back winner of the famous 12-hour race.

The 2002 racing season couldn't have started better for the Corvette Team. Fellows qualified the No. 3 on the GTS pole, followed by Pilgrim in the No. 4. Except for a few early laps with a Viper in front, the first half of the race was contested between the two Corvettes. They led the GTS class, running close together, until the No. 4 car's throttle stuck open. This careened Pilgrim into a tire wall, but he was able to limp back to the pits, where his crew patched up the No. 4 and got it back in the race after 12 laps, leaving them to battle hard for fourth in class. In contrast, the No. 3 Corvette's race was uneventful, with Fellows, O'Connell, and Gavin cruising to a landmark victory, eight laps ahead of

second in class. They finished ninth overall.

Sunday, May 5 was the traditional Le Mans test and prequalifying day at the Circuit de la Sarthe, and the best the Corvettes could do was third and fourth on the GTS timing charts behind a Ferrari and Viper. The Ferrari was a 550 Maranello, developed for the GTS class by David Richard's Prodrive Engineering in England, who was best known for building and showcasing the Subaru World Rally cars. This strictly private affair started with a used car that Prodrive commissioned to modify and race at Le Mans for a Swiss businessman without any factory affiliation. The lone Ferrari held everyone's attention, hitting over 210 mph on the long straights—almost equaling the Audi R8 prototypes—and over 15 mph faster than the Corvettes. The Corvette team, though, wasn't overly concerned—they believed they were faster on longer runs.

The American Le Mans Series' second race of the 2002 season was the Grand Prix of Sonoma at Sears Pointon on May 19, where the Corvette Team debuted a new pair of Pratt & Miller C5Rs. These next generation racing cars were successful right out of the box, starting first and second in GTS and finishing the same way with Fellows and O'Connell scoring the win. Their only real opposition

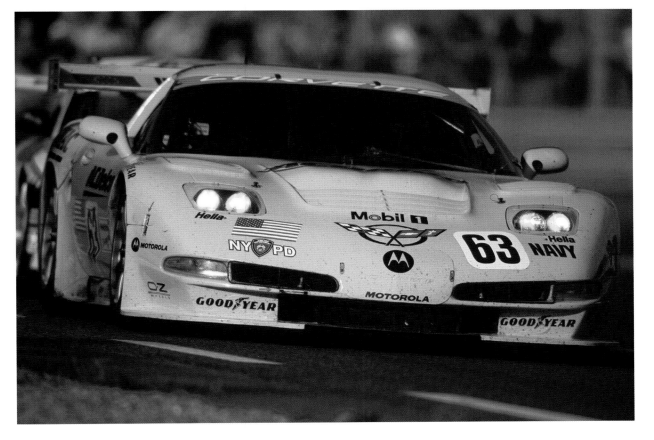

The Corvette team had a new pair of C5Rs for 2002, but last year's class winning cars returned to Le Mans for an encore performance, with new Hewland six-speed transaxles. Prodrive's Ferrari out qualified the Corvettes, but the 550 Maranello only lasted 12 hours, leaving the No. 63 Corvette driven by Ron Fellows, Johnny O'Connell, and Oliver Gavin to score back-to-back GTS wins.
*Richard Prince*

The No. 64 C5R Corvette finished second in GTS at the 2002 24 Hours of Le Mans, accomplishing something rarely seen at the Circuit De La Sarth: a 1-2 finish for a team two years in a row. Andy Pilgrim, Kelly Collins, and Franck Freon were teamed up again to finish 13th overall in this car, while the No. 63 came in 11th overall. *Richard Prince*

Dave Hill had been the Corvette engineering director for 11 years in 2003 when this photo was taken kneeling next to a Z06, and he also was the vehicle line executive. The sixth-generation Corvette was nearing completion by this time, and Dave would retire after the even more impressive Z06 version of the new platform reached production. *GM Media Archive*

came from the Konrad racing Saleen S7R, which battled with the No. 4 Corvette for second place late in the 2-hour, 45-minute race, but would have to settle for third in class. When Pilgrim and Collins finished second, the new Corvettes' sweep of their first outings was complete.

The new pair of C5Rs stayed in the United States for Le Mans, but last year's GTS class-winning Corvettes returned for an encore performance. As expected, the Prodrive Ferrari was fastest in qualifying, but Gavin's second quick time in the No. 63 Corvette was better than he practiced with Pilgrim, qualifying the No. 64 fifth in GTS. The Ferrari set a blistering pace for the first half of the race, but the Corvettes stuck to their game plan, and it paid off just past the 12-hour mark when the Ferrari dropped out with mechanical problems. In 2002, Corvette Racing accomplished something rarely seen at Le Mans—back-to-back one and two finishers in class. Fellows, O'Connell, and Gavin finished first in the No. 63 car, followed by Pilgrim, Collins, and Freon in the No. 64.

The ALMS race three was at Mid-Ohio late in June, and the new C5Rs were back in action, qualifying and finishing the race first and second. The Corvette Team swept both the qualifying and the race at the next four ALMS events, with Pilgrim and Collins in the No. 4 taking the next GTS victory at Road America on July 7. Race eight was at Laguna Seca in September. Prodrive's Ferrari made its ALMS debut there, and the Corvettes' winning streak came to an end with the yellow C5Rs finishing third and fifth in GTS. Both Corvettes came up short, with the No. 3 car's bodywork catching fire on Lap 41 from a broken exhaust system, and the No. 4 running out of fuel on Lap 105.

The next ALMS race was held on a tight, bumpy 1.57-mile street circuit in downtown Miami, and with the season finale at Road Atlanta only a week away, the Le Mans–winning C5Rs took the new cars' place for the last time. Fellows and O'Connell made a great comeback, easily winning the GTS class in the No. 3, while Pilgrim and Collins battled with the Ferrari for most of the race, finally pulling away in the last laps to finish second in class. This gave Pratt & Miller three weeks to rebuild the damaged No. 3 and get both of the lightweight Corvettes ready for the 1,000-mile Petit Le Mans, the series' second longest race of the year. Their fresh Millennium Yellow paint jobs included a broad anniversary red metallic stripe running from the nose over the roof to the rear spoiler, along with 50th anniversary graphics for this one event.

For this day-into-night 10-hour endurance race, Gavin again joined Fellows and O'Connell in the No. 3 Corvette, while Freon returned in the No. 4 with Pilgrim and Collins. Prodrive also added a third driver in the No. 33 Ferrari, which again was the fastest GTS car, but had to settle for 2nd in class behind the No. 3 Corvette. The team's No. 4, which had won the past two years, battled with the Ferrari for the lead early in the race until falling back with a high speed miss, and after 6 hours, both Corvettes were 1 lap down. An extended stay in the pits to repair the Ferrari's suspension put Fellows' No. 3 Corvette back on the lead lap, and he managed to close with the Italian car late in the race, passing for the win when the Ferrari tangled with a lapped car.

After being denied the ALMS GTS Driver's Championship the previous year, when the No. 3 car was out of the race after two laps, Ron Fellows won the 2002 title while the team won their championship as well. Chevrolet also won the ALMS Manufacturers' Championship, with their Z06 hardtops equally dominant in racing venues. The Z06 was as successful in showrooms as it was on the racetrack, and sales increased over the model's first year despite a hefty $2,650 price bump. Coupe and convertible sales dipped, but the surge in the Z06's popularity still increased by 140 to 35,767.

John Heinricy driving this hardtop-bodied Corvette in SCCA competition had been assistant chief engineer during the C5's development and was a C5R team driver at Daytona and Sebring in 1999. By 2003 the hardtop had become the most popular body style for production-based racing series, with the 42 Z06 kit cars built between 1999 and 2001 joined by many others.
*GM Media Archive*

## Corvette Turns 50

To commemorate 50 years of production, all 2003 Corvettes had 50th anniversary badges, and a special anniversary package was available for coupes and convertibles as the $5,000 RPO 1SC. 1SC included anniversary red metallic "xirallic crystal" exterior paint, champagne-painted wheels, unique fender badges, and a 50th anniversary shale interior with a darker gray-beige for the instrument panel. As advanced publicity, the 2002 Indy 500 Pace Car was a preproduction 50th anniversary Corvette coupe, and replica pace car graphics were available for $495.

Some new technology developed by Delphi was available for the coupe and convertible as RPO F55. Magnetic selective ride control replaced RPO F45's selective real time damping and offered faster response time. The F55 shock absorbers used an electromagnetic field instead of servos to adjust metering orifice sizes in response to changes in load and the road's surface, adjusting the shocks' damping rate to 1,000 times per second.

The breakthrough that made this possible was a synthetic magneto-rheological fluid that held iron particles in suspension; their alignment was adjusted by a computer-controlled magnetic field. This varied the fluid's flow rate through the shock's piston, with far more speed and precision than was mechanically possible.

Several new features were added to the base coupe and convertible's already impressive list of standard equipment for 2003, including fog lamps, sport seats, and a power passenger's seat, joining the already standard six-way power driver's seat. The formerly optional dual-zone air conditioning was also standard equipment, along with a parcel net and luggage shade for coupes. All models were equipped with LATCH (lower assist tether for children). To comply with more demanding occupant protection requirements, Z06 headliners were thicker, and the interiors of all A-pillars, along with coupe and Z06 hardtop B-pillars, were revised. After reaching a high of 12 color choices in 1998, C5s were limited to 8 for

After Le Mans Prodrive's Ferrari 550 Maranello had beaten the Corvettes in an ALMS event in 2002 and reappeared in Sebring in March 2003, along with a team car that heated up the GTS auction, the No. 80 Ferrari driven by Peter Kox, Tomas Enge, and Jamie Davis battled the eventual class-winning No. 3 Corvette for the lead deep into the race, but Ron Fellows, John O'Connell, and Franck Freon outlasted them again. *Richard Prince*

the remainder of production, with anniversary red and spiral gray replacing magnetic red, along with light pewter for 2003.

The dominant Corvette team ended the 2002 ALMS season one win short of sweeping the GTS class in the 10-race series, with Prodrive's Ferrari 550 Maranello the only other GTS class winner. Prodrive had a second Ferrari ready for the March 2003 12 Hours of Sebring, and that really heated up the GTS class auction, as the rival Corvettes and Ferraris ran bumper-to-bumper in the opening laps of the race. The Pilgrim—Collins' and Gavin's No. 4 Corvette—took the initial class lead, closely followed by Tomas Enge, Peter Kox, and Jamie Davies in the No. 80 Ferrari, and Fellows, O'Connell, and Freon close behind in the No. 3 Corvette. The Turner, Burt, and Davidson No. 88 Ferrari was the last car in the lead pack, battling for the class lead until both Ferraris dropped out with mechanical problems. Fellows,

O'Connell, and Freon's No. 3 Corvette sped ahead to finish first in GTS and eighth overall.

The Corvette team had won by outlasting the Prodrive Ferraris, not outrunning them, and after Sebring, they did some additional development in GM's Technical Center wind tunnel in preparation for Le Mans. The 8.45-mile Circuit de la Sarthe favored the Ferraris, with its long straights and high-speed turns, and to meet this challenge, the Corvettes improved their aerodynamics and brakes. The cars were renumbered from previous years in recognition of the Corvette's 50th anniversary, with the No. 64 car becoming the No. 50 and the No. 63 changing to No. 53 (numbered after the first year of production in 1953).

The Corvette team returned to Le Mans for the fourth time in June 2003 as the GTS favorites after sweeping the class for the past two years, with back-to-back 1-2 finishes. They were competing against

The C5R team returned to Le Mans in 2003 for the fourth time as the GTS class favorite, with new dark blue paint jobs to commemorate Corvette's 50th anniversary. The cars were renumbered for the occasion, with the No. 63 becoming the 53 for the first year of production. The No. 64 was changed to No. 50 for this special event. *Richard Prince*

During a night pit stop, the crew is poised to change the No. 50's Goodyear tires when refueling is completed, which had to be done at practically every stop, while the Ferraris could double stent their Michelins. To make the situation worse, for the first time at Le Mans both Corvettes had trouble, costing them the top step on the podium. *Richard Prince*

the most formidable opposition, however, since Team Oreca threw in the towel on its Dodge Viper program at the end of the 2000 season. The next serious challenge came from the Prodrive Ferrari in 2002 that qualified on the GTS pole and outran the Corvettes for the first half of the race until retiring with mechanical problems. Prodrive was back in 2003 with a pair of Veloqx Ferrari 550 Maranellos that, after a year of development on both cars, still had an advantage in top speed but, more importantly, ran on Michelin tires.

The French company had a tire that not only began with more grip than the Corvette's Goodyears, but also relinquished performance more slowly, allowing the Ferraris to double-stint their tires. This saved time in the pits, with the option of only changing tires every other stop for fuel, while the Corvettes required new Goodyear rubber almost every time they came in. To have any chance at all of continuing their string of class wins, at least one of the Corvettes had to race flawlessly, but unfortunately, for the first time, both cars had problems. Trouble started early for O'Connell in the No. 53; track temperatures exceeded 95 degrees, and the transmission felt tight until the crew sprayed it down, which did the trick…temporarily.

During the night their car had bigger problems. The transmission finally had to be replaced, along with the alternator pulley and battery, after running the last three 24-hour races trouble-free. The No. 50 Corvette found different trouble— Pilgrim tangled with a back marker at Arnage that spun him in the wrong direction. He turned off the traction control, did a quick 180, and was on his way, but this left both Corvettes to play catch up. They made a remarkable recovery with both cars on the Le Mans podium. The No. 53, driven by Fellows, O'Connell, and Freon finished 3rd in GTS, 21th overall, and the Pilgrim, Collins, and Gavin No. 50 finished 2nd in class, 11th overall.

Kox, Enge, and Davies stood on the top step of the GTS podium at the 2003 24 Hours of Le Mans, after driving their Prodrive Veloqx Ferrari 550 Maranello to victory. Not content with second- and third-place finishes, the Corvette team logged over 11,000 miles, testing in the off season to prepare for a comeback at Le Mans in 2004. To the delight of the French crowd, the C5Rs were on Michelin tires, and revisions to the chassis and aero package made the vehicles lighter. The results of this extensive development program were clearly evident, with a six-second per lap reduction over 2003 in qualifying and a rock solid 1-2 finish, relegating the best Prodrive Ferrari to third.

## End of the C5

For the fifth-generation Corvette's final year of production, the Z06 package received the only changes, with revised shock valving and stiffer upper control arm bushings, along with softer rear anti-roll bar bushings. There were commemorative editions of the coupe, convertible, and Z06, with red and white stripes over Le Mans' blue exterior paint, which closely resembled the 2003 C5Rs Le Mans' paint jobs. All commemorative editions featured crossed-flag embroidery on the seat headrests, unique wheel center caps, and silver front and rear emblems, which included the words "Commemorative 24:00 Heures du Mans 2 GTS Wins." Coupes and convertibles equipped with this package had two-tone shale interiors, similar to the previous year's anniversary edition, while Z06s stayed with black interiors.

In the C5's last two years of production, sales declined slightly, and with growing anticipation of the C6, they nose-dived in 2004. In the fifth-generation Corvette's eight years of production, coupes outsold the more expensive convertibles in every year except 2003. The C5 went out in style, with a 2004 convertible pacing the Indy 500 on May 30. This platform's innovative engineering and performance had taken the Corvette to a new level, and there was more to come.

For 2004, the fifth-generation Corvette's last year of production, a commemorative edition of all three models was available, with a paint scheme that closely resembled the C5R's at Le Mans in 2003. The package also included crossed flag headrest embroidery, unique wheel center caps, and silver front and rear emblems, which included the inscription "Commemorative 24:00 Heures Du Le Mans 2 GTS Wins." *GM Media Archive*

The C5R's were overall yellow again for their return to the 24 Hours of Le Mans, and to the delight of the French crowd, they were on Michelin tires. With 11,000 miles of development testing during the off season, the big yellow cars were six seconds a lap quicker than in 2003 and finished 1-2 in GTS, relegating Prodrive to third place. *Richard Prince*

# 2005-2012
## MORE OF THE SAME, ONLY BETTER

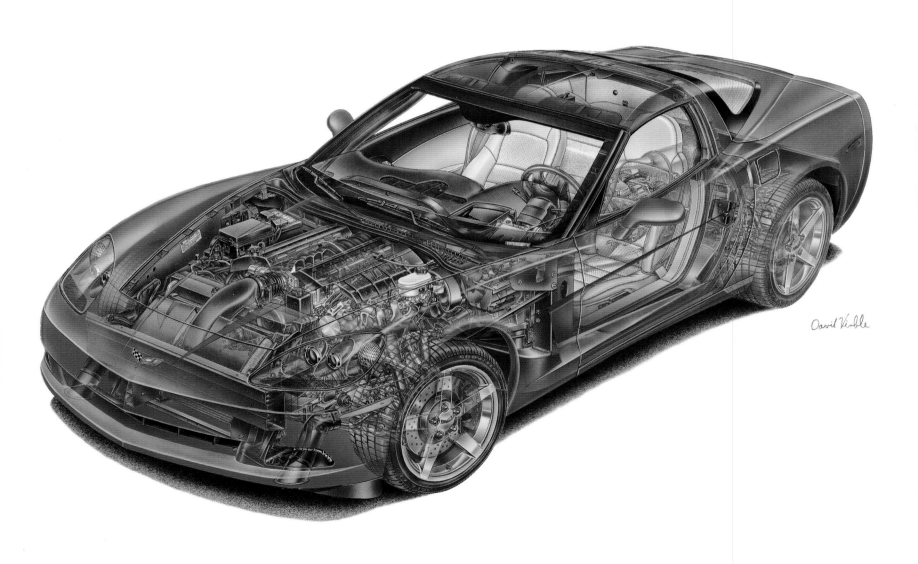

David Kimble

The sixth-generation convertible was introduced alongside the Corvette coupe in 2005, featuring a droptop that was 8.6 pounds lighter than the C5's with improved aerodynamics. The new folding top was the first to be available with a power option in 42 years, with a mechanism that was as weight conscious as the rest of the car, weighing only 11.2 pounds. *General Motors*

## The C6 Arrives

The C5 was a tough act to follow, but even before it entered production, Dave Hill and his engineers were thinking about the things they wished they had done differently, and the C6 gave them that chance. Hill characterized this approach as "building on success," pointing out that refining a still up-to-date driveline and chassis led to a better product than starting over again with a new design. Only the body and interior were completely new, but the sixth-generation Corvette was a lot more than a reskinned fifth generation. All of the exterior dimensions changed—the car's length was reduced by shorter body overhangs, and the width along with it.

Chief Designer Tom Peters crafted the new shape, which featured exposed headlights, unseen on a Corvette since 1962, faired into the rounded front fenders. The sixth generation's shorter overall length, wider rear tires, and increased cooling flow put it at an aerodynamic disadvantage to the slippery C5, which had an exceptionally low 0.290 Cd. It

took 400 hours in GM's wind tunnel testing both 1/3-scale models and full-size cars to get below this benchmark to a 0.286 Cd with acceptable lift and aero balance for 180 mph.

The C6 returned to just two body styles. A coupe and convertible were introduced together in 2005, and a Z06 version of the coupe was introduced in 2006. Despite its added features, the new Corvette's curb weight was 44 pounds less than a similarly equipped C5, thanks to lighter components like the coupe's magnesium-framed lift-off roof. The weight of the new convertible top was also reduced by 8.6 pounds and used thin wall castings in its frame. This new folding top was the first to be available with a power option in 42 years.

There was nothing new about keyless entry by 2005, but the C6 took it to a new level—both entry and ignition were controlled by a fob that didn't even have keys attached to it. After checking the fob's transponder code for a match, the car's security system enabled an engine start button and unlocked

Opposite page: Unlike the C5, only the sixth-generation Corvette's body and interior were completely new, wrapped around an updated chassis and driveline, which continued to have the same architecture. This was the first Corvette since 1962 to have exposed headlights, and all of the external dimensions also changed, with shorter overhangs reducing the car's length by 5.1 inches on a longer 105.7-inch wheelbase. *General Motors*

Not only was access to the new interior by keyless entry, but the C6 took it to a new level, with the keyless electronic fob also enabling an engine start button after the car's security system checked its transponder code. Displays from the new optional DVD-based navigation system, OnStar, and XM Satellite Radio appeared on a screen in the center of the dash, which was covered, along with the door panels, with a cast skin moldings. *GM Media Archive*

the doors, allowing access to the entirely new interior. The appearance and quality of the materials used in previous Corvette interiors, including the C5, had received a lot of criticism from the car magazines, but this one quieted most of the critics. The seat facings were premium quality low-gloss leather, with a cast skin process used for finishing the door panel trim and instrument panel covering, while hidden seams concealed the air bags.

Speedline manufactured the new cast-aluminum wheels, which were 1 inch larger in diameter than the C5s wheels. The 18-inch front wheels mounted P245/40ZR-18 third-generation Goodyear extended mobility tires (EMTs) that featured acoustically tuned directional tread patterns reminiscent of the original Gatorbacks. The 19-inch rear wheels mounted P285/352R-19 Goodyear Eagle EMTs.

Behind these restyled wheels and underneath its shapely new body, the sixth-generation Corvette's internal architecture was the same, but still superior, to the platform it replaced.

The new Gen IV LS2 V-8 also built on the success of the generation before it, helped by a displacement increase from 346ci (5.7L) to 364ci (6.0L), accomplished by enlarging the LS1's 3.90-inch bores to 4.00 inches. The stroke remained 3.62 inches in the first displacement increase for a Corvette small-block since the introduction of the 350 in 1969, and the LS2 was the first 400-hp base engine. The LS1 was introduced with the C5 Corvette, and it received just as thorough a makeover to become the LS2, keeping the same architecture.

The LS2's aluminum cylinder block was an entirely new casting, with LS6-inspired openings

Speedline manufactured the new cast-aluminum wheels, which were 1.0 inch larger in diameter than the C5's, with 18-inch fronts that were 8.5 inches wide, and 19 inch rears, 10.0-inch-wide mounting third-generation Goodyear extended mobility tires. Behind the restyled wheels and underneath the shapely new body, the sixth generation's architecture was the same only better than the exceptional platform it replaced. This is a convertible uniframe, which was the same as the coupe except for the lack of a halo bar behind the seats that supported the roof. This primary structure looked deceptively similar to the last generation, but was both a little lighter and slightly more rigid than the frame it replaced. *General Motors*

in the main-bearing bulkheads for chamber-to-chamber airflow to reduce pumping losses. The new Corvette's engine continued to be placed so close to the car's ground clearance line that the torque tube had to run uphill, and the oil pan was squeezed out to the sides with "bat wing" extensions. Even though there was only room for a very shallow pan, a newly designed baffle eliminated the need for wings while improving oil control during high G maneuvers. This lowered the LS2's oil capacity from 6.5 to 5.5 quarts, which, along with a smaller water pump and thinner wall exhaust manifold castings, made the LS2 15 pounds lighter than the LS1—with a larger displacement and more power.

The new Gen IV small-block displaced 18ci more than the Corvette's LS1 and produced 50 hp additional. Its compression ratio rose from 10.2

to 10.9:1. Intake airflow was increased 15 percent by a larger nylon six-intake manifold plenum and runners feeding larger intake ports in new aluminum cylinder heads. Exhaust ports were as big as they could get, with a less restrictive exhaust system, to allow 20 percent more airflow out of the engine, which was a favorable balance for making power. Stiffer valve springs allowed the redline to be raised 500 rpm above the LS1's 6,000, and the higher lift camshaft had to be less aggressive than the 2004 Z06's to cope with automatic transmissions.

The 2004 Z51 performance package cost buyers $395, while the 2005 version, with its increased content, added $1,495 to the base price of a C6 coupe or convertible. As in the past, it included stiffer springs, shocks, and anti-roll bars, along with engine oil, transmission, and power steering fluid coolers,

Like the C6, the new GEN IV LS2 base V-8 was a development of the generation before it, with a displacement increase from 5.7 to 6.0 liters, helping to produce an additional 50 hp, bringing it up to 400. The LS2's compression ratio was raised from the LS1's 10.2 to 10.9:1, with freer-flowing intake manifold, heads and exhaust system, hotter cam, and redesigned oil pan baffle that eliminated the "bat wing" side extensions. *General Motors*

but it now moved closer to the 2004 Z06. Goodyear Supercar EMT asymmetrical tires were added to the package, along with larger cross-drilled brake rotors and, for cars equipped with manual transmissions, special gear ratios with wider spacing similar to the 2004 Z06. The 2005 C6 was an improvement over the fifth generation in every way except one—even equipped with the Z51 package, the 2004 Z06 still outperformed it. But that changed in 2006 with the introduction of the next Z06.

## C6 Dominance
By 2005, Herb Fishel had retired, and Steve Wesoloski managed all of GM Racing's road racing programs out of Pratt & Miller's new 35,000-square-foot purpose-built facility in New Hudson, Michigan. They had moved from an industrial park in Wixom early in 2002, and their new location

was conveniently close to GM's Milford proving grounds and had room for further expansion. Like the C5 production Corvette, the R version was a phenomenal success, with three first- and second-in-class finishes at the 24 Hours of Le Mans, followed by three consecutive class wins at the 12 Hours of Sebring. The Corvette team racked up five consecutive American Le Mans Series (ALMS) championships, winning 45 of 66 events in the series' short history, and was so popular that there was no question about the program being discontinued.

The C6R had been under development for a year when the new cars debuted at Sebring in 2005, with Doug Fehan continuing as the program manager and Gary Pratt managing the team. Prodrive owner, David Richards, was an Aston Martin enthusiast, and he also had a new weapon to replace the Ferrari 550 Maranello—a Prodrive version of the

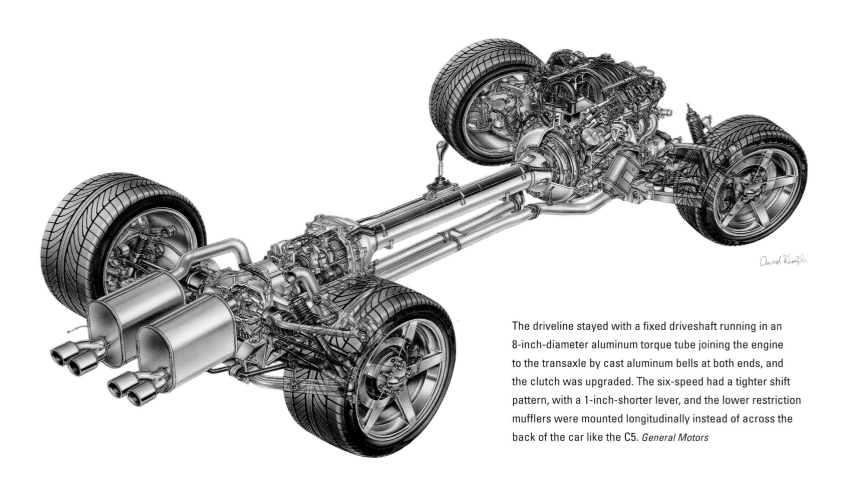

The driveline stayed with a fixed driveshaft running in an 8-inch-diameter aluminum torque tube joining the engine to the transaxle by cast aluminum bells at both ends, and the clutch was upgraded. The six-speed had a tighter shift pattern, with a 1-inch-shorter lever, and the lower restriction mufflers were mounted longitudinally instead of across the back of the car like the C5. *General Motors*

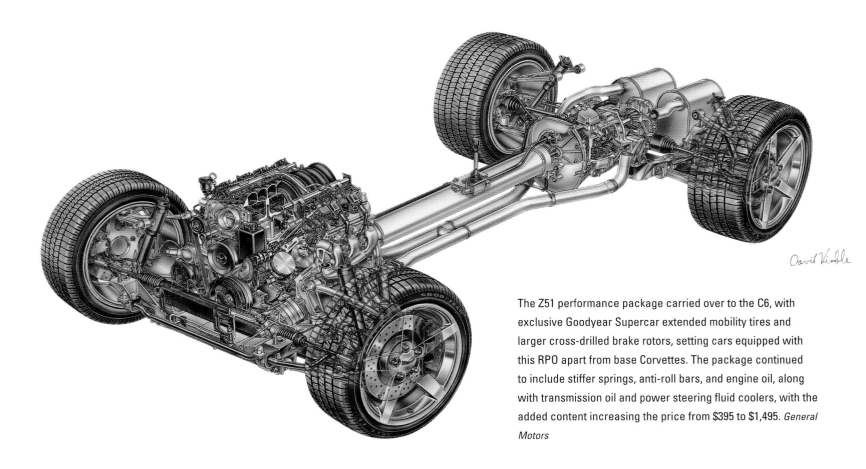

The Z51 performance package carried over to the C6, with exclusive Goodyear Supercar extended mobility tires and larger cross-drilled brake rotors, setting cars equipped with this RPO apart from base Corvettes. The package continued to include stiffer springs, anti-roll bars, and engine oil, along with transmission oil and power steering fluid coolers, with the added content increasing the price from $395 to $1,495. *General Motors*

When the C6R show car was ready for the press in January 2005, it offered an unannounced preview of the new Z06 a year before the latest super Corvette's introduction. The show car was built up on a modified C5R chassis used for early development to fill in for the actual C6R race cars, which were still under construction and wouldn't be ready until Sebring in March. *GM Media Archive*

Aston Martin DB9. This big Aston had replaced the DB7 in 2004 and, like the Ferrari, was powered by a front-mounted 6.0-liter aluminum 60-degree DOHC, 4-valve-per-cylinder V-12, making it an easy transition. The battle between Pratt & Miller and Prodrive would continue.

It was initially hoped that the latest C5R chassis, with its wheelbase stretched 1.2 inches, could simply be rebodied, but the new car's shorter overhangs and some rule changes meant the C6Rs had to be new cars. GTS became GT1 for the 2005 season, and the Federation Internationale de l'Automobile (FIA) paradoxically required that a greater portion of the car's original structure be used, while allowing more liberal engine modifications, but with the same approximately 600-hp cap on output. After all but disappearing from the late C5R frames, large portions of the factory uniframe were used in the new car's primary structures, including most of the hydroformed frame rails. The central backbone, rear bumper beam, and windshield frame were

also incorporated into a new tubular space frame that didn't give up any rigidity or gain any weight compared to earlier structures.

GM Racing's resident engineer designer, Roger Allen, was responsible for designing the LS7R. This was truly a dedicated racing engine that shared just enough with the Corvette's production Gen IV V-8s to satisfy the FIA, but it looked more like it belonged in an Indy car than a Corvette. The aluminum block and cylinder heads were about the only parts that resembled production components, but even they had fundamental differences; the heads' valve angle decreased from 15 to 12 degrees. Instead of iron liners, the big-bore block's cylinders were coated with nickel seal, and its shortened block skirts mated with a supportive lower crank case that formed a collocation pan for the dry-sump lubrication system.

## Corvette Rematch with Aston Martin

Like previous Team Corvette endurance racing engines since the 2000 season, the LS7R displaced

427ci with a 4.1800-inch bore and 3.875-inch stroke and had to breathe through FIA-mandated intake air restrictors that, like a NASCAR restrictor plate engine, limited rpm and power. To get the most out of what air was available, these engines had an innovative cross-ram intake manifold, with individual air intakes for all eight cylinders in a narrow aluminum housing topped by a single fuel rail. This intake housing stood over the block valley cover on tall carbon fiber runners that maximized low-end torque. It was sandwiched between two large plenums that contained filters and took in air from a pair of cone-shaped restrictors. The LS7R was developed at Kaytech and, with seven liters to fill breathing through tiny restrictors, ran out of air at about 5,400 rpm, where it produced 590 hp with 640 ft/lb of torque, coming at 4,400 rpm.

The C6R's carbon fiber bodywork was a preview of the 2006 Z06 with exaggerated styling clues and also previewed its new lead color, Velocity Yellow, which replaced Millennium Yellow the next year. Racing had a lot of influence on the C6's production body, so the completed version's appearance was a lot closer than the C5R had been, with the C6 headlights already exposed. Even though Richards eventually became Aston Martin's managing director, his Prodrive DBR9s had only limited factory connections but were still painted the traditional light metallic green. A Corvette won the GT class at the 24 Hours of Le Mans for the first time in 1960, defeating an Aston Martin, and the 2005 event was a rematch with the Corvette team's new C6Rs finishing 1-2 in GT1.

Sixth-generation Corvette production got off to a smooth start, and with good initial availability. Both coupes and convertibles were available at the same time, and the C6 outsold the C5 from the beginning. A slightly lower base price didn't hurt: a 2005 coupe sold for $44,245, which was $290 less than a 2004, while the new convertible cost $52,245, which was $140 less than its predecessor.

## Beauty Inside and Out

No exterior clues set the base 2006 Corvettes apart from the 2005 models, and not much in the way of new options did either—except for GM Powertrain's

This cutaway illustration shows the Ron Fellows, Johnny O'Connell No. 3 C6R ready for the 2005 12 Hours of Sebring painted in the team's new racing color: 2006 Velocity Yellow. The GTS class became GT1 in 2005, and the FIA required that a greater portion of the production chassis structure be retained, with the C6R's continuing to be built up on steel uniframes, even though the new Z06's would be aluminum.
*General Motors*

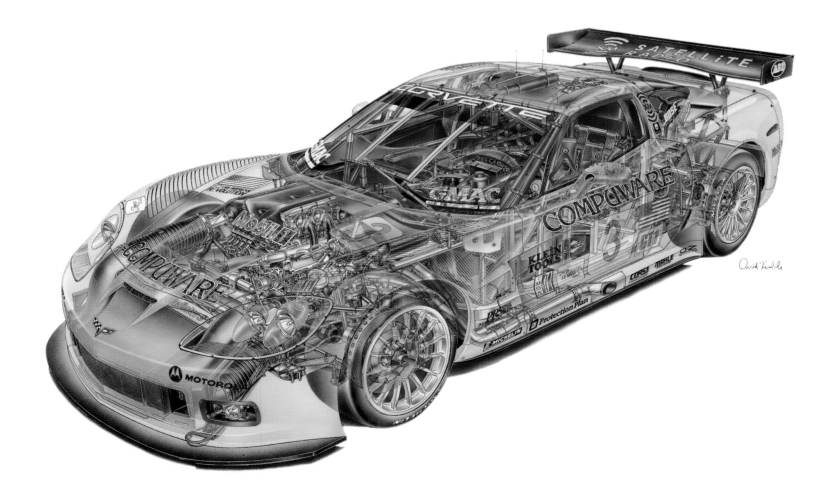

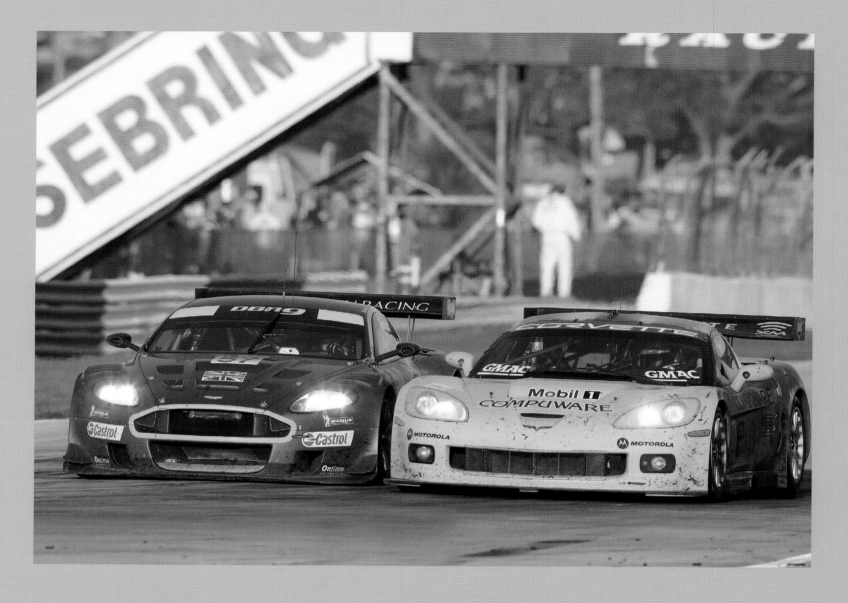

The C6Rs had been under development for a year when they debuted at Sebring in 2005 against new opposition from Prodrive, who had replaced their Ferraris with a pair of Aston Martin DBR9s. This matchup led to a lot of close racing, with the top GT1 contenders coming close to trading paint and an Aston finishing 1st in GTS ahead of the Corvettes. *Richard Prince*

first six-speed automatic transmission, the 6L80E. This option included racing-style paddle shifters on the steering wheel that were electronically controlled by a built-in 32-bit microprocessor. The paddle shifters allowed selection of two automatic modes: drive and sport. *Drive* was the smoothest mode; the transmission made firmer shifts in *sport* or changed over to manual control with the driver using the paddle shifters. Automatic transmissions had been the most popular choice since 1970, and 59 percent of 2005 Corvettes were equipped with the four-speed automatic, which was optional for no additional cost. For 2006, RPO MXO six-speed paddle shifters auto trans was expensive, adding $1,250 to the base price, but 56 percent of buyers still chose them, leaving automatic Corvettes in the majority.

All Hill said about the new Z06 while it was being developed was that "it would distance itself

further from the base Corvette"—and he wasn't kidding. The 2006 version was a complete bumper-to-bumper makeover of the base coupe, and it moved the Z06 to the top rung of the high-performance ladder and was the last achievement of Dave Hill's 12 years as Corvette's engineering director. Powered by a 7.0-liter 505-hp V-8 and only weighing 10 pounds more than the C5 version, its power-to-weight ratio was an impressive 6.20lb/hp, which landed it in very expensive company. This relationship is the golden fleece of performance, and landed this super Corvette between the megabuck Porsche Carrera GT, with 5.83lb/hp, and the Mercedes-Benz SLR McLaren, which had 6.25lb/hp, both of which cost over $400,000.

Far more than a sixth-generation coupe with a big engine, the first 427 to sit under the hood of a Corvette in 36 years was the center of attention. Unlike the big-blocks of old, this 427 was only 6mm taller, and at 458 pounds, it weighed no heavier than the LS2 6.0-liter small-block, making it truly a "big" small-block, an approach proven by six years of endurance racing. Each LS7 was hand assembled by an individual technician at GM's new performance engine build center in Wixom, Michigan. Specially trained master engine builders assembled 30 LS7s per day in the 100,000-square-foot facility, with each builder personally involved in every aspect of the process.

An engine oil tank took the place of the base Corvette's battery against the right side of the Z06 firewalls, and the LS7 engine got a double oil pump, with two "G" rotors in a compact housing. The back rotor pressurized the system, drawing oil from the remote tank and lubricating the engine, while the forward rotor scavenged the oil as it drained into the collection pan. From there it went through a

large cooler in front of the radiator on its way back to the eight-quart tank, which had both an oil filler cap and dipstick on its top. This engine's red line was unprecedented for a production pushrod V-8, and the dry-sump system ensured positive lubrication at the extremes of engine speed and the high lateral G-loading that this super Corvette was capable of.

With its 7,000 rpm red line allowing a lot of overrun, the LS7's 505 hp came at 6,300 rpm, which was 105 hp more than the base 6.0-liter base LS2, and it produced 470ft/lb of torque at 4,800 rpm. Thanks to the wonders of electronic engine management, fuel mileage was exceptional for an engine of this displacement and power output, and the car commanded an Environmental Protection Agency (EPA) combined fuel economy rating of 18.8 mpg. Electronics not only kept the Z06 above the gas guzzler threshold, but they also played a part in its

For easy head-on recognition, the No. 4 C6R had a black stripe at the top of its windshield, while the No. 3's was red. The DB9Rs had red and green windshield stripes with the same colors surrounding their grilles. The Prodrive team ran most of the ALMS events in 2005, but even with some favorable rules adjustments, the 6.0-liter V-12 powered cars rarely beat the 7.0-liter V-8 Corvettes. *Richard Prince*

The No. 64 Corvette is thundering down the Mulsanne straight in this photo during the 2005 24 Hours of Le Mans on the one circuit that gave the Aston Martin's high winding V-12 a distinct advantage. This was a historical rematch of the Corvettes' first trip to Le Mans in 1960, which was also America's sports car's first win defeating an Aston Martin. *Richard Prince*

exhaust system, allowing full throttle-back pressure to be kept to a minimum. The diameter of the stainless-steel exhaust pipes increased from 2 1/2 to 3 inches, with a pair of larger mufflers that each had two of the familiar round exhaust tips. The inboard outlet tips were normally closed by electronically controlled butterflies that only opened when the throttle plate angle and rpm reached a point way beyond normal driving, allowing the Z06 to pass drive-by noise test.

For the most part, the existing driveline was up to the job, with the clutch only requiring stiffer damping springs to deal with all of the additional power, but the manual transaxle assembly was unique. A special version of the Termec six-speed got a one-piece counter shaft that drove an oil cooler pump like the Z51's but had the base Corvette's closer gear ratios. The rear axle stayed with the 3.42:1 final drive ratio, but its ring and pinion set were larger

The hardtop body didn't carry over to the sixth generation Corvettes, and the Z06 returned in 2006 based on a coupe body, which was not only wider than the base coupe but featured distinctive styling. The Z06's lead color at its introduction was Velocity Yellow complemented by the upgraded red brake calipers; the color replaced Millennium Yellow for the second half of the decade. *GM Media Archive*

in diameter, which required a new housing that included its own small oil cooler.

Starting with the C4, RPO Z51 has been the Corvette's performance handling suspension, and for the C6 it became a far more comprehensive package that largely took the place of the Z06 for 2005. Even so, the reborn 2006 Z06 went a step further, with still stiffer springs, a larger diameter rear anti-roll bar, and recalibrated Sachs shocks. Suspension geometry and aluminum control arms remained unchanged, except that the upper arms had bow-ties extending from their aluminum frame mounts so camber could be adjusted using shims, which was more racer-friendly. The cross-drilled brake rotors featured larger 14.0-inch fronts and 13.4-inch rear diameters that were thicker and clamped by more powerful monolith 6-piston calipers at the front and 4-pistons in the rear.

To harness the LS7's 505 hp on the road and improve upon the Z51's already considerable lateral grip, the Goodyear F1 Supercar EMTs got wider, in fact, and the rears were the widest tires to find their way onto a Corvette. The newly styled ZO6 wheels were manufactured by Speedline, with a thick ring on the back, which was heated and stretched out over a spinning mandrel to form 9 1/2-inch wide front rims and 12-inch wide rears.

This third Z06 was the first to have distinctive bodywork, but it wasn't anything theatrical, just a pleasing reflection of the car's increased capabilities, with the fenders flared to cover the wider tires. The recontoured front fenders had prominent side ducts that displayed the Z06 badge, and a splitter on the bottom of the new front fascia improved high-speed underside aerodynamics. Most of the 7.0-liter engine's increased cooling air came through a larger

Power for the latest ultimate Corvette came from the LS7 V-8, which displaced 7.0 liters and produced 505 hp, while weighing only 10 pounds more than the C5's 5.7-liter 405-hp LS6. With all of its other weight-saving features, this gave the new Z06 a power-to-weight ratio of 6.20 lb/hp, putting it between the mega-buck Porsche Carrera GT, with 5.83 lb/hp, and the Mercedes-Benz SLR, which had 6.25 lb/hp.
*GM Media Archive*

Even with all of the added content, the new Z06 was 116 pounds lighter than the base coupe, thanks to the strategic use of lighter materials. The biggest single weight savings came from forming the uniframe out of aluminum instead of steel, reducing the primary structures weight by 132 pounds. *GM Media Archive*

egg-crate grille. A small scoop on top of the nose was functional, but only a distinctive styling clue. Cooling air for the front brakes came from narrow slots in the vertical flange at the back of the splitter and was directed to the center of the rotors by two-piece ducts, while the rear brake cooling scoops were on the sides of the rear fenders.

Except for a larger center high-mounted stop light (CHMSL) spoiler for additional rear downforce, the rest of the body remained the same as the base coupe, including the glass hatch rear window. With increased cooling airflow, aerodynamic add-ons, and much wider tires, the Z06's coefficient of drag increased from the base coupe's 0.286 to 0.340 and provided better lift numbers and high-speed stability. This was close to the last Z06's 0.31 Cd, and the latest version also came close to holding the line on mass; even with all of the added content it was 116 pounds lighter than

Unlike the C5 Z06, which remained a popular race car for years, the new version was just too much for a series like the Speed Challenge, but this didn't stop Z06 style bodies from appearing in competition. Lou Gigliotti continued making regular appearances in the Speed Challenge after the C6 came out, with his signature flame job on this Z06 look Corvette prepared by his LG Motorsports. *Richard Prince*

a base coupe. This lighter weight was accomplished by the strategic use of lighter materials, with the biggest weight savings coming from making the uniframe out of aluminum instead of steel. The aluminum primary structure was 132 pounds lighter than steel, with the frame rails created from tubing with twice the wall thickness and hydroformed in the same tooling.

Z06 roof panels had a cast-magnesium armature that was permanently bolted into the uniframe, bringing these cars' first torsional frequency up 2 Hz, which was higher than a base coupe with a removable roof panel. The balsa-wood core floor panels were skinned in carbon fiber that was also used for the front fenders and outer wheelhouses, which, along with casting the engine cradle in magnesium, all took weight off the front end. With the engine oil tank taking the battery's place under the hood, its relocation to the storage compartment behind the seats also made a small contribution to moving weight rearward. Altogether this gave the Z06 a slight rear weight bias, which evened out with a driver onboard to an ideal 50/50.

Like the other 2006 Corvettes, Z06s got a new three-spoke steering wheel. Interior choices were limited to ebony or a two-tone combination of ebony and titanium gray, or red with Z06 embroidery on the headrest. Additional weight was also shed from inside the Z06 by reducing acoustic insulation and deleting the hatch power pull-down, along with limiting the available options, like a power adjustable passenger's seat. The Z06 got its own preferred equipment group (RPO 1YY87), and it could be ordered with competition gray or polished aluminum wheels, and outside there were six color choices, including the new Velocity Yellow.

Performance numbers varied among different magazines, but all the times clocked were impressive. 0–60 mps was reached in the low 4-second range; the quarter mile covered in the low 12s to high 11s, with a top speed pushing 190 mph. Even with all of this speed, the latest Z06 was more civilized than its predecessor, with its low mass resulting from lightweight major components instead of stripping and decontenting the base chassis. There's a famous adage that says, "Speed costs money, how fast do you want to go?" In this case, that logic only applied up to a point. This more costly approach increased the price by $16,415 over the C5 Z06. With a base price of $65,000, the Z06 was still a bargain compared to its racing rival, the Aston Martin DB9, which went for $161,100 and couldn't come close to matching the Corvette's performance.

After a disappointing start to the 2005 ALMS season, with the C6R's finishing second and third at Sebring, the Corvette boys were back on the top step of the 12-hour race's podium in 2006. The trio of Corvette drivers were surrounded by green Prodrive fire suits, with the Aston Martin's finishing second and third in a reversal of the previous year's results.
*Richard Prince*

### The C6 on the Racetrack

Unlike the C5 Z06, which remained a popular race car for years after it was out of production, the latest version was just too much for series like the Speed Challenge. Z06-style bodies soon started appearing on Corvettes competing in that and other production-based series, but they were powered by modified 6.0-liter LS2s, with only the C6R competing with a 7.0-liter engine. Even though they were billed as an endurance racing version of the Z06, they stayed with a steel frame instead of the production aluminum structure because it was less susceptible to on-track battle damage. With the GT1 class's 2,400-pound minimum weight, there wasn't any penalty in keeping the steel frame, but after Le Mans in 2005, the ACO slapped a weight penalty on both the Corvettes and Aston Martins. They were concerned about the big-engined GT1 cars being faster than many of the P2 entries and "awarded" the Astons an additional 60 pounds, while the Corvettes were given another 180 pounds to slow them down.

After getting off to a disappointing start at the 2005 12 Hours of Sebring, finishing second and third in class, the 2006 season couldn't have started better at the Florida track. The C6Rs finished 1-2, despite the extra weight. The battle between the Pratt & Miller Corvettes and the Prodrive Aston Martins continued for the next two years before Prodrive moved on, with the GT1 class winding down. The Corvettes had the advantage most of the time; their lighter 7.0-liter pushrod V-8s had a lower center of gravity and more torque off the corners than the 6.0-liter DOHC V-12 Aston Martin lumps. Many concessions of the rules prevented Astons from returning to the American Le Mans Series (ALMS), but the Velocity Yellow cars usually came out on top.

Even with renewed excitement in the press over the Z06's return to production, Corvette sales slipped in the sixth generation's second year. Base coupe sales dropped almost 40 percent to 16,598, but this looked worse than it was because an additional 6,272 Z06 coupes were sold, bringing the combined total up to 22,870. The Z06, with a base price of $65,800, was the most expensive Corvette since the 1995 ZR-1, which was an RPO that, added to a base coupe, cost $68,043 and, in its best year, 1990, accounted for 3,049 cars.

The battle between the Pratt & Miller Corvettes and Prodrive's Aston Martins would go on for the next two years before Prodrive moved on with the GT1 class winding down. The Corvettes had the advantage most of the time, forcing Prodrive to ask the ALMS for rules concessions to keep them coming back to the United States. *Richard Prince*

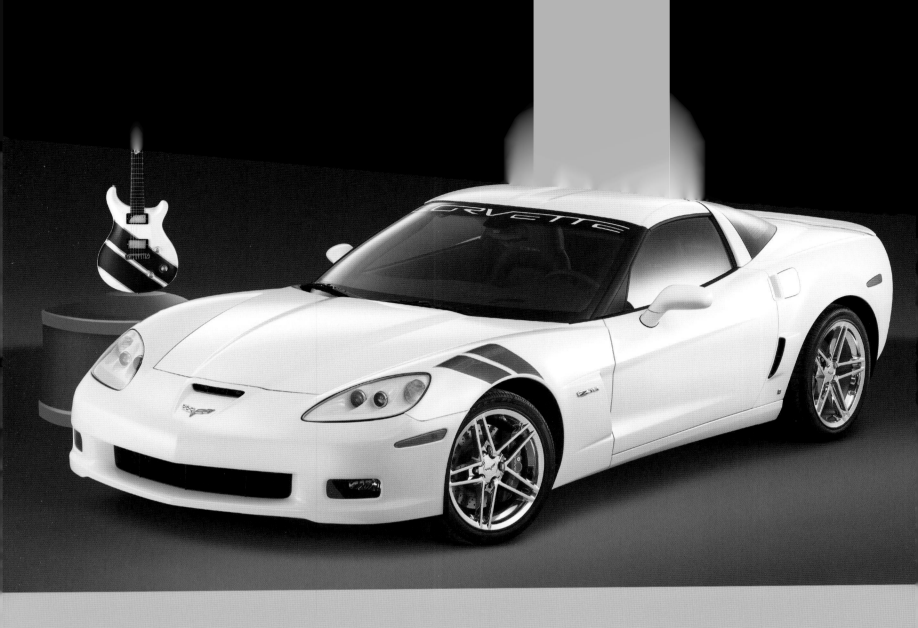

More than twice as many C6 Z06s were sold in their first year as ZR-1s, and convertibles made a small come back, gaining in popularity by 507 droptops for a total of 11,151.

The 2007 Corvettes again didn't have any exterior changes to set them apart from previous years, but there was a new extra-cost color, Atomic Orange, which replaced Daytona Sunset Orange Metallic. The 2006 coupes and convertibles' interiors had been available in only a single color and that remained standard, but two-tone seats became optional in ebony with cashmere and ebony with gray. Larger cross-drilled brake rotors were included, with RPO F55 magnetic selective ride control sized between the base and Z06 brake disc and was only available with the RPO Z51 performance package. This was also the beginning of a series of C6 special editions, with a Ron Fellows limited-edition Z06 introduced in February at the Chicago Auto Show to honor the multiple Le Mans and ALMS championship winner.

Chevy built 399 of these special Corvettes, painted Arctic White with Monterey Red front fender stripes, unique interior and exterior trim, and signed by the famous racer. There was also another Corvette Indy pace car replica, a convertible painted Atomic Orange, that previewed the 2008 restyled wheels and included special graphics and seat upholstery. Sales surged to a near record total of 40,561, the most since the 18-month 1984 model year, and 8,159 of them were Z06 coupes, an increase of 1,887 despite a $4,200 price increase to $70,000. Coupe and convertible prices also increased, but modestly, rising $395 and $575 respectively, but both limited editions were very pricey, with the Indy pace car replica going for $66,995, and the Ron fellows Z06 going for $77,500.

## The Gen IV LS3

For the 2008 model year, the LS V-8 family welcomed a new addition—the Gen IV LS3. It was introduced as the new Corvette base engine,

Ron Fellows stayed with the Corvette team, but stepped down as the lead driver of the No. 3 in 2007, and a special edition Z06 honored his contribution to the team. Ron Fellows Special Edition Z06 debuted on February 1, 2007, at the Chicago Auto Show. The top-notch car was painted Arctic White with Monterey Red slashes on the front fenders and unique trim. *GM Media Archive*

When Ron Fellows did appear in the No. 3 Corvette during the 2007 ALMS season, it was painted Arctic White to match his special edition, in contrast to the Velocity Yellow No. 4. The multiple Le Mans and ALMS championship winner signed all 399 of the production Z06's, making them a very limited edition with a total of 7,760 Z06s sold that year. *Richard Prince*

featuring a displacement increase from 6.0 liters (364ci) to 6.2 liters (376ci). The cylinder heads had larger valves and correspondingly bigger ports that, with a little lift added to the cam, increased output from 400 to 430 hp, with acoustic insulation added to the engine covers to lower valve train noise. An optional dual-mode exhaust system similar to the Z06 exhaust set-up was available for $1,250.

New base wheels that had debuted on the 2007 Indy pace cars were included with the 2008 coupes and convertibles. Interiors also had a new look, with a "cyber" graphic pattern console trim plate and bright surrounds that framed the cup holder and manual shifter. New metal door sill scuff plates were added, and the RPO 3LZ and 4LT combined up-level trim group featured a leather-wrapped instrument panel, door panels, and console. The console trim came with its own bias-graphic pattern and, adding RPO 4LT, put crossed Chevrolet and checked flag embroidery on the headrest of all models in sienna, linen, or ebony.

One of the few complaints that persisted from journalists about the C6 was steering that felt numb. Feel was improved by introducing a stiffer intermediate shaft along with more precise machining. To add in quicker gear changes, the manual transmission's linkage had shorter front-to-back throughs, while the automatic received upgraded hardware and software for quicker manual

paddle shifts. A Corvette paced the Indy 500 for the second year in a row, but this time it was a special Z06 running on E85 ethanol fuel, and the 2008 pace cars available for sale were powered by LS3s. Both coupe and convertible pace car replicas were available with black and silver paint schemes reminiscent of the first Corvette Indy pace car from 1978, and each car was signed and numbered by Emerson Fittipaldi, a former Formula 1 and Indy Car champion.

The pace car replicas were pricey; 234 of the coupes sold at a base price of $59,090, while the Z66 convertibles went for $68,160. There were also 505 special edition 427 Z06s sold for $84,195 each. These cars were painted Crystal Red with Dark Titanium interiors, featured unique "spider" chrome wheels, and were signed and numbered by recently retired Corvette Plant Manager Wil Cooksey. There were also 500 RPO ZHZ coupes built for the Hertz Fun Club rental fleet, with black stripes on Velocity Yellow, and they had seven-spoke chrome wheels. All four special editions only added 1,505 cars to 2008 total sales of 35,310, which was a 5,251 car downturn from the previous year but still ahead of 2006.

RPO ZR-1 first appeared on the Corvette option list in 1970 as a racing package for the new LT1 engine and returned in 1990 as the "King of the Hill" special performance package. With its 4-cam, 32-valve V-8, this was the ultimate Corvette up to this time, and the ZR-1 returned in 2009, not as an RPO but as a new model, which again was the fastest and most expensive Corvette ever. The last ZR-1 had been powered by the only DOHC 4-valve per cylinder engine in Corvette history, and this time the new ZR-1 was the first to be supercharged. The ZR-1's LS9 engine was hand assembled alongside the LS7 and Cadillac North Star LC3 at GM's Wixom performance build center, with its aluminum block and heads were topped by a newly designed Eaton roots-type supercharger.

This unit was similar to the 443-hp LC3's supercharger, but with a tighter twist on its four-lobe compressor rotors. The rotors were located below a pair of intercooler cores to carry coolant through the intake air heated by compression. The LS9 shared the LS3 base engine's 6.2-liter displacement, but with big-valve heads and dished pistons that lowered its compression ratio from 10.9 to 9:1. Lubrication was dry sump, using the LS7's double "G" rotor oil pumps and firewall-mounted tank. The LS9 pumped out a massive 638 hp, and even though the supercharger and its cooling system added almost 200 pounds, its power-to-weight ratio dropped from the Z06's 6.2 to 5.2 lb/hp.

To handle its prodigious power, ZR-1s were only available with beefed-up six-speed manual transmissions. They had a special heavy-duty double-disc clutch, but the rest of the driveline was shared with the Z06. They also used the Z06's aluminum uniframe and most of the same suspension components, except that their selective magnetic ride controls were reprogrammed to deal with the additional 133 hp. Brembo supplied the ZR-1's brakes to match the LS9's power

In addition to the four 2009 models, there were two special edition Corvette packages that could be ordered with most models (except the ZR-1) for a total of five different combinations. The most comprehensive special edition was the Competition Sport Package, which was available for the base and Z06 coupes. It featured gray stripes, wheels, and headlights. Interiors were ebony with titanium accents and included racing-style pedals, special engine covers, head-up display, along with NPP exhaust, Z51 suspension, and a rear axle cooler. The other special edition honored the C6R's racing success, with GT1 Championship special editions of the coupe, convertible, and Z06 available in the 2009 team racing colors, black or yellow.

All 2009 Corvettes featured variable-ratio power rack-and-pinion steering. The aluminum steering column shaft was replaced by steel for more precise control. They also came with steering-wheel-mounted audio controls, a stereo CD player, XM radio, MP3 jack, and OnStar communication as part

RPO ZR-1 returned to the Corvette option list for the third time in 2009, but now as a separate model, which, like the 1990 version, was the fastest, most expensive Corvette ever. This was the first production Corvette to have a supercharged engine, which produced a massive 638 hp from the same 6.2-liter displacement as the base 430-hp LS3 and could push these cars to over 200 mph. *GM Media Archive*

The ZR-1's carbon-fiber hood didn't have to be open to see that the LS9 was supercharged with the ribbed top of the blower's intercooler showing through a clear polycarbonate window. Raising the hood revealed a wide engine cover with blue accents, which were a reminder of the famous "Blue Devil" supercharged C5 development car that had been caught in spy photos at the Milford proving grounds.
*GM Media Archive*

of the standard electronics package. The Z06 carried over with 505 hp, but its LS7 engine's dry sump lubrication system increased oil capacity to 10.5 quarts, and both premium high-performance cars received the base coupe's power hatch pull down. The 2009 exterior emblems were brighter, and a new generation of Bosch ABS, traction control, and active handling systems, were all part of the base package.

## Corvette and the Recession

The global financial crisis in 2009 hit the automotive industry hard and led to the unthinkable—GM declared bankruptcy. In this declining economic climate, the Federation Internationale de l'Automobile (FIA) favored combining their GT classes with all the cars built to the current GT2 rules, where there was still strong support from the manufacturers. In the ALMS, the C6Rs had

frequently run unopposed in GT1, with their only competition coming from the team's Corvettes racing each other for most of the previous season. The Corvette racing program was able to continue after GM filed for bankruptcy court protection on June 1, but the future of the GT2 program that had been planned to start after Le Mans was in doubt.

Team Corvette's rival, Prodrive, had already moved on to LMP1 at the start of the 2009 season, running Aston Martin–powered prototype Lola coupes and leaving only a few customers racing the DBR9s. The 24 Hours of Le Mans was the C6R Corvette's final appearance in GT1 class competition, and Corvette was joined by only four other cars, two of which were older C6Rs entered by Alpha Adventures. A lone Prodrive Aston Martin DBR9 and a Lamborghini Murcielago made up the rest of the field, making the factory Corvettes odds-on favorites to finish first and second in class as they had so many times before. They ran true for much of the race, but in the last hour, the No. 64 Corvette lost drive, leaving the No. 63 to finish first in GT1.

The factory Corvettes and Aston Martins raced each other four times at Le Mans, and honors came out even with the C6Rs winning in 2005 and 2006, while the DBR9s won the last two French 24-hour races in 2007 and 2008. Even though Prodrive wasn't directly involved, Johnny O'Connell's, Jan Magnussen's, and Antonio Garcia's win in the No. 63 Corvette put the C6R one up on the Aston Martins, ending the program on a high note.

## Looking Ahead

For the next chapter in factory Corvette racing history, Pratt & Miller had to develop and build entirely new cars that were closer to production specifications, even though they remained dedicated racing cars. They were billed as a racing version of the new ZR-1, which meant they had to be built up on the production version's aluminum uniframe, but paradoxically, GT2 rules wouldn't allow the use of its supercharger. The ALMS handicappers did cut the Corvettes some slack to help them transition into GT2 by allowing them to continue using the LS7 GT1 engine, provided its displacement was reduced to 6.0 liters. Katech continued to build and maintain the LS7R engines until the end of the 2009 season, after which GM Racing took the endurance racing Corvette engine program in-house.

Except for flared fenders, GT2 C6R bodies were near duplicates of production ZR-1s. The cars were still Velocity Yellow, but the yellow now extended down between the taillights, and the black wrapped around on to the rear fenders. The black and yellow were separated by silver graphic splinters. The hood had the ZR-1's bulge but not its clear polycarbonate window and was dominated by a Compuware logotype's large blue dot. A flex-fuel E85 ethanol decal on the Corvettes' noses proclaimed the fuel they ran on in the American Le Mans Series (ALMS), switching to E10 for Le Mans.

For the C6R's fifth and final appearance at Le Mans in the GT1 class, the cars were numbered 63 and 64, with the No. 4 keeping its black paint job from the ALMS. The factory Corvettes and Aston Martins had raced each other four times with honors coming out even, but in 2009 there was only a lone, privately entered Aston to oppose the Corvette team. *Richard Prince*

GT1 had faded to four entries, in addition to the factory Corvettes, and two of these were older C6Rs, making the big black and yellow cars favorites for a 1-2 finish in class. This was the running order for most of the race, but the black No. 64 Corvette lost drive in the last hour, with the yellow No. 63 ending the GT1 program on a high note by finishing first in class.
*Richard Prince*

plastic sports car remained solid, and they knew the problem was the economy, not the product.

Until 2007 there had never been more than three Corvette models, but with a change of marketing strategy, the addition of special edition trim packages created more separate models. This approach led to nine models from which to choose in 2009, but none of the five special edition packages sold very well; the GT1 championship convertibles only found 17 buyers. Not one of these models returned in 2010, and the legendary Grand Sport name returned to take its place on a coupe and convertible that offered something more than a unique appearance. These new models combined the Z06 and ZR-1's aggressive styling with the base steel uniframe and LS3 engine, making the wide body more affordable.

## Racing Into the Next Decade

For the 2010 season, Pratt & Miller were scheduled to compete in all 10 ALMS events and the 24 Hours of Le Mans, with the factory GT2 Corvettes in a bid for the manufacturers and team championships. The only significant change in the program was the required replacement of the LS7R engine with a racing version of the LS9 developed and built by GM Racing in Wixom, Michigan. To ensure close racing, performance was equalized between the dissimilar cars competing in the ALMS GT2 class, and the ZR-1s weren't allowed to keep their superchargers. The Corvette 6.2-liter V-8s were also reduced in displacement to 5.5 liters, which proved to be a little too much of a handicap—Corvette power was reduced to less than most of its competitors.

The 2010 GT2 field was deep. Porsche 911 GT3 RSRs were still strong, but they were threatened by Ferrari F430 GT-Es and BMW M3 GTs, while the Doran Ford GT-Rs, along with the Jaguar XKRs were never a threat. The season didn't go as expected for the Corvette team, which was still winless when they arrived in France for the 2010 24 Hours of Le Mans in June. The year 2010 marked the 50th anniversary of Corvette's first win at the Circuit de la Sarthe, and John Fitch, the lead driver, was there to commemorate the occasion with the 1960 Cunningham Corvette. The GT2 C6Rs raced well and appeared to be on their way to a 1-2 finish in class when engine failure in the 16th hour retired first one and then the other team cars from the lead.

Back in the USA, Corvette's winless streak continued at GP of Mosport on August 29, which

## The Future of Corvette Racing

There was much speculation about whether or not the new GM emerging from reorganization would continue with the Corvette racing program, and that question was answered in August. The factory Corvettes rejoined the ALMS with Doug Fehan managing the new GT2 program and Gary Pratt managing the team as before, with an equally familiar driver lineup. O'Connell and Magnussen were in the new No. 3, and Olivier Beretta joined Oliver Gavin in the No. 4. They quickly returned to the podium with a win at Mosport late in the month. Unfortunately, this was the GT2 Corvettes' only victory in its short first season, but it was highly competitive against strong opposition and showed a lot of promise for the coming year.

The same could not be said for Corvette sales. In 2009, sales dropped by a staggering 52 percent from 2008. With credit all but frozen and most companies (including GM) suspending leasing, sales were down worldwide, and even a substantial across-the-board price reduction didn't help Corvette sales. Even though base coupes cost $2,100 less than in 2008, 11,059 fewer of them were sold. The Z06s were discounted $10,970, dropping their price to $73,225, and their sales *still* dropped by 18,354 cars. As bad as these numbers looked, GM's commitment to their

remained their only GT2 class win; the driver lineup was reshuffled for the 2010 event. Fehan explained in a television interview, "They paired up drivers that liked the same setup," which was accomplished by Magnussen and Beretta trading seats. This put Beretta in the No. 3 Corvette with O'Connell and Magnussen in with Gavin driving the No. 4. Beretta the No. 3 fifth. Fortunes didn't improve for the Corvette team; O'Connell damaged the left front corner of the No. 4 car before the race even started. After three hours, Magnussen crossed the finish line fourth in the No. 4, just ahead of Beretta in fifth driving the No.3 in the 12-car GT2 field.

Petit Le Mans at Road Atlanta on October 10 was the 13th ALMS season finale, and Corvette's last chance for a win in 2010. This 1,000 mile or 10-hour event always attracted many cars and drivers, and there were 17 entries in the GT2 class—4 Ferraris and 1 BMW qualified ahead of the Corvettes—but their chances didn't look good. Unlike the previous year's rain-shortened race, track conditions were perfect, and the Corvettes found their legs again, contending for the lead

and finally experiencing a little luck. In the third-fastest Petit ever, the 1,000-mile race was covered in 9:10:43, and it was Gavin's No. 4 Corvette that finished first in class. The No. 62 Ferrari ran out of gas on the last lap, and Beretta in the No. 3 Corvette finished sixth.

The drought was over on the racetrack, but not in Chevrolet showrooms. Corvette sales bottomed out at 12,194 cars in 2010, down almost 5,000 cars from 2009. Despite the lousy economy, the only model that gained in sales was the top-of-the-line ZR-1, with an additional 162 buyers undeterred by a $4,530 price increase, for a hefty $107,830 on the window sticker. At this production level, the Bowling Green assembly plant was barely open, but they were ready to respond as the economy improved and a new platform came along.

## The 2011 Corvette

Silver-colored and newly styled wheels set 2011 base coupes and convertibles apart from previous years, with optional Competition Grey paint and machined or chrome finishes also available. All Z06

For the next chapter in Corvette racing history, Pratt & Miller had to build an entirely new pair of C6Rs to GT2 class rules, which required race cars that remained much closer to production specifications. Even though the GT2 Corvettes weren't allowed to use superchargers, the new C6Rs were badged as ZR-1s, with their aluminum uniframes wrapped in a carbon-fiber near duplicate of the super Corvette's body.

*Richard Prince*

models arrived on new Goodyear F1 Supercar Gen 2 tires, had revised exhaust tuning, and presented two exciting new exclusive options—the CFZ carbon fiber and the Z07 ultimate performance packages. CFZ included a black carbon fiber splitter, rocker extensions, and roof panels, with a ZR-1 style spoiler, while Z07 packaged Brembo ceramic brakes with F55 magnetic ride control and Michelin Pilot Sport tires on gray 20-spoke ZR-1 style wheels.

After a model year without a limited or special edition Corvette, another one was introduced for 2011 to commemorate Corvette's 50th anniversary at Le Mans: the Z06 carbon limited edition. This model included the Z06 ultimate performance package, along with a carbon fiber hood, splitter, and rocker extensions painted the body color with exterior mirrors and headlight surrounds painted black. Color choices for the body were limited to the new Inferno Orange or Supersonic Blue, with the package's leather and suede interior stitched with body color matching thread. Z06 and ZR-1 buyers wanting hands-on involvement in building their new Corvettes could order RPO PBC, which allowed them to assemble the engine going in their car at the Wixom Performance Build Center.

## BMW Dominance

In a controversial move, the American Le Mans series pulled the coverage of their races off television and put it on the Internet, with 90-minute highlight shows airing the next day on ABC. The ALMS called this innovative broadcast deal the wave of the future, but fans were outraged, and it took most of the season for regular viewers to calm down. Another much less noticeable change was finally calling GT2 simply GT a year after the GT1 was phased out, joining the other production class GTC, which remained exclusively for Porsche 911 cups. GM advertised that when Chevrolet wanted to race the 638-hp ZR-1. they had to dial it back about 168 hp, and the ALMS handicappers had to deal with a similar problem to allow the 570-hp Ferrari 458 Italia into the GT field.

There were four new Ferraris on the Sebring starting grid in March, but last year's winning AF Corse team didn't get its vehicle in time, and Gianmaria Bruni qualified his No. 51 F430 on the GT pole. Gavin qualified the No. 4 Corvette C6 ZR-1 2nd and made an amazing start, quickly pushing past Bruni's Ferrari for the class lead with the Italian trading paint as the Ferrari forced its way back into the lead. Beretta's No. 3 Corvette started 8th, and with an hour to go had made it into 2nd. The No. 4 car was in 4th but after 12 hours it was the BMW M3s that came out on top. Hand/Priaulx/Mueller in the No. 56 BMW were the GT class winners, with Auberlen/Farfus/Werner's No. 55 BMW

2nd, followed by the No. 3 Beretta/Milner/Garcia Corvette 3rd and Gavin/Magnussen/Westbrooks No. 4 C6 ZR-1 4th.

Round 2 of the ALMS was a month later in April on the famous Long Beach street circuit, and the GT class Porsche 911s were allowed to shed a little weight, but it was the BMWs that showed their newfound muscle in qualifying. The Rahal/Letterman/Lanigan team had a new version of their factory-backed BMW M3s developed during the off season, and Joey Hand put the No. 56 on the GT pole, with Bill Auberlen qualifying third in the No. 55 BMW. Gavin qualified the No. 4 Corvette second with Tommy Milner, who had replaced O'Connell in the No. 3 C6 ZR-1 starting ninth, while O'Connell had been on the series broadcast team since Sebring. When the checkered flag fell, it was two wins for two for Joey Hand and Dirk Mueller in the No. 56 BMW, with Gavin and Magnussen finishing 2nd in the No. 4 Corvette.

Le Mans' prequalifying and practice were next in May, followed by the big 24-hour race on June 11 to 12, which would feature an epic battle between the latest Audi and Peugeot turbo diesel coupes in LMP1. There was also a large highly competitive

GT field divided into GTE-PRO with 18 entries, and GTE-AM added 10 more cars that had to be at least 1 year old with no more than 1 pro driver on each team. After missing the opportunity to celebrate the 50th anniversary of Corvettes' first win at Le Mans with a 1-2 finish in class due to mechanical failure, the factory Corvettes had an even greater opportunity this year. The year 2011 was the 10th anniversary of the Pratt & Miller Corvette team's first win at Le Mans, and the cars featured graphics of the 100th anniversary of Chevrolet on their hoods.

Qualifying was disappointing for the Corvette team, with Beretta starting the No. 73 10th, followed by Gavin in the No.74 in 11th, but the big yellow cars moved up quickly. There was a full course caution at the end of the first hour caused by a spectacular crash of Allan McNish's Audi after tangling with a Ferrari, and the Corvette team restarted 1st and 2nd in GTE-PRO. Disaster struck the Audi team for a second time around 11:00 p.m. when Mike Rockenfeller clobbered a Ferrari with his R18 at 200 mph, taking out enough barriers to keep the safety car out two and a half hours. This mishap left 1 factory Audi leading

For the 2010 season, Team Corvette was scheduled to compete in all 10 ALMS events and at the 24 Hours of Le Mans, in a bid for the manufacturer's and team championships, but things didn't go as hoped. The Corvette team leads a BMW M3 GT and a couple of Ferraris in this photo, but with new production-based engines that had their displacement reduced from 6.2 to 5.5 liters, they were overhandicapped and rarely stayed in front for long.
*Richard Prince*

The year 2010 was the 50th anniversary of the Corvette's first win at Le Mans, and the victorious 1960 Cunningham Corvette was there, along with its lead driver, John Fitch, to commemorate the occasion. In their first visit to the Circuit De La Sarth as a GT2 team, the Pratt & Miller crew lined up the first Corvette to win there between the current contenders on the start/finish line. *Richard Prince*

3 Peugeots, while the Corvette team pulled away from the rest of the GTE-PRO field, with Gavin, Magnussen, and Richard Westbrook leading the way.

After more than sixteen hours, the No. 74 Corvette was almost a full lap ahead when Magnussen careened onto the curb while exiting the Porsche curve, ironically to avoid a slow-moving Porsche 911, crashing out of the race. The accident thrust Toni Vilander's class pole winning No. 51 AF Corse Ferrari, 458 Italia into the lead, with Beretta in the No. 73 Corvette, a lap down in 2nd place. The Ferrari had electrical problems and started slowing, letting the surviving Corvette by with about an hour and a half to go, while the Ferrari still managed to finish 2nd in class. Even though it wasn't a 1-2 finish; Milner, Beretta, and Garcia won GTE-PRO with the Larbre competition Corvette, 1st in GTE-AM at Le Mans on the 10th anniversary of Team Corvette's first win at the Circuit de la Sarthe.

The ALMS resumed on July 9 with Round 3 on the 1.5-mile lime rock bull ring, and Joey Hand

in the No. 56 BMW E92 M3 picked up where he left off. He led the GT field from the start. By 30 minutes into the 3-hour race, both Corvettes were closely following Werner in the second BMW when he had to brake hard, trying to avoid a spinning Ferrari in the fast south bend. His reaction set off a chain reaction, piling the Corvettes into the BMW (and each other) and sending all three cars off the track and into the pits where the crews did an amazing job of patching up the shattered bodywork. After losing 15 laps in the pits, Auberlen took the No. 55 BMW back out and managed to finish 8th with Gavin and Milner's Corvettes 9th and 10th in the 14-car GT field. Hand and Mueller's BMW finished 1st for their 3rd win in a row.

Mosport occurred two weeks later on July 23, and because the BMWs qualified 1-2 once more, motorsport pundits and enthusiasts speculated who, if anyone, could break their three-race winning streak. Handicapping restrained the Corvettes to the point that only superior pit stops, strategy, and good luck would give them a chance. Luckily for the No. 4 car, those circumstances occurred: both BMW drivers made costly mistakes that led to stop-and-go penalties they never fully recovered from, while Gavin and Magnussen drove a flawless race in the No. 4 for the win. The No. 62 Melo/Vilander Risi "competizione" Ferrari was second with Werner/Auberlen third and Mueller/Hand fourth in the BMWs. The No. 3 Corvette, driven by Beretta/Milner, finished in sixth after Tommy Milner's spin in Turn 9. Round 5 at Mid-Ohio on August 6 was the halfway point in the ALMS season, and even though their winning streak had been broken, the white BMWs were still threatening to run away with the GT class. The handicappers made a performance adjustment, decreasing the size of the BMW's intake air restrictors. Their change didn't stop the cars from qualifying 1-2, but the No. 17 Falken-tire Porsche 911 won the race. Mosport was Corvette's last win of 2011, but the cars were far more competitive than in 2010,

and the No. 4's results were consistent enough to contend for the ALMS driver's championship. The Corvette boys came close, but Hand and Mueller clinched at Monterey in the BMW, with Gavin and Magnussen 33 points behind in second.

Corvette sales finally rose to almost 12 percent in 2011. The Grand Sport coupe continued to be the most popular model, followed by the base coupe, and Grand Sport convertibles were next. The Z06's additional 75 hp and lower weight accounted for 386 sales, but this surge in popularity didn't extend to the Z06 carbon limited edition—the lowest-selling model.

The fifth-generation Corvette was produced for eight years, and with a new platform delayed by the financial turbulence in 2009, the C6 also reached eight years in 2012, with a replacement a couple of years away. The 2012 interiors had larger seat bolsters for additional lateral support, padded console covers, and arm rests, along with new steering wheels with bright trim, and all included

The Corvette team was still winless for 2010 when they arrived in France, but the C6Rs were the class of the field during the race, running nose to tail leading GT2 into the night. By the 16th hour, the Corvettes appeared to be on their way to a 1-2 finish when disaster struck, with first one and then the other retiring from the class lead with engine failure. *Richard Prince*

audio controls. Every model could be ordered as a Centennial special edition to commemorate Chevrolet's 100th year, with a carbon flash paint job and red-striped satin black wheels. Brake calipers were red, along with the ebony interior's stitching that included micro fiber suede accents on the seats, steering wheel, shifter, and armrest, with a satin black stripe graphic.

The supercharged ZR-1 was the only Corvette with fuel mileage below the gas guzzler threshold, which was improved by a critical 1-MPG, with a 5th and 6th gear ratio change in the ME2 manual transmission. This lowered the gas-guzzler tax from $1,300 to $1,000 for ZR-1s, which could now be ordered with a performance package that included Michelin Pilot Sport Cup tires on lighter wheels. A narrower version of these tires replaced the Goodyear F1 Supercar Gen 2 tires that had come with the Z06 ultimate performance package also on lighter wheels with the full-width spoiler, but without magnetic ride control still included. Customers could have their 2012 Corvette's brake calipers painted red, yellow, or gray, with 10 exterior colors to choose from.

## The Next Chapter

Pratt & Miller opened another new chapter in Corvette racing history at the 2012 24 Hours of Daytona on January 28–29. Five Daytona Corvette prototypes were debuted. These were the first Corvette prototype racing cars since the Lola-built IMSA GTPs of the late 1980s. Pratt & Miller were already building Daytona prototypes for Coyote, and three of the Corvette bodies were on these chassis, with the other two on chassis supplied by customers.

The Grand-AM Rolex Sports Car series started in 2000, with their cost effective Daytona prototypes introduced for the 2003 season built to a National Association for Stock Car Auto Racing (NASCAR)–style rules package. At first, the DP cars were criticized as being "too ugly and too slow," with shovel-nosed carbon fiber bodies topped by an almost full width green house and powered by nearly stock 5.0-liter V-8s. The mid-engined tubular space frame chassis had unequal length A-arm independent suspension at both ends and was designed with an emphasis on safety, along with reparability. At first the DPs were often slower than the GT cars, but with development and adjustments

to the rules, they soon picked up speed and produced some of the best fender-banging road racing on TV.

The year 2012 was the 50th anniversary of the Daytona Continental 3-hour endurance race that evolved into the 24 Hours of Daytona in 1966, and, Dan Gurney's son Alex started 4th in the 50th running. Alex was in the new No. 99 Gainsco *Red Dragon* Corvette-bodied Gen 3 Riley, and much was made in the prerace buildup of the possibility that he might win the event 50 years after his father. The DP Corvettes were fast in practice, and Max Angelelli's No. 10 Suntrust Dallara was expected to qualify on the pole, but the 1st starting position was taken by Ryan Dalziel in a Riley Ford. The Suntrust Corvette was 2nd with the first of the Corvette-bodied Coyotes; the No. 90 *Spirit of Daytona* qualified in 5th, followed by the Action Express No. 9 in 7th, with their No. 5 at the back of the field in 14th.

Three manufacturers supplied engines for the Daytona prototypes: BMW, Chevrolet, and Ford. The balance of power was managed by the Grand-AM handicappers to ensure close and exciting competition. After lobbying to be allowed more horsepower for most of the season, Ford's fortunes finally turned at the Mid-Ohio 2011, when Ryan Dalziel won in a Riley with Ford power. The Ford's newfound strength was dialed back a little for the 2012 by lowering its rev limit to 500 rpm, but that didn't slow down Dalziel, who qualified the Starworks team new No. 8 Gen 3 Riley Ford on the pole at Daytona. Starworks' No. 8 and Michael Shank's No. 60 Riley Fords battled throughout the 24-hour race with A. J. Allmendinger driving a double stent at the end to finish 1st in the No. 60, 5 seconds ahead of the No. 8.

The Corvette Daytona prototypes were all essentially new cars built for a new program at Pratt & Miller's shops in New Hudson, Michigan, and they all performed well. Unfortunately, they didn't have luck on their side. All five DP Corvettes had some sort of problem. Max Angelelli drove the No. 10 Suntrust Dallara out after completing only 14 laps with valve train trouble after running at the front of the field. In the No. 99 Gansco Riley, Alex Gurney led briefly, but he was soon in the pits with a hole in the radiator followed by a lengthy trip to the garage for a broken water pump pulley, which took the *Red Dragon* out of contention. The highest finishing DP Corvette was the No. 5 Action Express Coyote of Darren Law, which came in 5th followed by Magnussen in the No. 90 Spirit of Daytona, a Coyote in 8th.

Even though the Grand-AM Rolex Sports Car series didn't have any international affiliations, its GT class attracted nine different makes of cars, including new contenders from Ferrari and Audi at Daytona. The newcomers were Prep1 cars like the Porsche GT3s that made up over half of the 45-car field based on production chassis, while the next most numerous Mazda RX-83s were built to Prep 2 rules, with tubular frames. These unique rotary-powered 4-door sports cars had dominated the GT class from their 2004 U.S. introduction. They were allowed to weigh 500 pounds less than any other car in the class, but time was catching up with them. Porsche had won last year's 24 Hours of Daytona, and it

was Porsche that qualified 1-2-3 at the 2012 event, with the first Mazda starting 4th. The Corvettes had always worried the handicappers, and the only one in the race qualified 41st.

Even though the series' handicappers had never favored the Corvettes or Camaros they had some success in Grand-AM racing. Three Pratt & Miller–built Prep 2 Camaros showed in the field and 2 of them finished in the top 10. Andy Lally won GT in the Magnus racing No. 44 Porsche followed by 2 more 911 GT3 cups with John Edwards finishing 4th driving the No. 57 Stevenson Motorsports No.57 Camaro that had won the last two races of the 2011 season. Even though the Camaros were winning some races, the new Daytona prototype rules were the best chance for Corvettes to start doing well in this top-tier racing series.

Petit Le Mans at Road Atlanta on October 10, 2010, was the ALMS finale, and the Corvette team's last chance for a win that year, but the 10-hour event always attracted a lot of cars and had 17 GT2 entries. The Corvettes found their legs again, contending for the lead, and finally had some good luck with the class-leading Ferrari running out of gas on the last lap, giving the No. 4 Corvette the win. *Richard Prince*

# INDEX

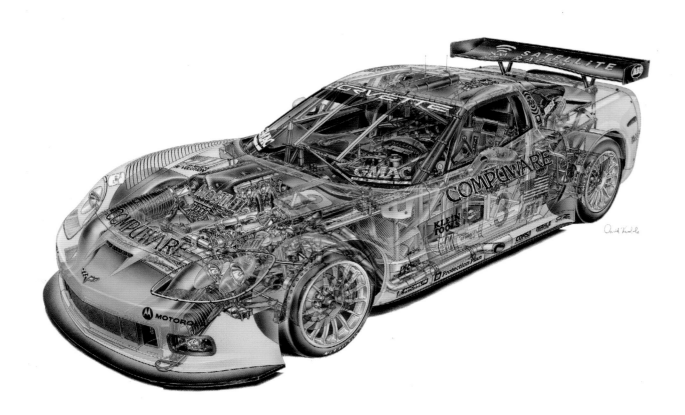